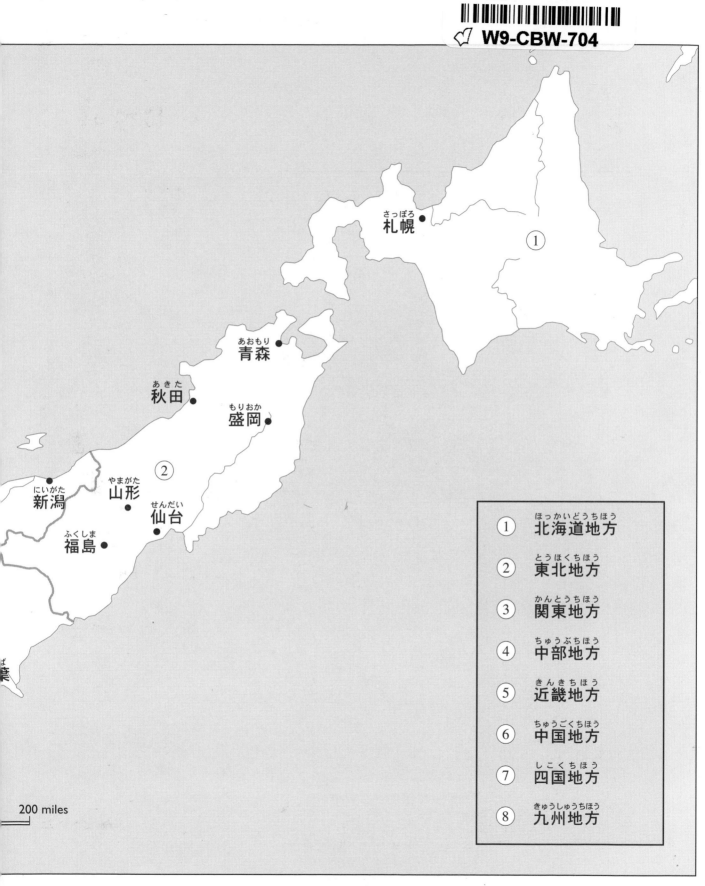

①	ほっかいどうちほう 北海道地方
②	とうほくちほう 東北地方
③	かんとうちほう 関東地方
④	ちゅうぶちほう 中部地方
⑤	きんきちほう 近畿地方
⑥	ちゅうごくちほう 中国地方
⑦	しこくちほう 四国地方
⑧	きゅうしゅうちほう 九州地方

200 miles

さっぽろ 札幌

あおもり 青森

あきた 秋田

もりおか 盛岡

にいがた 新潟

やまがた 山形

せんだい 仙台

ふくしま 福島

かぞく → Family

Kodomo - child

NAKAMA 1

JAPANESE COMMUNICATION, CULTURE, CONTEXT

Seiichi Makino
Princeton University

Yukiko Abe Hatasa
University of Iowa

Kazumi Hatasa
Purdue University

Houghton Mifflin Company
Boston   New York

Director, Modern Language Programs: E. Kristina Baer
Development Manager: Beth Kramer
Associate Sponsoring Editor: Hélène Hideko de Portu
Senior Development Editor: Sharon Alexander
Packaging Services Supervisor: Charline Lake
Senior Production/Design Coordinator: Sarah Ambrose
Senior Manufacturing Coordinator: Priscilla J. Abreu
Director of Strategic Marketing Initiatives: Elaine Uzan Leary

Cover design by Harold Burch, Harold Burch Design, New York City

Illustration by Travis Kain and Graham Lee

© Dave Bartruff: 1
© Cameramann International: 27, 34, 65, 199, 286
© Fujifotos/Image Works, Inc.: 59, 104, 323, 353, 395
© J. Burbank/Image Works, Inc.: 99, 241
Courtesy Ministry of Foreign Affairs, Consulate General of Japan: 131, 161
Courtesy Nanzan University, Nagoya, Japan: 137, 165
© Charles Gupton/Tony Stone Images: 247
© John Nordell/Image Works, Inc.: 279
© Orion Press/Tony Stone Images: 315
© Don Smetzer/Tony Stone Images: 387

Printed in the U.S.A.

Library of Congress Catalog Card Number: 97-72518

ISBN: 0-669-27583-2

9-VH-02 01

ABOUT THE AUTHORS

Professor Seiichi Makino received his Ph.D. in linguistics in 1968 from the University of Illinois at Urbana-Champaign. He is an internationally prominent Japanese linguist and scholar who is recognized throughout the world for his scholarship and for his many publications. Before beginning his tenure at Princeton University in 1991, he taught Japanese language, linguistics, and culture at the University of Illinois while training the lower-division coordinators. He is an experienced ACTFL oral proficiency trainer in Japanese and continually trains Japanese instructors internationally in proficiency-oriented instruction and in the administration of the Oral Proficiency Interview.

Professor Yukiko Hatasa received her Ph.D. in linguistics in 1992 from the University of Illinois at Urbana-Champaign. She is known nationwide, particularly among young Japanese professors and coordinators, as one of the premier Japanese methodologists in the United States and as an experienced coordinator of large teacher training programs. She is currently the coordinator of the Japanese language program at the University of Iowa and a senior lecturer at Monash University, Australia.

Professor Kazumi Hatasa received his Ph.D. in education in 1989 from the University of Illinois at Urbana-Champaign. He is currently an associate professor at Purdue University and a lecturer at Monash University, Australia. He is recognized internationally for his work in software development for the Japanese language and is distributing most of his work as freeware over the Internet. This book is accompanied by his software.

CONTENTS

TO THE INSTRUCTOR

OBJECTIVES OF THE PROGRAM

Nakama 1 is a complete, flexible introductory program designed to present the fundamentals of the Japanese language primarily to university students. *Nakama 1* focuses on proficiency-based foreign language learning. In other words, our textbook is very much concerned with the learner's level of proficiency in using Japanese for realistic, communicative purposes. At the end of *Nakama 1*, the successful learner's proficiency level should reach a basic survival level that roughly corresponds to the Novice High level of the proficiency guidelines of the American Council on the Teaching of Foreign Languages.

The originality of *Nakama 1* is that it strikes a balance between the curriculum focused only on speaking and listening over the first two years of instruction and the curriculum that equally emphasizes all four skills from the very beginning. In the first of these curricula, the sudden change from speaking and listening to reading and writing at the third-year level (intermediate) is difficult for students. It does not give students enough time to develop reading proficiency before graduation within a four-year college system. On the other hand, in the second curriculum, equal emphasis on all four skills from the beginning is overwhelming for students of Japanese.

In *Nakama 1*, speaking and listening are the foundation of language development. *Nakama 1* includes between 50 and 60 essential vocabulary words in each chapter but limits the number of grammar items. This is because initial vocabulary development is crucial for communicative fluency at the introductory level and because Japanese grammar is so foreign to English-speaking students. The first half of *Nakama 1* only introduces **kana** because of its phonetic nature. The high literacy rate of Japanese children is often attributed to a good association between sound and symbol in the case of **kana**. In the second half of *Nakama 1*, **kanji** is introduced gradually with stroke orders followed by reading practice at both the sentence and the paragraph level. Our purpose is to teach the basic concept of Chinese characters and familiarize students with all three writing systems so that they are better prepared for the second year, in which the focus shifts more toward **kanji**. Following are specific descriptions of the ways in which the four language skills and culture are developed in *Nakama 1*.

Speaking

At the beginning of each chapter, students learn new vocabulary through immediate interactive use. A chapter dialogue following the new vocabulary section provides a model conversation and motivates students in advance for active role-playing activities at the end of the chapter that incorporate the new language structures and functions they will have learned. Grammar explanations are streamlined so that students may focus on speaking and using the language. Students apply new language structures and communication strategies through pair-work and group activities.

Listening

Students practice their listening skills by using the Student Cassettes and by doing collaborative work in class. Each chapter dialogue, recorded on the Student Cassettes, is part of a lively story line and can be used for macro-listening to familiarize students with the chapter theme. After the language section, the dialogue can be used again for listening comprehension and speaking activities. The listening section features useful strategies, more listening activities, and *Dict-a-Conversations*, also recorded on the Student Cassettes, that focus on detail-listening skills.

Culture

Special care has been devoted in *Nakama 1* to providing practical insights into Japanese culture. The culture notes specifically discuss those realistic aspects of life in Japan that are crucial to using the language in the target culture. The notes in the culture section are closely related to the communication strategies covered later in each chapter. The topics discussed include greetings, the Japanese education system, college life, neighborhood relations, housing, popular pastimes, food, shopping, and what to do in case of sickness.

Writing

Nakama 1 introduces all three Japanese writing systems in an interactive, highly communicative manner. One of *Nakama's* key features is to train students to write Japanese from the beginning. The pace of introduction is carefully monitored so as not to overburden students. In Chapter 1, we introduce students to **hiragana,** the basic syllabary to write Japanese, as if **hiragana** were phonetic symbols. **Katakana,** introduced in Chapter 3, can be taught all at once or spread out over several chapters until Chapter 7. All **katakana** words appearing in Chapters 1 through 6 have **furigana** superscripts. Starting with Chapter 7, students learn to master 90 essential **kanji** by the end of *Nakama 1*.

Reading

After practicing new **kanji,** students are given a text where they can recognize the **kanji** they learned. Because the texts include words they don't know, students are required to make good use of the reading strategies provided before the readings in each chapter. To familiarize students with authentic Japanese texts, the reading texts in *Nakama 1* do not contain any word boundaries and are written in a combination of **kanji** and **kana. Hiragana** superscripts are provided for words containing **kanji** that were not introduced in the current or previous chapters. The rest of the chapter contains word boundaries, and unknown **kanji** words are written in **kana** except for the following two cases:

First, words containing **kanji** currently introduced are written in **kanji** and superscripted up to the reading section.

Second, words containing **kanji** that have been introduced as well as unintroduced kanji are superscripted throughout the chapter. For example, 書く is introduced in Chapter 11. Therefore, the verb **kaku** is written as 書^かく before the reading section of this chapter. The word **toshokan** (library), which has been introduced in Chapter 4, is written as 図書館^{としょかん} throughout the chapter because the **kanji** 図 and 館 have not been introduced. This method was taken so as to avoid showing inauthentic writing, such as と書かん, while providing a maximum exposure to newly introduced **kanji** without burdening students.

FEATURES OF NAKAMA

- Chapter dialogues present a lively story line that illustrates typical daily events in Japanese life and provide a realistic context in which to learn the chapter vocabulary and grammatical structures. Dialogue translations appear in an appendix to encourage guessing meaning from context.

- Specially created **manga** accompany each chapter dialogue and provide a listening comprehension activity. The listening activities and the *Dict-a-Conversation*, a unique feature of *Nakama,* are preceded by listening strategies to help students understand better the natural flow of Japanese.

- Grammar is presented functionally in the form of sample sentences in a clear, easy-to-comprehend boxed format, followed by language notes to keep explanations simple and focus on direct application in the はなして みましょう sections.

- Exercises progress from structured practice to a wide range of open-ended communicative activities that emphasize pair and group work.

- Culture notes in English explore aspects of contemporary life in Japan that are an essential component of communication.

- Helpful mnemonic devices acccompany the introduction of **hiragana** (Chapters 1–3) and **katakana** (Chapter 3.5). *Nakama 1* presents 90 **kanji** in Chapters 7 through 12, with stroke orders. Starting with Chapter 7, a **kanji** section in each chapter helps students master correct stroke orders when writing in Japanese and prepares students for the reading section.

- Each chapter reading is preceded by strategies. All readings feature **hiragana** superscripts to assist students with character reading.

- Communication sections in each chapter provide practical strategies to develop students' oral proficiency.

- Vocabulary is listed at the end of each chapter and organized into essential, passive, and supplementary groups for easy review. Essential vocabulary consists of the words that are introduced in the *New Vocabulary, Language,* and *Communication* sections for students' recognition and production. Passive vocabulary occurs throughout the chapter, but students are not expected to retain it. Supplementary vocabulary does not appear in the chapter but is relevant to the chapter theme and useful for class activities.

- Free text-linked student software may be downloaded from our Modern Language web site at http://www.hmco.com/college.

PROGRAM COMPONENTS
- Student's Text with Student Cassettes (0-669-46134-2)
- Workbook/Laboratory Manual (0-669-27585-9)
- Cassette program (0-669-27586-7)
- Free text-linked Web activities at http://www.hmco.com/college.
- Instructor's Resource Manual (0-669-27584-0)

MATERIALS FOR THE STUDENT
- Student's Text: *Nakama 1* has 12 chapters and is the main component of the program. You will find a description of the student text on pages xx–xxi of the To the Student section.

- Student Cassettes: These cassettes are designed to maximize learners' exposure to the sounds of natural spoken Japanese and improve their pronunciation. Included are dialogues, listening sections, and *Dict-a-Conversations* identified in the student text by a cassette icon. This set of cassettes comes shrinkwrapped with the student's textbook.

- Workbook/Laboratory Manual: An integral part of *Nakama*, the workbook/laboratory manual is designed to reinforce the association of sound, syntax, and meaning needed for effective communication in Japanese as well as the grammar and vocabulary presented in the textbook. Students who use the workbook/laboratory manual consistently will find this component of great assistance in developing their listening, speaking, reading, and writing skills and in targeting the specific lesson features that require extra review. Each chapter of the workbook/laboratory manual is correlated to the corresponding chapter in the textbook. The activities include sentence completion, dialogue completion, fill-in-the blank exercises, personal questions, and sentence combination exercises, among others.

- The workbook section provides a variety of practice to help students develop their reading and writing skills using the various grammatical patterns learned in each chapter. Occasionally, structured exercises are provided to strengthen students' accuracy with grammar points. Each chapter of the workbook features two communicative activities for each of the five grammar points introduced in the *Language* section of the textbook followed by one integration exercise.

- The laboratory manual exercises can be done at the language lab and are essential for developing pronunciation, language accuracy, and listening skills. The pronunciation section practices the sounds provided in Chapter 1 and the words listed in the *Essential Vocabulary* at the end of each chapter in the textbook. The listening and language accuracy section of each chapter of the laboratory manual features one to three activities for each of the five language points introduced in the corresponding chapter of the textbook.

- Cassette Program: The Cassette Program accompanying *Nakama* corresponds to the *Essential Vocabulary* section in the textbook and to the activities in the laboratory manual. The Cassette Program provides approximately six hours of taped exercises recorded by native speakers.

- Free text-linked student software may be downloaded from our Modern Language web site at http://www.hmco.com/college.

SUPPLEMENTARY MATERIALS FOR THE INSTRUCTOR

- Instructor's Resource Manual: The Resource Manual is made up of four sections. The first section, the Instructor's Guide, is written in both Japanese and English and provides a detailed description of the *Nakama 1* program with concrete suggestions and ideas for the effective implementation of chapter segments and supplementary activities. For example, Chapter 1 contains suggestions on how to teach **hiragana** and its pronunciation as if **hiragana** were phonetic symbols. The Instructor's Guide also features various games and pair activities to expand your teaching options.

  The second section, entitled Reproducible Materials, contains transparency masters and activity cards for the many activity suggestions in the Instructor's Guide.

  The Textbook Tapescript and Cassette Program Tapescript make up the third section of the Instructor's Resource Manual, which we have provided for your convenience.

  The Answer Keys to textbook, workbook, and laboratory manual activities are provided in the last section of the Instructor's Resource Manual and may be photocopied and distributed to students.

  The pages of the Instructor's Resource Manual are perforated for your convenience.

COURSE PLANNING

The following 150-hour semester syllabus reflects how *Nakama 1* can be used over two semesters of 15 weeks with classes meeting five times a week. Chapters 1 though 6 are taught the first semester and Chapters 7 through 12 the second semester. Two weeks have been set aside in each semester for review and testing all the skills taught in *Nakama 1:* listening, speaking, reading, writing, and culture acquisition.

	First Semester	**Second Semester**
Weeks 1 – 2	Chapter 1	Chapter 7
Weeks 3 – 4	Chapter 2	Chapter 8
Weeks 5 – 6	Chapter 3	Chapter 9
Week 7	Review and Testing	Review and Testing
Weeks 8 – 9	Chapter 4	Chapter 10
Weeks 10 – 11	Chapter 5	Chapter 11
Weeks 12 – 14	Chapter 6	Chapter 12
Week 15	Review and Final Exams	Review and Final Exams

The following 150-hour quarter syllabus reflects how *Nakama 1* can be used over three quarters of 10 weeks with classes meeting five times a week. Chapters 1 through 4 are taught in the first quarter, chapters 5 through 8 in the second quarter, and chapters 9 through 12 in the third quarter. One to two weeks have been set aside in each quarter for review and testing.

	First Quarter	Second Quarter	Third Quarter
Week 1	Chapter 1	Review and Chapter 5	Review and Chapter 9
Week 2	Chapter 1	Chapter 5	Chapter 9
Week 3	Chapter 2	Chapter 6	Chapter 10
Week 4	Chapter 2	Chapter 6	Chapter 10
Week 5	Review and Testing	Review and Testing	Review and Testing
Week 6	Chapter 3	Chapter 7	Chapter 11
Week 7	Chapter 3	Chapter 7	Chapter 11
Week 8	Chapter 4	Chapter 8	Chapter 12
Week 9	Chapter 4	Chapter 8	Chapter 12
Week 10	Review and Final Exams	Review and Final Exams	Review and Final Exams

Chapter 3.5 on **katakana** has been left out of the above syllabi because it should be up to the instructors to incorporate Chapter 3.5's contents into their instruction of Chapters 4 through 6.

Instructors teaching programs with fewer than 150 hours available in the year may want to cover fewer chapters or less material within the chapters. A suggested strategy is to identify the focus of the curriculum. If the curriculum focuses more on speaking and listening, instructors may want to cut down the **kanji** and reading sections. Instructors should not, however, reduce the items of vocabulary or of grammar, which are essential and were carefully selected. On the other hand, instructors might pick and choose from among the grammar activities.

TO THE STUDENT

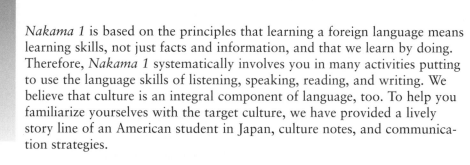

Nakama 1 is based on the principles that learning a foreign language means learning skills, not just facts and information, and that we learn by doing. Therefore, *Nakama 1* systematically involves you in many activities putting to use the language skills of listening, speaking, reading, and writing. We believe that culture is an integral component of language, too. To help you familiarize yourselves with the target culture, we have provided a lively story line of an American student in Japan, culture notes, and communication strategies.

ORGANIZATION OF THE TEXTBOOK

Nakama 1 consists of 12 chapters. In Chapter 1, you will learn the basic sounds of the Japanese language and the basic Japanese syllabary symbols called **hiragana**. You will also learn basic greetings and classroom instructions. At the end of this chapter, as of every chapter in *Nakama 1*, a list of essential and passive vocabulary is provided. Each of the following 11 chapters focuses on a common communicative situation and contains the features listed below.

- Chapter Opener: Each chapter opens with a photograph that sets the scene for the chapter and a list of chapter contents. The language functions introduced in the chapter are listed at the top of the chapter contents. Keeping in mind the functions while you go through the chapter will help you focus on results.

- *New Vocabulary*: The vocabulary is presented in thematic groups with basic communicative activities.

- *Dialogue*: The dialogues feature a lively story line: Alice Arisaka, an American student, spends a year studying in Japan. You will get to know a series of characters and follow them through typical events in their lives. First, you will look at the **manga** (a cartoon strip) and listen to the recorded dialogues on the Student Cassettes. Then, you will match the dialogue lines with the frames of the **manga**.

- *Culture*: Culture notes in English explore aspects of contemporary life in Japan that are an essential component of communication.

- *Language*: Grammar explanations are given in the form of sample sentences in a clear, easy-to-comprehend boxed format followed by language notes that keep explanations simple. Class activities that you can do in pairs or in groups immediately put the language structures into practice. Grammar accuracy, however, should not be overlooked. There is a high correlation between successful communication and grammar accuracy.

- *Reading*: The reading texts are systematically preceded by strategies designed to help you become a successful reader of Japanese. From Chapter 2, the text is written in the three scripts: **hiragana**, **katakana**, and **kanji** (Chinese characters). The reading of **katakana** until Chapter 6 is provided with small **hiragana** scripts (**furigana**) over the **katakana**. Starting with Chapter 7, a **kanji** section in each chapter precedes the reading section and prepares you for it. The reading of unintroduced **kanji** throughout the textbook is given with **furigana**. The readings include a small number of unknown words so that you can develop strategies to cope with authentic texts.

- *Listening*: Listening activities consist of strategies followed by practice. The listening strategy section introduces useful strategies for beginning students and is followed by practice that helps you apply the strategies for general comprehension. The next activity is a *Dict-a-Conversation* recorded on your Student Cassettes packaged with the textbook. After listening to the tape, you get to write down what you hear, which becomes your partner's lines. Then, you get to create your end of the dialogue.

- *Communication*: This segment will provide you with knowledge and practice of basic strategies that will facilitate your communication in Japanese.

- *Integration*: You will be asked to mobilize all the skills you have learned up to the current point through discussion, interview, and role-play formats.

- Vocabulary List: Vocabulary is listed at the end of each chapter and organized into essential, passive, and supplementary groups for easy review. *Essential Vocabulary* consists of the words that are introduced in the *New Vocabulary*, *Language*, and *Communication* sections for your recognition and production. Passive vocabulary occurs throughout the chapter, but you are not expected to retain it. Supplementary vocabulary does not appear in the chapter but is relevant to the chapter theme and useful for class activities.

- Appendices A–G: In the appendices, you will find the translation of the chapter dialogues; explanations of the accents of standard Japanese; verb and adjective conjugations; and lists of counter expressions, demonstrative words, and kanji.

- Index and Glossaries: At the end of your textbook, you will find an index for topics in the *Language* and *Culture* sections and Japanese-English and English-Japanese glossaries.

MATERIALS AND TIPS FOR THE STUDENT

- Student's Text with Student Cassettes: *Nakama 1* has 12 chapters and is the main component of the program.

- Student Cassettes: Two free 60-minute cassettes containing recordings of the dialogues, the *Dict-a-Conversation*, and other listening activities are packaged with your textbook. These cassettes are designed to maximize your exposure to the sounds of natural spoken Japanese and help you practice pronunciation.

- Workbook/Laboratory Manual: The workbook section provides a variety of practice to help you develop your listening, reading, and writing skills using the various grammatical patterns learned in each chapter.

Here are some tips to follow in using the workbook:

1. Before doing the activities, review the corresponding vocabulary and grammar sections in the textbook.

2. Do the activities with your textbook closed.

3. When you write, be creative without overstepping your linguistic boundaries.

4. Try to use the dictionary sparingly.

The laboratory manual exercises are essential for developing your pronunciation and listening skills. The pronunciation section practices the sounds provided in Chapter 1 and the words listed in the *Essential Vocabulary* at the end of each chapter in your textbook. The listening and accuracy section of each chapter of the laboratory manual features activities for each of the five language points introduced in the corresponding chapter of your textbook.

Here are some tips to follow when using the laboratory manual:

1. While doing the pronunciation exercises, listen carefully and try to imitate the speakers' pronunciation and intonation accurately.

2. Read the directions and exercise items before doing the listening comprehension activities.

3. Do not be concerned with understanding every word; your goal should be to do the task that is asked of you in the activity.

Through conscientious use of the workbook/laboratory manual, you should make good progress in your study of the Japanese language.

- Cassette Program: The Cassette Program accompanying *Nakama 1* corresponds to the *Essential Vocabulary* section in your textbook and to the activities in the laboratory manual. It provides approximately six hours of taped exercises recorded by native speakers and is available for student purchase as well as for use in the language lab.

- Free text-linked Web activities may be downloaded from our Modern Language web site at http://www.hmco.com/college.

We would like to hear your comments and reactions to *Nakama 1*. Reports on your experiences using this program would be of great interest and value to us. Please write us care of Houghton Mifflin Company, College Division, Modern Languages, 222 Berkeley Street, Boston, MA 02116.

ACKNOWLEDGMENTS

The authors and publisher thank the following people for their recommendations regarding the content of *Nakama 1*. Their comments and suggestions were invaluable during the development of this publication.

Noriko Akatsuka, *UCLA, Los Angeles, CA*
Aloysius Chang, *Washington State University, Seattle, WA*
Hiroko Kataoka, *University of Oregon, Portland, OR*
Chisato Kitagawa, *University of Massachusetts, Amherst, MA*
Chiyo Konishi, *Pennsylvania State University, Philadelphia, PA*
Junko Kumamoto-Healey, *University of Melbourne, Melbourne, Australia*
Yukari Kunisue, *formerly of Columbia University, New York, NY*
Yasumi Kuriya, *University of Iowa, Iowa City, IA*
Akira Miura, *University of Wisconsin, Madison, WI*
Shigeru Miyagawa, *MIT, Cambridge, MA*
John Mertz, *North Carolina State University, Raleigh, NC*
Hiroshi Nara, *University of Pittsburgh, Pittsburgh, PA*
Machiko Netsu, *International Christian University, Tokyo, Japan*
Yoko Pusavat, *California State University at Long Beach, Long Beach, CA*
Yoshiko Saito, *University of Texas at Austin, Austin, TX*
Zenryu Shirakawa, *Boston University, Boston, MA*
Alexander Vovin, *University of Hawaii, Honolulu, HI*
Paul Warnick, *Brigham Young University, Provo, UT*
Yasuko Ito Watt, *Indiana University, West Lafayette, IN*
Kikuko Yamashita, *Brown University, Providence, RI*

The authors and publisher also thank the following people for field-testing *Nakama 1*. Their comments contributed greatly to the accuracy of this publication.

Nobuko Chikamatsu, *DePaul University, Chicago, IL*
Fusae Ekida, *Purdue University, West Lafayette, IN*
Junko Hino, *Princeton University, Princeton, NJ*
Satoru Ishikawa, *Princeton University, Princeton, NJ*
Yoshiko Jo, *Princeton University, Princeton, NJ*
Sayuri Kubota, *University of Iowa, Iowa City, IA*

Yasumi Kuriya, *University of Iowa, Iowa City, IA*

Izumi Matsuda, *University of Washington, Seattle, WA*

Junko Mori, *University of Iowa, Iowa City, IA*

Fumiko Nazikian, *Princeton University, Princeton, NJ*

Kaoru Ohta, *University of Washington, Seattle, WA*

Mayumi Oka, *Princeton University, Princeton, NJ*

Amy Snyder Ohta, *University of Washington, Seattle, WA*

Mayumi Steinmetz, *Shoreline Community College, Seattle, WA*

Keiko Yamaguchi, *North Seattle Community College and Shoreline Community College, Seattle, WA*

The authors are especially grateful to Dr. Yasuko Makino, Asian Library, Columbia University, New York, for proofreading *Nakama 1*. They are also grateful to the following people and organizations for their valuable assistance during the development of this project: Kristina Baer, Director, Modern Language Programs; Beth Kramer, Development Manager; Hélène de Portu, Associate Sponsoring Editor; Sharon Alexander, Senior Development Editor; Charline Lake, Packaging Services Supervisor; Jeri Lambert, Project Manager; Travis Kain, illustrator; Graham Lee, illustrator; and Fusae Ekida for the handwritten characters in *Nakama 1*.

Tsuchiura train station sign

THE JAPANESE SOUND SYSTEM AND HIRAGANA

I. Introduction

Japanese is usually written with a combination of three types of characters: **hiragana, katakana,** and **kanji** or Chinese characters. **Hiragana,** the most basic type, is used for function words (words such as *in, at,* and *on*) and inflectional endings (to show negatives, tense, and so on) as well as words of Japanese origin. **Katakana** is used mainly for words borrowed from other languages, such as **keeki** (*cake*), and words for sounds, such as **wanwan** (the Japanese word for *bow-wow*). **Kanji,** which is of Chinese origin, is used for content words, such as nouns, verbs, and adjectives.

Hiragana evolved through the simplification of Chinese characters that occurred during the Heian period (794–1185). Because the Japanese had no writing system of their own, Chinese characters, which are logographs, were used to represent Japanese syllables with no regard for their meanings. For example, the character 安 (read [an] in Chinese) was used for the sound [a] with no regard for its meaning, *peace.* However, it was cumbersome to use some Chinese characters because Japanese words usually contain several syllables. Thus, Chinese characters were gradually simplified to their present-day form. This simplification was done by women who wrote letters and literary works. Thus, **hiragana** was once called **onna de** (*women's hand*).

Forty-six **hiragana** exist, each representing either a vowel or a combination of a consonant and a vowel (Figure 1). Diacritics in the shapes of two dots or a small circle show an alternative pronunciation (Figure 2). Glides are combinations of characters that represent more complex sounds (Figure 3). In Figures 1 to 3, pronounce each character by repeating it after your instructor and/or the accompanying tape. Each chart is read from top to bottom and right to left. Japanese may be written either vertically or horizontally from left to right as in English. In this chapter, whenever you see the Student Cassette symbol, be sure to listen to and repeat each sound.

Figure 1

n	w	r	y	m	h	n	t	s	k			Example	
ん	わ	ら	や	ま	は	な	た	さ	か	あ	a	か	ka
		り		み	ひ	に	ち	し	き	い	i	き	ki
		る	ゆ	む	ふ	ぬ	つ	す	く	う	u	く	ku
		れ		め	へ	ね	て	せ	け	え	e	け	ke
	を	ろ	よ	も	ほ	の	と	そ	こ	お	o	こ	ko

Figure 2

p	b	d	z	g	
ぱ	ば	だ	ざ	が	a
ぴ	び	ぢ	じ	ぎ	i
ぷ	ぶ	づ	ず	ぐ	u
ぺ	べ	で	ぜ	げ	e
ぽ	ぼ	ど	ぞ	ご	o

Figure 3

p	b	d	z	g	r	m	h	n	t	s	k	
ぴゃ	びゃ	ぢゃ	じゃ	ぎゃ	りゃ	みゃ	ひゃ	にゃ	ちゃ	しゃ	きゃ	ya
ぴゅ	びゅ	ぢゅ	じゅ	ぎゅ	りゅ	みゅ	ひゅ	にゅ	ちゅ	しゅ	きゅ	yu
ぴょ	びょ	ぢょ	じょ	ぎょ	りょ	みょ	ひょ	にょ	ちょ	しょ	きょ	yo

Hiragana あ～そ

In this section, you will learn fifteen **hiragana** and their pronunciation. The following charts show both printed and handwritten styles.

Printed Style

s	k		
さ	か	あ	a
し	き	い	i
す	く	う	u
せ	け	え	e
そ	こ	お	o

Handwritten Style

s	k		
さ	か	あ	a
し	き	い	i
す	く	う	u
せ	け	え	e
そ	こ	お	o

Study the following mnemonic pictures and keys. Although the illustrations do not accurately represent the shapes and sounds of the **hiragana,** they will help you remember the characters.

Ah! Ann is good at ice-skating.

あ is similar to [ah] but is shorter.

I have big *ears*.

い is similar to the vowel sound in *ear* but is shorter.

Ooh! This is heavy.

う [u] is similar to the vowel sound in [ooh] but is shorter and the lips are not as rounded.

I need *exercise*.

え is similar to the first vowel sound in *exercise*, but the mouth is more closed.

The ball will land *on* the green.

お is similar to the vowel sound [o] in *on* as the British pronounce it, but the lips are slightly more rounded.

Karate kick.

か is a combination of [k] and [a]. The Japanese [k] sound is pronounced with less forceful than its English equivalent.

This is a *key*.

き is similar to *key*, but the vowel sound is shorter. The [i] becomes a whispered sound before [p], [t], [k], [s], or [h].

This is a *cuckoo*.

く is similar to the first syllable of *cuckoo*, but the lips are not as rounded. The [u] becomes a whispered sound before [p], [t], [k], [s], or [h].

A man with a *cane*.

け is similar to the sound of [ca] in *cane* without the [y] sound.

A ten yen *coin* is worth a dime.

こ is similar to the sound of [co] in *coin* without the [y] sound.

Don't drink too much *sake*.

The Japanese [s] sound さ is not as strong as the English [s] sound because less air is forced out between the teeth.

This is how *she* wears her hair.

し is similar to *she*, but the vowel sound is shorter and the lips are spread wider. Japanese does not have the sound [si] as in *sea*. The [i] becomes a whispered sound before [p], [t], [k], [s], or [h].

Swimming is fun in the summer.

す is a combination of [s] and [u]. The Japanese [u] becomes a whispered sound before [p], [t], [k], [s], or [h]. The vowel sound is almost lost because it is very soft.

Hello, *Señor* García.

せ is similar to the sound of [se] in *señor*.

This character zigzags *so* much.

そ is similar to *so* but the vowel sound is shorter.

Practice

Read the following words, paying attention to whispered sounds and intonation. Characters with a bar over them (Ex. いけ) should be pronounced at a higher pitch than those without a bar. Highlighted characters (▢) are whispered sounds.

え	picture	いけ	pond
おかし	confectionery	いす	chair
き	tree	きく	chrysanthemum

かお	face	さけ	sake (rice wine)
あし	leg	えき	station
せかい	world	そこ	bottom
あさ	morning	しお	salt
あかい	red	あかい　かさ	red umbrella
あおい	blue	あおい　いす	blue chair

Useful Expressions   Introducing yourself

ha ji me ma shi te　　　　　de su　do o zo　yo ro shi ku
はじめまして。 ＿＿＿＿＿です。 どうぞ　よろしく。

How do you do?[1] I am ＿＿＿＿＿. Pleased to meet you.[1]

Example

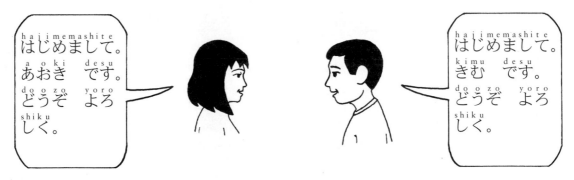

- ● The little circle at the end of each phrase represents a period in written Japanese.

Practice and Conversation

A. Today is the first day of Japanese class. Introduce yourself to your classmates. Then listen as your classmates introduce themselves to you. Try to remember their names.

B. Did you greet your classmates with a bow? If you didn't, greet them again with a bow. If you don't know how to bow properly, ask your instructor to show you.

---
[1] The English translation here is not a literal equivalent of the Japanese.

II. Hiragana た〜ほ

Study the following fifteen **hiragana** and their pronunciations.

Printed Style

h	n	t	
は	な	た	a
ひ	に	ち	i
ふ	ぬ	つ	u
へ	ね	て	e
ほ	の	と	o

Handwritten Style

h	n	t	
は	な	た	a
ひ	に	ち	i
ふ	ぬ	つ	u
へ	ね	て	e
ほ	の	と	o

Mnemonics and key	Pronunciation

The letters *t* and *a* make *ta*.

The Japanese sound た is produced by touching the tip of the tongue behind upper teeth and gum. The Japanese [t] sound is not as strong as the English [t] sound because less air is forced between the teeth.

Being a *cheerleader* isn't easy.

The sound ち is pronounced [chi] as in *cheer*. There is no [ti] sound in Japanese. The [i] sound becomes a whispered sound before [p], [t], [k], [s], and [h].

A *cat's* tail.

つ is similar to the final sound in *cats*. It appears not only at the end of a word, but also at the beginning and in the middle of a word. The [u] sound becomes a whispered sound before [p], [t], [k], [s], and [h].

Fruit on a *table*.

て is similar to the first syllable of *table*, without the [y] sound.

I've got a thorn in my *toe*.

と is similar to the sound of *toe* but the vowel sound is shorter.

This person is taking a *nap*.

な is similar to the sound of [na] in *nap*, but the vowel sound is more like [a] as in *ah*.

Look at my *knees*.

に is similar to the sound of *knees*, but the vowel sound is shorter.

Noodles and chopsticks.

ぬ is similar to the first syllable of *noodle*, but is shorter.

I caught a fish in my *net*.

ね is similar to the sound of [ne] in *net*.

See the "*No* Smoking" sign.

の is similar to the sound of *no*, but the vowel sound is shorter, and the lips are not as rounded.

I bought a *house*.

The Japanese [h] sound は is much softer than the English [h].

This is Mr. Hill. *He* is strong.

ひ is similar to the sound of *he*, but the vowel sound is shorter.

Mt. *Fuji* is beautiful.

The initial consonant [f] ふ is produced by bringing the lips together as if blowing out a candle.

I have a *headache*.

へ is similar to the sound of *head* without the [d] sound.

A house isn't a *home* without TV.

ほ is similar to the first part of *home,* without the [u] sound.

Practice

Read the following words, paying attention to whispered sounds and intonation.

て	hand	に̄く	meat
つき̄	moon	ひと̄	person
お̄な̄か	stomach	̄ねこ	cat
はな̄	nose	いぬ̄	dog
く̄ち̄	mouth	ふえ̄	flute
たき̄	waterfall	ほし̄	star
はな̄	flower	うち̄	house
た̄か̄い	high, expensive	た̄か̄い に̄く	expensive meat
ひく̄い	low	ひく̄い こ̄え	low voice

Useful Expressions   Greeting someone

Greeting people in the proper way is important in all cultures. In Japanese, the phrases used for greeting vary, depending on the time of day.

A. In the morning

o ha yoo   go za i ma su.
おはよう　ございます。   Good morning./Hello.

> **Example**
>
> o ha yoo   go za i ma su.
> A: おはよう　ございます。
> o ha yoo   go za i ma su.
> B: おはよう　ございます。

B. In the afternoon

ko n ni chi wa.
こんにちは。   Good afternoon./Hello.

> **Example**
>
> ko n ni chi wa.
> A: こんにちは。
> ko n ni chi wa.
> B: こんにちは。

C. In the evening

ko n ba n wa.
こんばんは。   Good evening./Hello.

Example

ko n ba n wa.
A: こんばんは。

ko n ba n wa.
B: こんばんは。

- よう in おはよう　ございます [ohayoo gozaimasu] is pronounced as a long [o]. You will learn more about long vowels in a later section.

- は in こんにちは [konnichi wa] and こんばんは [konban wa] is pronounced [wa].

- In general, these phrases are used in both casual and formal situations except for おはよう　ございます [ohayoo gozaimasu], which has a less formal version, おはよう [ohayoo]. おはよう [ohayoo] may be used with friends or family members but is considered rude to use with superiors and in formal situations.

- If you meet a person more than once on the same day, using these phrases each time would seem rather silly. In such cases, you should just bow slightly or make casual conversation.

- こんにちは [konnichi wa] and こんばんは [konban wa] are not used among family members.

Practice and Conversation

A. Imagine that class is about to begin. Greet your instructor and classmates, nodding slightly rather than bowing.

B. Greet a friend in the morning. Greet your instructor in the afternoon. Greet a friend in the evening.

C. Walk around the classroom. As your instructor announces whether it is morning, afternoon, or evening, greet five classmates with the appropriate phrase. Don't forget to bow slightly.

III. Hiragana ま〜ん

Study the following **hiragana** and their pronunciation.

Printed Style

n	w	r	y	m	
ん	わ	ら	や	ま	a
		り		み	i
		る	ゆ	む	u
		れ		め	e
	を	ろ	よ	も	o

Handwritten Style

n	w	r	y	m	
ん	わ	ら	や	ま	a
		り		み	i
		る	ゆ	む	u
		れ		め	e
	を	ろ	よ	も	o

Mom! I can't sit any longer.

The Japanese [m] sound ま is like the [m] in *mom* but is less forceful.

Who is twenty-one? *Me!*

み is similar to the sound of *me*, but the vowel sound is shorter.

Cows *moo*.

む is similar to the sound of *moo*, but the vowel sound is shorter.

An Olympic gold *medal*.

め is similar to the first syllable of *medal*.

You catch *more* fish with a hook.

も is similar to the sound of [mo] in *more*.

A *yacht*.

や is a combination of the [y] and [a] sounds. The [yi] and [ye] sounds do not exist in Japanese.

Can you play the *ukulele?*

ゆ is similar to the first syllable of *ukulele*.

Yo-yos were once very popular.

よ is similar to the first syllable of *yo-yo*, but the vowel sound is shorter.

A *rabbit*.

The [r] sound in Japanese ら is neither [l] nor [r] in English. It is produced by flicking the tip of the tongue against the gum behind the upper teeth.

A *ribbon*.

り is similar to the first syllable of *ribbon*. The position of the tongue is the same as in ら.

A *loop* at the end.

る is similar to the sound of *loop* without the [p] sound, but the vowel sound is shorter. The position of the tongue is the same as in ら.

Let's dance.

れ is similar to the sound of *let's* without the [ts]. The position of the tongue is the same as in ら.

A cowboy with his *rope*.

ろ is similar to the sound *rope* without the [p] sound, and the vowel sound is shorter. The position of the tongue is the same as in ら.

Wah!

For わ, your lips should not be as rounded, as when you pronounce the English sound *Wah*.

Oh! I can ride a unicycle.

を is pronounced [o], like お.

The *end*.

The pronunciation of ん changes according to the sound it precedes. Before [m], [n], [b], and [p] it becomes [m]. Before [t], [s], [d], and [z], it becomes [n]. Before [k], [g], and [ng] and at the end of a word, it becomes [ng].

Practice

Read the following words, paying attention to whispered sounds and intonation.

あたま	head	はれ	clear (weather)
みみ	ear	とり	bird
め	eye	むすめ	daughter
ひる	afternoon	かわ	river
よる	night	やま	mountain
あめ	rain	からし	mustard
ゆき	snow	くすり	medicine
くも	cloud	うま	horse
しろい	white	しろい　とり	white bird
くろい	black	くろい　め	black eyes

Useful Expressions   Addressing people; saying good-bye

A. Forms of address. The Japanese always use a title to address people other than family members.

se n see
せんせい
professor, teacher

se n see
〜せんせい
Professor 〜

sa n
〜さん
Mr./Mrs./Miss/Ms. 〜

Examples

たなかせんせい　　やまださん
Professor Tanaka　　Mr./Mrs./Miss/Ms. Yamada

- せい in せんせい [**sensee**] is pronounced as a long [e]. You will learn more about long vowels in a later section.

- It is customary to address an instructor simply as せんせい.

- The Japanese usually call others by their last names even when they have known them for a long time. First names are used among family members and close friends.

- 〜さん can be used for anyone except yourself.

B. Saying good-bye. The phrase for good-bye differs depending on who you are speaking with.

1. To instructors or social superiors:

   shi tsu ree shi ma su
   しつれいします。　Good-bye.

Student: せんせい、しつれい します。

Instructor: <ruby>さ<rt>sa</rt></ruby><ruby>よ<rt>yoo</rt></ruby><ruby>う<rt></rt></ruby><ruby>な<rt>na</rt></ruby><ruby>ら<rt>ra</rt></ruby>。

- The literal translation of しつれいします [shitsuree shimasu] is *I am committing a rudeness* or *I am disturbing you.*
- When saying good-bye, you should nod your head slightly.

2. To friends:

じゃあ、また。 See you later (literally: Well then, again).

さようなら。 Good-bye.

Student A: じゃあ、また。
Student B: さようなら。

- さようなら [**sayoonara**] is more often used when you do not expect to see the person for an extended period of time.

Practice and Conversation

Imagine that class is over. Say good-bye to your instructor and five classmates.

IV. Hiragana が〜ぽ: Voiceless and voiced consonants

The consonants [k], [s], [t], and [h] are voiceless. For example, when you pronounce [k], a voiceless consonant, your vocal chords do not vibrate, but when you pronounce [g], a voiced consonant, they do vibrate. Feel the difference by putting your hand on your throat when you pronounce [k] and [g].

					h		t	s	k	
ん	わ	ら	や	ま	は	な	た	さ	か	あ
		り		み	ひ	に	ち	し	き	い
		る	ゆ	む	ふ	ぬ	つ	す	く	う
		れ		め	へ	ね	て	せ	け	え
	を	ろ	よ	も	ほ	の	と	そ	こ	お

Voiceless consonants have voiced counterparts as shown in the following charts. The difference between voiced and voiceless consonants is the presence or absence of vibration. For example, try to pronounce [k] and [g] alternatively. The tongue position and the shape of the lips do not change. In both cases, the back of the tongue touches the back of the mouth, and then you quickly release the tongue to let the air flow. The only difference between the two is that your vocal chords vibrate when you pronounce [g] but do not when you pronounce [k]. A voiced consonant is indicated by two dots (゛) and an unvoiced consonant by the small circle (゜) at the upper right corner of a character. For example, the voiced consonant [b] in ば has the voiceless counterpart [p] in ぱ.

Printed Style

p	b	d	z	g (ŋ)	
ぱ	ば	だ	ざ	が	a
ぴ	び	ぢ	じ	ぎ	i
ぷ	ぶ	づ	ず	ぐ	u
ぺ	べ	で	ぜ	げ	e
ぽ	ぼ	ど	ぞ	ご	o

Handwritten Style

p	b	d	z	g (ŋ)	
ぱ	ば	だ	ざ	が	a
ぴ	び	ぢ	じ	ぎ	i
ぷ	ぶ	づ	ず	ぐ	u
ぺ	べ	で	ぜ	げ	e
ぽ	ぼ	ど	ぞ	ご	o

● Some people prefer to use [ŋ] instead of [g] because it sounds softer.

Reading hiragana

Read the following words, paying attention to voiced and voiceless consonants.

ひげ	beard	にほんご	Japanese language
ゆび	finger	かばん	bag
うで	arm	ちず	map
のど	throat	かぎ	key
ひざ	knee	かぜ	wind
からだ	body	えんぴつ	pencil
でんわ	telephone	てんぷら	tempura
ながい	long	ながい　うで	long arm
みじかい	short	みじかい　ゆび	short finger

Useful Expressions   Thanking; apologizing; getting attention

Speaking politely is important in all cultures. Here are some basic expressions of courtesy.

_{a ri ga too　　go za i ma su}
ありがとう　ございます。　　Thank you.

_{su mi ma se n}
すみません。　　I am sorry.

_{a noo　　su mi ma se n}
（あのう、）すみません。　　(Eh,) Excuse me.

_{doo　i ta shi ma shi te}
どういたしまして。　　You are welcome.

- ございます as in おはよう　ございます [ohayoo gozaimasu] and ありがとう　ございます [arigatoo gozaimasu] is a polite expression. Thus, おはよう [ohayoo] and ありがとう [arigatoo] are used in casual speech and are not used with older people or those of a higher social status.

Practice and Conversation

A. What would you say to your instructor if you forgot your homework?

B. Your instructor is talking to someone. You need to speak to him/her. How would you interrupt the conversation?

C. Your classmates are standing in front of the door, and you want to leave the room. What would you say to them?

D. A student sitting next to you picks up the pencil you just dropped. What would you say to him?

V. Hiragana ああ～わあ: Long vowels

When two of the same vowel appear consecutively in a word, each of the vowels retains the same length and quality. However, the two vowels are pronounced as a continuous sound rather than as two separate vowels. This is called a long vowel.

In general, long vowels are written by adding あ to the **hiragana** with the vowel [a], い to the **hiragana** with the vowel [i] or [e], う to the **hiragana** with the vowel [u] or [o]. Notice that い is added after the vowel [e] but is still pronounced as [e]. (See the following chart.) Similarly, う is added after the [o] sound but is pronounced as [o]. Some exceptions add え and お instead of い and う, respectively. You should not worry about them for now. You can learn them as you learn new vocabulary.

STUDENT

n	w	r	y	m	h	n	t	s	k	a		
ん	わあ	らあ	やあ	まあ	はあ	なあ	たあ	さあ	かあ	ああ		aa
		りい		みい	ひい	にい	ちい	しい	きい	いい		ii
		るう	ゆう	むう	ふう	ぬう	つう	すう	くう	うう		uu
		れい		めい	へい	ねい ねえ	てい	せい	けい	えい ええ		ee
	を	ろう	よう	もう	ほお ほう	のう	とう とお	そう	こう こお	おう おお		oo

Practice

Read the following words, paying attention to long vowels.

せんせい	teacher	がくせい	student
ふうせん	balloon	さとう	sugar
とおり	street	こうこう	high school
こおり	ice	とけい	clock, watch
おかあさん	mother	おとうさん	father
おばあさん	grandmother	おじいさん	grandfather
おねえさん	elder sister	おにいさん	elder brother
いもうと	younger sister	おとうと	younger brother
おおきい	big, large	おおきい ふうせん	big balloon
ちいさい	small	ちいさい とけい	small clock, watch

Useful Expressions   Asking for Japanese words and English equivalents

A. Asking for the Japanese word. There are a number of ways to ask someone how to say a word or phrase in Japanese. Study the following expressions, paying attention to the situation in which each is used.

1. If the object is close to you:

   これは[2] にほんごで なんと いいますか。

   What do you call this in Japanese?

---

[2] In this sentence, は is pronounced [wa].

Student: やまだせんせい、これは にほんごで　なんと
いいますか。

Professor Yamada, what do you call this in Japanese?

Yamada: 「ほん」と　いいます。

It's called **hon**.

やまだ

- To give the answer, say 〜と　いいます.
- The marks 「」 are the equivalent of quotation marks in English.

2. If the object is close to your instructor but at a distance from you:

それは　にほんごで　なんと　いいますか。

What do you call that in Japanese?

Student: やまだせんせい、それは　にほんごで　なんと
いいますか。

Professor Yamada, what do you call that in Japanese?

Yamada: 「いす」と　いいます。

It's called **isu**.

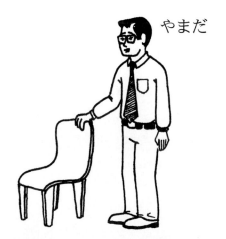

やまだ

3. If the object is at a distance from both you and your instructor:

あれは　にほんごで　なんと　いいますか。

What do you call that (over there) in Japanese?

Example

Student:　やまだせんせい、あれは　にほんごで　なんと
いいますか。

Professor Yamada, what do you call that (over there) in Japanese?

Yamada:「でんわ」と　いいます。

It's called **denwa**.

● これ、それ、and あれ are used to refer only to objects, never to people.

4. If you want to know the word for an object that is out of sight or that is an abstract concept:

〜は　にほんごで　なんと　いいますか。

How do you say 〜 in Japanese?

Example

Student:　やまだせんせい、「love」は　にほんごで　なんと
いいますか。

Professor Yamada, how do you say *love* in Japanese?

Yamada:「あい」と　いいます。

You say, **ai**.

B. Asking for the meaning of a Japanese word or phrase. Do you know what がくせい means? How about だいがく and せんこう? If you don't understand a Japanese word or expression, ask your instructor or classmate:

〜って　なんですか。

What does 〜 mean?

Student: せんせい、「すいか」って なんですか。
Professor, what does **suika** mean?

Teacher: 「Watermelon」です。
It means *watermelon*.

- To give the answer, say 〜です。
- The 、 mark indicates a commá in Japanese.

Practice and Conversation

A. Point at things that you are wearing and ask your instructor how to say them in Japanese.

B. Your instructor is in front of the class and you are sitting at a distance from him/her. What objects are near him/her? Ask your instructor what these objects are called in Japanese.

C. Look outside the window of your classroom and ask your instructor the Japanese word for something you see.

D. Ask your instructor the meanings of the following words: つくえ、こく ばん、まど、くるま

VI. Hiragana Small つ: Double consonants

Some Japanese words have a very slight pause between two sounds. This is called a double consonant, and it means that the consonant of the second syllable has the duration of one syllable. Double consonants are written with a small つ.

Horizontal Writing		Vertical Writing	
Printed Style	Handwritten Style	Printed Style	Handwritten Style
□ っか	□ っか	□ □ □	□ □ □
□ っき	□ っき	っ っ っ	っ っ っ
□ っく	□ っく	く き か	く き か
□ っけ	□ っけ		
□ っこ	□ っこ		

Practice

Read the following words, paying attention to double consonants.

にっき	diary	ざっし		magazine
がっき	musical instrument	せっけん		soap
がっこう	school	はっぱ		leaf
きっぷ	ticket	こっき		national flag
きって	stamp	さっか		writer
ねっとう	boiling water	しっぽ		tail
りっぱな	fine, magnificent	りっぱな　がっこう		fine school

Useful Expressions　Understanding your instructor's requests

Here are a few common expressions your instructor will use in class. Your instructor will also probably use words you don't understand. Learn to guess what he/she is saying from the context, situation, or facial expressions and gestures.

きいて　ください。	Please listen.
みて　ください。	Please look (at it).
かいて　ください。	Please write.
よんで　ください。	Please read.
いって　ください。	Please say it./Repeat after me.

Practice and Conversation

A. Listen to your instructor's request and guess what he/she wants you to do.

B. In pairs, take turns asking each other to do certain actions, using the phrases you know.

VII. Hiragana きゃ～ぴょ: Glides

Sounds containing a consonant and [y], such as [kya], [kyu], and [kyo], are called glides. Glides are written with the **hiragana** containing the vowel [i] and small や、ゆ、or よ.

ぱ	ば	だ	ざ	が	ん	わ	ら	や	ま	は	な	た	さ	か	あ
ぴ	び	ぢ	じ	ぎ			り		み	ひ	に	ち	し	き	い
ぷ	ぶ	づ	ず	ぐ			る	ゆ	む	ふ	ぬ	つ	す	く	う
ぺ	べ	で	ぜ	げ			れ		め	へ	ね	て	せ	け	え
ぽ	ぼ	ど	ぞ	ご		を	ろ	よ	も	ほ	の	と	そ	こ	お

i

pya	bya	ja	ja	gya	rya	mya	hya	nya	cha	sha	kya
ぴ	び	ぢ	じ	ぎ	り	み	ひ	に	ち	し	き
ゃ	ゃ	ゃ	ゃ	ゃ	ゃ	ゃ	ゃ	ゃ	ゃ	ゃ	ゃ

pyu	byu	ju	ju	gyu	ryu	myu	hyu	nyu	chu	shu	kyu
ぴ	び	ぢ	じ	ぎ	り	み	ひ	に	ち	し	き
ゅ	ゅ	ゅ	ゅ	ゅ	ゅ	ゅ	ゅ	ゅ	ゅ	ゅ	ゅ

pyo	byo	jo	jo	gyo	ryo	myo	hyo	nyo	cho	sho	kyo
ぴ	び	ぢ	じ	ぎ	り	み	ひ	に	ち	し	き
ょ	ょ	ょ	ょ	ょ	ょ	ょ	ょ	ょ	ょ	ょ	ょ

Printed Style

きゃ　きゅ　きょ

Handwritten Style

きゃ　きゅ　きょ

Practice

Read the following words, paying attention to glides.

こうちゃ	black tea	きんじょ	neighborhood
でんじゃ	train	ひゃく	one hundred
いしゃ	doctor	さんびゃく	three hundred
しゃしん	photo	りょこう	trip

- The combination of a glide and a double consonant is possible.

しゅっぱつ	departure	ちょっかく	right angle
しゃっくり	hiccup	しょっき	tableware

- Add あ or う to make a long vowel.

きょう	today	びょうき	sickness
きゅうり	cucumber	みょうじ	last name
にんぎょう	doll	しょうがつ	New Year's Day
りょう	dormitory	ぎゅうにゅう	milk

Useful Expressions   Making requests

Is it easy to understand your instructor? Does he/she speak too softly or too fast
for you?

A. When you want your instructor to repeat what he/she has just said:

もう　いちど　いってください。

(Excuse me.) Please say it again (literally: Please say it one more time).

B. When you want your instructor to speak more loudly:

おおきい　こえで　はなしてください。

Please speak loudly (literally: Please speak in a big voice).

C. When you want your instructor to speak slowly:

ゆっくり　いってください。　　　Please say it slowly.
ゆっくり　はなしてください。　　Please speak slowly.

Practice and Conversation

Your instructor has just said something that you don't completely understand.
Think of an appropriate request to make so that you can understand what
he/she said.

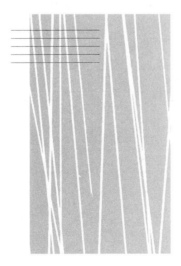

Suffixes

〜せんせい　　Professor 〜
〜さん　　Mr./Mrs./Miss/Ms. 〜

Expressions

ありがとう　ございます。Thank you.

あれは　にほんごで　なんと　いいます
　か。What do you call that (over there) in
　Japanese?

いって　ください。Please say it./Repeat after
　me.

おおきい　こえで　はなしてください。
　Please speak loudly.

おはよう　ございます。　Good
　morning./Hello.

かいてください。Please write.

きいてください。Please listen.

これは　にほんごで　なんと　いいます
　か。What do you call this in Japanese?

こんばんは。　Good evening./Hello.

こんにちは。Good afternoon./Hello.

さようなら。　Good-bye.

しつれいします。　Good-bye.

じゃあ、また。See you later (literally: Well
　then, again).

すみません。I am sorry。　（あのう、）
　すみません。(Eh,) Excuse me.

それは　にほんごで　なんと　いいます
　か。What do you call that in Japanese?

〜って　なんですか。What does 〜 mean?

どういたしまして。　You are welcome.

はじめまして。〜です。どうぞ　よろし
　く。　How do you do? I am _____. Pleased
　to meet you.

〜は　にほんごで　なんと　いいます
　か。How do you say 〜 in Japanese?

みてください。Please look (at it).

もう　いちど　いって　ください。
　Please say it again.

ゆっくり　いってください。Please say it
　slowly.

ゆっくり　はなしてください。Please
　speak slowly.

よんでください。Please read.

Passive Vocabulary

あおい	blue	いしゃ	doctor
あかい	red	いす	chair
あさ	morning	いぬ	dog
あし	leg	いもうと	younger sister
あたま	head	うち	house, home
あめ	rain	うで	arm
いけ	pond	うま	horse

え　picture
えき　station
えんぴつ　pencil
おおきい　big, large
おかあさん　mother
おかし　candy, confection
おじいさん　grandfather
おとうさん　father
おとうと　younger brother
おなか　stomach
おにいさん　older brother
おねえさん　older sister
おばあさん　grandmother
かお　face
かぎ　key
がくせい　student
がっき　musical instrument
がっこう　school
かぜ　wind
かばん　bag
からし　mustard
からだ　body
かわ　river
き　tree
きく　chrysanthemum
きって　stamp
きっぷ　ticket
ぎゅうにゅう　milk
きゅうり　cucumber
きょう　today
きんじょ　neighborhood
くすり　medicine
くち　mouth
くも　cloud
くろい　black
こうこう　high school
こうちゃ　black tea
こおり　ice

こっき　national flag
さけ　sake
さっか　writer
ざっし　magazine
さとう　sugar
さんびゃく　three hundred
しお　salt
しっぽ　tail
しゃしん　photo
しゃっくり　hiccup
しゅっぱつ　departure
しょうがつ　New Year's Day
しょっき　tableware
しろい　white
せかい　world
せっけん　soap
せんせい　teacher, professor
そこ　bottom
たかい　high, expensive
たき　waterfall
ちいさい　small
ちず　map
ちょっかく　right angle
つき　moon
て　hand
でんしゃ　train
てんぷら　tempura
でんわ　telephone
とおり　street
とけい　clock, watch
とり　bird
ながい　long
にく　meat
にっき　diary
にほんご　Japanese language
にんぎょう　doll
ねこ　cat
ねっとう　boiling water

のど throat
はっぱ leaf
はな nose
はな flower
はれ clear (weather)
ひくい low, flat
ひげ beard
ひざ knee
ひと person
ひゃく one hundred
びょうき sickness
ひる afternoon
ふうせん balloon
ふえ flute

ほし star
みじかい short
みみ ear
みょうじ last name
むすめ daughter
め eye
やま mountain
ゆき snow
ゆび finger
よる night
りっぱな fine, magnificent
りょう dormitory
りょこう trip

A formal bow

あいさつと　じこしょうかい

GREETINGS AND INTRODUCTIONS

Functions	Meeting someone for the first time; Introducing someone; Identifying someone
New Vocabulary	Countries, Nationalities and languages, Year in school and academic status, Majors, People
Dialogue	はじめまして (How do you do?)
Culture	Meeting and addressing people
Language	I. Identifying someone or something, using 〜は　〜です
	II. Asking はい／いいえ questions, using 〜は　〜ですか
	III. Recognizing the relationship between nouns with の
	IV. Asking for personal information, using question words
	V. Listing and describing similarities, using と and も
Reading	Using format as a clue
Listening	Listening for key words
Communication	あいづち (Giving feedback) 1

あたらしい ことば (NEW VOCABULARY)

Starting with this chapter, Japanese loan words are written in **katakana**. They have superscripts in **hiragana**, except for the symbol ー, which indicates a long vowel. For example:

コーヒー (*coffee*) is pronounced with an elongated [ko] and an elongated [hi].

A. くに (Countries). Look at the following map and answer the questions in Japanese.

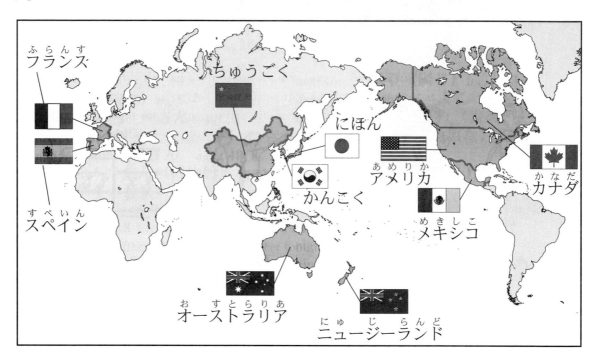

1. Have you ever been to any of these countries? If so, which ones?

2. Do you want to go to any of these countries? If so, to which ones?

3. Do you have a friend from one of these countries? If so, where is he/she from?

4. Is there a name of a country that you would like to say in Japanese? Refer to the vocabulary list on p. 55 or ask your instructor how to say it in Japanese.

B. くにと ことば (Nationalities and languages). Answer the following questions in Japanese.

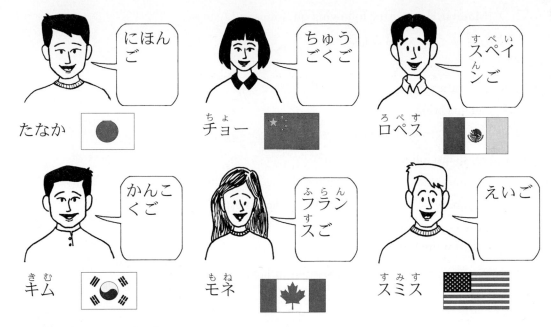

1. What is your native language?

2. What is your instructor's native language? What other languages does he/she speak?

3. Among the languages given, which ones do you understand?

4. What is your nationality? What is your instructor's nationality?

C. せんせい、がくせい、がくねん (Year in school and academic status). Write answers to the following questions in **hiragana.**

いちねんせい　freshman
にねんせい　sophomore
さんねんせい　junior
よねんせい　senior
だいがくいんせい　graduate student
がくせい　student
だいがくせい　college student
りゅうがくせい　exchange student
せんせい　instructor/professor
ともだち　friend

1. What year are you in?

2. How about your classmates?

D. せんこう (Majors). Answer the following questions in Japanese.

アジアけんきゅう　Asian studies
けいざいがく　economics
ぶんがく　literature
こうがく　engineering
けいえいがく　business administration

1. Which of these disciplines interest you?

2. In your opinion, which of these disciplines is the most difficult to learn ?

3. In your opinion, which of these disciplines is the easiest to learn?

4. Do you know how to say your major in Japanese? If not, ask your instructor, then write it down.

E. ひと (People). Answer the following questions in Japanese.

おとこ　male
おんな　female
おとこの　ひと　man (male person)
おんなの　ひと　woman (female person)

1. What is your gender?

2. Is your best friend a man or a woman?

3. If you had a choice, which gender would you like to be?

ダイアローグ　(DIALOGUE)

はじめに　(Warm-up)

A. Answer the following questions in English.

1. When you meet someone for the first time, how do you introduce yourself? Do you shake hands?

2. Suppose you have just been introduced to your host family in Japan. What kinds of things would you talk about?

B. In all the chapters, the dialogues are accompanied by **manga** (cartoon strips). It is important to familiarize yourself with the faces of the people in the two dialogues below because these characters will appear in the dialogues of subsequent chapters. First, study each frame of the **manga** and try to guess what it illustrates.

あ り す
アリス　　　　　　　り　　　　　　　　すずき
　　　　　　　　　リー

Next, proceed according to the following steps for each dialogue:

Step 1　Listen to the dialogue for Chapter 2 on the student cassette. It will be read once at normal speed. For each frame (numbered 1, 2, 3, etc.) of the **manga,** the person on the right speaks first.

Step 2　After listening to the tape, read the dialogue.

Step 3　Match each character's line in the dialogue with the corresponding frame number of the **manga.** The first one is done for you.

はじめまして　(How do you do?)

Alice Arisaka, a Japanese-American student,[1] is attending an orientation session at the International Student Center of Jōtō University in Tokyo. A student sitting next to Alice speaks to her.

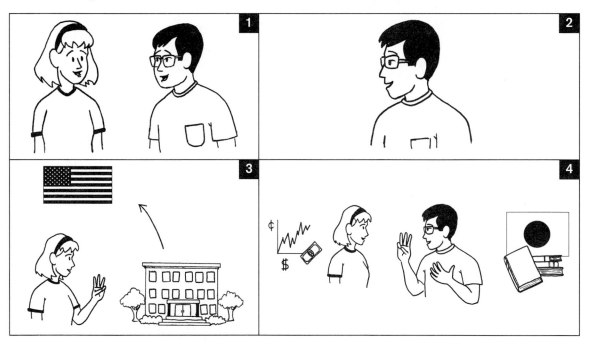

---

[1] In all illustrations of Alice, you will notice that her hair is not inked in. In Japanese **manga,** this indicates that a person is Caucasian.

1   リー：　あのう、すみませんが、　おなまえは　なんで
　　　　　　　　すか。

____ アリス：アリス　ありさかです。

____ リー：　ああ、ありさかさんですか。はじめまして。
　　　　　　　　ぼくの　なまえは　リー　です。どうぞ
　　　　　　　　よろしく。

____ アリス：こちらこそ。どうぞ　よろしく。

____ リー：　ぼくは　たいわんから　きました。ありさかさんは
　　　　　　　　どちらから　いらっしゃいましたか。

____ アリス：シカゴです。わたしは　ウエストサイド
　　　　　　　　だいがくの　さんねんせいです。

____ リー：　そうですか。ぼくも　さんねんせいです。
　　　　　　　　ぼくの　せんこうは　にほんぶんがくです。
　　　　　　　　ありさかさんの　せんこうは　なんですか。

____ アリス：けいざいがくです。

A staff member of the International Student Center and a Japanese man
approach them.

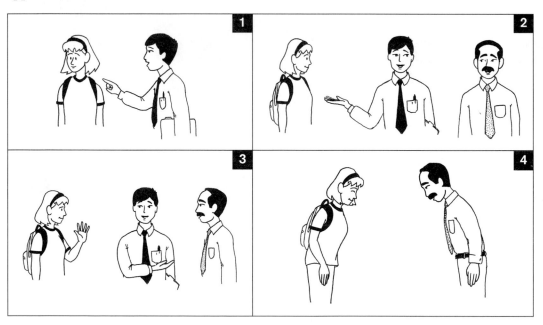

____ りゅうがくせいセンターの
　　　　ひと：　　　　　　　　　　　　ありさかさんですか。

____ アリス：　　　　　　　　　　　　ええ、そうです。

	りゅうがくせいセンターの ひと :	すずきさん、こちらは アリス　ありさかさんです。 ありさかさん、こちらは ホストファミリーの すずきさんです。
	アリス :	はじめまして。 アリスありさかです。 どうぞ　よろしく。
	すずき :	すずきです。よろしく。

わかりましたか　(Comprehension)

Complete the following chart with the information about Alice and Lee-san.

	Country/City くに／まち	Year in college 〜ねんせい	Major せんこう
アリス			
リー			

にほんの　ぶんか　(CULTURE)

First name or last name? How do you address your friends and class-mates? How about your professors?

When meeting a Japanese adult for the first time, use your last name to introduce yourself. It is not customary to use a Japanese adult's first name, especially when the person is older or has a higher social status. However, it is not uncommon to find close friends calling each other by their first names. Since many Japanese are aware that Westerners commonly use first names, a foreign student may be addressed with his/her first name, followed by さん such as クリスさん. Within a family, older family members address younger family members by their first names, but younger family members do not use the older members' first names. Instead, they use kinship terms such as mother, father, older brother, and older sister. When a foreign student stays with a Japanese host family, the host parents will address the student by either the first name only or the first name plus さん. The host sisters or brothers will most likely call him/her by the first name plus さん. In general, senior family members are called by kinship terms and junior members by their first name plus either さん (unisex), くん (for a young boy) or ちゃん (for a young girl or a small child). When in doubt, ask the members of your host family how they want to be addressed.

- *Bowing? Shaking hands? Why didn't Suzuki shake hands with Alice Arisaka when he was introduced to her?*

To be on the safe side, always bow when meeting a Japanese adult for the first time. Bow with your two feet together, bending slightly from your waist up. Your eyes should be downcast as you bow. You may bow more deeply and more than once if you wish to show greater respect. Shaking hands is not customary in Japan, but if someone extends his or her hand, then respond accordingly. Do not squeeze the person's hand too much.

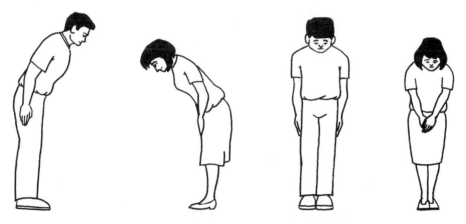

Photo of two people exchanging name cards with their hands clearly visible.

- *Name cards (めいし). Who uses name cards? When and how do people exchange name cards?*

  In Japan, exchanging name cards (めいし) is an important part of the ritual of meeting people for the first time. Professionals always have name cards, as do many graduate students. Undergraduate students usually do not have name cards because they are not considered full-fledged members of adult society. When a person expected to have a name card does not have one on hand, he/she usually apologizes for his/her oversight. When given a name card, you should take it with both hands and read it carefully to identify the person's title or rank and the name of the organization to which he/she belongs. Such information is essential to socializing with the proper degree of formality.

LANGUAGE

I. Identifying someone or something, using 〜は 〜です

A. Affirmative

Topic		Comment	
Noun	Particle	Noun	Copula Verb
わたし	は	さんねんせい	です。

I am a junior.

B. Negative

Topic		Comment	
Noun	Particle	Noun	Copula Verb
すずきさん	は	がくせい	じゃありません。 じゃないです。

Suzuki-san is not a student.

わたしは　いちねんせいです。でも、たなかさんは
いちねんせいじゃないです。

I am a freshman. But Tanaka-san is not a freshman.

ロペスさんは　メキシコじんです。おとこの　ひとです。
がくせいです。

Lopez-san is Mexican. He is a man. He is a student.

モネさんは　おんなの　ひとです。リーさんは　おんなの
ひとじゃありません。

Monet-san is a woman. Lee-san is not a woman.

- The Sentences X は Y です and X は Y じゃありません／じゃな
  いです are used to identify or characterize someone or something. They
  mean *X is Y* and *X isn't Y*. The copula verb です (and its variants) links the
  subject and predicate.

- じゃないです is more colloquial than じゃありません.

- Whereas the English verb *to be* sometimes indicates location, such as *Tokyo
  is in Japan,* です and じゃありません do not. Also, they do not change
  their forms according to the gender, number, and person (1st, 2nd, or 3rd)
  of the subject. Compare the following Japanese and English sentences.

わたしは　だいがくせい<u>です</u>。

I *am* a college student.

ありさかさんは　だいがくせい<u>です</u>。

Arisaka-san *is* a college student.

わたしたちは　だいがくせい<u>です</u>。

We *are* college students.

- In Japanese, besides nouns, verbs, and adjectives, there are also particles. A
  particle is usually one **hiragana**, although sometimes it can be two. Particles
  usually appear right after a noun or at the end of a sentence. Their purpose
  is to assign a grammatical function to the preceding noun. Some particles
  are similar to English prepositions. For example, noun + は (pronounced
  wa) marks the topic of a sentence about which the rest of the sentence
  makes a comment. The comment (〜です) is more important than the
  topic because the topic represents information already known to the speaker
  and the listener, whereas the comment provides the listener with new information.

はなして　みましょう　(Practice and Conversation)

A. Imagine that the following people live in your dormitory. Work with a partner and tell him/her about each person.

Example

たなかさんは　<u>にほんじん</u>です。<u>だいがくいんせい</u>です。
せんこうは　<u>かんこくご</u>です。

なまえ　〜じん　　　　〜ねんせい　せんこう

Name	Nationality	Year in School	Major
たなか	にほんじん	だいがくいんせい	かんこくご
チョー	ちゅうごくじん	だいがくいんせい	アジアけんきゅう
ブラウン	オーストラリアじん	よねんせい	けいざいがく
スミス	ニュージーランドじん	さんねんせい	こうがく
キム	かんこくじん	にねんせい	フランスご
モネ	カナダじん	いちねんせい	ぶんがく

B. Complete the following chart by circling the appropriate words and writing your major and nationality in Japanese.

Your status	だいがくせい　　だいがくいんせい
Major	
Year	いちねんせい　　にねんせい　　さんねんせい　　よねんせい だいがくいんせい
Nationality	アメリカじん　　ちゅうごくじん　　かんこくじん　　_____ じん

C. Introduce yourself to a classmate and tell him/her about yourself using the words in exercise B and X は Y です.

Example

はじめまして。たなかです。どうぞ　よろしく。

（わたしは）だいがくせいです。(Year) せいです。

せんこうは _____ です。わたしは (nationality) じんです。

Listen as your classmate introduces himself/herself and complete the chart.

Classmate's status	
Major	
Year	
Nationality	

D. Using the information from the charts in exercises B and C, talk to a third person about the differences between your classmate and yourself. Use わたしは　〜です and (your classmate's name) 〜さんは 〜じゃ ありません. If you need to talk about majors, use the expressions わたしの　せんこう (my major) and (your classmate's name) 〜さんの せんこう.

わたしは ＿＿＿＿ です。わたしの　パートナーは
＿＿＿＿ さんです。

わたしは ＿＿＿＿ じんです。 ＿＿＿＿ さんは
＿＿＿＿ じんじゃありません／じゃないです。

わたしは ＿＿＿＿ せいです。 ＿＿＿＿ さんは
＿＿＿＿ せいじゃありません／じゃないです。

わたしの　せんこうは ＿＿＿＿ です。 ＿＿＿＿ さんの
せんこうは ＿＿＿＿ じゃありません／じゃないです。

E.　Introduce your partner and yourself to another classmate.

Example

わたしは ＿＿＿＿ です。 ＿＿＿＿ じんです。
＿＿＿＿ せいです。

せんこうは ＿＿＿＿ です。

わたしの　パートナーは ＿＿＿＿ さんです。

＿＿＿＿ さんは ＿＿＿＿ じゃありません／じゃないです。
＿＿＿＿ です。

II.　Asking はい／いいえ questions, using 〜 は　〜ですか

Question			Answer		
	Copula Verb	Particle		Pronoun	Copula Verb
すずきさん	です	か。	はい、	そう	です。

Are you Suzuki-san?　　　　　　　　　Yes, I am.

Question		Answer		
Sentence	Particle		Pronoun	Copula Verb
すずきさんは　がくせいです	か。	ええ、	そう	です。

Is Suzuki-san a student?　　　　　　　Yes, she is.

	Answer	
	Pronoun	**Copula Verb**
いいえ、	そう	じゃありません。 じゃないです。

No, she isn't.

すずき ： ありさかさんですか。

　　　　Are you Arisaka-san?

アリス ： はい、そうです。

　　　　Yes, I am.

すずき ： ありさかさんは　にほんじんですか。

　　　　Are you Japanese, Arisaka-san?

アリス ： いいえ、そうじゃありません。アメリカじんです。

　　　　No, I'm not. I'm American.

● Use はい、そうです (*Yes, I am / you are / it is / she is / he is / they are / we are*) if the answer is affirmative. Use いいえ、そうじゃありません／いいえ、そうじゃないです (*No, I'm not / you aren't / it isn't / they aren't / we aren't*) if the answer is negative. そうじゃないです is stronger than そうじゃありません.

● While the Japanese pronoun あなた means *you*, it is not as commonly used as its English counterpart. Instead, the person's name is used. Thus, <u>アリスさんは　がくせいですか。</u> means either *Are you a student, Alice?* or *Is Alice a student?* depending on whom you are talking to.

● The topic is often omitted if it is clear from the context.

● The particle か is the particle used to mark a question.

はなして　みましょう　(Practice and Conversation)

A. Answer the following questions using ええ、そうです or いいえ、そうじゃありません／そうじゃないです.

> **Example**

　がくせいですか。<u>ええ、そうです。</u>
1. がっこうは　ウエストサイドだいがくですか。
2. いちねんせいですか。
3. せんこうは　にほんごですか。
4. アメリカじんですか。
5. せんせいは　にほんじんですか。
6. せんせいは　だいがくいんせいですか。

B. Work with a partner. Look at the chart and select a person you wish to be. Without telling your partner your new identity, have him/her try to guess who you are by asking questions with 〜は　〜ですか. Answer with ええ、そうです or いいえ、そうじゃありません／いいえ、そうじゃないです.

Example

A: にほんじんですか。

B: いいえ、そうじゃありません。

A: アメリカじんですか。

B: ええ、そうです。

A: せんこうは　えいごですか。

B: ええ、そうです。

A: スミスさんですか。

B: ええ、そうです。

Name	Nationality	Gender	Year in School	Major
スミス	アメリカじん	おとこの　ひと	さんねんせい	えいご
ブラウン	アメリカじん	おんなの　ひと	いちねんせい	アジアけんきゅう
ロペス	アメリカじん	おとこの　ひと	よねんせい	ぶんがく
たなか	にほんじん	おとこの　ひと	いちねんせい	スペインご
やまだ	にほんじん	おんなの　ひと	だいがくいんせい	けいえいがく
さとう	にほんじん	おんなの　ひと	にねんせい	こうがく

C. Survey your classmates to find out how many are in the same year as you and how many share your major. Use 〜さんは　〜ですか.

Example

A: きむらさんは　いちねんせいですか。

B: ええ、そうです。／いいえ、そうじゃありません／いいえ、そうじゃないです。

A: せんこうは　にほんごですか。

B: ええ、そうです。／いいえ、そうじゃありません／いいえ、そうじゃないです。

III. Recognizing the relationship between nouns with の

Noun	Particle	Noun Phrase			
		Noun 1	Particle	Noun 2	Copula Verb
やまださん	は	ウエストサイドだいがく	の	がくせい	です。

Yamada-san is a student at Westside University.

Noun Phrase				Noun	Copula Verb
Noun 1	Particle	Noun 2	Particle		
わたし	の	ともだち	は	りゅうがくせい	です。

My friend is a foreign student.

たなか：はじめまして、ウエストサイドだいがくの
　　　　たなかです。
> How do you do? My name is Tanaka and I'm from Westside University.

きむら：はじめまして、りゅうがくせいセンターの
　　　　きむらです。どうぞ　よろしく。
> How do you do? My name is Kimura and I'm from the International Student Center. I'm pleased to meet you.

　　　　たなかさんの　せんこうは　けいざいがくですか。
> Is your major economics, Tanaka-san?

たなか：いいえ。わたしの　せんこうは　こうがくです。
> No. My major is engineering.

● The particle の allows the first noun to modify the second noun. の can convey a variety of relationships between the two nouns, such as possession, group membership, location, and instrument. Thus, the interpretation sometimes depends on the context.

とうきょうだいがくの　リーさん

Lee-san *from Tokyo University*

とうきょうだいがくの　がくせい

student *at Tokyo University*

わたしの　ともだち

my friend

せんせいの　ほん

teacher's book; book *written by the teacher*

メキシコの　うち
（め き し こ）

house *in Mexico*

にほんの　ほん

book *about Japan*; book *from Japan*

にほんごの　ほん

book *written in Japanese*; book *about Japanese*

とうきょうの　すずきさん

Suzuki-san *who lives in Tokyo*; Suzuki-san *from Tokyo*

● The relationship called *appositive* can also be expressed with の. The following example is translated in English as *My host family, Suzuki-san*. In
contrast, すずきさんの　ホストファミリー is interpreted as *Suzuki's
host family*.

ホストファミリーの　すずきさん
（ほ す と ふ ぁ み り）

Suzuki-san *who is (my) host family*

すずきさんの　ホストファミリー
（ほ す と ふ ぁ み り）

Suzuki's host family

● In Japan, it is common to introduce oneself using the name of one's
company, college, or university.

はなして みましょう　(Practice and Conversation)

A. Look at the drawings in *New Vocabulary*, Section B on page 29. Imagine
that these people are your friends. Work with a partner and identify the
nationality of each person. Use 〜 じんの　がくせい. Also, describe the
flags (はた) pictured with them, using 〜 の　はた.

Examples

たなかさんは　にほんじんの　がくせいです。
たなかさんの　はたは　にほんの　はたです。

B. Work with a partner. Imagine that the following Japanese exchange students
are studying at your school. Introduce each person to your partner by identifying the school the person attends in Japan.

とうきょうだいがくの　やまださんです。

Name	やまだ	さとう	すずき	きむら
University	とうきょう だいがく	おおさか だいがく	わせだ だいがく	きょうと だいがく

C. Think of a friend. Tell a classmate your friend's name, school, and major using Noun の Noun.

Example

わたしの　ともだちは　＿＿＿＿さんです。

＿＿＿＿さんの　だいがくは　＿＿＿＿だいがくです。

＿＿＿＿さんの　せんこうは　＿＿＿＿です。

D. You meet a student from another school. Introduce yourself by identifying your school and using Noun の Noun.

Example

はじめまして。（わたしは）＿＿＿＿だいがくの
　　　　＿＿＿＿です。

E. You are the moderator of a panel discussion on environmental protection. Introduce the following experts using Noun の Noun.

やまだ	きむら	たなか	さとう
シカゴだいがく	EPA	とうきょう だいがく	にほんIBM

Example

（やまだ）こちらは　シカゴだいがくの　やまだせんせい
です。

IV. Asking for personal information, using question words

A. Asking about names and things, using なん

Question			
	Question Word	Copula Verb	Particle
おなまえは	なん	です	か。

What is your name?

Answer	
	Copula Verb
アリス	です。

It's Alice.

Question				
	Question Word	Counter	Copula Verb	Particle
キムさんは	なん	ねんせい	です	か。

What year are you in, Kim-san?

Answer		
Number	Counter	Copula Verb
さん	ねんせい	です。

I'm a junior.

B. Asking about places, using どこ and どちら

Question			
Question word (Place)	Particle	Verb	Particle
どちら	から	いらっしゃいました	か。

Where are you from (literally: Where did you come from)?

Answer		
Noun (Place)	Particle	Verb
にほん	から	きました。

I'm from Japan (literally: I came from Japan).

やまだ：キムさんは　どちらから　いらっしゃいましたか。

Kim-san, where are you from?

キム：　かんこくから　きました。　　　Kankoku

I'm from Korea.

やまだ：そうですか。なんねんせいですか。

I see. What year are you in?

キム：　いちねんせいです。

First year.

- なん, どこ, and どちら are question words. なん means *what*, and both どちら and どこ mean *where*. どちら is more polite than どこ. To ask the name of a school, use どこ or どちら.

- In Japanese, a question word is placed where the information would appear in the answer. A question word is not used as a topic or before the particle は.

  やまだ：たなかさんは　なんねんせいですか。

  What year are you in, Tanaka-san?

  たなか：わたしは　いちねんせいです。

  I'm a freshman.

  すずき：これは　なんですか。

  What is this?

  さとう：それは　かんこくごの　ほんです。

  That is a Korean language book.

- どちらから　いらっしゃいましたか (*Where are you from?*) is a polite way of asking about someone's hometown, country or state. どこから　きましたか is more informal. The particle から means *from*. いらっしゃいました and きました are the past tense forms of the verbs いらっしゃいます and きます, respectively; they both mean *come*. When responding to a question about your hometown, country or state, always use きました.

  Ira nshaimashtaka.

- It is possible to ask the name of someone's school with どこ or どちら. 「やまださんの　だいがくは　どこですか。」 is really a question about the name of Yamada-san's university and not its location, even though どこですか is used.

はなして　みましょう　(Practice and Conversation)

A. Ask a question for each of the following answers.

Example

スミスです。<u>おなまえは　なんですか。</u>

1. メキシコ から　きました。
2. アジアけんきゅうです。
3. リーです。
4. さんねんせいです。
5. フランスごです。
6. ちゅうごくから　きました。
7. だいがくいんせいです。
8. じょうとうだいがくです。

B. Ask your classmates what year they are in. Find out how many freshmen, sophomores, juniors, seniors, and graduate students are in your class.

Example

A: ＿＿＿＿＿ さんは　なんねんせいですか。

B: ＿＿＿＿＿ ねんせいです。

C. Ask your classmates what their majors are. Is anyone majoring in the same subject as you?

Example

A: ＿＿＿＿＿ さんの　せんこうは　なんですか。

B: ＿＿＿＿＿ です。

D. Ask your classmates and your instructor about their majors and home-towns. Find out who comes from the farthest place.

Example

A: ＿＿＿＿＿ さんは　どこから　きましたか。

or ＿＿＿＿＿ さんは　どちらから　いらっしゃいましたか。

B: ＿＿＿＿＿ から　きました。

V. Listing and describing similarities, using と and も

A. も ～also, ～too

Sentence 1
アリスさんは　だいがくせいです。

Alice is a college student.

Sentence 2		
Noun Phrase	**Particle**	
アリスさんの　ともだち	も	だいがくせいです。

Alice's friend is also a college student.

B. と and

Noun	Particle	Noun Phrase	Particle	
アリスさん	と	アリスさんの　ともだち	は	だいがくせいです。

Alice and Alice's friend are college students.

ブラウン：アリスさんの　せんこうは　けいざいがくですか。
          Alice, is your major economics?

アリス：　ええ、そうです。
          Yes, it is.

ブラウン：ぼくの　せんこうも　けいざいがくですよ。
          You know, my major is economics, too.

ブラウン：アリスさんと　リーさんは　よねんせいですか。
          Are Alice and Lee-san seniors?

アリス：　いいえ、さんねんせいです。
          No, they are juniors.

● The particle と is used only to connect nouns. It cannot be used to connect two or more sentences or verb phrases. To connect sentences, use the conjunction そして.

たなかさんと　わたしは　にほんから　きました。
Tanaka-san and I are from Japan.

わたしは　にほんから　きました。<u>そして</u>、たなかさんも
にほんから　きました。

I'm from Japan. *And* Tanaka-san is from Japan, too.

はなして　みましょう　(Practice and Conversation)

A. Work with a partner. The following is a list of new exchange students. Tell
your partner something about one of the students. Your partner should tell
you about another student who shares the same trait. Then, rephrase the
two statements using と.

Examples

A: リー_りさんは　ちゅうごくじんです。

B: チョー_{ちょ}さんも　ちゅうごくじんです。

A: リー_りさんと　チョー_{ちょ}さんは　ちゅうごくじんです。

A: キム_{きむ}さんの　せんこうは　フランス_{ふらんす}ごです。

B: ロペス_{ろぺす}さんの　せんこうも　フランス_{ふらんす}ごです。

A: キム_{きむ}さんと　ロペス_{ろぺす}さんの　せんこうは　フランス_{ふらんす}ご
です。

Name	Nationality	Year in School	Major
キム	かんこくじん	いちねんせい	フランスご
イー	かんこくじん	だいがくいんせい	ぶんがく
リー	ちゅうごくじん	よねんせい	こうがく
チョー	ちゅうごくじん	にねんせい	ちゅうごくご
ブラウン	オーストラリアじん	さんねんせい	けいざいがく
スミス	オーストラリアじん	にねんせい	ちゅうごくご
ロペス	アメリカじん	よねんせい	フランスご
たなか	アメリカじん	だいがくいんせい	こうがく
ワット	ニュージーランドじん	いちねんせい	けいざいがく
モネ	カナダじん	さんねんせい	ぶんがく

B. Work with a partner. Make a list of classmates who are in the same year as
you. Tell your partner about these classmates. Your partner should rephrase
your sentences, using と.

A: わたしは _____ ねんせいです。 _____ さんも
_____ねんせいです。

B: _____ さんと _____ さんは _____ ねんせいです。

C. Tell your partner which student shares your major and nationality. Your partner should rephrase your sentences, using も.

A: わたしと _____ さんの せんこうは _____ です。

わたしと _____ さんは _____ じんです。

B: _____ さんの せんこうは _____ です。

_____ さんの せんこうも _____ です。

_____ さんは _____ じんです。

_____ さんも _____ じんです。

D. Do any of your classmates come from your hometown or does anyone from your hometown attend your school? If so, tell your partner using も. (If not, tell your partner about two classmates who come from the same town.) Your partner should rephrase your sentences using と.

A: わたしは _____ から きました。わたしの
ともだちは _____ さんです。
_____ さんも _____ から きました。

B: _____ さんと _____ さんの ともだちの
_____ さんは _____ から きました。

じょうずな よみかた (READING)

Using format as a clue

Name cards are generally written in **kanji** and **katakana**. To a beginning student of Japanese, they may seem impossible to understand. Nevertheless, it is possible to identify a few facts if you know what to look for. This is a very important first step in acquiring reading skills.

The information provided on a name card is limited to one's name, title, one's company or organization, address, and phone and fax numbers. The information always follows a certain format. The name appears in the center, and to the right or above it the organization and title appear. The information in small type at the left or at the bottom gives the office address and phone number, followed by the home address and number.

A. Look at the name card below, on the left, and circle the telephone number and the name of the organization.

B. Look at the name card below, on the right. Although it is written vertically, the basic format is the same. Read the card from right to left and circle the card holder's name and address.

リーさんと アリスさん

よむまえに (Prereading)

● How much do you know about Alice? Try to say something about her using words you already know.

● Read the text below to answer questions about Alice and Mr. Lee.

● Most Japanese texts are written in a combination of **hiragana, katakana,** and **kanji.** Unlike English, there are usually no spaces between words. The text below is written in all three scripts rather than in **hiragana** and **katakana,** and without spaces so that you can become familiar with the format of authentic Japanese texts. While you read, pay attention to the three scripts and the division of words.

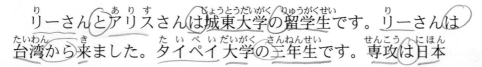

リーさんとアリスさんは城東大学の留学生です。リーさんは
台湾から来ました。タイペイ大学の三年生です。専攻は日本

文学です。アリスさんはシカゴから来ました。
ウエストサイド 大学の学生です。アリスさんも三年生です。でも、
専攻は 文学じゃありません。経済学です。アリスさんの
ホストファミリーは鈴木さんです。

(handwritten annotations: 来＝き, However, ⊕)

わかりましたか　(Comprehension)

A. Using **hiragana,** list the characteristics shared and not shared by Lee-san and Alice-san.

Similarities	Differences
三年生 Jr. さんねんせい 留学生 - Exchang. りゅうがくせい	専攻 - major せんこうです. 来身 国 - origin → くに です.

B. Write about yourself by completing the following paragraph. If you have not yet chosen your major, write （せんこうは）まだ　わかりません, meaning *I don't know my major yet.*

ぼく　は　御州　から　＿＿＿＿　きました。

ありぞな　だいがくの　だいが＿＿　ねんせいです。

せんこうは　＿＿＿＿　です。

ちゅうごく 文学

(handwritten annotations right margin: 東 - (とう), 西, 北, 南)

じょうずな　ききかた　(LISTENING)

Listening for key words

The dialogues in this section contain some unknown words and expressions and words to help you develop listening skills to deal with real-life situations. You may be surprised to find that natural speech is very redundant and that it is really not important to understand every word. Learn to focus on key words and to disregard the rest. For example, when someone is introduced to you, the most important word to understand is the person's name. Don't worry about the rest— just relax and listen.

A. Listen to the dialogue and write the names of the two people who are introduced.

B. すずきさんの　むすめ さん (Suzuki-san's daughter)

Situation: Remember that Alice and Suzuki-san met in the dialogue on page 33. Suzuki-san's daughter is standing next to him. He introduces her to Alice.

ことばの　リスト (Vocabulary)

むすめ　speaker's daughter

ちち　speaker's father

はは　speaker's mother

Read the following statements, then listen for the key words in the dialogue. Circle はい or いいえ , according to what you understood.

はい　いいえ　1. The name of Suzuki-san's daughter is Michiko.

はい　いいえ　2. Suzuki-san's daughter is a sophomore at Joto University.

はい　いいえ　3. Suzuki-san's daughter is majoring in economics.

はい　いいえ　4. Alice's father is Japanese.

  ## DICT-A-CONVERSATION

The Dict-a-Conversation combines listening and writing practice. The conversation activity is recorded on the student cassette. You will hear only one side of a conversation based on a topic covered in this chapter. After writing down what you hear, create the other (your) side of the conversation, following the steps below. In the Dict-a-Conversation your last name is Smith (スミス), unless you are told otherwise by your instructor. For this chapter, use only **hiragana** to transcribe and complete the conversation.

Step 1　Listen carefully to what your conversation partner says on the tape. If this activity is assigned as homework, you may listen to the tape as many times as you wish.

Step 2　Write the speaker's lines as you hear them.

Step 3　Next, write your (スミス) responses, questions, or statements. After **kanji** have been introduced, underline the parts that you can write in **kanji** and write the **kanji** below the underline. Do not write in **kanji** from the beginning.

Step 4　When you have finished, proofread the completed script and check your work.

1. You are meeting your host parent, Tanaka-san, for the first time at Narita Airport.

たなか：　＿＿＿＿＿＿＿＿＿＿＿＿＿＿＿＿＿＿＿＿＿

スミス：　＿＿＿＿＿＿＿＿＿＿＿＿＿＿＿＿＿＿＿＿＿

たなか： _____

2. At a party, you meet a Japanese woman named Ms. Yamada.

やまだ： _____
スミス： _____

やまだ： _____
スミス： _____

やまだ： _____
スミス： _____

やまだ： _____

ききじょうず　はなしじょうず　(COMMUNICATION)

あいづち　(Giving feedback) 1

Being a good listener is one of the most important factors in effective communication in Japanese. Strategies to become a good listener differ considerably among languages. For example, the Japanese tend to avoid frequent or prolonged eye contact because rather than interpreting prolonged eye contact as a sign of interest in the conversation, a Japanese person will tend to feel intimidated or uneasy. Thus, it is best to divert one's eyes from time to time. Instead of eye contact, the Japanese use various other strategies to indicate they are listening. For example, they nod occasionally to show attentiveness. For this reason, Japanese students often nod in the classroom. Another common type of feedback is the frequent use of ええ or はい, which means *yes*. These expressions do not necessarily indicate agreement. They simply mean that the person is listening. If the listener remains silent even though he/she is looking at the speaker, the speaker may consider the listener to be impolite, cold, or even uninterested. In Japan, it is also considered inappropriate to eat or drink in the classroom. Equally inappropriate is putting one's feet or legs up on a chair or desk. Japanese instructors who are not used to such behavior may think these acts show a student's lack of seriousness or respect, or boredom.

A. Listen to your instructor talk about himself/herself. Sit up straight and nod occasionally to indicate interest while listening.

B. Work with a partner. Tell him/her about a friend. While listening, your partner should nod or say ええ or はい between sentences. Practice avoiding prolonged eye contact.

そうごう れんしゅう (INTEGRATION)

インタビュー (Interview)
いんたびゅ

1. Interview your classmates about their status, major, country, and home-town. First, write down a greeting, then prepare a list of questions. Survey your classmates, interviewing as many people as you can. Fill in the following survey form with the information you gather.

   Greeting phrase: _____

   Questions: (year)   _____

               (major)   _____

               (hometown/country)   _____

なまえ	～ねんせい	せんこう	～から きました

2. Based on the results of your survey, introduce one of your classmates to another classmate and write what is said by each person during the conversation.

   _____ : _____

   _____ : _____

   _____ : _____

   _____ : _____

ロールプレイ (Role Play)
ろ る ぷ れ い

1. You are at an airport to pick up a Japanese person named Yamada, whom you have never met. Approach the person and ask if he/she is the right person. Then introduce yourself.

2. You want to practice speaking Japanese so you go to the International Student Center on campus. Introduce yourself to a Japanese student and start a conversation with him/her.

Nouns

アジアけんきゅう（アジア研究）Asian studies

アメリカ　America, United States

いちねんせい（一年生）freshman, first-year student
(The suffix せい may be dropped as in いちねん.)

えいご（英語）English

オーストラリア　Australia

おとこ（男）male

おとこの　ひと（男の人）man

おんな（女）female

おんなの　ひと（女の人）woman

がくせい（学生）student

カナダ　Canada

かんこく（韓国）South Korea

くに（国）country

けいえいがく（経営学）business administration

けいざいがく（経済学）economics

こうがく（工学）engineering

こうこう（高校）high school

さんねんせい（三年生）junior, third-year student
(The suffix せい may be dropped.)

スペイン　Spain

せんこう（専攻）major

せんせい（先生）teacher, professor

だいがく（大学）college, university

だいがくせい（大学生）college student

だいがくいん（大学院）graduate school

だいがくいんせい（大学院生）graduate student

ちゅうごく（中国）China

ともだち（友達）friend

なまえ（名前）name

にねんせい（二年生）sophomore, second-year student
(The suffix せい may be dropped.)

にほん（日本）Japan

ニュージーランド　New Zealand

ひと（人）person, people

フランス　France

ぶんがく（文学）literature
にほんぶんがく（日本文学）(Japanese literature)

メキシコ　Mexico

よねんせい（四年生）senior, fourth-year student
(The suffix せい may be dropped.)

りゅうがくせい（留学生）exchange student

Pronouns

そう　so

ぼく（僕）I (normally used by a male)

わたし（私）I

Copula verb

です　(to) be

Adverbs

いいえ　no
はい／ええ　yes

Question Words

どこ　where
どこから　きましたか。（どこから
　来ましたか。）Where are you from?
どちら　where (more polite than どこ),
　which way

どちらから　いらっしゃいましたか。
　Where are you from?
なに／なん（何）what
　なんですか。（何ですか。）What is it?

Demonstrative Words

こちら　this person, this way

Particles

か　question mark
と　and
の　noun modifier marker (of, 's)

は　topic marker
も　similarity marker (also, too)

Suffixes

〜がく（〜学）study of 〜
　けいざいがく（経済学）study of
economics
〜ご（〜語）language
　にほんご（日本語）Japanese language
　スペインご（スペイン語）Spanish
language
〜じん（〜人）-nationality
　アメリカじん（アメリカ人）American
　オーストラリアじん（オーストラリ

ア人）Australian　カナダじん（カナダ
人）Canadian　にほんじん（日本人）
Japanese　かんこくじん（韓国人）
Korean　ちゅうごくじん（中国人）
Chinese　メキシコじん（メキシコ人）
Mexican
〜せい（〜生）-student
　だいがくせい（大学生）college student
　だいがくいんせい（大学院生）gradu-
ate student　いちねんせい（一年生）

freshman りゅうがくせい（留学生） | ～ねん（～年）year
exchange student | いちねん（一年）first year

Conjunction

そして　also, and

Expressions

そう　so
いいえ、そうじゃありません。No, that's not so.
～から　いらっしゃいました。～ came from ～. (polite)

～から　きました。（～から　来ました。）～ came from ～. (casual)
こちらこそ。It is I who should be saying that. Thank you. I'm sorry.
はい（ええ）、そうです。Yes, that's so.

Passive Vocabulary

Nouns

センター　center
　りゅうがくせいセンター（留学生センター）exchange student center
たいわん（台湾）Taiwan
ちち（父）(the speaker's) father

はは（母）(the speaker's) mother
はた（旗）flag
パートナー　partner
ホストファミリー　host family

Pronouns

あなた　you

Verbs

いらっしゃいます　come/s (present tense, polite form)
きます（来ます）come/s (present tense, casual form)

Adverbs

いま（今）now

から　from

お〜　polite prefix
　　おなまえ（お名前）polite form of なまえ（名前）(name)

（せんこうは）まだ　わかりません。（（専攻は）まだ　分かりません）I don't know
　　(my major) yet.
そうですか。I see. Is that so. Really?

Supplementary Vocabulary

The words in this section in every chapter of **Nakama 1** do not appear in the
course of the chapter but are useful terms and are thematically related to the
chapter content.

Names of Countries

イギリス　England　　　　　　ドイツ　Germany
イタリア　Italy　　　　　　　　ロシア　Russia

Academic Majors

いがく（医学）medical science　　　じんるいがく（人類学）anthropology
おんがく（音楽）music　　　　　　　すうがく（数学）mathematics
かがく（化学）chemistry　　　　　　せいじがく（政治学）political science
きょういくがく（教育学）education　　びじゅつ（美術）fine arts
けんちくがく（建築学）architecture　　ぶつりがく（物理学）physics
コンピュータサイエンス　computer　　れきし（歴史）history
　　science
しゃかいがく（社会学）sociology
しんりがく（心理学）psychology

Interior of a traditional Japanese house

にほんの　うち

JAPANESE HOUSES

Functions	Describing a house and the things in it
New Vocabulary	A building; A room; Describing buildings and rooms; Question words
Dialogue	すずきさんの　うち　(Suzuki-san's house)
Culture	Japanese houses
Language	I. Describing things and people, using adjective + noun
	II. Referring to places, things, and people, using この、その、あの、and どの
	III. Describing the location of people and things, using 〜に　〜が あります／います and ここ、そこ、あそこ
	IV. Using location nouns: なか、そと、となり、よこ、ちかく、うしろ、まえ、うえ、した、みぎがわ、and ひだりがわ
	V. Using よ and ね
Reading	Using visual clues
Listening	Listening for general ideas
Communication	あいづち (Giving feedback) 2

A. たてもの (A building). Answer the following questions in Japanese.

うち　house　　　アパート　apartment　　　りょう　dormitory

1. Which type of building do you currently live in?
2. Which types of buildings have you lived in before?
3. Which type of building do your parents live in?

B. へや (A room). Look at the drawing of a bedroom and label each item in Japanese. You may use **hiragana** for loan words. Then fill in the chart on the next page with the items that you would find in a bedroom and a living room.

もの　thing, object	ふとん　futon	ソファ　sofa
ベッド　bed	たんす　chest	テーブル　table
いす　chair	おしいれ　closet	スタンド　lamp
つくえ　desk	まど　window	しゃしん　photo
ほんだな　bookshelf	ドア　door	とけい　clock
でんわ　telephone	いぬ　dog	とだな　cabinet
テレビ　television	ねこ　cat	え　picture
ステレオ　stereo	ほん　book	

Bedroom	Living Room

C. たてものと　へやを　あらわすことば (Describing buildings and rooms). Select a word from exercise A or B that would be described by each adjective. Then classify the listed adjectives into two groups according to whether you think they are positive or negative features of a room, a house, or an object.

おおきい　big
ちいさい　small
あたらしい　new
ふるい　old
ひろい　spacious, wide
せまい　cramped, narrow
あかるい　bright

たかい　tall, high
いい　good
きれい(な)　clean, pretty
しずか(な)　quiet
りっぱ(な)　fine, splendid
すてき(な)　attractive, nice
ゆうめい(な)　famous

D. しつもんの　しかた (Question words). Try to answer the questions in as few words as possible. Can the answer be a noun or an adjective? Before using a noun in your answer, be sure that the question asks for a person, a place, or a thing.

なに／なん	what	おなまえは　<u>なん</u>ですか。 <u>なん</u>ねんせいですか。
どこ	where	<u>どこ</u>から　きましたか。
どちら	where (polite)	<u>どちら</u>から　いらっしゃいましたか。
どんな + noun	what kind of ～	やまださんの　へやは　<u>どんな</u>　へやですか。 What kind of room is your room, Yamada-san?
だれ	who	<u>だれ</u>の　へやですか。 Whose room is it?
どの + noun	which ～	やまださんは　<u>どの</u>　ひとですか。 Which person is Yamada-san? やまださんの　りょうは　<u>どの</u>　たてもの ですか。 Which building is Yamada-san's dormitory?

ダイアローグ　(DIALOGUE)

はじめに　(Warm-up)

A. How would you describe in English a typical Western-style house to a Japanese friend?

B. Have you ever visited a Japanese house? How would you describe a Japanese house in English? Try describing the photo of a traditional Japanese house on the opening page of this chapter.

C. Remember to follow these steps when working with the dialogue.

1. Look at the **manga**.
2. Listen to the dialogue.
3. Match the characters' lines in the dialogue with the frames of the **manga**.

すずきさんの　うち　(Suzuki-san's house)

STUDENT

Mr. Suzuki, Michiko, and Alice arrive at the Suzukis' house.

<u>　1　</u>　　すずき：　　　　　　　　　　さあ、アリスさん、ここですよ。

(Mr. Suzuki opens the door.)

　　　　　　　　　　　　　　　　　　　　ただいま。

_____　すずきさんの　おくさん：　あ、おかえりなさい。　*Okayrinasai*

_____　すずき：　　　　　　　　　おかあさん、こちら、
　　　　　　　　　　　　　　　　　アリスさん。アリスさん、
　　　　　　　　　　　　　　　　　かないと　むすこの
　　　　　　　　　　　　　　　　　けんいちです。

_____　アリス：　　　　　　　　　はじめまして。アリス
　　　　　　　　　　　　　　　　　ありさかです。どうぞ
　　　　　　　　　　　　　　　　　よろしく。

_____　おくさん：　　　　　　　　はじめまして。どうぞ
　　　　　　　　　　　　　　　　　あがってください。

_____　アリス：　　　　　　　　　おじゃまします。

After some conversation and tea, Mrs. Suzuki takes Alice to her room.

_____　おくさん：　アリスさん、ここに　おふろと
　　　　　　　　　　おてあらいが　あります。

_____　アリス：　はい。

_____　おくさん：　そして、アリスさんの　へやは　この
　　　　　　　　　　へやですよ。

_____　アリス：　まあ、きれいな　へやですね。

_____　おくさん：　あの　おしいれの　なかに　ふとんが
　　　　　　　　　　あります。あとで、いっしょに
　　　　　　　　　　しきましょうね。

_____　アリス：　はい、ありがとう　ございます。あのう...

_____　おくさん：　はい？

_____　アリス：　その　へやは　だれの　へやですか。

_____　おくさん：　みちこの　へやです。

わかりましたか　(Comprehension)

Answer the following questions in Japanese.

1. すずきさんの　むすこさんの　なまえは　なんですか。
2. アリスさんの　へやは　どんな　へやですか。
3. おしいれの　なかに　なにが　ありますか。

にほんの　ぶんか　(CULTURE)

Public restrooms (トイレ). What do you know about public restrooms in Japan?

Both Japanese and Western-style toilets are used in Japan, and most public restrooms offer a choice. Paper towels, soap, and toilet paper are not always provided, so it is wise to carry your own supply. Restroom doors are often marked W.C. for *water closet*. The Japanese sign for *restrooms* reads お手洗, 御手洗 or 便所. The sign for *men* reads 男; the sign for *women* reads 女. More easily recognizable icons for male and female are also common. The door to a restroom, public or private, is kept closed when it is not occupied. Therefore, you should always knock on the door to see if it is occupied.

トイレ

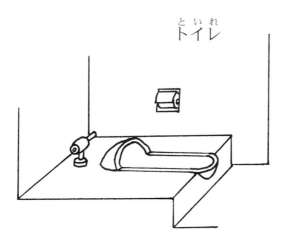

The Japanese bath (おふろ). Do you know that in Japan people wash their body before entering the bathtub?

The Japanese bathroom, or おふろ, is used solely for bathing. The toilet is never in the same room. The bathroom has a tiled area where you wash and rinse yourself completely before entering the tub. The bathtub water is usually very hot (about 110°F). You may add cold water, but be careful not to cool it too much, because other people will be using the おふろ after you. When you finish, do not drain the water! Also remember to replace the cover to retain the heat.

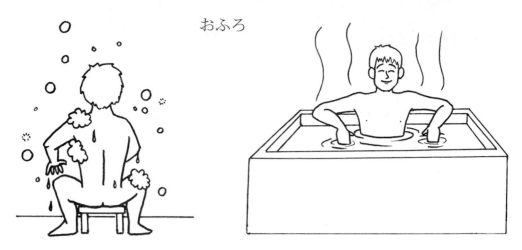

おふろ

- *Japanese-style rooms (わしつ). Did you know the word futon comes from Japanese?*

  Many houses have Western-style bedrooms, but many families still favor Japanese-style rooms with たたみ (*straw mat*) floors which can be used for many purposes as futons are folded and put away during the day. Look at the photo below, of a typical Japanese-style room with a ふとん spread out on the たたみ. A futon sofa is an American invention.

- *Closed door policy. When do you close the door?*

  The door to a room, whether Japanese or Western style, is almost always closed. A closed door doesn't necessarily mean *don't disturb,* so knock to find out if anyone is in the room. Also don't be surprised if a Japanese person enters your room without knocking. It often happens among family members.

I. Describing things and people, using adjective + noun

	い-adjective (Prenominal)	Noun	Copula Verb
りょうは	ふるい	たてもの	です。

The dormitory is an old building.

	な-adjective (Prenominal)	Noun	Copula Verb	
やまださんの　うちは	すてきな	うち	です	ね。

Ms. Yamada's house is a nice house.

い-adjectives
    Dictionary form:　おおきい
    Prenominal form:　おおきい＋うち　→　おおきい　うち

な-adjectives
    Dictionary form:　きれい
    Prenominal form:　きれいな＋うち　→　きれいな　うち

たなか：　やまださんの　へやは　きれいな　へやですね。
        Ms. Yamada's room is a pretty/neat room, isn't it?

スミス：　ええ。そして、あかるい　へやですね。
        Yes, and it's a bright room.

● There are two types of adjectives in Japanese. One is called an い-adjective because it ends in い when it comes before a noun, as in おおきい　うち (*big house*) and ちいさい　うち (*small house*). The other type is called a な- adjective because it ends in な before a noun, as in りっぱな　うち (*fine house*) and きれいな　うち (*pretty house*). These are called the prenominal forms.

● The dictionary form is the form in which dictionaries list adjectives and verbs. You will learn about the dictionary form in chapter 7.

はなして みましょう (Practice and Conversation)

A. Answer the questions, using the adjectives in the following box. Note that ～さん refers to you.

Example

A: ～さんの へやは どんな へやですか。
B: ちいさい へやです。

おおきい	ちいさい	あたらしい	ふるい	ひろい	せまい
あかるい	たかい	いい			
きれい	しずか	りっぱ	すてき	ゆうめい	

1. ～さんの だいがくは どんな だいがくですか。
2. りょうの へやは どんな へやですか。
3. ～さんの うちは どんな うちですか。
4. ～さんの へやは どんな へやですか。
5. ～さんの ともだちの アパートは どんな たてものですか。
6. にほんごの せんせいは どんな せんせいですか。

B. Work with a partner. Using two or more adjectives, tell each other what the following things are like. Try to use adjective + noun and write your answers in the chart.

Example

わたし／ぼくの へやは ふるい へやです。

	わたし／ぼく	(パートナー)
へや		
つくえ		
とけい		

C. Work with a different partner. Tell your new partner about the things you described in exercise B.

Example

わたし／ぼくの へやは きれいな へやです。
～さんの へやも きれいな へやです。

II. Referring to places, things, and people, using この, その, あの, and どの

A. Referring to things or people close to the speaker, using この

	Noun	Particle			
この	へや	は	あかるい　へや	です	ね。

This room is a bright room, isn't it?

B. Referring to things or people close to the listener, or slightly removed from both the speaker and the listener, using その

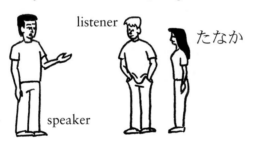

	Noun	Particle			
その	ひと	は	たなかさん	です	か。

Is that person Tanaka-san?

C. Referring to things or people far away from both the speaker and the listener, using あの

	Noun	Particle				
あの	うち	は	すずきさんの　うち	です	か。

Is that house over there Suzuki-san's house?

D. Asking which person or thing is being referred to, using どの

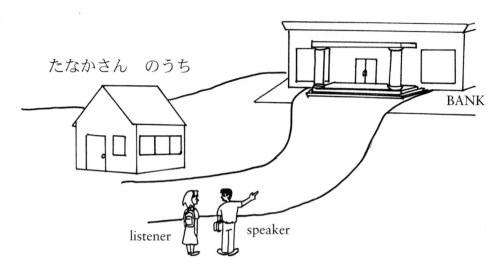

たなかさん　のうち

BANK

listener　　　speaker

Question				
	Question Word	Noun		
ぎんこうは	どの	たてもの	です	か。

Which building is the bank?

Answer		
	Noun	
あの	たてもの	です。

It's that building over there.

アリス：　たなかさんの　うちは　どの　うちですか。
ありす
Which house is your house, Tanaka-san?

たなか：　その　うちです。
It's that house.

アリス：　ああ、りっぱな　たてものですね。
ありす
Oh, it's a splendid building, isn't it?

たなか：　いいえ。
Not at all.

- この, その, あの, and どの must be followed by a noun or a noun phrase.
- どの cannot be used as part of the topic of a sentence with は.
- その can be used to refer to something that has just been mentioned.

A: ありさかさんは　ウエストサイド<ruby>ウエストサイド<rt>うえすとさいど</rt></ruby>だいがくの　がくせいです。
Arisaka-san is a student at Westside University.

B: <u>その</u>　ひとは　にほんじんですか。
Is he/she (literally: that person) Japanese?

はなして　みましょう　(Practice and Conversation)

A. Look at the following drawing of a bedroom. アリス<rt>ありす</rt>さん is in the left side of the room (location A), and you are at location B. Make comments about the room to アリス<rt>ありす</rt>さん by changing the following sentences into your comments. Use この, その, あの, どの.

Example

いい　ベッド<rt>べっど</rt>ですね。→　その　ベッド<rt>べっど</rt>は　いい　ベッド<rt>べっど</rt>ですね。

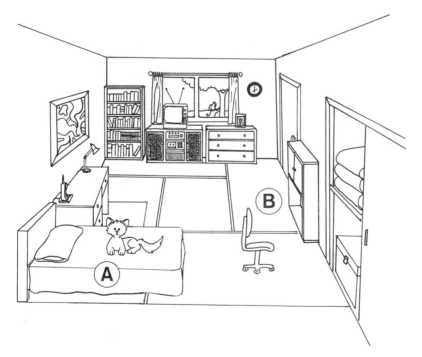

1. おおきい　おしいれですね。
2. きれいな　つくえですね。
3. あたらしい　テレビ<rt>てれび</rt>ですね。
4. ふるい　いすですね。
5. りっぱな　ねこですね。

B. Look again at the picture of the room in exercise A. You are staying in this room, but most of the things in the room belong to your host brother, ひろし. Choose three things that belong to him, then make statements about them. You are at location A, and the listener is at location B.

Example

(You pick the bed.) ベッド
　この　ベッドは　ひろしさんの　ベッドです。

1. とだな　2. ステレオ　3. ねこ　4. ほん　5. でんわ

C. Work with a partner. Look at the drawing of the living room. You are sitting on the sofa (location A), and your partner is at location B. Your partner will pick up some items. Make a statement about each item, using この、その、あの.

Example

Your partner:　ソファ
You:　　　　　この　ソファは　きれいな　ソファですね。

III. Describing the location of people and things, using 〜に　〜が あります／います and ここ、そこ、あそこ

A. Describing the location of things

Question					
Location	Particle	Noun (Subject)	Particle	Verb	
あそこ	に	おしいれ	が	あります	か。

Is there a closet over there?

Answer	
	Verb
はい、	あります。
いいえ、	ありません。

Yes, there is./No, there isn't.

すずき： リーさんのへやに　ステレオが　ありますか。
り す て れ お

Is there a stereo in your room, Mr. Lee?

リー： ええ、あります。／いいえ、ありません。
り

Yes, there is. / No, there isn't.

B. Describing the location of people

Question					
Location	Particle	Question Word	Particle	Verb	
そこ	に	だれ	が	います	か。

Who is there?

Answer		
Noun (Subject)	Particle	Verb
すずきさん	が	います。

Suzuki-san is there.

たなか： そこに　なにが　いますか。
What is there?

すずき： ねこが　います。
A cat is there.

たなか： この　たてものに　でんわが　ありますか。
Is there a telephone in this building?

すずき： ええ、あります。／いいえ、ありません。
Yes, there is./No there isn't.

- The particle に indicates the location of something or someone.
- The verbs あります and います mean *be* or *exist,* and they indicate that something or someone is at a location marked by the particle に. Use あります to talk about the location of a thing. Use います to talk about the location of a person or an animal.
- ここ, そこ, あそこ, and どこ are used to identify a location. ここ means *here* or *this place* and refers to a place close to the speaker and listener. そこ means *there* or *that place* and refers to a place close to the listener or between, or some distance from, the speaker and the listener. あそこ means *over there* or *that place over there*. It refers to a place far away from the speaker and the listener. どこ is a question word meaning *where,* as in どこから　きましたか in Chapter 2.
- The location may be marked by には instead of just に if the location is the topic of a sentence.

にほんには　ふじさんが　あります。
As for Japan, Mt. Fuji is there.

はなして　みましょう　(Practice and Conversation)

A. Look at the drawing of the bedroom on the next page. You are at location B, and アリス (ありす) さん is at location A. Form sentences using ここ, そこ, and あそこ.

Example

つくえ　→　ここに　つくえが　あります。

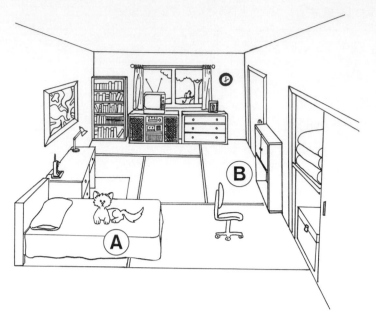

1. まど　　3. ねこ　　　5. ドア^{どあ}　　7. アリスさん^{ありす}
2. いぬ　　4. おしいれ　6. いす

B. Work with a partner. Look at the drawing of the living room. You are sitting on the sofa (location A). Your partner will choose location B, C, or D. In order to find out your partner's location, ask where different objects are in the room.

Example

A: そこに　まどが　ありますか。

B: はい、あります。or　いいえ、ありません。

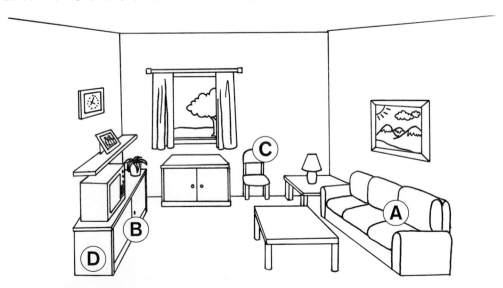

C. Work in groups of four. One person will think of a famous city or a foreign country. The others will try to guess the name of the city or the country by asking what kind of people or buildings are found there. Use そこ to refer to that city or country.

Examples

A: そこに　なにが　ありますか。

B: ＿＿＿＿＿が　あります。

A: ＿＿＿＿＿ですか。

B: はい、そうです。

D. Interview a classmate about his/her home and room. Find similarities and differences between your home and your classmate's, then list them in the chart. Note that ～に　すんでいます means *live(s)/reside(s) in* ～.

Example

A: ～さんは　アパート／りょう／うちに　すんでいますか。

B: アパート／りょう／うちに　すんでいます。

A: ～さんの　へやに　どんな　ものが　ありますか。

B: ＿＿＿＿＿が　あります。

A: ＿＿＿＿＿も　ありますか。

B: ええ、あります。 or　いいえ、ありません。

	Similarities	Differences
Home		
Room		

IV. Using location nouns: なか, そと, となり, よこ, ちかく, うしろ, まえ, うえ, した, みぎがわ, and ひだりがわ

Place				Subject		
Noun	Particle	Location Noun	Particle	Noun	Particle	Verb
たんす	の	うえ	に	ねこ	が	います。

There is a cat on the chest of drawers.

（うちの）なか   inside (the house)

（うちの）そと   outside (the house)

（うちの）となり   next (to the house)
(used with the same kind of object)

（うちの）よこ   next or adjacent (to the house)
(used with a different kind of object)

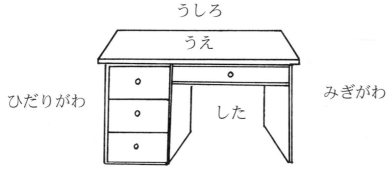

（つくえの）ちかく   close (to the desk)
（つくえの）うしろ   behind (the desk)
（つくえの）まえ   in front (of the desk)
（つくえの）うえ   on or above (the desk)
（つくえの）した   below or underneath (the desk)
（つくえの）みぎがわ   to the right (of the desk)
（つくえの）ひだりがわ   to the left (of the desk)

キム： 　つくえの　したに　なにが　いますか。
(きむ)
　　　　　What is under the desk?

ロペス： いぬが　いますよ。
(ろぺす)
　　　　　A dog is there.

● If two things next to each other belong to the same category of objects or people, use となり. If they belong to a different category, use よこ. For example, if you are talking about a chair next to a desk, say つくえの となり, but if you are talking about a person next to a building, say たてものの　よこ.

はなして　みましょう　(Practice and Conversation)

A. Look at this drawing of a room. Describe the things around the desk with location nouns.

Example

　　つくえの　うえに　ほんが　あります。

B. Look at the drawing of this room. Some objects are missing, and their locations are marked with question marks. Ask your partner what is in each location and write in the name of the object in the appropriate place. Your partner will answer the questions using the information in the drawing on page 80.

Example

A: つくえの　うえに　なにが　ありますか。

B: でんわが　あります。

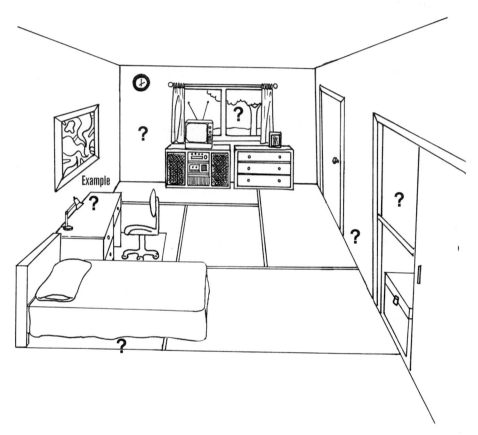

C. Work with a partner. Your partner will look at the drawing of the bedroom on page 74, and you will look at the drawing on page 80. Ask each other where various objects are, and find the differences and similarities between the two pictures.

Example

A: へやの　ひだりがわに　どんな　ものが　ありますか。

B: つくえが　あります。ベッドも　あります。

V. Using よ and ね

A. Giving information, using よ

Sentence	Particle
あそこに　おおきい　いぬが　います	よ。

There is a big dog over there, you know.

B. Seeking agreement, using ね

Sentence	Particle
たなかさんの　へやには　すてきな　えが　あります	ね。

There is a nice picture in Tanaka-san's room, isn't there?

ワット：　あの　おおきい　たてものは　ジョーンズさんの
　　　　　アパートですね。

That big building is Jones-san's apartment, isn't it?

すずき：　いいえ、そうじゃありませんよ。りょうですよ。

No, it isn't. It's a dormitory, you know.

ワット：　あ、そうですか。

Oh, I see.

- The particle よ is used when the speaker wishes to emphasize to the listener that he/she is imparting completely new information. Like *you know* in English, it is used more often in conversation and should not be overused.

- The particle ね is used when the speaker is seeking the listener's agreement or confirming a fact. It is similar to ～ *isn't it?* in English.

はなして　みましょう　(Practice and Conversation)

A. Look at the drawing of the bedroom on the next page, and answer the following questions, using よ.

Example

へやの　なかに　どんな　ものが　ありますか。
ちいさい　ベッドが　ありますよ。

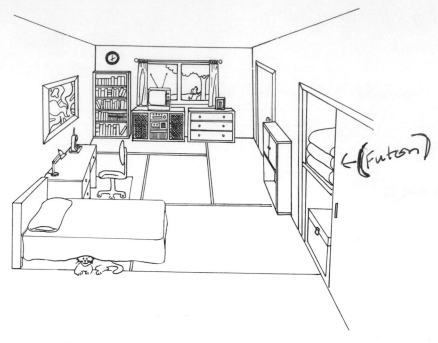

(Futon)

1. ベッドの　したに　なにが　いますか。
2. ステレオの　うえに　でんわが　ありますか。
3. まどの　ひだりがわに　ほんだなが　ありますか。
4. つくえの　したには　ねこが　いますか。
5. へやの　そとに　なにが　いますか。
6. へやの　みぎがわに　どんな　ものが　ありますか。

B. Work with a partner. Try to recall the contents of the living room in the drawing on page 74 of your textbook. State the location of various objects. Your partner will check the drawing on page 74 and verify the accuracy of what you say.

Example

A: ソファの　うしろに　まどが　ありますね。

B: いいえ、ありませんよ。

C. Work with a partner. Recall what the person has told you about him/herself (name, major, year, residence, hometown, friends, and so on). Then confirm the facts you remember, using ね.

Example

A: おなまえは　スミスさんですね。

B: ええ、そうです。or いいえ、ブラウンです。

Using visual clues

Photos, illustrations, and graphs can often help you understand what you read. For example, it's much easier to understand a description of a room or house if a floor plan is given as well. Such visuals not only help create a context for a text, but they may also provide other information that may not be included in the text.

リーさんのアパート

よむまえに　(Prereading)

Look at the following floor plan and determine what kinds of information it conveys.

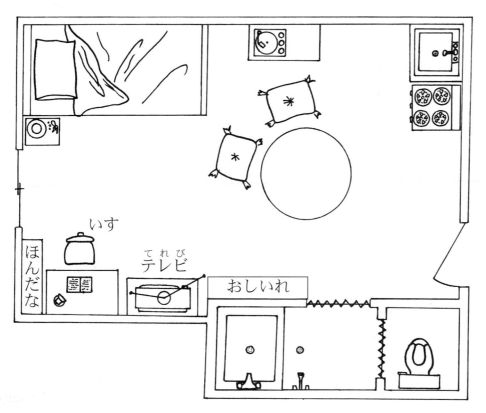

いす

ほんだな

テレビ

おしいれ

ことばの　リスト (Vocabulary)

〜に　すんでいます　live/reside at 〜	お手洗　restroom
台所　kitchen	おく　inner part
お風呂　bathroom	

- Read the following passage. Then look at the floor plan and circle the objects mentioned in the text. Starting with the passage below, every text in the *Reading* section of every chapter in *Nakama 1* will contain some unknown words and grammar. This will help you become accustomed to dealing with unknown materials.

リーさんはアパートに住んでいます。リーさんのアパートは
あまり大きくありません。アパートには台所とお手洗があります。
でも、お風呂はありません。部屋の右側には台所があります。
ドアの横にはお手洗があります。お手洗はとても小さいです。
部屋のおくには窓があります。窓の左側に、本棚と机があります。
机の横に戸棚があります。そして、戸棚の上にテレビがあります。
窓の前にはベッドがあります。ベッドの近くにステレオが
あります。

わかりましたか　(Comprehension)

A. Imagine that you are standing in the doorway, looking into the room. Verify the layout of the apartment along with the picture. Are all the objects in the room properly described?

B. Describe each object in the room as thoroughly as you can using different location nouns.

C. Describe the place where you live in a few sentences.

じょうずな　ききかた　(LISTENING)

Listening for general ideas

Conversations are often full of redundancy and unimportant details, so it is not necessary to understand every single word. Instead, it is more important to pick up a few key words and to get a general idea of what the conversation is about. If you need to know specific details or information, you can always ask questions about them for clarification.

(Practice)

Listen to the following three conversations and write the general idea conveyed in each one. You may use Japanese or English.

1. _____

2. _____

3. _____

 DICT-A-CONVERSATION

Remember these four Dict-a-Conversation steps and that your last name is
Smith (スミス):

Step 1 Listen carefully to what your conversation partner says on the tape. You may listen to the tape as many times as you wish.

Step 2 Write the speaker's lines as you hear them.

Step 3 Write your own responses, questions, or statements on the appropriate lines.

Step 4 When you have finished, check your completed script.

You are telling your friend, Kimura-san, about your room.

きむら : _____
スミス : _____

きむら : _____
スミス : _____

きむら : _____
スミス : _____

きむら : _____
スミス : _____

ききじょうず はなしじょうず (COMMUNICATION)

あいづち (Giving feedback) 2

In Chapter 2, you learned that the Japanese give feedback in several ways during a conversation and that はい and ええ do not necessarily indicate agreement. Besides indicating that the listener is following the conversation, はい and

ええ can mean that the listener sympathizes with the speaker or that the listener agrees with the speaker's opinion. For a person unfamiliar with this, the Japanese use of はい and ええ can lead to misunderstanding. For example, it is not uncommon to hear of an American who thought that a business negotiation was going well because the Japanese counterpart kept agreeing but that the deal fell through, leaving him/her bewildered.

はい and いいえ are also used between phrases as well as sentences. In the following example, Suzuki-san constantly interrupts Kimura-san, who consequently never finishes a sentence.

きむら： きのう　コンサートが　あって...
There was a concert yesterday, and. . .

すずき： ええ、
Yeah./Uh-huh.

きむら： おもしろいって いうから　いってみたんですが...
I went because I heard it would be interesting, but. . .

すずき： ええ、ええ
Yes, yes.

きむら： ぜんぜん　しゅみに　あわなくて...
It wasn't at all to my taste, and. . .

In contrast to Western standards, Suzuki-san is not being rude by interrupting because Kimura-san expects constant feedback from Suzuki-san. Indeed, Kimura-san would feel uncomfortable if Suzuki-san waited for him/her to finish the sentence. In fact, this type of interruption is very common with other types of conversational feedback in Japanese.

Work with a partner. Both of you are in front of the library, and your partner is pointing out different buildings on the campus. Say はい or ええ at appropriate intervals to indicate that you understand what he/she is saying.

そうごうれんしゅう　(INTEGRATION)

インタビュー　(Interview)

Work in groups of three or four. Each person will be interviewed by the other members of your group about his/her apartment, house, or dormitory room. The interviewers will take notes about what is said, and then each person will draw a picture of the room. After each interview, compare your drawings with those of other members of your group.

ロールプレイ (Role Play)

1. You want to go to the hospital. You see a tall, white building in the distance as you pass by a police officer. Ask the police officer if the building is a hospital.

2. You have invited a Japanese friend to your home. Show your friend around your home.

3. You have just arrived at your host family's home in Japan, and one of the family members is showing you the home. Check the locations of various rooms and objects.

たんご　(ESSENTIAL VOCABULARY)

Nouns

アパート　apartment
いす　chair
いぬ（犬）dog
うち（家）home; house
え（絵）picture
おしいれ（押し入れ）Japanese-style closet
しゃしん（写真）photograph
スタンド　lamp
ステレオ　stereo
ソファ　sofa
たてもの（建物）building
たんす　chest; drawers
つくえ（机）desk
テーブル　table

テレビ　television
でんわ（電話）telephone
ドア　door
とけい（時計）clock; watch
とだな（戸棚）cabinet
ねこ（猫）cat
ふとん（布団）futon
ベッド　bed
へや（部屋）room
ほん（本）book
ほんだな（本棚）bookshelf
まど（窓）window
りょう（寮）　dormitory

Location Nouns

うえ（上）on; above; over
うしろ（後ろ）behind; back of
した（下）under; beneath
そと（外）outside

ちかく（近く）near; vicinity
となり（隣）next to
なか（中）in; inside
ひだりがわ（左側）to the left; left side

まえ（前）in front of; in the front
みぎがわ（右側）to the right; right side
よこ（横）next to; at the side of

Verbs

あります　am/is/are, exist/s (inanimate things) The dictionary form is ある.
います　am/is/are, exist/s (people or animals) The dictionary form is いる.

な-adjectives

きれい（な）clean; pretty; neat
しずか（な）（静か（な））quiet　*shizuka*
すてき（な）（素敵（な））attractive; nice

ゆうめい（な）（有名（な））famous
りっぱ（な）（立派（な））fine; splendid; gorgeous

い-adjectives

あかるい（明るい）bright　*akarui*
あたらしい（新しい）new　*atarashii*
いい　good
おおきい（大きい）big
せまい（狭い）cramped; narrow

たかい（高い）tall; high
ちいさい（小さい）small
ひろい（広い）spacious; wide　*hiroi*
ふるい（古い）old　*furui*

Adverbs

あまり　(not) very　*amari*
　　(used with a negative form)
どうぞ　please
　　どうぞ　あがってください。（どうぞ
　　上がってください。）Please come in.

どうも　very
　　どうも　ありがとうございます。（ど
　　うも　有難うございます。）Thank you
　　very much.
とても　very　*totemo*
　　(used with an affirmative form)

Question Words

だれ　who
だれの + noun　whose + noun

どの + noun　which + noun
どんな + noun　what kind of + noun

Demonstrative Words

あそこ   over there; that place
ここ   here; this place
そこ   there; that place

あの + noun   that + noun over there
この + noun   this + noun
その + noun   that + noun

Expressions

ああ   oh
あがってください。（上がってください。）Please come in.
おかえりなさい。（お帰りなさい。）
   Welcome back./Welcome home.

おじゃまします。（お邪魔します。）
   Thank you (for allowing me to come in) (literally: I will intrude on you).
ただいま。（ただ今。）I'm back!

Passive Vocabulary

Nouns

おくさん（奥さん）(someone else's) wife
おてあらい（お手洗）restroom *otearai*
おふろ（お風呂）bathroom; bathtub *ofuro*
かない（家内）(the speaker's) wife *kanai*

だいどころ（台所）kitchen *daidokoro*
トイレ toilet *toirei*
むすこ（息子）son *musuko*

Verbs

すんでいます（住んでいます）   live/s, reside/s (present tense)

Supplementary Vocabulary

Parts of a House

いま（居間）family room *ima*
ガレージ garage *gareji*
クローゼット   Western-style closet
げんかん（玄関）front entrance
＊こどもべや（子供部屋）child's room
しんしつ（寝室）bedroom *shinshitsu.*
せんめんじょ（洗面所）washbowl area
ダイニングキッチン   eat-in kitchen

ちかしつ（地下室）basement
とこのま（床の間）alcove
にわ（庭）garden; yard *niwa*
ベッドルーム   bedroom
ベランダ   verandah
ものおき（物置）storage
ようしつ（洋室）Western-style room
リビングルーム   living room; family room

ろうか（廊下）hallway *rōka.*
わしつ（和室）Japanese-style room *washitsu.*

Household Articles

いけばな（生け花）flower arrangement
カーテン　curtain
げたばこ（下駄箱）shelf for putting shoes
　located in the entranceway of a house
コンピュータ　computer *konpyuta.*
ざぶとん（座布団）cushion for sitting on
　tatami floor
シャワー　shower
じゅうたん　carpet
しょうじ（障子）paper sliding-door

スイッチ　switch
せっけん（石鹸）soap
せんたくき（洗濯機）washing machine
たたみ（畳）tatami mat
でんき（電気）light; electricity
でんしレンジ（電子レンジ）microwave
　oven
はちうえ（鉢植え）potted plants
ファックス　fax machine
れいぞうこ（冷蔵庫）refrigerator

Location Nouns

aida

あいだ（間）between つくえと　ほんだ
なの　あいだ（机と本棚の間）
　between the desk and the bookshelf
おく（奥）inner part (of a house or a room) *oku.*
さき（先）ahead
てまえ（手前）this side *temae*
はし（端）end

ひだりはし（左端）left end
みぎはし（右端）right end
むかい（向かい）opposite side, across (the
　street)
むこう（向こう）beyond

Adjectives describing rooms and buildings

な-adjectives

にぎやか（な）（賑やか（な））lively　*nigiyaka(na)*

い-adjectives

きたない（汚い）dirty; messy
くらい（暗い）dark *kurai*

ひくい（低い）low
わるい（悪い）bad *warui*

カタカナ

K A T A K A N A

Introduction

In this section, you will learn how to read and write **katakana**. It is important to learn **katakana** because there are many loan words, especially from English, in modern Japanese. Also, your names are likely to be written in **katakana**. The following chart shows the printed style of **katakana** and the reading of each in **hiragana**. Note that the use of small [tsu] ツ for double consonants, the two dots on the right shoulder to indicate voiced syllables, and the small [ya] ヤ, [yu] ユ, and [yo] ヨ to indicate glides are the same as **hiragana**. A dash ー indicates a long vowel as explained in Chapter 2.

ん ン	わ ワ	ら ラ	や ヤ	ま マ	は ハ	な ナ	た タ	さ サ	か カ	あ ア
		り リ		み ミ	ひ ヒ	に ニ	ち チ	し シ	き キ	い イ
		る ル	ゆ ユ	む ム	ふ フ	ぬ ヌ	つ ツ	す ス	く ク	う ウ
		れ レ		め メ	へ ヘ	ね ネ	て テ	せ セ	け ケ	え エ
		ろ ロ	よ ヨ	も モ	ほ ホ	の ノ	と ト	そ ソ	こ コ	お オ

Katakana ア〜ソ

Study the following fifteen **katakana** and the mnemonic devices given. Practice reading and writing them in your Workbook.

I'd like an *ice cream* cone.　ア　ア

 I need an *easel* to draw.　イ　イ

 It's the *wick* of a candle.　ウ　ウ

 An *egg* is on an egg stand.　エ　エ

 Oh, what an *odd* way to walk.　オ　オ

 A *karate* kick.　カ　カ

 This is a *key*.　キ　キ

 A baby is sleeping in a *cradle*.　ク　ク

 This is a crooked *K*.　ケ　ケ

 This letter has two *corners*.　コ　コ

This is a *saddle* on a horse. サ サ

Sh. . . , a cat is sleeping. シ シ

I like a *swing*. ス ス

Hello, *Señor* García. セ セ

I'm *sewing* with a needle. ソ ソ

れんしゅう (Practice)

Read the following words in **katakana** and guess what they mean.

キス	ケーキ	サーカス	ケース	アイス
シーソー	コース	エース	オアシス	

Katakana タ〜ホ

Study the following カタカナ and the mnemonic devices given. Practice reading and writing them in Workbook.

Mnemonics and Key	Printed Style	Handwritten Style
A crooked *tie*.	タ	タ
A *chick* is trying to fly.	チ	チ

	The cat *gets* up on her feet.	ツ	ツ
	The cat's *tail* is wagging to the left.	テ	テ
	An Indian *tomahawk*.	ト	ト
	A *knife*.	ナ	ナ
	A *neat* tennis court.	ニ	ニ
	Noodles are difficult to eat with chopsticks.	ヌ	ヌ
	A *neckerchief* is around my neck.	ネ	ネ
	Someone's *nose*.	ノ	ノ
	A *hat*.	ハ	ハ
	A *heel*.	ヒ	ヒ
	A child's *hood*.	フ	フ

I have a bad *headache*.　　　　　　　　　　　ヘ　　　　　　　　ヘ

I will *hold* a cross.　　　　　　　　　　　　ホ　　　　　　　　ホ

れんしゅう　(Practice)

Read the following words in **katakana** and guess what they mean.
Remember that the small ツ indicates a double consonant.

カタカナ　　ネット　　　セーター　　カヌー　　　　ノート

エチケット テキスト　　カッター　　ハイヒール　ホット

ニット　　　テスト

Katakana マ〜ン

Study the following カタカナ and the mnemonic devices given. Practice
reading and writing them in your Workbook.

Mnemonics and Key	Printed Style	Handwritten Style
A giant *mushroom*	マ	マ
Who's three? *Me!*	ミ	ミ
The *moon* is sleeping.	ム	ム
The knife is *melting*.	メ	メ
A *monster* appears in Tokyo.	モ	モ

	A *yacht* on the ocean.	ヤ	ヤ
	It's a *U-boat*!	ユ	ユ
	Yoga is fun.	ヨ	ヨ
	A *rabbit* with long ears.	ラ	ラ
	This *ribbon* has long tails.	リ	リ
	A tree with deep *roots*.	ル	ル
	Let's write a capital L.	レ	レ
	A *loaf* of bread.	ロ	ロ
	A *wine* glass.	ワ	ワ
	A needle is sharp at the *end*.	ン	ン

れんしゅう (Practice)

Read the following words in **katakana** and guess what they mean.

ワシントン	テキサス	モンタナ
ユタ	オクラホマ	ミシシッピー
アイオワ	ミネソタ	イリノイ
オハイオ	アーカンソー	テネシー
ノースカロライナ	サウスカロライナ	メイン
アメリカ	メキシコ	オーストラリア
ニュージーランド	イタリア	スイス
フランス	ロシア	

Transcribing katakana

The following rules for transcribing **hiragana** also apply to **katakana**.

- Two dots (゙) indicate a voiced sound, and a small circle (゚) indicates the [p] sound, as in ガ [ga], ギ [gi], パ [pa]
- Small ヤユヨ indicate sounds in キャ [kya], シュ [shu], ミョ [myo], etc.
- Small ツ indicates a double consonant as in ホットドッグ (*hot dog*).

The following conventions are used to transcribe English words into **katakana**.

- The English sounds -er, -or, and -ar are heard as [aa] in Japanese. A dash indicates the long vowels.

  カーター Carter   ハート heart

  When **katakana** is written vertically, the long vowel marker (ー) is written vertically.

  カ　ハ
  ー　ー
  タ　ト
  ー

- The English [v] is heard in Japanese as [b]. Thus, [va], [vi], [vu], [ve], and [vo] will be [ba], [bi], [bu], [be], and [bo], respectively, in Japanese.

  カバー cover   バイオリン violin

- The English [l] and [r] are both heard as an [r] in Japanese.

  ライト right *or* light   リーダー reader *or* leader
  ロビー lobby *or* robby

- The English [th], as in *think* and *third*, is heard as [s]. The [th], as in *that* or *mother,* is heard as [z].

  サンクスギビング　Thanksgiving　　　マザーグース　Mother Goose
  サードベース　third base

- If an English word ends in [k], [g], [m], [f], [v], [l], [s], [z], [th], [p], or [b], the vowel [u] is added in Japanese. The vowel [u] is also added when these sounds are followed immediately by consonants in English.

  ミルク　milk　　　リング　ring　　　ホテル　hotel
  ミス　Miss　　　ジャズ　jazz

- If an English word has [t] or [d], the vowel [o] is added in Japanese.

  コスト　cost　　　スピード　speed　　　ラスト　last
  ベッド　bed

- The English vowel sounds in *bus* and *cut* or *bat* or *gas* are both heard as [a] in Japanese.

  バス　bus　　　カット　cut　　　バット　bat　　　ガス　gas

- In order to approximate as closely as possible the pronunciation of loan sounds such as people's names, the following combinations are commonly used. Note that these combinations are never used in **hiragana**.

ウェ [we]	ウェイン Wayne	フィ [fi]	マーフィー Murphy
ウォ [wo]	ウォルター Walter	フェ [fe]	フェイ Fay
シェ [she]	シェリル Cheryl	フォ [fo]	フォード Ford
チェ [che]	チェイス Chase	ジェ [je]	ジェーン Jane
ティ [ti]	カーティス Curtis	ディ [di]	ディーン Dean
ファ [fa]	ジェニファー Jennifer	デュ [du]	デューク Duke

Does your name contain any of the sounds listed above?

れんしゅう　(Practice)

A. Read the following words. Do you recognize any of them?

アジアけんきゅう、アメリカ、オーストラリア、カナダ、
スペイン、フランス、メキシコ、ニュージーランド、
アパート、ステレオ、ソファ、テーブル、テレビ、ドア、
ベッド、キャンパス、コンピュータ、スーパー、デパート、
デーパック、ノート、ボールペン、ラボ、レストラン、
コーヒー、シャワー

B. Guess what the following words are in English.

1. Foods and beverages

ハンバーガー、ステーキ、ホットドッグ、カレー、
スパゲッティ、サンドイッチ、サラダ、トマト、レタス、
オレンジ、レモン、フルーツ、バター、チーズ、ケーキ、
アイスクリーム、チョコレート、クッキー、ポテトチップ、
ミルク、ジュース、ビール、コーラ、ワイン

2. Sports

フットボール、バスケットボール、テニス、サッカー、
ジョギング、スキー、スケート、バレーボール、
ラケットボール、ゴルフ、サーフィン

3. Music

ピアノ、バイオリン、ギター、オーケストラ、
トランペット、ジャズ、ロック、クラシック

4. Household items

キッチン、リビングルーム、ランプ、オーブン、
トースター、ラジオ、レコード、ビデオ、カメラ、
カレンダー、コンピュータ

5. Countries

メキシコ、ブラジル、イギリス、ドイツ、オランダ、
イタリア、スイス、イスラエル、ロシア、オーストラリア、
ニュージーランド、インド、タイ、ベトナム、
サウジアラビア

6. Cities

ニューヨーク、ボストン、シカゴ、ロサンゼルス、
サンフランシスコ、トロント、モントリオール、ロンドン、
パリ、ベルリン、モスクワ、カイロ、シドニー、
バンコック、ホンコン

CHAPTER 4

だいよんか

Students chatting on campus

にほんの　まちと　だいがく

JAPANESE TOWNS AND UNIVERSITIES

Functions	Asking about a location and making statements about towns, buildings, rooms, and objects
New Vocabulary	Town buildings; Campus buildings; Classrooms and offices; Colors
Dialogue	あれは　なんですか。 (What is that over there?)
Culture	Japanese towns and neighborhoods; The Japanese educational system; Entrance examinations
Language	I. Describing and commenting on places, using adjectives (polite affirmative and negative forms) and とても and あまり
	II. Referring to things mentioned immediately before, using noun/adjective + の (pronoun)
	III. Referring to things, using これ、それ、あれ、and どれ
	IV. Using は and が
	V. Expressing location, using ～は　～に　あります／います and ～は です
Reading	Reading for a general idea
Listening	Guessing and predicting content
Communication	Getting someone s attention 1

あたらしい ことば (NEW VOCABULARY)

A. まち (Town buildings). Underline the Japanese words in the drawing for buildings or places in a neighborhood. Then fill in the chart, placing each word in one of two categories: public or private.

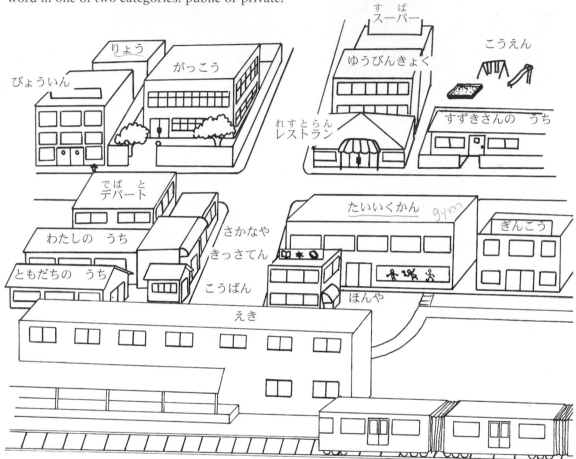

えき　station
ぎんこう　bank
ゆうびんきょく　post office
スーパー　supermarket
こうえん　park
がっこう　school
びょういん　hospital

レストラン　restaurant
ほんや　bookstore
きっさてん　coffee shop
こうばん　police box
さかなや　fish market
デパート　department store

Public	Private

B. きゃんぱす
   キャンパスのたてもの (Campus buildings). Draw a map of your
   school campus (or obtain a campus map) and label the following buildings
   and facilities in Japanese. If there is a word you don't know how to say in
   Japanese, ask your instructor.

がくせいかいかん　student union　*gakusei kai kan*

としょかん　library　*toshyo kan*　(図書館)

たいいくかん　gym　*taiikukan*

らぼ
ラボ　laboratory　*ra bo*

きょうようがくぶ　school of liberal arts

ほうがくぶ　law school　*hoogakubu*

けいざいがくぶ　school of economics

こうがくぶ　school of engineering　*koogakubu*

しょくどう　cafeteria　*shyokudoo*

きょうしつ　classroom　*Kyoo shitsu*

じむしつ　business office

けんきゅうしつ　professor's office, research room　*Kenkyuushitsu*

C. きょうしつと　じむしつ (Classrooms and offices). Complete the chart
   on the next page by classifying the following items as personal or school
   related. Some items may belong to both categories.

こくばん　blackboard

えんぴつ　pencil

ぼ　る　ぺん
ボールペン　ballpoint pen

け　ご　む
けしゴム　eraser

の　と
ノート　notebook

じしょ　dictionary

きょうかしょ　textbook

かばん　bag, briefcase

で　ぱっく
デーパック　backpack

こん　ぴゅ　た
コンピュータ　computer

Personal	School Related

D. いろ (Colors). Rank the following colors according to your preference, then ask your classmates what their favorite colors are for shoes, clothing, and cars. (〜が　すきです means *like 〜/am fond of 〜*.)

Example

り
リー：　　どの　いろが　すきですか。
What color do you like?

あ り す
アリス：　あかい　いろが　すきです。
I like red.

あかい　red　*akai*
あおい　blue　*aoi*
しろい　white　*shiroi*
くろい　black　*Kuroi*
きいろい　yellow　*Kiroi*
ちゃいろい　brown
みどり (noun)　green

だ い あ ろ く
ダイアローグ　**(DIALOGUE)**

はじめに　**(Warm-up)**

A. Look at the photograph on page 99 and describe what you see.

B. How does this campus compare with your campus?

C. Do you think Japanese universities are similar to your university in size, facilities, and number of faculty ?

あれは　なんですか。 (What is that over there?)

Alice and Michiko are on the campus of じょうとう　だいがく.

____ アリス：あそこに　おおきい　たてものが　ありますね。

____ みちこ：ええ。

____ アリス：あれは　なんですか。

____ みちこ：ああ、あれは　としょかんですよ。

____ アリス：（magnicifent）りっぱな　たてものですね。

____ みちこ：ええ。じょうとうだいがくの　としょかんは
とても　ゆうめいですよ。

____ アリス：そうですか。いいですね。あのう、がくせい
かいかんは　どの　たてものですか。

____ みちこ：その　しろいのですよ。

____ アリス：ああ、そうですか。あまり　おおきく
ありませんね。

____ みちこ：ええ。

____ アリス：じゃあ、どれが　けいざいがくぶの
たてものですか。

____ みちこ：ここですよ。

____ アリス：ここですか。あのう、じむしつは　どこですか。

____ みちこ：みぎがわに　ちゃいろい　ドアが　ありますね。

____ アリス： ええ。

____ みちこ： あそこですよ。

____ アリス： ああ、そうですか。

わかりましたか (Comprehension)

Complete the chart with the adjectives used in the dialogue to describe the following nouns.

Adjective	Noun
	としょかん
	がくせいかいかん
	けいざいがくぶの　たてもの

にほんの　ぶんか　(CULTURE)

● *Japanese towns and neighborhoods. Do you know what a* こうばん *is?*

Japanese neighborhoods tend to develop around a train station and to include stores, restaurants, banks, post offices, bus terminals, and other services. A police box (こうばん), often found in front of a station, usually has several officers on duty around the clock.

People often stop at a police box to ask for directions because locating a specific address can be difficult in large cities, where houses are not always numbered consecutively.

A Japanese police box.

● *The Japanese educational system. Do you know the percentage of high school graduates who go to college in Japan?*

Education is considered very important in Japan. Parents spend about one third of their income on their children's education. Attendance in elementary school (six years) and junior high school (three years) is mandatory, and over ninety-five percent of junior high school graduates go on to senior high school (three years). The high school dropout rate is only about two percent. About forty percent of high school graduates enroll in college. Half the female graduates attend a junior college, while practically all male graduates attend a four-year college.

● *Entrance examinations. What kind of examination is required to enter college?*

Entrance examinations play a major role in the college admission process, although the system is changing gradually. For public universities, students first take a national examination, then another examination prepared by that university. For private universities, students take only examinations prepared by that university. Examinations are given from January through March, and a student may take several examinations during this period.

Most schools admit new students each April, which is the beginning of an academic year. A high school graduate who fails the entrance examination must wait a year to retake it. The period in which students spend day after day studying for entrance exams is sometimes described as しけんじごく (*examination hell*).

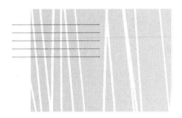

LANGUAGE

I. Describing and commenting on places, using adjectives (polite affirmative and negative forms) and とても and あまり

Question			
Topic		**い-adjective (polite, affirmative)**	
すずきさんの　うち	は	おおきいです	か。

Is Suzuki-san's house big?

Answer		
	Adverb	**い-adjective (polite, negative)**
いいえ、	あまり	おおきくありません。
いいえ、	あまり	おおきくないです。

or (before second row)

No, it's not very big.

Question			
Topic		**な-adjective (polite, affirmative)**	
すずきさんの　へや	は	しずかです	か。

Is Suzuki-san's room quiet?

Answer		
	Adverb	**な-adjective (polite, negative)**
いいえ、	あまり	しずかじゃありません。
いいえ、	あまり	しずかじゃないです。

or (before second row)

No, it's not very quiet.

い-adjectives

Dictionary form[1]	おおきい	いい
Polite affirmative form	おおき<u>い</u>＋です	いい＋です
Polite negative form	おおき<u>く</u>＋ありません	<u>よく</u>＋ありません
or	おおき<u>く</u>＋ないです	<u>よく</u>＋ないです

な-adjectives

Dictionary form	りっぱ
Polite affirmative form	りっぱ＋です
Polite negative form	りっぱ＋じゃありません
or	りっぱ＋じゃないです

いしだ：　　　アリスさんの　うちは　きれいですね。

あ り す

Alice-san's house is beautiful, isn't it?

ジョーンズ：　そうですね。でも　へやは　あまり　ひろく
じ ょ ん ず　　　ありませんよ。

or　　　　　でも　へやは　あまり　ひろくないですよ。

It is. But the rooms aren't very spacious, you know.

---

[1] See Chapter 7 for more information about dictionary forms.

- The い-adjective いい, meaning *good*, has a slight irregularity in the negative form.

- The alternative negative form, 〜ないです, is considered colloquial and is used only in spoken language.

- Note that the negative form of a な-adjective is the same as that of a noun + です.

Negative of noun + です
だいがくせいじゃありません。
だいがくせいじゃないです。

Negative of な-adjective
きれいじゃありません。
きれいじゃないです。

- The adverbs とても and あまり are often used with adjectives, and both may be translated as *very* in English. とても occurs with an affirmative form, and あまり occurs with a negative form.

この　たてものは　とても　きれいです。
This building is *very* pretty.

この　たてものは　あまり　きれいじゃありません。
This building is *not very* pretty.

- 〜くないです and 〜じゃないです are stronger, respectively, than 〜くありません and 〜じゃありません。

はなして　みましょう　(Practice and Conversation)

A. Look at the chart on the next page describing the conditions of different buildings. Then answer the questions, paying attention to はい, いいえ, とても, and あまり.

Examples

A: ゆうびんきょくは　おおきいですか。

B: いいえ、おおきくありません。

or いいえ、おおきくないです。

A: ぎんこうは　おおきいですか。

B: はい、とても　おおきいです。

	ゆうびんきょく	ぎんこう	スーパー	びょういん
おおきい	いいえ	とても	あまり	はい
あたらしい	とても	いいえ	はい	あまり
いい	あまり	いいえ	はい	とても
きれい	はい	いいえ	はい	はい
しずか	いいえ	はい	あまり	いいえ
りっぱ	あまり	とても	いいえ	はい

1. スーパーの　たてものは　いいですか。
2. ゆうびんきょくは　あたらしいですか。
3. びょういんは　きれいですか。
4. びょういんは　りっぱですか。
5. ゆうびんきょくは　しずかですか。

B. Work with a partner. Ask your partner about his/her belongings, using the adjectives in the box.

> おおきい　ちいさい　あたらしい　ふるい　ひろい　せまい
> あかい　あおい　しろい　くろい　きいろい　ちゃいろい
> あかるい　たかい　いい　きれい　しずか　りっぱ　すてき

Example

A: ～さんの　かばんは　あかいですか。

B: いいえ、あかくありません。or いいえ、あかくないです。

C. Work with a new partner. Tell him/her about your belongings and your previous partner's belongings.

Examples

わたしの　デーパックは　ちいさいです。
～さんの　デーパックも　ちいさいです。

ぼくの　へやは　しずかです。
でも、～さんの　へやは　あまり　しずかじゃありません。
　　　　　　　　　　　　　or　　しずかじゃないです。

D. Work with a new partner. Ask your partner about the buildings in his/her neighborhood. Then write a description of the buildings, using both adjective + noun and 〜は 〜adjective.

Example

A: 〜さんの　うちの　ちかくに　どんな　たてものが
　　ありますか。

B: <u>ぎんこう</u>が　あります。

A: どんな　たてものですか。

B: <u>たかい　たてものです。そして、あまり　きれいじゃあ
　　りません。</u>

II. Referring to things mentioned immediately before, using noun/adjective + の (pronoun)

A. い-adjective + の

あの　しろい　たてものは　びょういんです。

That white building over there is a hospital.

Adjective (Prenominal)	Pronoun	Particle	
ちゃいろい	の	は	ぎんこうです。

The brown one is a bank.

B. な-adjective + の

その　ちいさい　たてものは　ほんやです。

That small building is a bookstore.

Adjective (Prenominal)	Pronoun	Particle	
きれいな	の	は	きっさてんです。

The pretty one is a coffee shop.

C. Noun + の

Question					Answer		
	Noun	**Pronoun**			**Noun**	**Pronoun**	
この　かばんは	だれ	の	です	か。	やまださん	の	です。

Whose bag is this?　　　　　　　　　　　　　　　　　　　　　　　It's Yamada-san's.

イー：　　この　りっぱな　かばんは　だれのですか。
　　　　　　Whose is this fine bag?

やまだ：　その　おおきいのですか。たなかさんのですよ。
　　　　　　That big one? It's Tanaka-san's.

- の is a pronoun that means *one* or *ones* in English, as in the *red one* or *that big one*. It is usually used for things, and it is rarely used for people.

- The pronoun の must be directly preceded by an adjective or a noun. It cannot be used with the particle の; the demonstrative adjectives この, その, or あの; or the interrogative word どの.

- When the pronoun の is modified by a noun, that noun should immediately precede it, as in key sentence C. When the pronoun の is modified by an adjective, use the prenominal form of the adjective.

はなして　みましょう　(Practice and Conversation)

A. Look at the following chart and identify the owner of each item.

	よしださん	たなかさん	すずきさん	スミスさん
デーパック	あかい	あおい	くろい	しろい
うち	しずか	きれい	ふるい	あたらしい

Example

あかい　デーパック
<u>あかい　デーパックは　よしださんの</u>です。

1. ふるい　うち
2. あおい　デーパック
3. くろい　デーパック
4. しずかな　うち
5. きれいな　うち
6. しろい　デーパック
7. あたらしい　うち

B. Look at the chart in exercise A and tell to whom each house or backpack belongs, using の.

Example

デーパック ／ あかい しろい
あかい デーパックは よしださんのです。しろいのは
スミスさんのです。

1. うち ／ ふるい あたらしい
2. デーパック ／ あおい あかい
3. デーパック ／ くろい しろい
4. うち ／ きれい ふるい
5. デーパック ／ しろい あおい
6. うち ／ しずかな あたらしい

C. Make a list of items found in your classroom. Then ask your classmates who owns those items.

Example

A: あのう、すみません。この あかい ボールペンは
だれのですか。

B: せんせいのですよ。

Item	Owner
あかい ボールペン	せんせい

III. Referring to things, using これ, それ, あれ, and どれ

Question					Answer	
Demonstrative Pronoun						
それ		は	なん	です	か。	にほんごの じしょ	です。

What is that?　　　　　　　　　　　　It's a Japanese dictionary.

せんせい： これは　スミスさんの　かばんですか。

Is this your bag, Smith-san?

スミス： いいえ。わたしのは　あれです。

No. Mine is that (thing) over there.

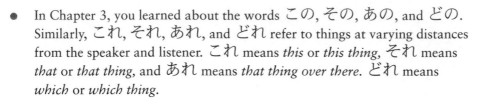

- In Chapter 3, you learned about the words この, その, あの, and どの. Similarly, これ, それ, あれ, and どれ refer to things at varying distances from the speaker and listener. これ means *this* or *this thing,* それ means *that* or *that thing,* and あれ means *that thing over there.* どれ means *which* or *which thing.*

- これ, それ, あれ, and どれ are pronouns and cannot be followed by another noun. Use この, その, あの, and どの before a noun.

これは　ぼくの　えんぴつです。

This is my pencil.

この　えんぴつは　ぼくの　えんぴつです。

This pencil is my pencil.

- これ, それ, あれ, and どれ refer to things, not to people. Use この, その, あの, and どの followed by かた (respectful term) or ひと to refer to a person.

この　かたは　たなかせんせいです。

This (person) is Professor Tanaka.

- The actual distances that these words indicate vary depending on context. それ would imply much greater distance when it is used to point out a building than when it is used to point to an item in a room.

はなして　みましょう　(Practice and Conversation)

A. Look at the following drawing of a classroom. Brown-san is at location A, and Kimura-san is at location B. Brown-san is asking Kimura-san the Japanese words for various objects in the room. Complete the following questions, using これ, それ, あれ, and どれ.

> **Example**
>
> A: あれは　にほんごで　なんと　いいますか。
> B: いぬと　いいます。

1. A: ＿＿＿＿は　にほんごで　なんと　いいますか。
   B: まどと　いいます。
2. A: ＿＿＿＿は　にほんごで　なんと　いいますか。
   B: ド<ruby>ア<rt>あ</rt></ruby>と　いいます。
3. A: ＿＿＿＿は　にほんごで　なんと　いいますか。
   B: テ<ruby>レ<rt>れ</rt></ruby>ビと　いいます。
4. A: ＿＿＿＿は　にほんごで　なんと　いいますか。
   B: コ<ruby>ン<rt>ん</rt></ruby>ピューータと　いいます。
5. A: ＿＿＿＿は　にほんごで　なんと　いいますか。
   B: デーパックと　いいます。

B. Work with a partner. Look at the drawing in exercise A. You are at location A, and your partner is at location B. An eraser, a pencil, and some books are scattered around the room. First let your partner decide who, among the following people, owns each item and mark the person's name on the drawing in his/her book.

たなかせんせい　やまださん　アリスさん　キムさん
スミスさん　リンさん

Then ask who owns each item and write the owner's name in the appropriate place in your book. When you are done, have your partner check your answers.

A: これ／それ／あれは　だれの　<u>ほん</u>ですか。

B: これ／それ／あれは　<u>やまださんの</u>です。

or

A: これ／それ／あれは　<u>やまださんの　ほん</u>ですか。

B: はい、そうです。or　いいえ、そうじゃありません。

C. Work with a partner. Look at the drawing of a street. and ask your partner to locate certain places, using これ, それ, and あれ. Assume that both of you are standing in front of the police box.

A: これ／それ／あれは　＿＿＿＿＿＿　ですか。

B: はい、そうです。 or いいえ、そうじゃありません。

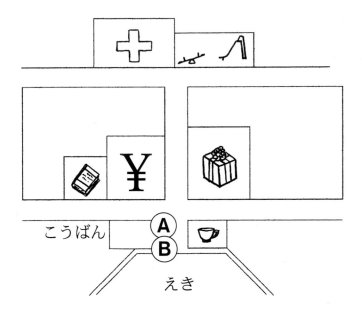

こうばん　　Ⓐ　　☕

Ⓑ

えき

D. Work with a partner. Your instructor will give you a map of a college campus. Your partner is a new student, and you are showing him/her the campus. First decide where you and your partner are, then describe the buildings around you.

(Assume that you are in front of the library.)
これは　としょかんです。

IV. Using は and が

A. Using が

Question				Answer	
Question Word	**Particle (subject)**				
どれ	が	アリス^{ありす}さんの　かばんです	か。	それ	です。

Which is Alice-san's bag?　　　　　　　　　　　　　　　　　　It's that one.

B. Using は

Question						
Noun	**Particle (topic)**	**Question Word**	**Particle**			
これ	は	だれ	の	かばん	です	か。

Whose bag is this?

Answer	
スミス^{すみす}さんの	です。

It's Smith-san's.

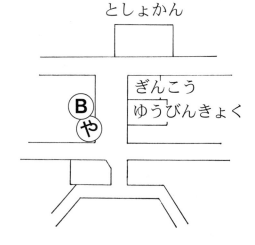

ブラウン^{ぶらうん}： あれは　ぎんこうですか。
　　　Is that (over there) a bank?

やまだ：　いいえ、あれは　としょかんです。
　　　No, that (over there) is a library.

ブラウン^{ぶらうん}： そうですか。じゃあ、どれが
　　　ぎんこうですか。
　　　I see. Then, which one is the bank?

やまだ：　その　しろいのですよ。
　　　It's that white one.

ブラウン^{ぶらうん}： ああ、そうですか。じゃあ、となりの
　　　たてものは　なんですか。
　　　Oh, I see. Well, what is the building next to it?

やまだ：　それは　ゆうびんきょくです。
　　　That is a post office.

- The particle が marks the grammatical subject of a sentence. Always use が when the subject is (or contains) a question word, as in どの　ひとが　せんせいですか. The particle は cannot be used with a question word because は marks the topic of a sentence, which is information already known to the speaker.

- If a question word is used in the part of a sentence that follows the topic, は is used.

  じむしつは　どこですか　　Where is the business office?

- Once the subject noun has been mentioned, は is often used for the subject that refers to the same item in subsequent sentences.

あそこに　ねこが　いますね。

There is a cat over there.

それは　くろい　ねこですか。

Is it a black cat?

(In sentence 1, the information about the cat's existence is new. In sentence 2, the fact is already familiar, so は is used.)

- それ can be used to refer to something mentioned previously. In this usage, それ means *it* in English. Likewise, その〜 and そこ can be used in the same way. In this case, それ refers to something invisible.

あそこに　かばんが　あります。　あれは　たなかさんのです。

There is a bag over there.　　　　　It is Tanaka-san's.

or　あの　かばんは　たなかさんのです。

That bag is Tanaka-san's.

がくせいかいかんの　なかに　しょくどうが　あります。そこは　とても　きれいです。

There is a cafeteria in the student union. It (that place) is very clean/nice.

はなして　みましょう　(Practice and Conversation)

A. First circle the question words, then complete the following sentences using either が or は.

Example

だれ　＿が＿　がくせいですか。

1. リーさん ＿＿＿＿＿＿　どの　ひとですか。
2. どれ ＿＿＿＿＿＿　びょういんですか。

3. どの　コンピュータ　__は が__　あたらしいですか。
4. きっさてん　__は__　どこですか。
5. アリスさん　__は__　どんな　ひとですか。
6. だれ　__が__　いますか。
7. デパート　__は__　どこに　ありますか。
8. きむらさん　__は__　どちらから　いらっしゃいましたか。
9. あの　あたらしい　たてもの　__は__　なんですか。

B. Survey your classmates to find out which building or person best fits the descriptions given in the chart. Use a question word + noun as the grammatical subject in your question. Note that いちばん (literally: *number one*) before an adjective means *the most ～*, and いちばん　おおきい means *the biggest*.

Example

A: どの　たてものが　いちばん　おおきいですか。

B: としょかんが　いちばん　おおきいです。

いちばん　きれいな　たてもの	がくせいかいかん
いちばん　ちいさい　たてもの	
いちばん　しずかな　ひと	
いちばん　ゆうめいな　ひと	

C. Work with a partner. Ask your partner about the results of the survey in exercise B. Use は in your questions.

Example

A: いちばん　おおきい　たてものは　どれですか。

B: としょかんです。

V. Expressing location, using ～は　～に　あります／います and ～は　です

A. Expressing the location of an object

Question					
Noun	Particle	Question Word	Particle	Verb	
こうばん	は	どこ	に	あります	か。

Where is the police box?

Answer		
Noun Phrase (location)	Particle	Verb
えきの　ちかく	に	あります。

It's near the station.

Question				
Noun	Particle	Question Word	Verb	
こうばん	は	どこ	です	か。

Where is the police box?

Answer	
Noun Phrase (location)	Verb
えきの　ちかく	です。

It's near the station.

B. Expressing the location of a person or an animal

Question					
Noun	Particle	Question Word	Particle	Verb	
アリスさん	は	どこ	に	います	か。

Where is Alice-san?

Answer		
Noun Phrase (location)	Particle	Verb
あそこ	に	います。

She is over there.

Question				
Noun	Particle	Question Word	Verb	
アリスさん	は	どこ	です	か。

Where is Alice-san?

Answer	
Noun Phrase (location)	Verb
あそこ	です。

She is over there.

ロペス：アリスさんは　どこに　いますか。／アリスさんは
　　　　どこですか。
　　　Where is Alice-san?

みちこ：びょういんに　います。／びょういんです。
　　　She is in the hospital.

ロペス：びょういんは　どこに　ありますか。／びょういんは
　　　　どこですか。
　　　Where is the hospital?

みちこ：あそこに　あります。／あそこです。
　　　It's over there.

- Although 〜に　〜が　あります／います is similar to 〜は　〜に　あります／います, the usage is very different. Use 〜は　〜に　あります／いますか to focus on the location of a person or thing. Use 〜に　〜が　あります／いますか to focus on the person or thing whose location is being established.

- 〜です can be used instead of 〜に　あります／います.

はなして みましょう (Practice and Conversation)

A. Look at the following drawing of a classroom. Answer the following questions, using location nouns and 〜は 〜に あります/います.

Example

こくばんは どこに ありますか。／こくばんは どこ
ですか。

<u>せんせいの うしろに あります。／せんせいの うしろ
です。</u>

1. コンピュータは どこに ありますか。
2. いぬは どこに いますか。
3. せんせいの かばんは どこに ありますか。
4. ノートは どこに ありますか。
5. まどは どこに ありますか。
6. テレビは どこに ありますか。
7. えんぴつは どこに ありますか。
8. けしゴムは どこに ありますか。 <u>けしゴムは へやの てまえのつくえ
のうえのほんのえんぴつ
のみぎがわにあります。</u>

B. Work with a partner. Look at the following drawing of a street. Your partner will ask you where various buildings are located. Both of you are in front of the station. Answer his/her questions based on the drawing.

Example

A: さかなやは　どこに　ありますか。／　さかなやは　どこですか。

B: ほんやの　ひだりがわに　あります。／ほんやの　ひだりがわです。

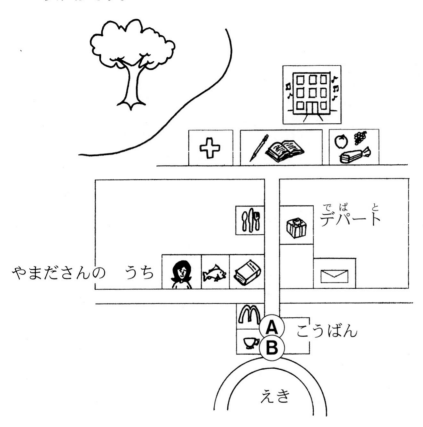

C. Work with a partner. Ask your partner about the locations of various buildings on campus and take notes. Then check the answers with a campus map.

Example

A: ラ^{らぼ}ボは　どこに　ありますか。／ラ^{らぼ}ボは　どこですか。

B: この　たてものの　なかに　あります。／この　たてものの　なかです。

D. Work with a partner. Your partner will draw the objects listed below the drawing of the room in his/her book. Then ask your partner where each object is located and draw the items in your book. When you are done, check your drawing with your partner's.

Example

A: かばんは　どこに　ありますか。／かばんは　どこ
　　です か。

B: ドア<ruby>ド<rt>ど</rt>ア<rt>あ</rt></ruby>の　みぎがわに　あります。／ドア<ruby>ド<rt>ど</rt>ア<rt>あ</rt></ruby>の　みぎがわ
　　です。

1. つくえ
2. いす
3. ソファ<ruby>ソ<rt>そ</rt>ファ<rt>ふぁ</rt></ruby>
4. デーパック<ruby>デ<rt>で</rt>パック<rt>ぱっく</rt></ruby>
5. かばん

6. えんぴつ
7. きょうかしょ
8. ノート<ruby>ノ<rt>の</rt>ト<rt>と</rt></ruby>
9. コンピュータ<ruby>コ<rt>こ</rt>ンピュ<rt>んぴゅ</rt>タ<rt>た</rt></ruby>

じょうず　な　よみかた　(READING)

Reading for a general idea

Written texts are not as redundant as conversations. There are fewer repeated words and no sound clues. However, you can still get the general idea by focusing on the title and frequently occurring words and expressions.

Read the following text, paying attention to the title and repeated words. What is the general idea?

城東大学

城東大学は東京の郊外にあります。学生は約三万人で、教授は約二千人います。でも、キャンパスはあまり大きくありません。城東大学には経済学部と文学部と商学部と法学部があります。留学生センターもあります。

田中先生の研究室

よむまえに　(Prereading)

Look at the following drawing, and describe the room to a partner.

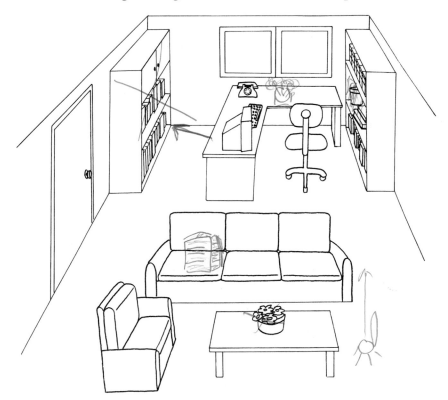

ことばの　リスト　(Vocabulary)

奥　the inner part of a building, or room

手前　this side (side closer to the speaker)

鉢植え　potted plant

たくさん　many, a lot

- Read the passage paying attention to the three types of scripts. There are four discrepancies between the text and the drawing. Underline the sentences with the wrong information in the text.

田中先生の研究室はとても広いです。部屋の右側には大きい本棚があります。本棚には本がたくさんあります。本棚の横には窓があります。窓の前には小さい鉢植えがあります。そして、窓の近くには先生の机があります。窓は部屋の奥にあります。机は部屋の左側にあります。机の上にはコンピュータと電話があります。部屋の手前には小さいソファがあります。ソファの上にも本がたくさんあります。ソファの横に小さい椅子があります。

わかりましたか　(Comprehension)

A. Rewrite the four sentences you underlined in the text to make them match the drawing.

1. _____

2. _____

3. _____

4. _____

B. Write a short description of your campus or your classroom.

じょうずな　ききかた　(LISTENING)

Guessing and predicting content

In Chapters 2 and 3, you learned that you don't have to understand every single word to understand a conversation and that it is important to pick up a few key words. Face-to-face conversations give many clues (e.g., facial expressions, gestures, and intonation) as to what the person is saying. Context, general knowledge, and previous experiences in similar situations will also help you guess words you may have missed or don't know.

 **(Practice)**

Listen to the conversations, which take place on a busy street near Jōtō University. Because there is a lot of background noise, you will not hear some of the words. From the context, guess what the missing words are and write them down.

1. _____

2. _____

3. _____

4. _____

  ## DICT-A-CONVERSATION

Your Japanese friend, Kimura-san, is showing you, Smith-san, around the campus, and you are asking about various buildings.

<ruby>スミス<rt>す み す</rt></ruby> : (Pointing at a nearby building) _____

きむら : _____

<ruby>スミス<rt>す み す</rt></ruby> : _____

きむら : _____

<ruby>スミス<rt>す み す</rt></ruby> : _____

きむら : _____

<ruby>スミス<rt>す み す</rt></ruby> : _____

きむら : _____

ききじょうず　はなしじょうず　(COMMUNICATION)

Getting someone's attention 1

In Chapter 1, you learned the phrase, あのう、すみません (*excuse me*) as a way of getting someone's attention. In modern Japanese, すみません is commonly used for three different functions: to apologize, to get someone's attention, and to thank someone. すみません is probably the phrase most commonly used to get someone's attention. It is often preceded by あのう (*ah . . .*) or ちょっと (*well . . .*) and followed by が (*but*), as in あのう すみませんが, ちょっと　すみませんが, and あのう　ちょっと すみませんが.

あのう by itself may also be used to get someone's attention. For example, if someone wants to initiate a conversation at a meeting or a party, the person can say あのう and wait for the listener to respond. あのう is also used as a conversation filler when you cannot think of the right word. If you want to ask someone a personal question, though, first say しつれいですが or あのう しつれいですが (literally: *I am being rude, but . . .*). For example, あのう しつれいですが、にほんの　かたですか is a polite way of asking someone whether the person is Japanese.

Finally, along with あのう or すみません, おねがいします (literally: *I am requesting*) may also be used to get the attention of someone who provides a service, such as a store clerk or waiter.

A. You are looking for a certain building or facility, and your classmates are all strangers. Ask someone for its location using the appropriate expression.

B. Ask a classmate personal questions using the appropriate expressions.

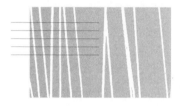

そうごうれんしゅう　(INTEGRATION)

だいがくさがし　(Choosing a university)

In this activity, half the class are recruiters from a university or college, and the other half are prospective students. Each recruiter must decide which school to represent and fill in the information card with the pertinent information. Each prospective student should talk to as many recruiters as possible, take notes on each school using the checklist provided, and make a choice on which school to attend at the end of the activity.

Recruiter's Information Card	
1. Name of the school	_____
2. Location of the school	_____
3. Size of the school	_____
4. Departments and programs	_____
5. Facilities on campus	_____
6. Other information	_____

Student's Checklist				
School				
Location				
Size				
Departments and programs				
Facilities				
Other information				

ろ　る ぷれ い
ロールプレイ　(Role Play)

1. You are showing your campus to a visitor from Japan who doesn't speak English. Tell the visitor about your campus as he/she asks you questions.

2. You've just left the train station, and you want to go to 〜 (decide where you want to go). Ask a passerby where it is.

たんご　(ESSENTIAL VOCABULARY)

Nouns

いろ（色）color
えき（駅）station
えんぴつ（鉛筆）pencil
がくせいかいかん（学生会館）student union
がっこう（学校）school
かばん（鞄）bag, briefcase
きっさてん（喫茶店）coffee shop
きゃんぱす
キャンパス　campus
きょうかしょ（教科書）textbook
きょうしつ（教室）classroom
きょうようがくぶ（教養学部）school of liberal arts
ぎんこう（銀行）bank

けいざいがくぶ（経済学部）school of economics
ご む
けしゴム（消しゴム）eraser
けんきゅうしつ（研究室）professor's office, research room
こうえん（公園）park
こうがくぶ（工学部）school of engineering
こうばん（交番）police box
こくばん（黒板）blackboard
こん ぴゅ た
コンピュータ　computer
さかなや（魚屋）fish market
じしょ（辞書）dictionary
しょくどう（食堂）dining room/hall, cafeteria

じむしつ（事務室）business office
スーパー　supermarket
たいいくかん（体育館）gym
デーパック　backpack
デパート　department store
ところ（所）place
としょかん（図書館）library
ノート　notebook
びょういん（病院）hospital

ほうがくぶ（法学部）law school
ボールペン　ballpoint pen
ほんや（本屋）bookstore
まち（町）town
みどり（緑）green
ゆうびんきょく（郵便局）post office
ラボ　laboratory
レストラン　restaurant

い-adjectives

あおい（青い）blue
あかい（赤い）red
きいろい（黄色い）yellow

くろい（黒い）black
しろい（白い）white
ちゃいろい（茶色い）brown

Question Words

どれ　which, which one

Demonstrative Words

これ　this, this one
それ　that, that one nearby
あれ　that, that one over there

Particles

が　subject marker
ね　isn't it, etc.; seeking confirmation marker
よ　"you know"; emphasis marker

Suffixes

〜がくぶ（〜学部）school of 〜　こうがくぶ（工学部）school of engineering

おねがいします。（お願いします。）Excuse me (to get the attention of a store clerk).

しつれいですが（失礼ですが）Excuse me, but . . . (used before asking a personal question).

ちょっと　すみませんが（ちょっと　済みませんが）Excuse me, but . . . (used to make a request, to ask a question).

Passive Vocabulary

Location Nouns

おく（奥）the inner part of a house or room

てまえ（手前）this side (the side closer to the speaker)

な-adjectives

すき（な）（好き（な））like

Adverbs

いちばん（一番）most, best

ずいぶん　quite

たくさん　many, much, a lot

Expressions

～がすきです（～が好きです）like, be fond of (all persons, present tense)

Supplementary Vocabulary

Colors (Nouns)

オレンジ　orange

きみどり（黄緑）light green

クリームいろ（クリーム色）cream, off-white

グレー　gray

ピンク　pink

ベージュ　beige

みずいろ（水色）light blue

むらさき（紫）purple

がくせいしょくどう（学生食堂）school cafeteria; often shortened to がくしょく（学食）

けいじばん（掲示板）bulletin board

こうどう（講堂）auditorium

せいもん（正門）main entrance

ちゅうしゃじょう（駐車場）parking lot, parking garage

ほんぶ（本部）administration office

Teaching at a Japanese university

まいにちの　せいかつ　1

DAILY ROUTINE 1

Functions	Describing one's daily schedule
New Vocabulary	Routine activities 1; Numbers; Telling time; Days of the week; Other time expressions
Dialogue	じゅぎょうが　あります。 (I have class.)
Culture	College life 1
Language	I. Telling time using numbers, counters, and the particle に
	II. Telling what one does and where one does it, using the particles に, で, and を
	III. Expressing routines, future actions, or events, using the polite present forms of verbs
	IV. Expressing frequency of actions, using adverbs
	V. Expressing approximate time or duration, using ごろ or ぐらい
Reading	Using script types as clues to word boundaries
Listening	Distinguishing sounds in words and phrases
Communication	Getting someone's attention 2

A. まいにちの　せいかつ (Routine activities 1). Use the following verbs to answer the questions below.

おきます　wake/s up

シャワーを　あびます　take/s a shower

あさごはんを　たべます　eat/s breakfast

がっこうに　いきます　go/es to school

きょうしつに　きます　come/s to the classroom

じゅぎょうが　あります　have/has class

べんきょうします　study/studies

じゅぎょうが　おわります　class ends

えいがが　はじまります　the movie begins

ひるごはんを　たべます　eat/s lunch

うちに　かえります　go/es home

ばんごはんを　たべます　eat/s dinner

しゅくだいを　します　do/es homework

おふろに　はいります　take/s a bath

ほんを　よみます　read/s a book

テレビを　みます　watch/es television

ねます　go/es to bed

コーヒーを　のみます　drink/s coffee

1. Which one of these activities do you do every day?

2. Which activities do you do often?

3. Which do you do sometimes?

4. Which don't you do very often?

5. Which don't you do at all?

B. すうじ (Numbers). Read the following numbers aloud and answer the questions in Japanese.

0	ゼロ, or れい	6	ろく	12	じゅうに
1	いち	7	なな, or しち	13	じゅうさん
2	に	8	はち	20	にじゅう
3	さん	9	きゅう, or く	30	さんじゅう
4	よん, or し	10	じゅう	40	よんじゅう
5	ご	11	じゅういち		

70 ななじゅう, or しちじゅう
90 きゅうじゅう
99 きゅうじゅうきゅう or きゅうじゅうく

Note: Some numbers have more than one pronunciation.

1. What are the last four digits of your social security number?
2. What is your telephone number (でんわばんごう)? Use の, as in 123 の 4567.
3. What is your instructor's office telephone number?
4. How many rooms are in your house or apartment?
5. Take another look at the list of numbers above and try to deduce from the list the pattern for counting in Japanese. How would you say the following numbers?

   50   60   23   64   27   89

C. 〜じ, 〜じかん, 〜ふん (Telling time). What time is it now? How long does your class last?

Note: ※ indicates a sound change.

	〜じ (o'clock)	〜じかん (hours)	〜ふん (minutes)
Question	なんじ	なんじかん	※なんぷん
1	いちじ	いちじかん	※いっぷん
2	にじ	にじかん	にふん
3	さんじ	さんじかん	※さんぷん
4	※よじ	※よじかん	よんふん／※よんぷん
5	ごじ	ごじかん	ごふん
6	ろくじ	ろくじかん	※ろっぷん
7	しちじ	しちじかん	しちふん／ななふん
8	はちじ	はちじかん	※はっぷん／はちふん
9	※くじ	※くじかん	きゅうふん
10	じゅうじ	じゅうじかん	※じゅっぷん／※じっぷん
11	じゅういちじ	じゅういちじかん	※じゅういっぷん
12	じゅうにじ	じゅうにじかん	じゅうにふん
20	にじゅうじ	にじゅうじかん	※にじゅっぷん／※にじっぷん
21	にじゅういちじ	にじゅういちじかん	※にじゅういっぷん

D. ～ようび (Days of the week). Answer the following questions in Japanese. Note that each day ends with ようび.

にちようび	Sunday	もくようび	Thursday
げつようび	Monday	きんようび	Friday
かようび	Tuesday	どようび	Saturday
すいようび	Wednesday		

1. Which day is the busiest one for you?

2. Which days do you like the best?

3. Which days do you have Japanese class?

4. Which days do you go to the library?

E. ほかのじかんのいいかた (Other time expressions). For each routine activity in section A, choose a logical time expression from the list below.

あさ	morning
ひる	afternoon
ばん	night
ごぜん	A.M./morning
ごご	P.M./afternoon
こんばん	tonight
まいにち	every day
まいあさ	every morning
まいばん	every night
いま	now
きょう	today
いつ	when

ダイアローグ (DIALOGUE)

はじめに (Warm-up)

A. Answer the following questions in Japanese.

1. What kind of courses are you taking now?

2. On which days of the week do they meet?

3. At what time do they meet?

4. At what time is your last class over?

B. Remember the three steps in the dialogue: 1. Look at the **manga.** 2. Listen to the dialogue on the tape. 3. Match the dialogue and the **manga,** filling in the frame number.

じゅぎょうが　あります。　(I have class.)

Alice and Mr. Lee run into each other on campus.

_____ アリス：　あ、リーさん、こんにちは。

_____ リー：　ああ、こんにちは。　いまから　じゅぎょう
　　　　　　　　　　　ですか。

_____ アリス：　ええ、けいざいがくの　じゅぎょうが

　　　　　　　　　　　あります。リーさんは？

_____ リー：　ぼくは　きょうは　じゅぎょうが
　　　　　　　　　ありません。

_____ アリス：　そうですか。　いいですね。

_____ リー：　けいざいがくの　じゅぎょうは　なんじごろ
　　　　　　　　おわりますか。

_____ アリス：　にじはんに　おわります。

_____ リー：　そうですか。その　あとも　じゅぎょうが
　　　　　　　　ありますか。

_____ アリス：　いいえ、でも　あした　テストが　あります
　　　　　　　　　　　から、としょかんで　いちじかんぐらい
　　　　　　　　　　　べんきょうします。

The bell rings.

____ リー：　あっ、じゅぎょうですね。

____ アリス：　そうですね。　じゃあ、また。

____ リー：　じゃあ、また。

わかりましたか　(Comprehension)

A. List two activities that Alice does today.

1. _____

2. _____

B. Read each statement. If the statement is true, circle はい; if it is false, circle いいえ.

はい　いいえ　1. けいざいがくの　じゅぎょうは　にじはんに
　　　　　　　　　おわります。

はい　いいえ　2. リーさんは　よじごろ　うちに
　　　　　　　　　かえります。

はい　いいえ　3. アリスさんは　としょかんに　いちじかんぐ
　　　　　　　　　らい　います。

にほんの　ぶんか　(CULTURE)

● *The academic year in Japan. When does your school year begin and end? When do you have vacations?*

Japanese colleges and universities usually start in April and end in January or February. Summer vacation starts at the end of July, and the fall session begins in September or October. Winter break is usually very short, starting around the end of December and ending at the beginning of January.

● *College classes. How often and for how long do your classes meet?*

The usual class period in Japan is 90 or 100 minutes. Apart from seminars and some science classes, most classes are straight lectures with little interaction between the professor and the students. Classes usually meet once a week for a year (with summer vacation and winter break in between), so students take many classes concurrently. Exams are usually held only once, at the end of an academic year, and the exam period lasts a couple of weeks.

● *College housing. Where do most college students live in your country?*

The majority of Japanese colleges are commuter schools and few have dormitories, which are rarely found on campus. Thus, most Japanese college students live at home or in an apartment. The average commute is about one hour but can be as long as two hours in large cities.

● *Financial aid. Who pays for your college education?*

Many parents pay for their children's college education in Japan. Although scholarships are available from various sources, student loans are nonexistent. A number of students have part-time jobs, or アルバイト (from the German *Arbeit*, meaning *work*). A common form of アルバイト is as a かていきょうし, or a private tutor for junior and senior high school students who are preparing for college entrance examinations.

LANGUAGE

I. Telling time using numbers, counters, and the particle に

A. Telling time with counters 〜じ／〜ふん

Question				Answer				
Question Word	**Counter**			**Number**	**Counter**	**Number**	**Counter**	
なん	じ	です	か。	ご	じ	はっ	ぷん	です。

What time is it?　　　　　　　　　　It's 5:08.

B. Expressing specific points in time with に

Question				
Question Word	**Counter**	**Particle**	**Verb**	
なん	じ	に	おきます	か。

What time do you get up?

Answer				
Number	**Counter**	**Half**	**Particle**	**Verb**
はち	じ	はん	に	おきます。

I get up at 8:30.

さとう ： あのう、すみません。いま　なんじですか。
It's 10:43.

ブラウン ： じゅうじ　よんじゅうさんぷんです。
It's 10:43.

さとう ： にほんごの　じゅぎょうは　なんじに
はじまりますか。
What time does Japanese class begin?

ブラウン ： じゅういちじはんに　はじまります。
It begins at 11:30.

- There are two ways of counting to ten in Japanese. One uses the traditional Japanese numbering system introduced on page 258; the other uses a system borrowed from Chinese. In this chapter, you learn the Chinese origin numbers shown on page 132. Look at page 133 for a list of counter expressions used in this system.

- The numbers between 11 and 19 are formed by the word for ten, followed by the word for the single digit.

  11 = 10 + 1 じゅういち＝じゅう＋いち
  12 = 10 + 2 じゅうに　＝じゅう＋に
  13 = 10 + 3 じゅうさん＝じゅう＋さん

- The multiples of ten from 20 to 90 are formed by the single-digit number followed by 10.

  20 = 2 × 10 にじゅう＝に×じゅう
  30 = 3 × 10 さんじゅう＝さん×じゅう
  40 = 4 × 10 よんじゅう＝よん×じゅう

- Numbers like 23 and 35 are formed by combining a single digit followed by ten and single digit.

  23 = (2 × 10) + 3 = 20 + 3   にじゅうさん＝にじゅう＋さん
  35 = (3 × 10) + 5 = 30 + 5   さんじゅうご＝さんじゅう＋ご

- Remember that the numbers 4, 7, and 9 have two pronunciations. The number 40 is more likely to be read よんじゅう than しじゅう. The number 70 can be either ななじゅう or しちじゅう, and the number 90 is always read きゅうじゅう.

- Depending on the counters used, the pronunciation of the numbers will change. For example,

  よん → よじ　よじかん　　いち → いっぷん

- To specify A.M., use ごぜん before the time expression. To specify P.M., use ごご before the time expression. For example, ごぜん　くじ 9:00 A.M. ごご　はちじ　8:00 P.M.

- To express half past the hour, use さんじゅっぷん or はん. For example, さんじさんじゅっぷん／さんじはん　3:30

- The particle に indicates a point in time and corresponds to *at, in,* or *on* in English. It may be used to express clock time, the day, the month, or the year (see Supplementray Vocabulary for an extended list). For example,

  ごじに　　*at* 5 o'clock
  げつようびに　　*on* Monday
  ごがつに　　*in* May
  1996 ねんに　　*in* 1996

  Note that one group of words does not take に: きょう, いま, あさ, ばん, いつ, まい〜 (every 〜), こん〜 (this 〜), らい〜 (next 〜)

- When two or more time expressions are used, list them in the order of day and time and connect them with の. A few words like まいにち do not require の. For example,

  げつようびの　ごごさんじに　じゅぎょうが　あります。
  I have a class at 3 P.M. on Monday.
  まいにち　はちじに　おきます。
  I wake up at 8:00 every day.

はなして みましょう (Practice and Conversation)

A. Say the following using Chinese origin numbers.

2	5	6	8	10	11	17
20	49	53	75	94	81	62

B. Work in groups of three. One person writes a different number in arabic numerals on five separate slips of paper. As he/she shows one number at a time, see who can say the number first.

C. Say the following time expressions in Japanese.

1. 4:10
2. 2:25 *ni ji, ni jugo fun*
3. 3:03 *san ji, san pun*
4. 11:44 *juichijxo juyonpun*
5. 12:30
6. 6:40
7. 8:09
8. 1:56

9. 4:17 P.M.
10. 9:18 A.M.
11. 7:11 P.M.
12. 9:02 A.M.
13. 6:55
14. 9:03
15. 3:53
16. 8:30

D. Work with the class. Ask your classmate when his/her last class ends and whose class ends the latest and the earliest.

Example

A: きょう なんじに じゅぎょうが おわりますか。

B: いちじに おわります。

E. Ask your partner about his/her class schedule for the week and complete the following chart.

Example

A: げつようびに じゅぎょうが ありますか。

B: ええ、あります。

A: そうですか。 いつ ありますか。

B: ごぜんはちじに にほんごの じゅぎょうが あります。
そして、くじに ぶんがくの じゅぎょうが あります。

はなして みましょう (Practice and Conversation)

A. Complete the following sentences with the appropriate particles.

Example

としょかん ／ べんきょうします
としょかんで べんきょうします。

1. ごぜん はちじ ／ おきます
2. ほん ／ よみます
3. おふろ ／ はいります
4. ひるごはん ／ たべます
5. つくえの うえ ／ あります
6. ゆうびんきょく ／ いきます
7. しゅくだい ／ します
8. テレビ ／ みます
9. うち ／ ねます

B. Ask your classmates where they go after class and what they do. Note that じゅぎょうの あとで means *after class*.

Example

A: じゅぎょうの あとで どこに いきますか。

B: こうえんに いきます。

A: こうえんで なにを しますか。

B: ほんを よみます。

C. Work with a partner. Report to him/her what you and your classmates do after class.

Example

スミスさんは こうえんで ほんを よみます。
リーさんは としょかんで しゅくだいを します。
わたしも としょかんに いきます。

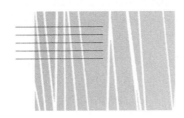

abe , tabe , nomi , iki , ki

III. Expressing routines, future actions, or events, using the polite present forms of verbs

Question			
	Verb		
こうえん	に	いきます	か 。

Answer	
	Verb
いいえ、	いきません。

Do you go to parks?
or, Are you going to a/the park?

No, I don't.
or, No, I am not.

Japanese verbs are classified into three classes: irregular verbs, る-verbs, and う-verbs. There are only two irregular verbs (きます and します). These verb classes will become more useful as you learn different forms of inflections in Chapter 7.

	Polite Affirmative Form	**Polite Negative Form**	**Verb Class**
to come	きま<u>す</u>	き<u>ません</u>	Irregular
to do	しま<u>す</u>	し<u>ません</u>	Irregular
to get up	おき<u>ます</u>	おき<u>ません</u>	る-verb
to go to bed	ね<u>ます</u>	ね<u>ません</u>	る-verb
to eat	たべ<u>ます</u>	たべ<u>ません</u>	る-verb
to go	いき<u>ます</u>	いき<u>ません</u>	う-verb
to go home	かえり<u>ます</u>	かえり<u>ません</u>	う-verb
to read	よみ<u>ます</u>	よみ<u>ません</u>	う-verb

- In contrast to English, Japanese verbs have two forms: polite and plain. The polite form is used among acquaintances, people of different age-groups, and strangers in public places. It is also used in television and radio broadcasts and letters. The plain form is used among family members, young children, and close friends of the same age as well as in newspaper and magazine articles. You will first learn the polite form in this textbook.

- Japanese verbs have only two tenses: past and present. The present tense indicates present or future time, depending on the context.

- べんきょうします is an irregular verb because it is a compound verb of べんきょう and します. You will learn more verbs (noun +します) like this one in later chapters.

- In addition to expressing the location of objects, the verb あります can be used to express possession. You will use 〜は　〜が　あります.

ぼくは　じゅぎょうが　あります。

I have class.

やまださんは　テレビ^{てれび}が　ありません。

Yamada-san does not have a TV.

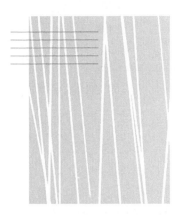

はなして　みましょう　(Practice and Conversation)

A. Answer the following questions.

Example

まいにち　としょかんに　いきますか。
<u>ええ、いきます。</u> or <u>いいえ、いきません。</u>

1. まいにち　だいがくに　きますか。
2. あさごはんを　たべますか。
3. まいあさ　コーヒー^{こひ}を　のみますか。
4. どようびに　じゅぎょうが　ありますか。
5. げつようびの　ばん　テレビ^{てれび}を　みますか。
6. まいばん　ほんを　よみますか。
7. こんばん　おふろに　はいりますか。

B. Fill in the blanks with the appropriate particles in the chart on the next page, as in the box in the upper left corner. An X indicates no particle. Then ask your classmates はい／いいえ questions based on the statements in the chart. If someone answers はい, write his/her name in the box. Insert the name of one classmate per column or row.

Example

A: ミラー^{みら}さんは　まいあさ　あさごはんを　たべますか。

B: はい、たべます。

Write ミラーさん in the box in the upper left corner.

_____さん	_____さん	_____さん	_____さん
まいあさ　X ごはん　を たべます	きょう ___ テレビ ___ みます	まいにち__ コーヒー ___ のみます	こんばん ___ うち__います
もくようび ___ あさ ___ じゅぎょう ___ あります	としょかん ___ べんきょう します	すいようび ___ しゅくだい ___ します	うち__ ひるごはん ___ たべます
おふろ ___ ほん ___ よみます	じゅうにじ はん ___ じゅぎょう ___ おわります	こんばん ここ ___ きます	カフェテリア ___ べんきょうします
まいばん ___ おふろ ___ はいります	いま ___ うち ___ かえります	ごごはちじ ___ うち ___ かえります	まいあさ ___ シャワー ___ あびます

C. Work with a partner. First write your routine activities in the following chart; then ask your partner about his/her routine and fill out the schedule.

Example

A: 〜さんは　まいあさ　なにを　しますか。

B: シャワーを　あびます。そして、しんぶんを　よみます。

A: あさごはんを　たべますか。

B: いいえ、たべません。

A: （お）ひるに　なにを　しますか。

continue . . .

	Your Routine Activities	Your Partner's Routine Activities
あさ ひる ばん		

IV. Expressing frequency of actions using adverbs

A. Always いつも

		Adverb					Verb (affirmative)
やまださん	は	いつも	くじ	に	じゅぎょう	に	きます。

Yamada-san always comes to class at nine o'clock.

B. Usually たいてい

		Adverb			Verb (affirmative)
わたし	は	たいてい	じゅういちじ	に	ねます。

I usually go to bed at eleven o'clock.

C. Often, frequently よく

		Adverb			Verb (affirmative)
わたし	は	よく	きっさてん	に	いきます。

I often go to a coffee shop.

D. Sometimes ときどき

		Adverb		Verb (affirmative)
ぼく	は	ときどき	じゅうじごろ	おきます。

I sometimes get up around ten o'clock.

E. Not very often/not that often あまり plus negative

		Adverb			Verb (negative)
わたし	は	あまり	ほん	を	よみません。

I don't read books very (that) often.

F. Not at all ぜんぜん plus negative

		Adverb			Verb (negative)
スミスさん	は	ぜんぜん	コーヒー	を	のみません。

Smith-san doesn't drink coffee at all.

スミス： いつも　あさごはんを　たべますか。
    Do you always eat breakfast?

さとう： いいえ、ぜんぜん　たべません。　スミスさんは？
    No, not at all. How about you, Smith-san?

スミス： わたしは　たいてい　たべますよ。
    I usually do.

さとう： そうですか。
    I see.

- とても may be used before よく to express activities that someone does often and for a long time.

  やまださんは　とても　よく　べんきょう　します。
  Yamada-san studies very hard.

- The position of an adverb of frequency in a sentence is relatively flexible. Such an adverb usually appears immediately before the verb, but it may appear before the direct object without any significant change in meaning.

  やまださんは　じゅぎょうに　あまり　きません。
  Yamada-san does not come to class very often.

  やまださんは　あまり　じゅぎょうに　きません。
  Yamada-san does not come to class very often.

- あまり and ぜんぜん can also be used with adjectives. In this case, あまり means *not very*, and ぜんぜん means *not at all*.

この　だいがくは　あまり　おおきくありません。

The college is not very big.

この　へやは　ぜんぜん　きれいじゃありません。

This room is not at all clean.

- Remember that あまり and ぜんぜん must always be used with the negative form of a verb or adjective.

はなして　みましょう　(Practice and Conversation)

A. Create your own sentence by choosing one of the frequency words:
いつも, たいてい, よく, ときどき, あまり, and ぜんぜん.

Example

レストランで　ごはんを　たべます。
レストランで　ごはんを　よく　たべます。

1. びょういんに　いきます。
2. としょかんで　べんきょうします
3. シャワーを　あびます
4. うちで　しゅくだいを　します。
5. おふろに　はいります。
6. あさ　ほんを　よみます。

B. Work with your partner. Ask your partner which activity he/she does frequently and what he/she does not do frequently. Then fill in the chart.

Example

A:　〜さんは　ほんを　よく　よみますか。

B:　いいえ、あまり　よみません。

	パートナー	わたし
いつも		
よく		
ときどき		
あまり		
ぜんぜん		

C. Write down what you do or don't do frequently in the chart in exercise B. Tell a classmate what you do; then ask whether he/she does the same. Find a classmate who shares similar interests.

Example

A: わたしは　ときどき　としょかんに　いきます。
　　〜さんは　よく　としょかんに　いきますか。

B: or　はい、わたしも　ときどき　としょかんに
　　　　いきます。
　　or　はい、よく　いきます。
　　or　いいえ、わたしは　あまり　いきません。
　　or　いいえ、わたしは　ぜんぜん　いきません。

V. Expressing approximate time or duration, using ごろ or ぐらい

A. Expressing an approximate point in time with ごろ

		Point in Time	Suffix	
わたし	は	しちじ	ごろ	おきます。

I get up around seven o'clock.

B. Expressing approximate duration with ぐらい

	Duration	Suffix	
まいにち	しちじかん	ぐらい	ねます。

I sleep about seven hours every day.

キム：　なんじに　おきますか。
　　　　What time do you get up?

たなか：　ろくじはんごろ　おきます。
　　　　　I get up around 6:30.

キム：　そうですか。なんじかんぐらい　ねますか。
　　　　I see. Approximately how many hours do you sleep?

たなか：　そうですね。はちじかんぐらい　ねます。
　　　　　Well, I sleep about eight hours.

- ごろ indicates an approximate point in time. The particle に may be used optionally, as in ろくじごろに　きます.

- Use 〜じかん to talk about duration or how long (how many hours) it takes someone to do something. 〜ふん is used for duration (how many minutes) as well as for a point in time. Durations such as *1 hour and 15 minutes* and *3 hours and 40 minutes* can be expressed as いちじかんじゅうごふん and さんじかんよんじゅっぷん. いちじじゅうごふん and さんじよんじゅっぷん mean 1:15 and 3:40, respectively.

- ぐらい indicates approximate duration, amount, or frequency. Some people say くらい instead of ぐらい; there is no difference in meaning. When you want to express an approximate amount of time, such as *about eight hours,* make sure to use the counter じかん, not じ, as in はちじかんぐらい.

はなして　みましょう　(Practice and Conversation)

A. Complete the following sentences using ごろ or ぐらい.

Example

さんじはん／じゅぎょうが　おわります。
<u>さんじはんごろ　じゅぎょうが　おわります。</u>

1. しちじ／おきます。
2. にじかん／べんきょうします。
3. ごじよんじゅうごふん／うちに　かえります。
4. いちじかん／テレビを　みます。
5. はちじかん／ねます。
6. ろくじはん／ばんごはんを　たべます。
7. くじ／がっこうに　きます。

B. Work with a partner. Your partner will ask the following questions. Answer them with ごろ or ぐらい. Your partner will write your answer in the blanks.

Example

A: なんじに　ここに　きますか。
B: <u>ごご　いちじごろ　きます。</u>

1. なんじに　だいがくに　　　　　　　＿＿＿＿＿　ごろ　or　ぐらい
   いきますか。

2. なんじに　うちに　　　　　　　　　＿＿＿＿＿　ごろ　or　ぐらい
   かえりますか。

3. なんじかん　じゅぎょうが　　　　　＿＿＿＿＿　ごろ　or　ぐらい
   ありますか。

4. なんぷん(かん)　シャ<small>しゃ わ</small>ワーを　　＿＿＿＿＿　ごろ　or　ぐらい
   あびますか。

5. なんじに　この　きょうしつに　　＿＿＿＿＿　ごろ　or　ぐらい
   きますか。

6. うちで　なんじかん　　　　　　　　＿＿＿＿＿　ごろ　or　ぐらい
   べんきょうしますか。

C. Work with a partner. Tell your partner about your least busy day of the
week. (いちばん　ひまな　ひ) Use ごろ and ぐらい. Ask your part-
ner what his/her least busy day is like.

Example

A: わたしは　じゅうにじごろ　おきます。　　～さんは
　　なんじごろ　おきますか。

B: そうですね。わたしは　じゅうじごろ　おきます。
　　じゅうじかんぐらい　ねます。
　　・・・・

じょうずな　よみかた　(READING)

Using script types as clues to word boundaries

Japanese words, unlike English words, are usually not separated by space.
However, there are certain ways to identify word boundaries. For example,
katakana and **kanji** are always used for content words such as nouns, verbs, and
adjectives. Thus, if you see a series of **katakana** in a sentence, you can be sure
that it is a word. **Hiragana** is always used for particles such as は, が, の, and
に and for the endings of verbs and adjectives. Other content words are written
in **hiragana** as well. When several **hiragana** occur in the middle of a sentence,
you should read them carefully because they may contain more than one word.

Read the following sentences and try to find the word boundaries using the
script types as a clue. Insert a slash to indicate a word boundary.

私<small>わたし</small>は毎朝<small>まいあさ</small>、六時三十分<small>ろくじさんじゅっぷん</small>に起<small>お</small>きます。　そして、シャワーを浴<small>しゃ わ</small>び<small>あ</small>
ます。それから、たいてい喫茶店<small>きっさてん</small>で朝御飯<small>あさごはん</small>を食<small>た</small>べます。

ジョンソンさんの　いちにち　(A typical day in Johnson-san's life)

よむまえに　(Prereading)

Write five Japanese sentences about your daily life.

ことばの　リスト (Vocabulary)

アルバイト　part-time job

かていきょうし　private tutor

ジョギング　jogging

ですから　so, therefore

The following is a composition written by Terry Johnson about her daily routine.

私の一日

テリー　ジョンソン

私は毎朝六時半に起きます。そして、二十分ぐらい　ジョギングをします。八時ごろ朝ごはんを食べます。そして、八時半に大学に行きます。日本語の授業は毎朝九時に始まります。その後、よく図書館で勉強します。昼ごはんはたいてい学生会館のカフェテリアで食べます。月曜日と水曜日と金曜日の午後は経済学と文学の授業があります。火曜日と木曜日の午後は授業がありません。ですから、ときどきアルバイトをします。たいてい六時ごろアパートに帰ります。晩ごはんを食べてから、二時間ぐらい勉強します。テレビはあまり見ません。いつも　十一時半に寝ます。

わかりましたか　(Comprehension)

A. Answer the following questions in Japanese.
   1. ジョンソンさんは　まいにち　じゅぎょうが　ありますか。
   2. ジョンソンさんは　どんな　じゅぎょうが　ありますか。

3. げつようびには　どの　じゅぎょうが　ありますか。
4. ジョンソンさんは　がくせいかいかんに　よく
   いきますか。
5. ジョンソンさんは　かようびに　なにを　しますか。

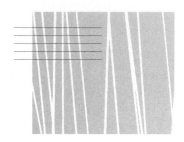

じょうずな　ききかた　(LISTENING)

Distinguishing sounds in words and phrases

Listening to conversations in Japanese is like reading long sentences without **kanji** or other clues to distinguish word boundaries. It takes practice to be able to distinguish words and phrases from a succession of sounds. Listening for repeated words, familiar words, intonation, and pauses can help you find word boundaries.

A. Your instructor will say some sentences at a normal speed. Write words that you pick up. Then, in groups of four, reconstruct the sentences you heard.

B. みっつの　ライフスタイル (Three different lifestyles). Listen to three people talk about their daily lives. Decide which person's life is most like yours. Try to explain the reasons for your choice. There are some conversational fillers and unknown words. Don't worry about them. Try to pick out a few words at a time, write them down, and try to get the general idea of each monologue. Then try to guess which one of the following people fits each description.

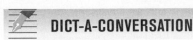
DICT-A-CONVERSATION

Imagine that you, Smith-san, are on your college campus and you run into your friend Ogawa-san.

おがわ： _____

スミス： _____

おがわ： _____

スミス： _____

おがわ： _____

スミス： _____

おがわ： _____

スミス： _____

おがわ： _____

ききじょうず　はなしじょうず　(COMMUNICATION)

Getting someone's attention 2

Talking to someone in a non-native language can be a strain, especially if the person is a stranger. This is certainly also true in Japan, where people tend to be less open to strangers. One reason for this may be that Japan was isolated from the Western world for over 250 years under the government's seclusion policy from the seventeenth to the mid-nineteenth century. During that period, Japan remained a relatively homogeneous nation. Moreover, under the feudal order, a strong sense of hierarchy was developed. This distinction between in-groups and out-groups remains strong in modern Japan. An in-group is one's family, people at one's place of work, classmates, and so on. The Japanese are very aware of the degree of intimacy that should be maintained between those in the in-group and those in the out-group, and they act accordingly. Any foreigner, by definition, belongs to the out-group; thus, along with the fear of not being able to communicate, a Japanese person will often deliberately avoid contact with a foreigner, even at the risk of appearing indifferent. (These are general tendencies, and much variation exists among individuals.)

Thus, it is important to use the appropriate phrases in approaching a stranger or a person you don't know well. The following is a summary of some useful expressions and other strategies.

To approach people:
あのう（ちょっと）
すみませんが／しつれいですが
あのう　すみませんが／しつれいですが
ちょっと　すみませんが／しつれいですが、

あのう　ちょっと　すみませんが／しつれいですが
おねがいします (used to get the attention of someone, such as a store clerk, who provides services)

To thank someone:
すみません
ありがとう　ございます

To give feedback as a listener:
Nodding
Avoiding prolonged eye-contact
ええ／いいえ

A. Imagine that you are in Japan and want to ask someone the time. Approach the person to get his/her attention. Ask the time. Thank him/her. Try to act out the scene with a partner.

B. Imagine that you are on a college campus and are looking for a person from Japan to talk to. You have just found an Asian person but you are not sure if the person is in fact Japanese. Approach the person and find out if he/she is Japanese. If the person is from Japan, introduce yourself.

そうごうれんしゅう　(INTEGRATION)

おかださんの　まいにち　(Okada-san's daily routine)

STUDENT

Divide into three groups: groups A, B, and C. Listen to the interview with Okada-san and record a memo in the following form. Check with the classmates in your group that the information you recorded is correct. Then form groups of three, each member coming from a different group (one from group A, another from group B, and the other from group C). Exchange the information you recorded and note any discrepancies in that information among the three original groups.

～ようび	なにを　しますか。
にちようび	
げつようび	
かようび	
すいようび	
もくようび	
きんようび	
どようび	

ロールプレイ　(Role Play)

Imagine that you are talking with a Japanese friend. Explain to him/her how a
typical American college student may spend a week.

たんご　(ESSENTIAL VOCABULARY)

Nouns

あさ（朝）morning
あさごはん（朝御飯）breakfast
いま（今）now
えいが（映画）movie
かようび（火曜日）Tuesday
きょう（今日）today
きんようび（金曜日）Friday
げつようび（月曜日）Monday
コーヒー　coffee
こんばん（今晩）tonight
シャワー　shower
じゅぎょう（授業）class, course
しゅくだい（宿題）homework
すいようび（水曜日）Wednesday

せいかつ（生活）daily life, daily routine,
　daily activities
どようび（土曜日）Saturday
にちようび（日曜日）Sunday
ばん（晩）night, evening
ばんごはん（晩御飯）supper, dinner
ひる（昼）afternoon
ひるごはん（昼御飯）lunch
べんきょう（勉強）study
まいあさ（毎朝）every morning
まいにち（毎日）every day
まいばん（毎晩）every night
もくようび（木曜日）Thursday

Irregular Verbs

きます（来ます）come/s
　The dictionary form is くる（来る）.

します　do/es
　The dictionary form is する.

る-verbs

あびます（浴びます）take/s (a shower)
シャワーを　あびます（シャワーを
浴びます）take/s a shower
　The dictionary form is あびる（浴びる）.

おきます（起きます）get/s up, wake/s up
　The dictionary form is おきる（起きる）.
たべます（食べます）eat/s
　The dictionary form is たべる（食べる）.

ねます（寝ます）go/es to bed
The dictionary form is ねる（寝る）.

みます（見ます）see/s, watch/es
The dictionary form is みる（見る）.

The dictionary form is the form in which verbs are listed in Japanese dictionaries. You will learn the dictionary forms in chapter 7.

う -verbs

いきます（行きます）go/es
The dictionary form is いく（行く）.
おわります（終わります）end/s, is/are over
The dictionary form is おわる（終わる）.
かえります（帰ります）return/s, go/es home
The dictionary form is かえる（帰る）.
のみます（飲みます）drink/s
The dictionary form is のむ（飲む）.

はいります（入ります）take/s (a bath), enter/s
The dictionary form is はいる（入る）.
おふろに　はいります（お風呂に入ります）take/s a bath.
はじまります（始まります）begin/s (intransitive)
The dictionary form is はじまる（始まる）.
よみます（読みます）read/s
The dictionary form is よむ（読む）.

Adverbs

いつも　always
ぜんぜん（全然）not at all (used with the negative form of verbs)

たいてい　usually
ときどき（時々）sometimes
よく　often

Question Words

いつ　when

Particles

で　at, in, on, etc. (location of action or event)
としょかんで　べんきょうします
（図書館で　勉強します）

に　at, on, in (point in time)
じゅうじに　ねます（十時に寝ます）
sleep/s at 10 o'clock

に　to (goal, activity + に)
えいがに　いきます（映画に行きます）go/es to a movie

を　(direct object marker)
ほんを　よみます（本を読みます）
read/s a book

Prefixes

お〜（御〜）polite prefix
　おふろ（お風呂）
まい〜（毎〜）every 〜
　まいしゅう（毎週）every week　まいあさ（毎朝）every morning
　まいばん（毎晩）every night　まいにち（毎日）every day

Suffixes

〜ようび（〜曜日）days of the week

Counters

〜じ（〜時）〜 o'clock
〜じかん（〜時間）(for) 〜 hour/s
〜じはん（〜時半）half past 〜
〜ふん（〜分）〜 minute/s

Passive Vocabulary

Nouns

アルバイト　part-time job
かていきょうし（家庭教師）private tutor
ジョギング　jogging

Conjunctions

ですから　so, therefore

Expressions

あした　テストが　ありますから
（明日テストがありますから）
　I have a test tomorrow, so . . .
いまから（今から）from now on
そのあとも（その後も）after that, too

ぼくは　きょうは　じゅぎょうが　あり
ません。　I don't have class today.
（は in きょうは is contrastive. See Language,
part IV, in Chapter 5.）（僕は今日は授業が
ありません。）

Supplementary Vocabulary

Months

いちがつ（一月）January
にがつ（二月）February
さんがつ（三月）March
しがつ（四月）April
ごがつ（五月）May
ろくがつ（六月）June
しちがつ（七月）July

はちがつ（八月）August
くがつ（九月）September
じゅうがつ（十月）October
じゅういちがつ（十一月）November
じゅうにがつ（十二月）December

Days of the Month

ついたち（一日）the first (day)
ふつか（二日）the second
みっか（三日）the third
よっか（四日）the fourth
いつか（五日）the fifth
むいか（六日）the sixth
なのか（七日）the seventh
ようか（八日）the eighth
ここのか（九日）the ninth
とおか（十日）the tenth
じゅういちにち（十一日）the eleventh
じゅうににち（十二日）the twelfth
じゅうさんにち（十三日）the thirteenth
じゅうよっか（十四日）the fourteenth
じゅうごにち（十五日）the fifteenth
じゅうろくにち（十六日）the sixteenth
じゅうしちにち（十七日）the seventeenth
じゅうはちにち（十八日）the eighteenth
じゅうくにち（十九日）the nineteenth
はつか（二十日）the twentieth

にじゅういちにち（二十一日）the twenty-first
にじゅうににち（二十二日）the twenty-second
にじゅうさんにち（二十三日）the twenty-third
にじゅうよっか（二十四日）the twenty-fourth
にじゅうごにち（二十五日）the twenty-fifth
にじゅうろくにち（二十六日）the twenty-sixth
にじゅうしちにち（二十七日）the twenty-seventh
にじゅうはちにち（二十八日）the twenty-eighth
にじゅうくにち（二十九日）the twenty-ninth
さんじゅうにち（三十日）the thirtieth
さんじゅういちにち（三十一日）the thirty-first

Years

〜ねん　〜年　year
　きゅうじゅうはちねん　'98

CHAPTER 6

Students in a library

まいにちの　せいかつ　2
生活

DAILY ROUTINE 2

Functions	Talking about one's daily activities
New Vocabulary	Routine activities 2; Adjectives to describe routine activities; Time expressions
Dialogue	にちようびに　えいがを　みました (I saw a movie on Sunday)
Culture	College life 2
Language	I. Expressing a means, using で; Expressing starting and end points, using から〜まで; Expressing "to whom," using に; Expressing "together with," using と
	II. Talking about past events, using polite past verbs and polite past adjectives
	III. Expressing frequency and extent, using counter expressions
	IV. Using double particles with the topic marker は, the contrast marker は, and the similarity marker も
	V. Giving a reason, using 〜から, and expressing contrast, using が
Reading	Identifying missing words
Listening	Making sense out of missing pronouns
Communication	Using そうですか and そうですね

あたらしい　ことば　(NEW VOCABULARY)

A. せいかつの　ことば (Routine activities 2). Answer the questions below in Japanese.

ごはんを　つくります　fix/es a meal　*tsukurimasu.*

せんたくを　します　do/es laundry　*sentaku*

そうじを　します　clean/s /dust/s a room　*sooji*

アルバイトを　します　has/have a part-time job

ざっしを　よみます　read/s a magazine　*zasshi*

レポートを　かきます　write/s a paper　*kakimasu*

おんがくを　ききます　listen/s to music　*ongaku を kikimasu.*

うんどうを　します　do/es (physical) exercise　*undoo*

ビデオを　みます　watch/es a video

かいものに　いきます　go/es shopping　*kaimonoḥi)ikimasu.*

でんしゃで　いきます　go/es by train

バスで　きます　come/s by bus

しんぶんを　かいます　buy/s a newspaper　*kaimasu*

しごとを　します　work/s

ひとりで　べんきょうします　study/studies alone

ルームメートと　でかけます　go/es out with a roommate　*dekakemasu*

クラスメートと　はなします　talk/s with a classmate　*hanashimasu*

しけん／テストが　あります　have/has an examination/test

くるまで　えきに　いきます　go/es to the station by car

じてんしゃで　だいがくに　いきます　go/es to college by bicycle

がっこうから　うちまで　あるいて　かえります　go/es home from school on foot

ともだちに　てがみを　かきます　write/s a letter to a friend

りょうしんに　でんわを　かけます　make/s a phone call to (one's) parents　*goryooshin ni denwa o kakemasu.*

にほんごの　クラスが　あります　have/has Japanese class

1. Which activities do you do every day?

2. Which activities do you often do?

3. Which activities do you sometimes do?

4. Which activities don't you do very often?

5. Which activities don't you do at all?

B. ライフスタイルを　あらわすことば　(Adjectives to describe routine activities). For each adjective, write down one place, time, activity, or event that matches the adjective.

_____ おもしろい　interesting　omoshiroi

_____ たのしい　fun　tanoshii

_____ やさしい　easy　yasashi

_____ むずかしい　difficult　muzukashii

_____ いそがしい　busy (doing things)　isogashii

_____ ひま（な）　free, not busy　hima (na)

_____ たいへん（な）　tough　taiten (na)

_____ ざんねん（な）　unfortunate, sorry　zannen(na)

C. じかん　(Time expressions). List the activities in exercise A that you did, do, or will do in the future.

きのう　yesterday

あした　tomorrow

せんしゅう　last week

こんしゅう　this week

らいしゅう　next week

しゅうまつ　weekend

こうこうの　とき　during high school

ダイアローグ　(DIALOGUE)
だ い あ ろ ー く

はじめに　(Warm-up)

A. Answer the following questions.

1. What did you do last Saturday? last Sunday?

2. How often do you clean your room (or apartment)?

3. How often do you have exams for your classes?

4. Do you watch movies? How often?

5. What are the names of some movies that you found interesting?

B. Remember the three steps in the dialogue: 1. Look at the **manga**. 2. Listen to the dialogue on the tape. 3. Match the dialogue and the **manga**, filling in the frame number.

にちようびに えいがを みました (I saw a movie on Sunday.)

Alice and Mr. Lee are talking about what they did last weekend.

___ アリス： リーさん、せんしゅうの しゅうまつに
なにを しましたか。

___ リー： どようびは アパートの そうじと
せんたくを しました。でも、にちようびには
えいがを みました。

___ アリス： そうですか。 えいがは どうでしたか。

___ リー： あまり おもしろくありませんでした。

___ アリス： そうですか。 それは ざんねんですね。
リーさんは よく えいがを みますか。

___ リー： ええ、よく みますよ。 アリスさんは。

___ アリス： ときどき みますよ。 にしゅうかんに
いちどぐらい みますね。

___ リー： そうですか。 こんしゅうも みましたか。

___ アリス： いいえ。げつようびに しけんが ありました
から、しゅうまつは でかけませんでした。

___ リー： そうですか。

わかりましたか (Comprehension)

A. Write three things that Lee-san did last weekend.

1. _____
2. _____
3. _____

B. Read each statement. If the statement is true, circle はい; if it is false, circle いいえ.

はい　いいえ　1. リーさんは　にちようびに　せんたくを
　　　　　　　　　しました。

はい　いいえ　2. リーさんは　どようびに　アパートを
　　　　　　　　　そうじしました。

はい　いいえ　3. リーさんは　おもしろい　えいがを　みました。

はい　いいえ　4. アリスさんは　ときどき　えいがを
　　　　　　　　　みます。

はい　いいえ　5. アリスさんは　せんしゅうの　しゅうまつに
　　　　　　　　　えいがを　みました。

にほんの　ぶんか (CULTURE)

* *Do you want to go to a graduate school? Why do people go to graduate schools in your country?*

A large number of college students are full-time students. They usually graduate in four years and start working immediately after graduating. College graduates do not usually return to graduate school later. Undergraduates who are interested in graduate school tend to go there directly after graduating. Graduate schools are generally regarded as institutions that produce academicians and researchers. In Japan, law and business degrees are earned at the college level. Medical and dental schools accept students directly from high schools and take six years.

Japanese college students at a school festival.

- *What do you think of college life in your country?*

The following is a summary of a small survey of college freshmen (250 male students and 250 female students) who attended four-year colleges in the Tokyo metropolitan area (60 schools participated). While particular characteristics of a metropolitan area should be noted, the survey gives a general picture of college life in Japan.

1. 83% of the respondents went to private colleges.

2. 60% of male respondents were ろうにん, while 32% of female respondents were ろうにん. (ろうにん refers to a person who fails college entrance exams and then studies for those exams in the subsequent year.)

3. 80% of the respondents participated in club activities (e.g. athletics).

4. 80% of the respondents lived with their parents (male 71%, female 89%).

5. 98% of the respondents who did not live with their parents received monthly support from them (average amount 126,000 yen). The average rent was 55,000 yen.

6. The most popular answers to the question asking why they went to college were (a) to think about a future career path, (b) because a college education is the norm, (c) it is advantageous to getting a job, and (d) to make friends.

7. What was respondents' image of college before they entered? (a) たのしい (enjoyable/fun), (b) じゆう (free), (c) あかるい (bright), (d) おもしろい (interesting/fun), (e) きらくな (carefree).

8. How did college change their lifestyle? The respondents answered that free time, time for television, and time for sleep increased, while study time at home and time to talk with their family decreased. Stress also decreased.

9. The average attendance rate of the respondents was 70%; 42% of all classes were interesting, while the rest were uninteresting.

10. The respondents were satisfied in their relationships with friends, in their participation in club activities, and in how they spent their free time.

11. 90% of the respondents had done part-time work (アルバイト). The most common jobs were waiter/waitress, private tutor, store clerk at fast-food restaurants and convenience stores, helper for events, delivery (male), and manual labor (male). The average monthly earnings were 76,000 yen.

12. Popular possessions were audio equipment, televisions, credit cards, VCRs, and telephones.

I. Expressing a means, using で; expressing starting and end points, using から～まで; expressing "to whom," using に; expressing "together with," using と

A. Expressing a means, using で

Question				
	Question Word (means)	**Particle**	**Verb**	
だいがくに	なん	で	いきます	か。

How do you go to school (literally: By what means do you go to school)?

Answer		
Means	**Particle**	**Verb**
じてんしゃ	で	いきます。

I go by bicycle.

B. Expressing starting and ending points, using から～まで

Place	Particle	Place	Particle	Verb
うち	から	だいがく	まで	あるいて　いきます。

I walk to school from my house.

Time	Particle	Time	Particle			
よじ	から	ごじ	まで	うんどう	を	します。

I exercise from four o'clock to five o'clock.

C. Expressing "to whom," using に

		Noun	Particle			
わたし	は	ともだち	に	てがみ	を	かきます。

I will write a letter to a friend.

D. Expressing "together with," using と

		Noun	Particle			
わたし	は	ルームメート	と	かいもの	に	いきます。

I will go shopping with a roommate.

キム： うちから　がっこうまで　なんで　いきますか。
How do you go to school from your house?

おがわ： じてんしゃで　いきます。
I go by bicycle.

キム： あした　なにを　しますか。
What are you going to do tomorrow?

おがわ： ともだちと　かいものに　いきます。そして、りょう
しんに　ほんを　かいます。
I'm going shopping with a friend, and I will buy a book for my parents.

● When you want to say *on foot*, use あるいて, as in <u>だいがくに　あるいて　いきます</u>.

● When you want to say *alone*, use ひとりで, as in <u>わたしは　ひとりでべんきょうします</u>.

はなしてみましょう　(Practice and Conversation)

A. Look at the following pictures of Okada-san's daily routine, and complete the statements using the appropriate particles.

Example

バス／がっこう／いきます。
バスで　がっこうに　いきます。

1. くじはん*が*／じゅういちじ*まで*／じゅぎょう*が*／あります。
2. アメリカじんの　ともだち*と*ごはん*を*たべます。
   <small>あめりか</small>
3. としょかん*で*べんきょうします。
4. うち*が*スーパー*まで*じてんしゃ*で*いきます。
   <small>す ぱ</small>
5. ごじはん*に*うち*で*ごはん*を*つくります。
6. しちじはん／じゅうじ／しゅくだい／します。
7. クラスメート*と*でんわ*に*かけます。
   <small>く ら す め　と</small>
8. りょうしん*に*てがみ*を*かきます。

B. Work with a partner. First answer the questions, then ask the same questions to your partner. See how many times your partner's answer is the same as yours.

Example

あさごはんを　たべますか。／だれと　たべますか。
A: あさごはんを　たべますか。
B: ええ、たべます。
A: だれと　たべますか。
B: ひとりで　たべます。

1. なんじごろ　がっこうに　きますか。／なんで　きますか。
2. きょう　なんじから　なんじまで　じゅぎょうが
   ありますか。
3. しゅうまつに　よく　でかけますか。／だれと
   でかけますか。
4. よく　でんわで　はなしますか。／だれと　はなしますか。
5. テレビを　みますか。／たいてい　なんじから
   なんじまで　テレビを　みますか。
6. ここから　えきまで　なんで　いきますか。

C. Work with a partner. Study the pictures in exercise A for one minute, and memorize as much information as you can. Then cover the pictures. Your partner will ask you questions based on the pictures. You get one point for each correct answer. You get two points if you can answer the questions about the means (〜で), with whom (〜と), from 〜 to (〜から〜まで), and to whom (〜に).

Example

おかださんは　なんで　だいがくに　いきますか。
バスで　いきます。

D. Work with a partner. Study the pictures in exercise A, then ask your partner if he/she does similar things. Note the differences and similarities between Okada-san's activities and your partner's.

Example

A: おかださんは　バスで　だいがくに　きます。
　　〜さんも　バスで　きますか。
B: いいえ、わたしは　あるいて　きます。

II. Talking about past events, using polite past verbs and polite past adjectives

A. Expressing a past action, using polite past verbs

Question		
	Verb (past)	
きのう　しんぶんを	よみました	か。

Did you read the newspaper yesterday?

Answer	
	Verb (past)
いいえ、	よみませんでした。

No, I didn't.

	Polite Affirmative Form		Polite Negative Form	
	Present	**Past**	**Present**	**Past**
	～ます	～ました	～ません	～ませんでした
to eat	たべます	たべました	たべません	たべませんでした
to buy	かいます	かいました	かいません	かいませんでした
to do	します	しました	しません	しませんでした

B. Describing and commenting about the past, using polite past adjectives and the copula verb です

1. はい／いいえ questions

Question		
	な-adjective (past)	
レポートは	たいへんでした	か。

Was the paper hard to do?

Answer		
		な-adjective (past)
いいえ、	あまり	たいへんじゃありませんでした。 たいへんじゃなかったです。

No, it wasn't very hard to do.

2. Information questions

Question		
	How was 〜	
きのうの　えいがは	どうでした	か。

How was the movie yesterday?

Answer		
	い-adjective (past)	
とても	おもしろかった	です。

It was very interesting.

い-adjectives

Affirmative present form:	あかいです
Affirmative past form:	あか<u>かった</u>です
Negative present form:	あか<u>く</u>ありません
	あか<u>く</u>ないです
Negative past form:	あか<u>く</u>ありません<u>でした</u>
	あか<u>くなかった</u>です

Dictionary Form	Polite Affirmative Form	
	Present	**Past**
おもしろい (interesting)	おもしろ<u>い</u>です	おもしろ<u>かった</u>です
いい (good)	い<u>い</u>です	<u>よかった</u>です

Dictionary Form	Polite Negative Form	
	Present	**Past**
おもしろい (interesting)	おもしろ<u>く</u>ありません おもしろ<u>く</u>ないです	おもしろ<u>く</u>ありません<u>でした</u> おもしろ<u>くなかった</u>です
いい (good)	<u>よく</u>ありません よ<u>く</u>ないです	<u>よく</u>ありません<u>でした</u> よ<u>くなかった</u>です

な-adjectives

Affirmative present form:	ひまです
Affirmative past form:	ひま<u>でした</u>
Negative present form:	ひま<u>じゃありません</u>
Negative past form:	ひま<u>じゃ</u>ありません<u>でした</u>
Negative present form:	ひまじゃ<u>ない</u>です
Negative past form:	ひま<u>じゃなかった</u>です

The copula verb です

Affirmative present form:	がくせいです
Affirmative past form:	がくせい<u>でした</u>
Negative present form:	がくせいじゃありません
Negative past form:	がくせい<u>じゃ</u>ありません<u>でした</u>
Negative present form:	がくせいじゃ<u>ない</u>です
Negative past form:	がくせい<u>じゃなかった</u>です

Dictionary Form	Polite Affirmative Form	
	Present	Past
しずか (quiet)	しずかです	しずかでした
じゅぎょう (class)	じゅぎょうです	じゅぎょうでした

Dictionary Form	Polite Negative Form	
	Present	Past
しずか (quiet)	しずかじゃありません しずかじゃないです	しずかじゃありませんでした しずかじゃなかったです
じゅぎょう (class)	じゅぎょうじゃありません じゅぎょうじゃないです	じゅぎょうじゃありませんでした じゅぎょうじゃなかったです

アリス： せんしゅうの　どようびに　なにを　しましたか。
　　　　 What did you do last Saturday?

さとう： ビデオを　みましたよ。
　　　　 I saw a video.

アリス： そうですか。どうでしたか。
　　　　 I see. How was it?

さとう： とても　おもしろかったですよ。
　　　　 It was very interesting. / I liked it very much.

- The い-adjective いい has the same irregularity in the past tense form as in the negative form (see Chapter 3). The correct forms are よかったです, よくありませんでした, and よくなかったです (colloquial form). The first い becomes よ.

- な-adjectives and the copula verb です conjugate the same way.

はなして　みましょう　(Practice and Conversation)

A. The following chart shows what Brown-san did yesterday. Using the cues below, ask はい／いいえ questions.

Example

はちじに　おきます。
ブラウンさんは　はちじに　おきましたか。

7:00 A.M.	Wake up, take a shower, read a newspaper	4:00 P.M.	Go home (by bus, alone)
8:30 A.M.	Go to school (10-minute walk from home)	5:00 P.M.	Fix dinner
9:00 A.M.	Japanese class (9:00–9:50 A.M.)	6 P.M.	Eat dinner (with a roommate)
10:00 A.M.	Break	7:30 P.M.	Watch a video (7:30–9:00 P.M.), do laundry
11:00 A.M.	English class (11:00–11:50 A.M.)		
12:00 P.M.	Lunch with a friend (until 1:30 P.M.)	9 P.M.	Study (9:00–10:00 P.M.)
1:30 P.M.	Go shopping (to department store by bus, with a friend), purchase bag	10:00 P.M.	Call parents, talk on the phone
2:00 P.M.		11:00 P.M.	Write a letter to a friend
3:00 P.M.		12:00 A.M.	Go to bed

1. そうじを　します。
2. コーヒーを　のみます。
3. しんぶんを　よみます。
4. レポートを　かきます。
5. りょうしんに　でんわを　かけます。
6. ごはんを　つくります。
7. えいごの　クラスが　あります。

8. ともだちと　でんわで　はなします。

9. ビデオを　みます。
^{び で お}

10. せんたくを　します。

11. おんがくを　ききます。

B. Work with a partner. Ask your partner the はい／いいえ questions you created in exercise A. Your partner will answer the questions based on the chart in exercise A.

Example

A: ブラウンさんは　はちじに　おきましたか。
^{ぶ ら う ん}

B: いいえ、おきませんでした。しちじに　おきました。

C. Work with a partner. Fill in the table below as completely as possible, with the activities you did yesterday. Your partner will ask you questions about your activities and then fill in his/her own table. Compare the two tables when you are done to see how well they match.

Example

A: きのう　なんじに　おきましたか。

B: はちじごろ　おきました。

A: くじごろ　なにを　しましたか。

B: がっこうに　いきました。

5 A.M.		4 P.M.	
6 A.M.		5 P.M.	
7 A.M.		6 P.M.	
8 A.M.		7 P.M.	
9 A.M.		8 P.M.	
10 A.M.		9 P.M.	
11 A.M.		10 P.M.	
12 P.M.		11 P.M.	
1 P.M.		12 A.M.	
2 P.M.		1 A.M.	
3 P.M.			

D. Change the following adjectives into the affirmative past form and the negative past form. Pay attention to the two kinds of adjectives: い-adjectives and な-adjectives. Use とても for the affirmative form and あまり for the negative form.

Example

おおきい
とても　おおきかったです。あまり　おおきくありませんでした。

1. おもしろい
2. きれい
3. ちいさい
4. いい
5. たのしい

6. しずか
7. ざんねん
8. たいへん
9. ひま

E. Work with a partner. Ask your partner about classes he/she took during high school. Find out which ones were interesting, not interesting, easy, difficult, and so on. Then complete the following chart.

Example

A: こうこうの　とき、どの　じゅぎょうが　おもしろかったですか。
B: えいごの　じゅぎょうが　おもしろかったです。
A: こうこうの　とき、どの　クラスが　おもしろくなかったですか。
B: フランスごの　クラスが　おもしろくなかったです。

	Affirmative 😊	Negative 😞
おもしろい／じゅぎょう		
たいへんな／じゅぎょう		
いい／じゅぎょう		

F. Work with a partner. Ask your partner about his/her high school life; then complete the following chart.

Example

A: こうこうの　せいかつは　どうでしたか。
B: とても　たのしかったです。

A: こうこうの　じゅぎょうは　どうでしたか。
B: あまり　むずかしくありませんでした。／むずかしくな
　　かったです。

こうこうの　せいかつ	
こうこうの　じゅぎょう	
こうこうの　せんせい	
こうこうの　クラスメート	

G. Work with a partner. Ask your partner about memorable things he/she did last week.

Example

A: せんしゅうの　しゅうまつに　なにを　しましたか。
B: せんしゅうの　きんようびに　ともだちと　ビデオを　みました。
A: どうでしたか。
B: とても　おもしろかったです。
A: そうですか。

III. Expressing frequency and extent, using counter expressions

A. Frequency of action

		Time Frame	Particle	Counter Expression			
わたし	は	にしゅうかん	に	いちど	えいが	を	みます。

I watch a movie once every two weeks.

B. Extent of action

		Time Frame	Particle	Counter Expression			
わたし	は	いちにち	に	にじかんぐらい	ほん	を	よみます。

I read about two hours a day.

A: いっしゅうかんに　なんどぐらい　せんたくを　しますか。
About how many times a week do you do laundry?

B: いちど　します。
I do it once.

A: まいにち　なんじかんぐらい　しごとを　しましたか。
About how many hours a day did you work?

B: いちにちに　さんじかんぐらい　しました。
I worked about three hours a day.

- There are two sets of counters commonly used to express frequency: かい and ど. ど used most often in いちど (once), にど (twice), and さんど (three times), while かい is used with any number. The following list shows counters used from 1 to 10. Pay attention to the sound change in 1, 6, 8, and 10.

  1. いっかい
  2. にかい
  3. さんかい
  4. よんかい
  5. ごかい
  6. ろっかい
  7. ななかい
  8. はっかい
  9. きゅうかい
  10. じゅっかい

- Commonly used counter expressions for lengths of time

  いちにち　one day
  いっしゅうかん　one week
  にしゅうかん　two weeks
  さんしゅうかん　three weeks
  いっかげつ　one month
  にかげつ　two months
  さんかげつ　three months
  ろっかげつ／はんとし　six months / half a year
  いちねん　one year
  にねん　two years
  さんねん　three years
  よねん　four years
  じゅうねん　ten years

- どのくらい (or どのぐらい) is a generic question word meaning *how long, how often,* or *how much.* Use it if you cannot decide time, frequency, or quantity expression to use.

チョー： どのくらい　べんきょうしますか。
How often/How long/How much do you study?

さとう： まいにち　べんきょうします。
I study every day.

or　さんじかんぐらい　べんきょうします。
I study for about three hours.

or　さんページ　べんきょうします。
I study three pages.

ブラウン： いちにちに　どのくらい　しんぶんを　よみますか。
How often/How long/How much do you read the newspaper every day?

やまだ： いちにちに　にど　よみます。
I read it twice a day.

or　いちじかんぐらい／さんじゅっぷんぐらい　よみます。
I read it for about one hour / about thirty minutes.

or　はちページぐらい　よみます。
I read about eight pages.

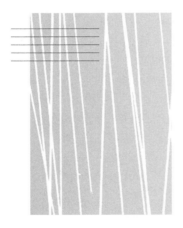

はなしてみましょう　(Practice and Conversation)

A. Rephrase the following sentences using frequency/extent and time frame.

Example

	Frequency/ Extent	Time Frame
ビデオを　みます。 にしゅうかんに　いちど　ビデオを みます。	once	two weeks

	Frequency/ Extent	Time Frame
1. ざっしを　かいます。	once	two weeks
2. えいがを　みます。	twice	one month
3. としょかんで　べんきょうします。	five hours	one week
4. アルバイトを　します。 <small>あ る ば い と</small>	ten hours	one week
5. ともだちに　てがみを　かきます。	four times	one year
6. ごはんを　つくります。	three times	one day
7. デパートに　いきます。 <small>で ぱ　 と</small>	once	one month

B. Answer the following questions. Note that ごりょうしん is a more polite expression for りょうしん and is used for someone else's parents.

Example

A: きむらさんは　よく　えいがを　みますか。
B: にしゅうかんに　いちどぐらい　みます。

1. よく　へやを　そうじしますか。
2. いちにちに　なんじかんぐらい　べんきょうしますか。
3. よく　えいがを　みますか。
4. よく　うんどうを　しますか。
5. よく　ごりょうしんに　でんわを　かけますか。
6. よく　せんたくを　しますか。
7. いっしゅうかんに　どのくらい　アルバイトを　します<small>あ る ば い と</small>か。

C. Work with a partner. Find out how often he/she did the following things when he/she was in high school. Compare it with your own experience.

Example

A: いっしゅうかんに　なんかいぐらい　うんどうしましたか。
B: さんかいぐらい　しました。

うんどうを　します／いっしゅうかん	
アルバイトを　します／いっしゅうかん <small>あ る ば い と</small>	
べんきょうを　します／いちにち	
ねます／いちにち	
ともだちと　でかけます／いっしゅうかん	

D. Work with a new partner. Tell your partner how your college lifestyle is different from your high school lifestyle. Find out how often he/she did the following things when he/she was in high school and compare it with your own experience.

Example

ぼく／わたしは　こうこうの　とき　まいにち　うんどうを
しました。
でも、いまは　いっしゅうかんに　いちど　します。

E. First guess and write down how often or how much a typical college student does the following activities. Then conduct a survey of your classmates and find out how close your guess is to the results of your survey.

Example

Suppose you write *once a week* next to せんたくを　します as your guess,

A: まいしゅう　せんたくを　しますか。

B: ええ、します。

A: いっしゅうかんに　なんど　しますか。

B: にどぐらい　します。

Write *twice a week* in the column for the survey results.

Suppose you write *5 hours a week* next to でんわで　はなします as your guess,

A: よく　でんわで　はなしますか。

B: ええ、はなします。

A: いっしゅうかんに　どのくらい　はなしますか。

B: ごじかんぐらい　はなします。 or いちにちに　いちじ
   かんぐらい　はなします。

Write *7 hours a week* (*1 hour a day*) in the column for the survey results.

	How Often	
	Your Guess	**Survey Results**
せんたくを　します		
そうじを　します		
かいものに　いきます		

	How much	
	Your Guess	Survey Results
でんわで　はなします		
しゅくだいを　します		
うんどうを　します		

IV. Using double particles with the topic marker は, the contrast marker は, and the similarity marker も

A. Double particles with the topic marker は and the similarity marker も

Sentence			
Noun (place)	Particle	Particle	
この　だいがく	に	は	りっぱな　としょかんが　あります。

This university has a fine library.

Sentence			
Noun (place)	Particle	Particle	
とうきょうだいがく	に	も	あります。

Tokyo University also has a fine one.

B. Contrasting with は

Sentence			
		Noun (object)	Particle	
わたし	は	しんぶん	を	よく　よみます。

I often read the newspaper.

Sentence			
	Noun (object)	Particle (contrast)	
でも、	ざっし	は	あまり　よみません。

But I don't read magazines very often.

C. Noun contrast

Sentence				
		Noun (place)	Particle	
わたし	は	うち	で	ごはんを　たべます。

I eat meals at home.

Sentence			
Noun (place)	Particle	Particle (contrast)	
がっこう	で	は	たべません。

I don't eat at school.

さとう： どようびには　なにを　しました か。
　　　　 What did you do on Saturday?

スミス： あさから　ばんまで　アルバイトを　しました。
　　　　 I worked from morning until night.

さとう： たいへんですね。らいしゅうの　どようびにも
　　　　 アルバイトが　ありますか。
　　　　 That's hard, isn't it? Are you going to work next Saturday, too?

スミス： いいえ、らいしゅうは　ありません。
　　　　 No, I am not going to do that next week.

● As you remember from Chapter 2, a topic is a part of the sentence about which the speaker wishes to make some statement, and it usually comes at the beginning. Therefore, the particle は to indicate the topic can be used with any type of noun. Similarly, the particle も to indicate similarity can be used with any type of noun. Both は and も replace を (direct object) or が (subject), as in the following examples:

わたしは　あさごはんを　たべました。たなかさんも　たべました。

I ate breakfast. So did Tanaka-san.

レポートは　あした　かきます。しゅくだいも　あした します。

I am going to write a report tomorrow. I will also do homework tomorrow.

● With other particles, は for topic and も for similarity are added to the particle as in the following examples. These are called double particles.

にほん<u>には</u>　ひとりで　いきました。かんこく<u>にも</u>
ひとりで　いきます。

I went to Japan by myself. I will also go to Korea by myself.

とうきょう<u>では</u>　えいがを　みました。きょうと<u>でも</u>
えいがを　みました。

I saw a movie in Tokyo. I also saw one in Kyoto.

りょうしん<u>には</u>　きょう　てがみを　かきます。
せんせい<u>にも</u>　きょう　てがみを　かきます。

I am going to write a letter to my parents today. I am also going to write a letter to my professor.

<ruby>十<rt>じゅう</rt></ruby>じ<u>には</u>　じゅぎょうが　あります。<ruby>十一<rt>じゅういち</rt></ruby>じ<u>にも</u>
じゅぎょうが　あります。

I have a class at ten o'clock. I also have another at eleven o'clock, too.

- Relative time expressions like きょう and あした do not take the particle
に. は and も are added directly to the noun, as in the following example:

きょう<u>は</u>　うんどうを　します。あした<u>も</u>　します。

I will exercise today. I will also do that tomorrow.

- Besides indicating a topic, は can indicate contrast. The は in the second
key sentence B contrasts ざっし to しんぶん. The は particle for contrast can be used with any type of noun as well. Like は for topic and も
for similarity, は for contrast replaces を (direct object) or が (subject), as
in the example below:

にほんごの　しけんが　あります。でも、けいざいがくの
しけん<u>は</u>　ありません。

I have a Japanese exam. But I don't have an economics exam.

- Similarly, with other particles, は for contrast is added to the particle, as in
the examples below:

としょかんで　べんきょうします。でも、
がくせいかいかん<u>では</u>　しません。

I study in the library. But I don't study in the student union.

ここに　ねこが　います。あそこ<u>には</u>　いません。

There is a cat here. There isn't one over there.

- は for contrast is often used in negative sentences. Often, the contrast is
implicit rather than explicit, as in the following example:

すずき： あした　いきますか。
　　　　Are you going tomorrow?

ブラウン：いいえ、あした<u>は</u>　いきません。
　　　　No, I am not going tomorrow (but I may go some other time).

- Occasionally particles can be omitted if they can be easily determined from the context. For example, the time particle に is often deleted when the noun indicates a day, as in げつようび:

げつようび（に）は　にほんごの　じゅぎょうが　あります。

はなしてみましょう　(Practice and Conversation)

A. Create two sentences: one that shares a similarity with the first sentence and another that contrasts with the first sentence.

Example

あさごはんを　たべます。
<u>ばんごはんも　たべます</u>。<u>でも、ひるごはんは　たべません</u>。

1. バスは　じゅうじに　きました。
2. やまださんと　いきます。
3. バスで　だいがくに　いきます。
4. きのう　しごとを　しました。
5. きょう　ともだちに　でんわを　かけました。

B. Work with a partner. Ask a question using the words in column A. Your partner will answer the question using the words in column B and the information in column A (underlined in the example) to form a topic.

Example

A	B
いつ／コーヒーを　のみます。	あさ

A: いつ　<u>コーヒーを</u>　のみますか。
B: <u>コーヒー</u>ですか。　<u>コーヒー</u>は　あさ　のみますね。

A	B
どこ／おもしろい　ほんを　かいました。	だいがくの　ほんや
なに／びょういんに　いきました。	くるま
いつ／そうじを　しました。	きのう

どこ／スミスさんと　いきました。	きっさてん
なに／えきから　いきました。	バス
だれ／レポートを　かきました。	せんせい
いつ／たなかさんと　でかけます。	しゅうまつ

C. Work with a partner. Write down which day(s) you do the following activities and which day(s) you don't. Then ask your partner when he/she does or does not do them.

Example

A: たいてい　なんようびに　アルバイトを　しますか。

B: げつようびに　します。すいようびにも　しますよ。

A: そうですか。　きんようびにも　しますか。

B: いいえ、きんようびには　しません。

	わたし		パートナー	
	します	しません	します	しません
アルバイトを　します				
うんどうを　します				
スーパーに　いきます				
そうじを　します				

D. Work with a new partner. Think of three cities and write their names in the following chart. Discuss how a student's daily life might be different if he/she lived in these cities. Then list as many of these differences as you can.

Example

Suppose you choose ニューヨーク, シカゴ, (your hometown)

A: ニューヨークには　いい　にほんの　レストランが　ありますね。

B: ええ。シカゴにも　ありますよ。

A: この　まちにも　ありますか。

B: いいえ、この　まちには　ありません。

Town 1	Town 2	Town 3

V. Giving a reason, using 〜から, and expressing contrast, using が

A. Expressing cause and effect in a single sentence

Sentence		
Clause (reason)		**Clause (result)**
	Particle (reason)	
あした　りょうしんが　きます	から、	アパートの　そうじを しました。

Since my parents are coming tomorrow, I cleaned my apartment.

B. Expressing contrast, using が

Sentence		
Clause		**Clause**
	Particle (contrast)	
きょうは　いそがしいです	が、	あしたは　ひまです。

I am busy today, but I will be free tomorrow.

チョー：なにを　しましたか。
　　　　What did you do?

やまだ：レポートが　ありましたから、うちで　べんきょう
　　　　しました。
　　　　I studied at home because I had a report to write.

チョー：そうですか。たいへんでしたね。
　　　　I see. That was hard, wasn't it?

やまだ：ええ、たいへんでしたが、おもしろかったです。
　　　　Yes, it was hard, but interesting.

- If a sentence contains both a reason and a result, the clause for the reason (the one ending with から) must come before the clause indicating the result.

- 〜から can be used by itself to state a reason:

アリス：よく　テレビを　みますか。
　　　　Do you watch TV often?

さとう：いいえ、いそがしいですから。
　　　　No, because I am busy.

- Since が connects two clauses in a contrasting or negative relationship, the contrast marker は is often used with が:

えいがは　みませんでしたが、テレビは　みました。

I didn't watch movies, but I watched television.

ゆうびんきょくには　いきませんでしたが、ぎんこうには
いきました。

I didn't go to the post office, but I went to the bank.

- が can be used in the sentence that opens a conversation or introduces a topic. In this case, it is called a weak "but," because it does not introduce a strong negative relation. This is the use of が similar to the use of "but" in English in the sentence *Excuse me, but could you turn on the television?*:

あのう　すみませんが、いま　なんじですか。

Excuse me, but what time is it?

わたしの　うちは　あれですが、たなかさんのは　どの
たてものですか。

My house is that one over there, but which building is Tanaka-san's?

はなしてみましょう　(Practice and Conversation)

A. Combine the following pair of sentences using 〜から. Make sure to start with the sentence that expresses a reason and is followed by から.

きょうは　べんきょうします。　あした　しけんが
あります。
あした　しけんが　ありますから、きょうは　べんきょう
します。

1. まいにち　しごとを　します。いそがしいです。
2. きょうは　いそがしいです。かいものに　いきません。
3. しちじに　おきます。はちじに　じゅぎょうが　あります。
4. ともだちが　うちに　きます。ごはんを　つくります。
5. ひまです。おんがくを　ききます。

B. Work with a partner. Discover as many differences as you can in lifestyle between you and your partner. Then write them in the following chart.

A: ぼくは　まいにち　はちじに　おきますが、〜さんは
　　なんじに　おきますか。

B: わたしは　じゅうじごろ　おきます。

わたし／ぼく	パートナー

C. Work with a partner. Ask your partner what he/she often did in high school. Then ask whether he/she still does the same things.

A: こうこうの　とき　よく　なにを　しましたか。
B: そうですね。よく　ともだちに　てがみを
　　かきましたね。
A: いまも　よく　かきますか。
B: いいえ、いまは　あまり　かきません。いそがしいです
　　から。

D. Think of one activity that you do often now but didn't when you were in high school. Ask your classmate what he/she does often now but didn't during high school. Discover which lifestyle changes commonly take place at college and why. Note that すんでいました means *was living; was residing.*

Example

A: なにを　よく　しますか。

B: ひとりで　よく　ごはんを　つくります。

A: こうこうの　ときも　つくりましたか。

B: いいえ、こうこうの　ときは　りょうしんの　うちに　すんでいましたから、ぜんぜん　つくりませんでした。

じょうずな　よみかた　(READING)

Identifying missing words

In Japanese it is not necessary to include pronouns in a text when they can be inferred from the context. Missing words are most often either the subject or the topic of a sentence, although they can be other types of words such as the object and expression of time or place. For example, in the sentences わたしは　が くせいです。 さんねんせいです。, the topic of the second sentence, わたしは, is missing because it is mentioned in the first sentence and can be inferred from the context. This type of deletion makes a paragraph more cohesive. As you become more proficient in Japanese, this will become second nature to you.

Identify missing nouns, if there are any, from each sentence in the text.

1. キムさんは毎日八時に起きます。そして、九時に学校に行きます。

2. きょうは宿題をしません。あしたします。

3. アリスさんに電話をかけました。手紙も書きました。

みちこさんの　せいかつ　(Michiko-san's daily life)

よむまえに　(Prereading)

Create five sentences about your daily life.

ことばの　リスト (Vocabulary)

八つ　eight

クラスをとっています　taking classes

心配です／〜のことを　心配しています　worried about

Read the following paragraph to answer the questions below.

私は今、毎日試験がありますから、とても忙しいです。
私の大学では試験はあまりありませんが、大きいのが一年に一度
あります。私はクラスを八つとっていますから、とても大変です。
きのうも午後十一時ごろまで図書館で　友達と勉強しました。
あしたは英語の試験があります。英語の授業はあまり難しく
ありませんでしたから、試験のことはあまり心配していません。
でも、経済学の授業はとても難しかったですから、とても
心配です。経済学の試験は土曜日にあります。

わかりましたか　(Comprehension)

A. Answer the following questions in Japanese.

1. みちこさんの　まいにちの　せいかつは　どうですか。
2. みちこさんの　だいがくでは　よく　しけんが
   ありますか。
3. みちこさんの　だいがくでは　いちねんに　どのぐらい
   しけんが　ありますか。
4. みちこさんは　きのう　なにを　しましたか。
5. どの　じゅぎょうが　やさしかったですか。
6. どの　じゅぎょうが　たいへんでしたか。
7. けいざいがくの　しけんは　いつ　ありますか。

B. Identify missing nouns, if there are any, from each sentence in the text.

C. Write a short composition that describes your daily routine.

Making sense out of missing pronouns

In conversation, as in writing, pronouns are often omitted when they can be inferred from the context. Imagine that two people are talking to each other. One person asks a question without using an overt subject pronoun; the missing subject likely is *you*. Then the other person makes a statement without using a subject; the missing subject likely is the speaker himself/herself. As you become more proficient in Japanese, you will understand who is mentioned without listening for the subject pronouns.

A. Listen to the following short dialogues. In each conversation, the subject in the man's speech is either *I* or *you*, but it's missing. Identify which one is the missing subject.

1. I   you   4. I   you

2. I   you   5. I   you

3. I   you

B. わたしの　せいかつ Listen to the following conversations; then listen to the statements. If a statement is true, circle はい; if it is false, circle いいえ.

1. a. はい　いいえ   2. a. はい　いいえ
   b. はい　いいえ   b. はい　いいえ
   c. はい　いいえ   c. はい　いいえ
   d. はい　いいえ   d. はい　いいえ
   e. はい　いいえ   e. はい　いいえ
   f. はい　いいえ   f. はい　いいえ

  DICT-A-CONVERSATION

You, Smith-san, are talking with your classmate, Sato-san, who is working part time. He did not come to class yesterday. You are asking him questions.

スミス：きのう　じゅぎょうに　きましたか。

さとう：＿＿＿＿＿＿＿＿＿＿＿＿＿＿＿＿＿＿

スミス：＿＿＿＿＿＿＿＿＿＿＿＿＿＿＿＿＿＿

さとう： _____
スミス： _____
さとう： _____
スミス： _____
さとう： _____

ききじょうず　はなしじょうず　(COMMUNICATION)

Using そうですか and そうですね

そうですか and そうですね are often used in conversations. They are very important devices because they make the conversation go smoothly. However, it is sometimes difficult to know which one to use. There are two そうですか: one with a falling intonation and one with a rising intonation. そうですか with a falling intonation means *I see* (*and I didn't know that*). It is used when you just received new information and is often preceded by ああ. On the other hand, そうですか with a rising intonation means *Is that so?* It is used to question what you have just heard and is often preceded by えっ, which means *What!*

そうですね is used with a falling intonation. It means *That's right*. Thus, it is not appropriate to use そうですね when you have just heard something new. そうですね is often preceded by ええ or はい.

Work with your partner. Read the following sentences one at a time. Respond to each, using the three following phrases. You may choose more than one answer as long as you know why you have chosen it.

ああ、そうですか。　↓
えっ、そうですか。　↑
ええ、そうですね。　↓

1. やまだせんせいは　いい　せんせいです。
2. やまだせんせいは　けいざいがくの　せんせいです。
3. ブラウンさんは　にほんじんです。
4. このしゅくだいは　むずかしいですね。
5. きのうは　いそがしかったですね。
6. あした　にほんに　いきます。

そうごうれんしゅう (INTEGRATION)

にほんの　だいがくせいと　アメリカの　だいがくせい
(American and Japanese college students)

The illustration shows a typical day of two Japanese college students: Mr. Yamada and Mr. Sato. Mr. Yamada lives with his parents, while Mr. Sato lives in an apartment, as he is from another area of Japan. Work as a group. First describe what each person does in a typical day. Then find some differences and similarities between the routines of the two students. Finally, discuss how their routines are different from or similar to your daily routine.

	やまだ	さとう
7:30		
8:00		
9:00		
9:30		
10:00		
11:30		
12:00		
1:00		
2:30		
3:00		
4:00		

	やまだ	さとう
5:00		
6:00		
6:30		
7:00		
8:00		
9:00		
10:00		
11:30		
12:00		
1:00		

ロールプレイ (Role play)

You are doing a telephone survey of people's daily routines and activities. First, create five questions you would like to ask someone. Then make a phone call. Ask for the person politely. Once he/she comes to the phone, say すみません。 アンケートちょうさ<ruby>あんけ<rt></rt></ruby><ruby>と<rt></rt></ruby>なんですが、よろしいですか。 (Excuse me. I am doing a survey. Is that okay with you?) Ask the five questions and take notes. When you are done, reverse roles with your partner. Talk to several people and discover any similarities among your classmates. Compare your notes with others who asked similar questions.

たんご　(ESSENTIAL VOCABULARY)

Particles

から　from
　はちじから　くじまで　べんきょう
　します。（八時から　九時まで　勉強
　します。）　study/studies from 8 o'clock to 9
　o'clock

で　with; by means of
　くるまで　いきます。
　（車で　行きます。）　go/es by car

と　with
　ともだちと　はなします。
　（友達と　話します。）　talk/s with a friend

に　to (indirect object marker, person + に)
　ともだちに　でんわを　かけます。
　（友達に　電話を　かけます。）
　call/s a friend

に　time frame
　いっしゅうかんに　いちど（一週間に
　一度）　once a week

まで　until
　はちじから　くじまで　べんきょう
　します。（八時から　九時まで　勉強
　します。）　study/studies from 8 o'clock to
　9 o'clock

Nouns

あした（明日）tomorrow
アルバイト　part-time job (from the German *Arbeit*)
うんどう（運動）(physical) exercise
おんがく（音楽）music
かいもの（買物）shopping
きのう（昨日）yesterday
クラス　class
クラスメート　classmate

くるま（車）automobile, car
ごりょうしん（ご両親）(somebody else's) parents
こんしゅう（今週）this week
ざっし（雑誌）magazine
しけん（試験）examination, test
しごと（仕事）work, permanent job
じてんしゃ（自転車）bicycle
しゅうまつ（週末）weekend
しんぶん（新聞）newspaper

せんしゅう（先週）last week
せんたく（洗濯）laundry
　せんたくを　します（洗濯をします）
　　do/es laundry
そうじ（掃除）cleaning
　そうじします（掃除します）clean/s
てがみ（手紙）letter
テスト　test
でんしゃ（電車）(electric) train

バス　bus
ビデオ　videotape
らいしゅう（来週）next week
りょうしん（両親）(the speaker's) parents
ルームメート　roommate
レポート　report, term paper

い-adjectives

いそがしい（忙しい）busy (doing things)
おもしろい（面白い）interesting
たのしい（楽しい）fun

むずかしい（難しい）difficult, hard
やさしい（易しい）easy

な-adjectives

ざんねん（な）（残念（な））unfortunate, sorry
たいへん（な）（大変（な））tough, hectic, hard
ひま（な）（暇（な））free, idling

う-verbs

かいます（買います）buy/s
　The dictionary form is かう（買う）.
かきます（書きます）write/s
　The dictionary form is かく（書く）.
ききます（聞きます）listen/s
　The dictionary form is きく（聞く）.

つくります（作ります）make/s
　The dictionary form is つくる（作る）.
はなします（話します）talk/s
　The dictionary form is はなす（話す）.

る-verbs

かけます　make/s (a telephone call)
　でんわを　かけます（電話を　かけます）make/s a telephone call
　The dictionary form is かける.
でかけます（出かけます）go/es out
　The dictionary form is でかける（出かける）.

あるいて（歩いて）on foot
ひとりで（一人で）alone, by oneself

Counters

〜かい（〜回）times (frequency)　　〜ど（〜度）times (frequency)
〜かげつ（〜か月）month (duration)　　〜ねん（〜年）year (duration)
〜しゅうかん（週間）week (duration)

Expressions

〜のとき　　at the time when 〜
　こうこうの　とき（高校の　時）when I was in high school

Passive Vocabulary

Expressions

じゅぎょうを　やっつ　とっています。（授業を　八つ　とっています。）I am
　taking eight classes.
しんぱいです。（心配です。）am/is/are worried
すみません。アンケートちょうさなんですが、よろしいですか。（すみません。
　アンケート調査なんですが、よろしいですか。）Excuse me. I am doing a survey.
　May I . . .?
〜の　ことは　しんぱいしていません。（〜のことは　心配していません。）is/are
not worried about 〜

Supplementary Vocabulary

Other daily activities

おてあらいに　いきます。（お手洗いに
　行きます。）go/es to the restroom
かおを　あらいます（顔を　洗います。）
　wash/es (one's) face
　The dictionary form is あらう.
かじを　します（家事を　します。）
　do/es household work

ゴミを　だします（ゴミを　出します。）
　take/s out the trash
　The dictionary form is だす（出す）.
ゴミを　すてます（ゴミを　捨てます。）
　discard/s the trash
　The dictionary form is すてる（捨てる）.

さんぽを　します（散歩を　します。）
stroll/s, go/es for a walk
The dictionary form is する.

しゅくだいを　だします。（宿題を出し
ます。）　turn/s in homework
The dictionary form is だす（出す）.

しょっきを　あらいます（食器を
洗います。）　do/es the dishes
The dictionary form is あらう（洗う）.

てを　あらいます（手を　洗います。）
wash/es (one's) hands
The dictionary form is あらう（洗う）.

はを　みがきます（歯を　磨きます。）
brush/es (one's) teeth
The dictionary form is みがく（磨く）.

ビデオを　かります。（ビデオを
借ります。）　rent/s a video
The dictionary form is かりる（借りる）.

へやを　かたづけます（部屋を
片付けます。）　tidy/tidies up a room
The dictionary form is かたづける
（片付ける）.

Playing baseball on Sunday

すきな こと と すきな もの

ACTIVITIES AND HOBBIES

Functions	Describing likes, dislikes, and preferences
New Vocabulary	Food; Beverages; Sports; Music; Pastimes and interests
Dialogue	どんな スポーツが すきですか。 (What kinds of sports do you like?)
Culture	Popular pastimes in Japan
Language	I. Expressing likes and dislikes, using すき and きらい
	II. Making noun phrases, using の and the dictionary (plain present affirmative) forms of verbs
	III. Listing nouns, using や
	IV. Making comparisons, using いちばん and 〜の ほうが 〜より
	V. Requesting and giving an explanation or a confirmation, using the prenominal and plain present forms + んです
Kanji	Introduction to kanji
Reading	Word formation
Listening	Identifying conversation fillers
Communication	Giving positive feedback with も and marking a contrast with は

あたらしい　ことば

A. たべもの (Food). Name the following items and answer the questions in Japanese.

さかな　fish　sakana　　　　にんじん　carrots　ninjin

にく　meat　niku　　　　トマト　tomato　tometo

たまご　egg　tamago　　　バナナ　banana　banana

やさい　vegetables　yasai　　オレンジ　orange　orenji

くだもの　fruits　kudamono　りんご　apple　ringo

レタス　lettuce　retasu

1. スーパーで　なにを　よく　かいますか。　　(often buy)

2. なにを　あまり　たべませんか。

3. スーパーに　どんな　たべものが　ありますか。

4. Is there any other food that you want to know how to say in Japanese?　casseroles
   Ask your instructor what the Japanese word is for it.　salads　chicken

B. のみもの (Beverages). Name the following items and answer the questions in Japanese.

コーヒー　coffee　　　　　ワイン　wine

こうちゃ　black tea　　　　ビール　beer

コーラ　cola

1. あさ　なにを　よく　のみますか。

2. ばん　なにを　よく　のみますか。

3. きっさてんに　どんな　のみものが　ありますか。ありませんか。

C. スポーツ (Sports). Match the Japanese words with their English equivalents. Then answer the questions in Japanese.

_h._ 1. テニス   a. bowling

_i_   2. バスケットボール   b. aerobics

_j_   3. フットボール   c. jogging

_e._ 4. ゴルフ   d. baseball

_b_   5. エアロビクス   e. golf

_g._ 6. スキー   f. hiking

_c._ 7. ジョギング   g. skiing

_a._ 8. ボーリング   h. tennis

_f_   9. ハイキング   i. basketball

_d_ 10. やきゅう   j. football

1. どの　スポーツを　よく　しますか。
2. どの　スポーツを　よく　みますか。

D. おんがく (Music). Find the following words in the grid and circle them.

クラシック　classical   ポップス　pop music
ジャズ　jazz   ギター　guitar
ロック　rock and roll

ポ	ラ	シ	ッ	ク	ズ
ッ	ク	ジ	ギ	タ	ー or l
プ	ッ	ラ	ピ	ャ	ア
ス	プ	ピ	シ	ポ	ロ
ノ	ノ	ー or l	ア	ッ	ッ
ジ	ャ	ズ	コ	ノ	ク

E. レジャーと　しゅみ　(Pastimes and interests). Work with classmates in groups of three or four. One member of the group acts out one of the following activities and hobbies. The other members try to tell what the activity or hobby is in Japanese. Verbs are presented in the dictionary form (plain present affirmative).

こうえんで　あそぶ　(to) play in the park
テニスを　する　(to) play tennis
川で　およぐ　(to) swim in a river

りょこうを　する　(to) travel
ドライブに　いく　(to) go for a drive
ファミコンを　する　(to) play computer games
本を　よむ　(to) read books
うたを　うたう　(to) sing songs
おんがくを　きく　(to) listen to music
コンサートに　いく　(to) go to a concert
えを　かく　(to) draw
りょうりを　する　(to) cook
山の　しゃしんを　とる　(to) take pictures of mountains
レストランで　しょくじを　する　(to) dine at a restaurant
パーティを　する　(to) have a party
おいしい　りょうりを　たべる　(to) eat delicious food

ダイアローグ

はじめに

1. What activities are popular among your classmates?

2. What do you think are the most popular activities among Japanese students?

どんな　スポーツが　すきですか。 (What kinds of sports do you like?)

Alice and Mr. Ishida are talking about sports.

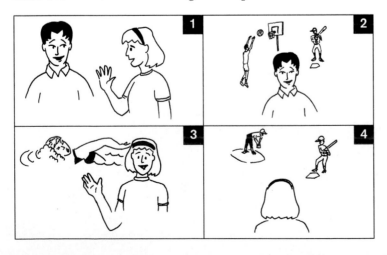

____ アリス： 石田さんは どんな スポーツが すきですか。

____ 石田： そうですね。やきゅうや バスケットボールを
よく しますね。 アリスさんは。

____ アリス： わたしは およぐのが すきですね。
バスケットボールも すきですよ。

____ 石田： そうですか。やきゅうは どうですか。

____ アリス： やきゅうですか。ざんねんですが、やきゅうは (unfortunate, sorry)
あまり よく わからないんですよ。 (I don't understand)

____ 石田： そうですか。じゃあ、おんがくは どうですか。

____ アリス： そうですね。しずかな おんがくが
すきですね。とくに、クラッシックや ジャズは (especially, particularly)
すきですね。

____ 石田： じゃあ、クラッシックと ジャズと どちらの
ほうが すきですか。

____ アリス： どちらも だいすきですよ。

わかりましたか

A. If the following statement is true, circle はい; if it is false, circle いいえ.

はい いいえ 1. 石田さんは スポーツを よく します。

はい いいえ 2. アリスさんは バスケットボールが
すきです。

はい いいえ 3. 石田さんは およぐのが すきです。

はい いいえ 4. アリスさんは ジャズが すきです。

はい いいえ 5. アリスさんは よく やきゅうを します。

B. Complete the following passage by writing an appropriate word in each blank.

石田さんは　よく ＿＿＿＿＿＿ します。アリスさんは ＿＿＿＿＿＿
が　すきです。 ＿＿＿＿＿＿ も　すきです。

にほんの　ぶんか

- *Popular pastimes in Japan. What pastimes do you think Japanese people enjoy?*

A recent survey indicates that the following are the most popular pastimes among Japanese people between the ages of twenty and twenty-nine. The ranking of activities is based on the number of respondents who participated in the activities and not on the frequency of their participation. Watching television was not included in this survey.

おとこの　人	おんなの　人
1. ドライブに　いく	1. ドライブに　いく
2. カラオケ (karaoke) に　いく	2. レストランで　しょくじを　する
3. おさけを　のみに　いく (to go out for drinks)	3. おんがくを　きく
4. ビデオを　みる	4. カラオケ (karaoke) に　いく
5. レストランで　しょくじを　する	5. ビデオを　みる
6. おんがくを　きく	6. こくないりょこう (domestic traveling) を　する
7. ボーリングを　する	7. はくぶつかん (museum) に　いく
8. パチンコ (pachinko game) を　する	8. ゆうえんち (amusement park) に　いく
9. こくないりょこう (domestic traveling) を　する	9. おさけを　のみに　いく (to go out for drinks)
10. ゲーム (game such as cards) を　する	10. ボーリングを　する

The same survey also lists the most popular sports. Again, the ranking of activities is based on the number of people who participated in the sport and not on how frequently they participated.

おとこの　人	おんなの　人
1. ボーリングを　する	1. ボーリングを　する
2. キャッチボール を　する (to play catch)	2. プール (pool)で　およぐ
3. スキーを　する	3. たいそう (calisthenics) を　する
4. ゴルフの　れんしゅうを　する	4. スキーを　する

5. プール (pool) で　およぐ
6. ソフトボール (softball) を　する
7. テニス を　する
8. たいそう (calisthenics) を　する
9. ジョギングを　する
10. トレーニング (physical training) を　する

5. テニスを　する
6. バドミントン (badminton) を　する
7. ゴルフの　れんしゅうを　する
8. ジョギングを　する
9. サイクリング (cycling) を　する
10. バレーボール (volleyball) を　する

According to the same survey, traditional arts such as いけばな (flower arrangement), さどう (tea ceremony), and しょどう (calligraphy) are ranked very low in terms of the number of participants. However, in terms of time spent, these activities are ranked high, after listening to music, calisthenics, and playing musical instruments.

LANGUAGE

I. Expressing likes and dislikes, using すき and きらい

Topic (person, animal)		Noun (thing that he/she likes)	Particle	
アリスさん	は	テニス	が	すきです。

Alice-san likes tennis.

Conjunction	Noun (thing that he/she does not like)	Particle	
でも	やきゅう	は	すきじゃありません。 すきじゃないです。

But, she does not like baseball.

アリス : はやしさんは　どんな　のみものが　すきですか。
　　　　What drinks do you like, Hayashi-san?

はやし : そうですね。　ぼくは　ワインが　大^{だい}すきですね。
　　　　Well, I like wine very much.

アリス : じゃあ、ビールは　どうですか。
　　　　How about beer?

はやし : ビールは　ちょっと...
　　　　Beer is a bit . . . (I don't like beer very much.)

- In English, *like* is a verb, but in Japanese すき is a な-adjective. The negative is じゃありません. The word for *dislike* or *hate,* きらい, is also a な-adjective. Because すき／きらい are adjectives, the object is indicated by が, never を.

- すき and きらい can also be used before nouns. In this case, すきな means *favorite,* and きらいな is the opposite of favorite.

<u>すきな</u>　くだものは　りんごです。

My favorite fruit is the apple. (The fruit I like is the apple.)

<u>きらいな</u>　くだものは　バナナです。

The fruit that I don't like is the banana.

- Because きらい can be a strong word, you might want to avoid using it to answer a question. You can use expressions such as 〜は　ちょっと… (〜 *is a bit . . .*) and あまり.

- In Chapters 3 through 6, 〜は　どうですか means *How is* 〜? Another meaning of 〜は　どうですか is *How about* 〜?

たなか:　私は　ワインが　すきです。

        I like wine.

ロペス:　じゃあ、ビールは　どうですか。

        Well, how about beer?

たなか:　ビールも　すきですよ。

        I like beer, too.

- 大すきです means *like very much* or *really like.*

はなしてみましょう

A. Look at the drawings on the next page. Describe what Yamada-san likes, doesn't like very much, and positively dislikes. Use は to contrast his likes and dislikes.

Example

山田さんは　りんごが　すきです。

でも、トマトは　あまり　すきじゃありません。

すきです	あまり すきじゃありません	きらいです	すきです	あまり すきじゃありません	きらいです

B. Work with a partner. Ask him/her about his/her preferences, using the items in the table below. Try to use the particles も and は correctly.

Example

A: 〜さんは　レタスが　すきですか。

B: はい、すきです。

A: にんじん<u>も</u>　すきですか。

B: いいえ、にんじんは　あまり。

A: トマト<u>は</u>　どうですか。

B: はい、トマト<u>は</u>　すきです。

Categories	Items		
たべもの	レタス	にんじん	トマト
いろ	あか (red color)	しろ (white color)	あお (blue color)
のみもの	コーラ	ビール	ワイン
スポーツ	テニス	フットボール	エアロビクス
おんがく	クラシック	ジャズ	ポップス

Cameron

C. Work with a new partner. Tell your new partner what your previous partner likes and dislikes.

Example

～さんは　～が　すきです。（～も　すきです。）でも、～は
すきじゃありません。（～も　すきじゃありません。）

or ～は　～と　～が　すきですが、～と　～は　すきじゃあり
ません。

D. Survey your classmates to find out which of the four items below your classmates like or dislike the most.

Example

A: どんな　くだものが　すきですか。

B: ～が　すきです。

A: どんな　くだものは　あまり　すきじゃないですか。

B: ～は　あまり　すきじゃありません。

	Most Liked	Least Liked
くだもの		
のみもの		
スポーツ		
おんがく		

II. Making noun phrases using の and the dictionary (plain present affirmative) forms of verbs

Noun phrase				
Verb (plain present affirmative)				
私_{わたし}は	本_{ほん}を　よむ	の	が	すきです。

I like reading books.

Dictionary (plain present affirmative) form

It is important to know which group a given verb belongs to, in order to conjugate the verb. When you know the dictionary (plain present affirmative) form, then it is relatively easy to identify which group a given verb belongs to, by using the following three steps:

1. Irregular verbs: The following are the only two irregular verbs in Japanese: する (します, do) and くる (きます, come). In addition, する can be combined with a noun, to form a compound verb, as in べんきょうする.

2. る-verbs: A verb is a る-verb if in the dictionary form, it ends with the letter る, preceded by the sounds /e/ or /i/.

3. う-verbs: All other verbs are う-verbs. Note: ある is an う-verb even though it ends with る because the preceding sound is /a/. There are some exceptions to this rule. Among them, the ones you have learned are: かえる and はいる are う-verbs.

You can derive the dictionary (plain present affirmative) form in the following way.

Irregular verbs

Polite present affirmative form		Dictionary (plain present affirmative) form
きます (come)	→	くる
します (do)	→	する
べんきょうします (study)	→	べんきょうする

る-verbs

Change ます to る.

Polite present affirmative form		Dictionary (plain present affirmative) form
います (exist/s)	→	いる
おきます (get/s up)	→	おきる
たべます (eat/s)	→	たべる
ねます (sleep/s)	→	ねる

う -verbs

Remove ます from the polite present affirmative form and change the last vowel sound to /u/.

Polite present affirmative form			Dictionary (plain present affirmative) form	
あります (exist/s)	ari + ~~masu~~	→	aru	ある
かいます (buy/s)	kai + ~~masu~~	→	kau	かう
かきます (write/s)	kaki + ~~masu~~	→	kaku	かく
のみます (drink/s)	nomi + ~~masu~~	→	nomu	のむ
はなします (talk/s)	hanashi + ~~masu~~	→	hanasu	はなす
よみます (read/s)	yomi + ~~masu~~	→	yomu	よむ

スミス：田中<ruby>たなか</ruby>さんは　なにを　するのが　すきですか。
What do you like to do, Tanaka-san?

田中<ruby>たなか</ruby>：そうですね。　私<ruby>わたし</ruby>は　りょうりを　するのが　すきですね。
Let's see. I like to cook.
スミスさんは　どうですか。
How about you, Smith-san?

スミス：ぼくは　クラシックを　きくのが　すきです。
I like to listen to classical music.

- The plain present affirmative form of a verb is also called the dictionary form because it is used in dictionaries.

- In English, the gerund (-ing form of a verb) and the infinitive (to + verb) may be used as nouns, for example, *Seeing is believing* or *To play a musical instrument is fun*. In a similar manner, Japanese adds の to the plain present affirmative form of a verb to make a noun. It is also used to make a noun phrase out of a sentence, just like English *to* or ～ing, as in *Seeing is believing* or *To study Japanese is not an easy task*. This の is different from the pronoun の (one) and from particle の in noun の noun.

私<ruby>わたし</ruby>は　えいがを　みるのが　すきです。

I like watching movies.

えいがを　みるのは　おもしろいです。

Watching movies is fun.

はなしてみましょう

A. The following pictures illustrate activities that きむらさん likes. Describe
them, using 〜のが　すきです.

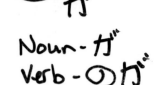

Noun - ガ
Verb - のガ

Example

きむらさんは　テニスを　するのが　すきです。

B. Work with a partner. Look at the pictures in exercise A. Choose five activities that you think your partner likes. Ask your partner whether he/she likes
to do them.

Example

A: 〜さんは　およぐのが　すきですか。

B: はい、すきです。 or いいえ、　あまり　すきじゃありま
せん。

C. Look at the following chart and describe each person's likes and dislikes.

Example

やまだ
山田さんは　パーティに　いくのが　すきですが、パーティ
を　するのは　あまり　すきじゃありません。

	☺	☹
やまだ 山田	パーティに　いきます	パーティを　します
おがわ 小川	あそびます	べんきょうします
やまもと 山本	レストランで　しょくじを　します	うちで　たべます
おおかわ 大川	えいがを　みます	ファミコンを　します
ささき	コンサートに　いきます	うたを　うたいます
たなか 田中	しゃしんを　とります	えを　かきます

くる (Kuru)
K.masu 来

Asobu
Asobimasu ~ Play

D. Work with a partner. Find out what he/she likes to do. どんな　こと *koto - things activities* means *what kinds of things/activities*. Then ask him/her other questions.

<u>Example</u>

A: 〜さんは　どんな　ことを　するのが　すきですか。

B: 私は　おいしい　りょうりを　たべるのが　すきです。

A: そうですか。どこで　よく　たべますか。なにを　よく　たべますか。

III. Listing nouns, using や

	Direct Object				
	Noun	Particle	Noun	Particle	
私は	スキー	や	テニス	を	よく　します。

I often ski and play tennis, among other things.

小川：　どんな　たべものが　すきですか。
What kinds of food do you like?

ブラウン：やさいや　くだものが　すきです。
I like vegetables and fruit, among other things.

アリス：　どこで　よく　べんきょうしますか。
Where do you often study?

ささき：　としょかんや　がくせいかいかんで　よく
べんきょうします。
I often study in the library and the student union, among other places.

● Like the particle と, や means *and*. The important difference is that nouns connected with や form a list of representative examples, whereas と is used to give an all-inclusive list.

私は　<u>りんごと　オレンジ</u>が　すきです。

I like apples and oranges. (There is no implication as to whether I like other fruit.)

私は　<u>りんごや　オレンジ</u>が　すきです。

I like apples and oranges. (This sentence has an implication that I like other fruit.)

- と and や can connect only noun phrases. You will learn how to connect verbs and adjectives in Chapter 9.

はなしてみましょう

A. Answer the following questions, using either や or と. - HOMEWORK

Example

どんな　スポーツを　しますか。
<u>テニスや　スキーを　します。</u>

1. しゅうまつに　どこに　よく　いきますか。
2. どんな　本^{ほん}を　よく　よみますか。
3. 今日^{きょう}は　なんじに　じゅぎょうが　ありますか。
4. どんな　おんがくを　よく　ききますか。
5. どこで　ひるごはんを　たべますか。

B. Work in groups of three. Each person thinks of a country and a few famous things about that country. The other members of the group guess the country, using the famous things as clues.

Example

A: この　くにには　ヨセミテ (Yosemite) や
　　イエローストーン (Yellowstone) が　あります。

B: アメリカですか。

A: はい、そうです。

C. Work with a partner. Find at least three things that your partner likes in each category. Keep track of them in the chart on the next page.

Example

A: どんな　たべものが　すきですか。

B: 〜や　〜が　すきです。

A: 〜も　すきですか。

B: ええ、すきです。／いいえ、〜は　ちょっと。

A: じゃあ、〜は　どうですか。

B: 〜は　すきです。

	すきな　もの		
のみもの たべもの おんがく スポーツ いろ			

D. Work with a partner. Describe the buildings and facilities of your hometown and neighborhood to your partner.

Example

私（わたし）の　まちは　とても　大（おお）きいです。まちには　りっぱな
としょかんや　びょういんが　あります。私（わたし）の　うちの
ちかくには　〜や　〜が　あります。

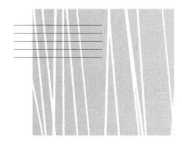

IV. Making comparisons, using いちばん and 〜の　ほうが　〜より

A. Expressing superlatives, using いちばん

Question						
Noun Phrase (scope)		Question Word		Superlative		
スポーツの　中（なか）	で	なに	が	いちばん	すきです	か。

Which sport do you like the best?

Answer			
Subject		Superlative	
やきゅう	が	いちばん	すきです。

I like baseball the best.

B. Asking about preferences

Question							
Noun (choice A)	Particle	Noun (choice B)	Particle	Question Word	Particle	Noun	Particle
とうきょう	と	きょうと	と	どちら	の	ほう	が すき ですか。

Which do you like better, Tokyo or Kyoto?

Answer						
Noun (preferred)	Particle	Noun	Particle	Noun (less preferred)	Particle	
きょうと	の	ほう	が	（とうきょう	より）	すきです。

I like Kyoto better (than Tokyo).

C. Expressing a lack of preference

Noun A	Particle	Noun B	Particle	
とうきょう	も	きょうと	も	すきです。

I like both Tokyo and Kyoto.

Noun A	Particle	Noun B	Particle	
とうきょう	も	きょうと	も	すきじゃありません。

I don't like either Tokyo or Kyoto.

田中：　この　クラスで　だれが　いちばん　よく
べんきょうしますか。

Who studies the most in this class?

チョー：山田さんが　いちばん　よく　べんきょうします。／
山田さんです。

Yamada-san studies the most. / It's Yamada-san.

田中：　ペプシコーラと　コカコーラと　どちらの　ほうが
　　　　おいしいですか。

> Which is more delicious, Pepsi Cola or Coca Cola?

チョー：ペプシコーラも　コカコーラも　おいしいです。

> Both Pepsi Cola and Coca Cola are delicious.

　　　　でも、私は　ペプシコーラの　ほうが　すきです。

> But, I like Pepsi better.

田中：　木村さんと　山本さんと　どちらの　ほうが　よく
　　　　べんきょうしますか。

> Who studies more, Kimura-san or Yamamoto-san?

チョー：山本さんの　ほうが　よく　べんきょうします。

> Yamamoto-san studies more.

- いちばん means *number one* or *first*. To form a superlative, いちばん must be followed by an adjective or an adverb. いちばん　先生 is a common mistake; the correct form is いちばん　いい　先生.

- The phrase 〜の　中で means *among* 〜 or *within* 〜. 〜の中 is omitted if the preceding noun is a place noun.

  たべものの　中で　なにが　いちばん　すきですか。

  Which food do you like the best?

  日本で　どの　まちが　いちばん　ふるいですか。

  Which town is the oldest in Japan?

- When a comparison is being made between two nouns, both of the items being compared always precede より. 〜より can be omitted if obvious from the context.

- If you want to say *a little more* and *much more* when making a comparison, use すこし and ずっと, respectively.

  エベレスト山の　ほうが　富士山より　<u>ずっと</u>　たかいです。

  Mt. Everest is much higher than Mt. Fuji.

  とうきょうの　ほうが　ニューヨークより　<u>すこし</u>　大きいです

  Tokyo is a little bigger than New York.

- 〜も　〜も can be used in a positive or a negative statement. *A* も *B* も + *affirmative statement* means *both A and B* , and *A* も *B* も + *negative statement* or in a negative statement means *neither A nor B.*

やきゅうも　バスケットボールも　すきです。

I like both baseball and basketball.

ロックも　ジャズも　あまり　すきじゃありません。

I like neither rock nor jazz very much.

はなして　みましょう

A.　Answer the following questions.

Example

おんがくの　中で　なにが　いちばん　すきですか。
ジャズが　いちばん　すきです。

1. スポーツの　中で　なにが　いちばん　すきですか。
2. たべものの　中で　なにが　いちばん　きらいですか。
3. のみものの　中で　なにを　いちばん　よく　のみますか。
4. どんな　おんがくを　いちばん　よく　ききますか。
5. この　クラスで　だれが　いちばん　よく　べんきょう
   しますか。

B.　Work with a partner. Ask your partner about things and places that have the most in some attribute using the given adjective and noun. Then check the answers.

Example

川／大きい

A:　アメリカで　いちばん　大きい　川は　どれですか。

B:　ミシシッピー川です。

1. 川／大きい
2. 山／たかい
3. まち／ふるい
4. たてもの／ゆうめい
5. 小さい／しゅう (state)
6. きれい／こうえん

C. Order the two items in parentheses based on the meaning of the adjective.
Then create a comparative sentence.

Example

すき　（こうちゃ／コーヒー）
こうちゃの　ほうが　コーヒーより　すきです。

1. 大変（たいへん）　（日本語（にほんご）／スペイン語（ご））
2. 大（おお）きい　（ニューヨーク／とうきょう）
3. いそがしい　（先生（せんせい）／学生（がくせい））
4. むずかしい　（経済学（けいざいがく）／工学（こうがく））
5. いい　（あたらしい　うち／ふるい　うち）
6. しずか　（大（おお）きい　いぬ／小（ちい）さい　いぬ）

D. Work with a partner. Find out at least two things he/she likes; then ask
him/her to rank those things. If he/she likes both equally, write *Both* in
column 1.

Example

A:　どんな　くだものが　すきですか。

B:　りんごや　オレンジが　すきです。

A:　りんごと　オレンジと　どちらの　ほうが　すきですか。

B:　オレンジの　ほうが　すきです。or オレンジも　りんご
　　も　すきです。

	1	2
くだもの	オレンジ	りんご
のみもの		
たべもの		
おんがく		
スポーツ		

E. Work with a partner. Ask your partner what he/she likes in each of the following categories. He/She must name at least three things. Then ask your
partner what he/she likes better and rank them.

Example

A: どんな　のみものを　よく　のみますか。

B: コーヒーや　コーラを　よく　のみます。

A: こうちゃも　のみますか。

B: ええ、のみますよ。

A: じゃあ、どれが　いちばん　すきですか。

B: そうですね。コーヒーが　いちばん　すきですね。

A: じゃあ、こうちゃと　コーラと　どちらの　ほうが　すきですか。

B: コーラの　ほうが　すきです。／コーラも　こうちゃも　すきです。

	1	2	3
のみもの			
たべもの			
おんがく			
スポーツ			

V. Requesting and giving an explanation or a confirmation, using the prenominal and plain present forms + んです

A. はい／いいえ questions

Question				
	Verb (plain affirmative)			
うちに	かえる	ん	です	か。

Are you going home? (I think you are.)

Answer				
ええ、	もう	ごじ	です	から。

Yes, because it's already five o'clock.

Question						
Question Word			**Verb (plain negative)**			
どうして	さかな	を	たべない	ん	です	か。

Why don't you eat fish?

Answer				
		な-adjective (prenominal)		
さかな	は	きらいな	ん	です。

I don't like fish.

Plain Present Negative Forms

The plain present negative forms are used in the 〜んです construction as well as in many other structures in Japanese. The following is the formation of the plain present negative forms of adjectives and verbs.

Adjectives and the copula verb

		Polite present negative form	Plain present negative form
い-adjectives	ひろい (spacious)	ひろくないです (or ひろくありません)	→ ひろくない
い-adjectives	いい (good)	よくないです (or よくありません)	→ よくない
な-adjectives	りっぱ (gorgeous)	りっぱじゃないです (or りっぱじゃありません)	→ りっぱじゃない
な-adjectives	きれい (pretty, clean)	きれいじゃないです (or きれいじゃありません)	→ きれいじゃない

		Polite present negative form	Plain present negative form
Noun + Copula verb	<ruby>日本人<rt>にほんじん</rt></ruby>	<ruby>日本人<rt>にほんじん</rt></ruby>じゃ ないです (or <ruby>日本人<rt>にほんじん</rt></ruby>じゃあ りません)	<ruby>日本人<rt>にほんじん</rt></ruby>じゃない
Noun + Copula verb	ここ (here)	ここじゃ ないです (or ここじゃあ りません)	ここじゃない

Irregular verbs

Polite present affirmative form		Plain negative form
<u>き</u>ます(come/s)	→	<u>こ</u>ない
<u>し</u>ます(do/es)	→	<u>し</u>ない
べんきょう<u>し</u>ます(study/studies)	→	べんきょう<u>し</u>ない

る-verbs

Change ます to ない.

Polite present affirmative form		Plain negative form
い<u>ます</u>(exist/s)	→	い<u>ない</u>
おき<u>ます</u> (wake/s up)	→	おき<u>ない</u>
たべ<u>ます</u>(eat/s)	→	たべ<u>ない</u>
ね<u>ます</u>(sleep/s)	→	ね<u>ない</u>

kiku/kikanai nomu/nomanai くる こない Suru, shinai
iku/ikanai kuru, konai
neru/nenai iru/inai

う -verbs

Remove ます from the polite present affirmative form. Change the vowel sound /i/ to /a/ and add ない.

Polite present affirmative form			Plain negative form	
かきます (write/s)	/kaki/ + /masu/	→	/kaka/ + /nai/	かかない
のみます (drink/s)	/nomi/ + /masu/	→	/noma/ + /nai/	のまない
はなします (talk/s)	/hanashi/ + /masu/	→	/hanasa/ + /nai/	はなさない
よみます (read/s)	/yomi/ + /masu/	→	/yoma/ + /nai/	よまない

If there is no consonant before the /i/ sound of the polite present affirmative form as in かいます, change /i/ to /wa/ instead of /a/. The plain present negative form of あります is ない.

Polite present affirmative form			Plain negative form	
かいます (buy/s)	/kai/ + /masu/	→	/kawa/ + /nai/	かわない
あります (exist/s)	/ari/ + /masu/	→	/nai/	ない

Formation of the 〜んです Construction

〜んです is preceded by an adjective or a verb. Right before 〜んです, the prenominal form of an adjective or a noun + な is used for an affirmative sentence. For a negative sentence, use the plain negative form.

Adjectives and copula verb	Polite present affirmative form	〜んです (affirmative)	〜んです (negative)
い-adjectives	ひろいです (It's spacious.)	ひろいんです	ひろくないんです
い-adjectives	いいです (It's good.)	いいんです	よくないんです
な-adjectives	りっぱです (It's gorgeous.)	りっぱなんです	りっぱじゃないんです
な-adjectives	きれいです (It's pretty.)	きれいなんです	きれいじゃないんです
Copula verb	日本人です (It's a Japanese person.)	日本人なんです	日本人じゃないんです
Copula verb	ここです (It's here.)	ここなんです	ここじゃないんです

In the case of verbs, the plain affirmative or negative form of a verb is used before 〜んです.

Irregular verbs

Polite present affirmative form	～んです (affirmative)	～んです(negative)
<u>き</u>ます(come/s) 来	くるんです 来	こないんです 来
<u>し</u>ます(do/es)	するんです	しないんです
べんきょう<u>し</u>ます(study/studies)	べんきょうするんです	べんきょうしないんです

る-verbs

Polite present affirmative form	～んです (affirmative)	～んです(negative)
い<u>ます</u>(exist/s)	いるんです	いないんです
おき<u>ます</u> (wake/s up)	おきるんです	おきないんです
たべ<u>ます</u>(eat/s)	たべるんです	たべないんです
ね<u>ます</u>(sleep/s)	ねるんです	ねないんです

う-verbs

Polite present affirmative form	～んです (affirmative)	～んです(negative)
あります(exist/s)	あるんです	ないんです
かいます(buy/s)	かうんです	かわないんです
かきます(write/s)	かくんです	かかないんです
のみます(drink/s)	のむんです	のまないんです
はなします(talk/s)	はなすんです	はなさないんです
よみます(read/s)	よむんです	よまないんです

- ～んです is used to confirm a speaker's assumption, to give or request an explanation or a reason. In key sentence A on page 219, the speaker assumes that the listener is going home, so he/she asks for confirmation or details by using ～んですか. The listener then gives a reason for going home. If ～ますか is used instead of ～んですか, the speaker makes no assumption and simply asks whether he/she is going home.

やまだ
山田：　うちに　かえりますか。
Are you going home? (I have no clue as to what you are going to do.)

ロペス：ええ、かえります。
Yes, I am.

- どうして (*why*) asks for a reason, as in key sentence B on page 220, and it is frequently used with 〜んです, implying that an explanation is being asked for. The answer to such a question will also be given with 〜んです as well as 〜から, indicating that the explanation is being given. In general, から makes more explicit reasoning than 〜んです.

- どうしてですか means *Why is that?*

- 〜んです can be used to make an excuse or to explain the reasons for a situation without indicating it explicitly. For example, in the following example, Mr. Kimura gives an excuse when Alice approaches him.

> アリス： あのう、すみませんが。Excuse me.
>
> 木村_{きむら}： すみません。いま ちょっと いそがしいんです。
>   Sorry, I'm slightly tied up right now.

- 〜んです can also imply surprise. For example, Tanaka-san indicates her surprise by using 〜んですか in the following example.

> スミス： あした びょういんに いきます。
>   I'm going to a hospital tomorrow.
>
> 田中_{たなか}： えっ、びょういんに いくんですか。
>   What? Are you going to the hospital?
>
> スミス： ええ、ともだちが しゅじゅつを するんですよ。
>   (しゅじゅつを する have surgery)
>   Yes, my friend is having surgery.

はなして みましょう

A. You have gotten to know Alice a little. Ask questions to confirm the things you think you know about her.

Example

アリスさんは ニューヨークが すきです。
<u>アリスさんは ニューヨークが すきなんですか。</u>

1. アリスさんは さかなを あまり たべません。
2. アリスさんの うちは とても 大_{おお}きいです。
3. アリスさんの へやは とても きれいです。
4. アリスさんは ぜんぜん りょうりを つくりません。
5. アリスさんは よく レストランで しょくじを します。
6. アリスさんの くるまは あまり よくありません。
7. アリスさんは にんじんが すきじゃありません。

B. Work with a partner. Tell your partner which things you don't do often and why you don't. Your partner will write this down.

Example

A: ぼくは　あまり　うんどうを　しません。

B: どうして　しないんですか。

A: うんどうを　するのは　きらいなんです。

B writes: <u>A さんは　うんどうがきらいですから、あまり</u>
<u>しません。</u>

C. Work with a partner. Think of three things that college students in your country typically do on weekends. Ask your classmate if he/she is planning to do them this weekend, and if not, why. Find out the most common reasons why people don't do these things.

Example

A: こんしゅうの　しゅうまつに　でかけますか。

B: いいえ、でかけません。

A: どうして　でかけないんですか。／どうしてですか。

B: げつようびに　テストが　あるんです。

D. Work with a partner. You are planning to travel abroad together. First decide where to go; then ask each other about what you would like to do and why.

Example

You have decided to go to Japan.

A: にほんで　なにを　しますか。

B: そうですね。りょこうを　しますね。

A: どこに　いくんですか。

B: きょうとに　いきます。

A: どうして　きょうとに　いくんですか。

B: きょうとには　ふるい　たてものが　たくさん　あるん
です。

In addition to **hiragana** and **katakana,** the Japanese writing system makes extensive use of **kanji,** which are characters borrowed from Chinese. When the Japanese adopted **kanji,** they also adopted the Chinese way of reading them. At the same time, the Japanese gave the Chinese characters Japanese readings for existing Japanese words. Consequently, a **kanji** character has two or sometimes more readings. The Chinese reading of a **kanji** is called the **on** reading and the Japanese reading the **kun** reading. For example, the **on** reading for the **kanji** 大 (big) is だい, as in 大学（だいがく）. Its **kun** reading is おお, as in 大（おお）きい. Chinese words incorporated into Japanese are usually given **on** readings, as in 大学（だいがく）, 学生（がくせい）, or 先生（せんせい）.

A **kanji** can be used only for its specific meaning. Thus, even if 五 (*five*) is read ご, one may not use it to replace the **hiragana** ご in おはようございます or あさごはん.

Kanji originated as pictographs, and some of these still retain their pictorial qualities. For example, 川 (river) developed from the picture 〲, 月 (moon) from 𖤘, and 山 (mountain) from 𖤙. The exact number of existing **kanji** has never been clear, but it is estimated to be more than 40,000. Approximately 3,000 **kanji** are commonly used in Japan. The Ministry of Education has designated 1,945 **kanji** for use in publications such as newspapers and magazines.

Learning **kanji** can be laborious. However, once a certain number of **kanji** have been learned, it becomes easier because one can make associations on the basis of their components. In dictionaries, **kanji** are classified according to 214 basic component shapes, or radicals, each of which has a meaning. The following **kanji,** which share the common radical 言, have something to do with language: 訳 (translation), 話 (talk), 語 (language), and 読 (reading).

A **kanji** is written according to a fixed stroke order. The general rule is to write from top to bottom and left to right, and horizontal lines are usually drawn before vertical lines.

In Japanese, **kanji** are used mostly for nouns and the stems of verbs, adjectives, and adverbs. Grammatical markers, such as particles and inflectional endings, are not written in **kanji.** For example, in the following sentence, the nouns わたし and さかな are written in **kanji** 私 and 魚, and the verb stem た of たべます is written in **kanji** 食. The particles は and を as well as the verb ending べます are written in **hiragana.**

私は魚を食べます。（わたしは　さかなを　たべます。*I eat fish.*）

Note the following format for the **kanji** charts used in this book.

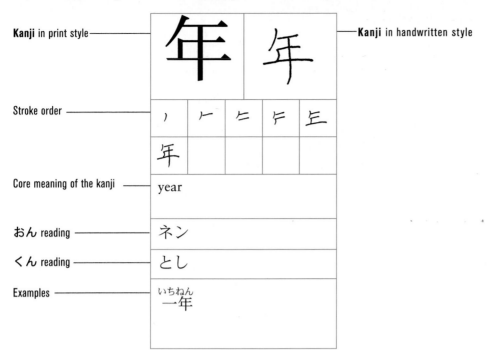

Kanji in print style — Kanji in handwritten style

Stroke order

Core meaning of the kanji — year

おん reading — ネン

くん reading — とし

Examples —
いちねん
一年

Writing kanji: Stroke order

Stroke order is very important not only in writing but also in reading, especially when you read handwritten style **kanji.** In the handwritten style, lines are often connected, and some strokes are simplified. The following are the basic rules for writing **kanji:**

1. Write from left to right.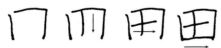

2. Write from top to bottom.

3. Write ⌐⌐ in the following way.

4. When you enclose a square, write the bottom line at the end.

5. It is also important to distinguish the following three types of strokes:

stop 生   release 大   hook 学

Some **kanji** are made from pictures:

☁ ⛰	山	mountain	
🌾 ⊞	田	rice field	
🏠 学	学	study, learn	

(A child in a school)

☀ ⊟	日	sun, day
大 人	人	person
生 生	生	life, to live

Some **kanji** that represent abstract ideas are made from symbols:

二 上	上	on, up, above
中 中	中	in, middle, center
大 大	大	big, large

⊤ ⊤	下	under, below
米 本	本	root, book
小 小	小	small

山 山	日 日	田 田
丨 山 山	丨 冂 月 日	丨 冂 冂 毌 田
mountain	sun, day	rice field
サン	ニチ、ニ、ジツ、カ	デン
やま	ひ、び	た だ
やまだ 山田さん やました 山下さん	にほん 日本 にちようび 日曜日 まいにち 毎日	たなか 田中さん やまだ 山田さん

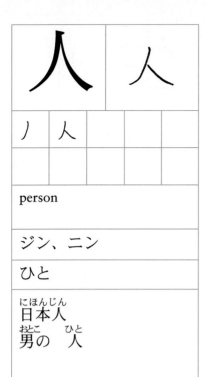

人

| ノ | 人 | | |

person

ジン、ニン

ひと

<ruby>日本人<rt>にほんじん</rt></ruby>

<ruby>男<rt>おとこ</rt></ruby>の <ruby>人<rt>ひと</rt></ruby>

上

| 丨 | 卜 | 上 | |

on, up, above

ジョウ

うえ、かみ

つくえの <ruby>上<rt>うえ</rt></ruby>

<ruby>木<rt>き</rt></ruby>の <ruby>上<rt>うえ</rt></ruby>

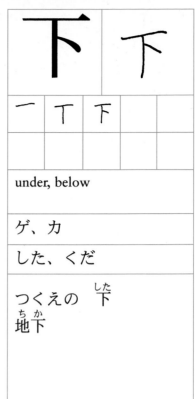

下

| 一 | 丁 | 下 | |

under, below

ゲ、カ

した、くだ

つくえの <ruby>下<rt>した</rt></ruby>

<ruby>地下<rt>ちか</rt></ruby>

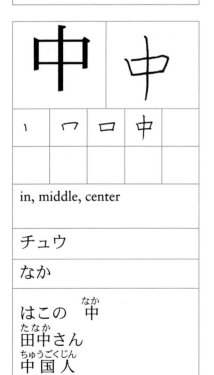

中

| 丨 | 口 | 口 | 中 |

in, middle, center

チュウ

なか

はこの <ruby>中<rt>なか</rt></ruby>

<ruby>田中<rt>たなか</rt></ruby>さん

<ruby>中国人<rt>ちゅうごくじん</rt></ruby>

大

| 一 | ナ | 大 | |

big, large

ダイ

おお（きい）

<ruby>大学<rt>だいがく</rt></ruby>

<ruby>大<rt>おお</rt></ruby>きい <ruby>人<rt>ひと</rt></ruby>

<ruby>大学生<rt>だいがくせい</rt></ruby>

<ruby>大川<rt>おおかわ</rt></ruby>さん

小

| 丨 | 小 | 小 | |

small

ショウ

ちい（さい）、お

<ruby>小<rt>ちい</rt></ruby>さい <ruby>車<rt>くるま</rt></ruby>

<ruby>小川<rt>おがわ</rt></ruby>さん

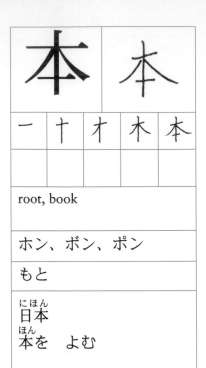

一 | 十 | 才 | 木 | 本

root, book

ホン、ボン、ポン

もと

にほん
日本
ほん
本を　よむ

ヽ | ゛ | ゛゛ | ゛゛ゝ

学 学 学

to study, learn

ガク、ガッ

まな（ぶ）

がくせい
学生
だいがく
大学
がくせいかいかん
学生会館
がっこう
学校

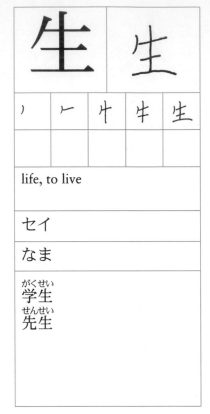

丿 | ﾉ一 | 牛 | 生 | 生

life, to live

セイ

なま

がくせい
学生
せんせい
先生

丿 | ﾉ一 | 牛 | 生 | 先

先

ahead, previous

セン

さき

せんせい
先生
せんしゅう
先週

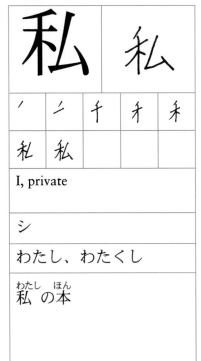

丿 | ﾉ二 | 千 | 禾 | 禾

私 私

I, private

シ

わたし、わたくし

わたし　ほん
私 の 本

丿 | 刂 | 川

river

セン

かわ、がわ

かわ
アマゾン川
かわ
川の　そば
おおかわ
大川さん

れんしゅう
練習　(Practice)

Read the following sentences written in **hiragana, katakana,** and **kanji.**

1. 山田さんは日曜日に大学に行きます。
2. 田中先生は日本人の日本語の先生です。
3. 私の車は小さいです。でも、山下さんの車はとても大きいです。
4. つくえの上に大きい猫がいます。まどの下に小さい犬がいます。
5. その箱の中に私の本があります。
6. リンさんは中国から来ました。

じょうずな　よみかた

Word formation

Many words consist of one or more words or of prefixes and suffixes. It is important to make use of these word clusters to guess meanings and to increase your vocabulary. For example, the suffix 〜や indicates a store or a shop, and さかな means *fish*. So what does さかなや mean? How about にくや and くだものや?

よむまえに

Break down the following words and determine their meaning.

Example

だいがくいんせい
大学院生
だいがくいん and 〜せい, *graduate school* and *student* = *graduate student*

1. フランス人
2. うんどうします
3. そうじします
4. 大学生
5. 三年生
6. 毎日
7. すしや
8. 大すき

いとうさんの　しゅみ

ことばの　リスト

たとえば　for example

モーツァルト　Mozart

ベートーベン　Beethoven

　私の趣味はスポーツと音楽です。スポーツの中では　テニスが一番好きです。それから、エアロビクスとスキーも大好きです。でも、野球やゴルフはあまり好きじゃありません。バスケットボールは見るのは好きですが、するのはあまり好きじゃないんです。

　音楽は明るい音楽の方が好きです。ポップスやジャズはとても好きです。クラシックは好きな音楽もありますが、きらいなのもあります。たとえば、モーツァルトは大好きです。でも、ベートーベンはあまり好きじゃありません。

わかりましたか

A. Answer the following questions in Japanese.

1. いとうさんの　しゅみは　なんですか。
2. いとうさんは　スキーと　バスケットボールと　どちらの　ほうが　すきですか。
3. いとうさんは　どんな　スポーツが　きらいですか。
4. いとうさんは　どんな　おんがくを　よく　ききますか。
5. いとうさんは　だれの　おんがくを　ききますか。

B. Underline the following transitional words in the text, and observe how they help indicate what the relationship is between the sentences.

それから　in addition, also, and

でも　but

C. Write a short paragraph about your hobbies.

じょうずな　ききかた

Identifying conversation fillers

There are many conversation fillers in English, such as *mm, you know, uh, aha,* and *well.* The equivalents of these in Japanese are ふうん, でね, あのう, ええ, and そうですね. These words have little meaning, but they do serve a purpose, as they keep the channels of communication open when the person responding does not know what to say.

A. Listen to the following short statements and conversations. Circle the fillers you hear.

1. あのう　　ええ　　そうですね　　でね　　ふうん
2. あのう　　ええ　　そうですね　　でね　　ふうん
3. あのう　　ええ　　そうですね　　でね　　ふうん
4. あのう　　ええ　　そうですね　　でね　　ふうん
5. あのう　　ええ　　そうですね　　でね　　ふうん

B. 日本人の　学生に　聞く　(Interviews with Japanese students). Listen to the interviews between the reporter for a student newspaper and four Japanese students who are visiting a college campus. Fill in the chart with their names, what they like, and what they like to do.

	なまえ	すき
Interview 1		
Interview 2		
Interview 3		
Interview 4		

  DICT-A-CONVERSATION

You, Smith-san, are at a party and meet a Japanese student, Sugiyama-san. After introducing yourself, you start to talk to him about his hobbies.

スミス：　　すぎやまさんの　しゅみは　なんですか。

すぎやま：　_____

　　　　　　_____

スミス：　＿＿＿＿＿＿＿＿＿＿＿＿＿＿＿＿＿＿＿＿

すぎやま：　＿＿＿＿＿＿＿＿＿＿＿＿＿＿＿＿＿＿＿＿

スミス：　＿＿＿＿＿＿＿＿＿＿＿＿＿＿＿＿＿＿＿＿

すぎやま：　＿＿＿＿＿＿＿＿＿＿＿＿＿＿＿＿＿＿＿＿

スミス：　＿＿＿＿＿＿＿＿＿＿＿＿＿＿＿＿＿＿＿＿

すぎやま：　＿＿＿＿＿＿＿＿＿＿＿＿＿＿＿＿＿＿＿＿

ききじょうず　はなしじょうず

Giving positive feedback with も and marking a contrast with は

Like そうですか and そうですね, you can use the particles も (similarity) and は (contrast) to carry on a conversation more smoothly. When the person you are talking to mentions something that you have in common, use も to give the person positive feedback.

アリス：　山田さんは　どんな　スポーツを　みるのが
　　　　　すきですか。

山田：　　やきゅうを　みるのが　すきです。

アリス：　ああ、そうですか。私<u>も</u>　やきゅうが　とても　すき
　　　　　ですよ。

By establishing a point in common, the conversation can now progress into subtopics, such as which sports teams you like. In other situations, however, you may not share common interests, in which cases you can use は to mark the contrast:

アリス：　山田さんは　どんな　スポーツを　みるのが　すきで
　　　　　すか。

山田：　　やきゅうを　みるのが　すきです。

アリス：　ああ、そうですか。　私<u>は</u>　テニスが　とても　すき
　　　　　ですよ。

Be careful not to dwell too much on differences as this may become disruptive. You might want to include an interest of yours in a follow-up question about the other person's interests, as in the following exchange:

アリス：　山田さんは　どんな　スポーツを　みるのが
　　　　　すきですか。

山田：　　やきゅうを　みるのが　すきです。

アリス：　ああ、そうですか。　テニスも　すきですか。
　　　　orテニスは　どうですか。

山田：　　ええ、テニスも　よく　みます。
　　　　orそうですね、テニスは　あまり　（すきじゃありません。）

Carrying out a conversation is like playing catch: You must take turns speaking and listening while focusing on common topics. It is important to be aware of these strategies when speaking in a second language. Being a good listener is key to being a successful communicator.

Work with a partner. Choose a topic of conversation from the following list or create a topic of your own. Talk about your individual preferences regarding the topic and incorporate the communicative strategies you have learned.

1. leisure activities
2. music
3. sports

4. food
5. movies
6. books

そうごうれんしゅう

Work in groups of three. Look at the travel advertisements on the following pages. Decide with the other members of the group which travel plan is the best and explain why you think so.

ことばの　リスト

やすい (inexpensive), たかい (expensive) , プラン (plan)

Example

A:　どの　りょこうプランが　すきですか。

B:　(pointing at one plan) わたしは　これが　すきです。

C:　(pointing at a different one) ぼくは　これの　ほうが　すきです。
　　このほうが　やすいですから。

ロールプレイ

1. You are at a party and you meet a person. Approach him/her, introduce yourself, and start a conversation. Find out about him/her to see if he/she shares your interests.

2. You are planning a blind date for a friend of yours. Find out what kind of person he/she likes.

3. You are looking for an apartment. Tell your agent what your preferences are.

Nouns

うた（歌）song *uta*
エアロビクス　aerobics
オレンジ　orange
クラシック　classical music
こうちゃ（紅茶）black tea
コーラ　cola
ゴルフ　golf
さかな（魚）fish
ジャズ　jazz
しゅみ（趣味）hobby
ジョギング　jogging
しょくじ（食事）dining *Shyokuji*
　しょくじを　する（食事をする）(to) dine *Shyokuji*
スキー　skiing
スポーツ　sports
たべもの（食べ物）food
たまご（卵）egg
テニス　tennis
トマト　tomato
ドライブ　driving (pleasure driving)
にく（肉）meat
にんじん（人参）carrot
のみもの（飲み物）beverage, drink

パーティ　party
ハイキング　hiking
バスケットボール　basketball (sometimes abbreviated バスケット or バスケ)
バナナ　banana
ビール　beer
ファミコン　family computer (computer game, Nintendo)
フットボール　(American) football
ボーリング　bowling
ポップス　pops (popular music)
やきゅう（野球）baseball
やさい（野菜）vegetable
やま（山）mountain
りょうり（料理）cooking, food (cuisine)
　りょうりを　する（料理をする）(to) cook
りょこう（旅行）traveling
りんご　apple
レジャー　leisure
レタス　lettuce
ロック　rock and roll
ワイン　wine

う -verbs

あそぶ（遊ぶ）(to) play, (to) have fun
うたう（歌う）(to) sing
およぐ（泳ぐ）(to) swim

とる　(to) take
　しゃしんを　とる（写真をとる）(to) take a picture

い -adjectives

おいしい　delicious, tasty, good *oishii*

な-adjectives

きらい（な）（嫌い（な）） dislike; hate
すき（な）（好き（な）） liked
だいすき（な）（大好き（な）） like very much

Conjunctions

そして　　and　　*soshite*
それから　　and, in addition, also　*sorekara*
でも　　but　　*demo*

Adverbs

すこし（少し） a little, a few　*skoshi*
ずっと　　much more, by far　*zu'to*

Expressions

どうですか。 How about 〜?　*doodesuka*

Passive Vocabulary

Nouns

あか（赤） the color red　*aka*
あお（青） the color blue　*ao*
しゅう（州） state (in the United States,
　Canada, and Australia)

しゅじゅつ（手術） surgical operation　*shyujyutsu*
しろ（白） the color white　*shiro*
てんいん（店員） salesperson　*tenyin*

Adverbs

もう　　already　*moo*

Conjunctions

とくに（特に） especially, particularly　*tokuni*

Expressions

わからないんですよ。（分からないんですよ） I don't understand.

Food and beverages

いちご（苺）strawberry
えび（海老）shrimp
おちゃ（お茶）green tea
キャベツ　cabbage
ぎゅうにく（牛肉）beef
きゅうり　cucumber
ジュース　juice
たまねぎ　onion
とりにく（鳥肉）chicken

ねぎ　scallion
ピーマン　green pepper
ぶたにく（豚肉）pork
ぶどう　grape
ほうれんそう　spinach
みかん　mandarin orange
ミルク　milk
メロン　melon

Sports

からて（空手）karate
キャッチボール　playing catch
けんどう（剣道）kendo (Japanese-style fencing)
サッカー　soccer
じゅうどう（柔道）judo

すいえい（水泳）swimming
スケート　skating
ソフトボール　softball
たいそう（体操）calisthenics, gymnastics
つり（釣り）fishing
バレーボール　volleyball

Pastimes and interests

いけばなを　する（生け花を　する）
　flower arrangement ((to) arrange flowers)
カラオケで　うたう（カラオケで　歌う）(to) sing with karaoke (singing place)
きってを　あつめる（切手を　集める）
　(to) collect stamps
ゲームを　する　(to) play a game
サイクリングに　いく（サイクリングに　行く）(to) cycle
ハイキングに　いく（ハイキングに　行く）(to) go hiking

はくぶつかんに　いく（博物館に　行く）(to) go to a museum
パチンコを　する　(to) play pachinko
ピアノを　ひく　(to) play the piano
ピクニックに　いく（ピクニックに　行く）(to) go on a picnic
ゆうえんちに　いく（遊園地に　行く）
　(to) go to an amusement park

CHAPTER 8

だい　八か

Entrance to a Japanese department store

かいもの

SHOPPING

Functions	Making an inquiry or a request; Expressing quantities and numbers
New Vocabulary	Clothing and accessories; Sizes, amounts, and prices; Shopping; Departments in a department store
Dialogue	デパートで (At the Department Store)
Culture	Japanese department stores; Customer service; Methods of payment
Language	I. Making a request, using the て-form of a verb + 下さい
	II. Using Chinese origin numbers, 100 and above
	III. Referring to quantities with numbers and counters, using まい, 本, ひき, さつ and Japanese origin numbers
	IV. Referring to prices and floor levels, using 円 and かい
	V. Abbreviating verbal expressions, using です
Kanji	Using **kanji** for numbers; Variations in the pronunciation of **kanji**
Reading	Scanning
Listening	Recognizing the characteristics of speech
Communication	Asking someone to repeat or reword a phrase

あたらしい ことば

A. ようふくと アクセサリー (Clothing and accessories).

ネックレス necklace

くつ shoes *Kutsu*

ハンドバッグ handbag

セーター sweater *seta*

スカート skirt

コート coat

ジャケット jacket

ネクタイ tie *nekutai*

シャツ shirt *Shyatsu*

ベルト belt

ズボン pants/trousers

くつした socks *Kutsu shita*

かばん bag, briefcase

パンツ shorts, briefs *pantsu*

Tシャツ t-shirt

ジーンズ jeans

かさ umbrella *Kasa*

1. What are the people in the picture wearing?

2. What are you wearing?

3. What is your teacher wearing?

4. What have you bought recently?

5. Besides the items listed above, what else do you own? Ask your instructor what those additional items are called in Japanese.

B. 大きさ、りょう、ねだん (Sizes, amounts, and prices).

たかい expensive *takai*

やすい inexpensive *Yasui*

たくさん a lot *takusan*

すこし a little, less *skoshi*

もっと a lot more *motto*

もうすこし a little more *moskoshi*

もう すこし大きい a little bigger *mo skoshi ookii*

もう すこし 小さい a little smaller *chisai*

もっと大きい a lot bigger *motto ookii*

もっと小さい a lot smaller *motto chisai*

You are thinking about going shopping. The following table lists the items the store carries. Describe those items in column A and the items that you want in column B. For example, if you want to buy a size-L coat without spending much money, write たかい *and* ちいさい in column A and もっと　やすい *and* もっと　おおきい in column B.

Item	Price/Quantity	Size	A (description)	B (what you want)
くろい　コート	¥50,000	S		
スカート	¥2,000	45 inches		
Ｔシャツ	¥500	L		
ジーンズ	¥8,000	32 inches		
バナナ	1			
りんご	30			

C. かいもの (Shopping). Describe each of the following pictures using the verb phrases below. Then, answer the questions about the items you own.

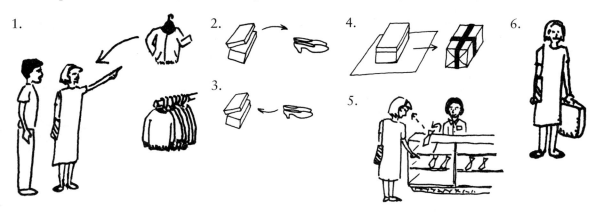

1. ～を　とる　(to) take, pick up

2. ～を　はこから　だす　(to) take ～ out of a box

3. はこに　～を　いれる　(to) put ～ in a box

4. ～を　つつむ　(to) wrap

5. ～を　みせる　(to) show ～

6. ～を　もつ　(to) hold ～
　　～を　もっている　(to) own ～

1. どんな　ふくを　もっていますか。
2. どんな　かばんを　もっていますか。
3. どんな　くるまを　もっていますか。

D. うりば (Departments in a department store). Guess where various departments are found in a local, large department store. Then list a few items that are sold in each department.

ふじんふくうりば　women's clothing
しんしふくうりば　men's clothing
しょくひんうりば　food
かばんうりば　luggage
アクセサリーうりば　accessories
レコードうりば　music
ぶんぼうぐうりば　stationery

	うりば	Items
七階 （7 F）		
六階 （6 F）		
五階 （5 F）		
四階 （4 F）		
三階 （3 F）		
二階 （2 F）		
一階 （1 F）		
地下一階 （B 1）		

ダイアローグ

はじめに

A. 日本語で　こたえて下さい。Answer the following questions in Japanese.

1. よく　デパートに　いきますか。デパートで　なにを　よく　かいますか。

2. Describe a typical department store where you live.

B. Remember to follow these three steps when working with the dialogue: (1) Look at the **manga.** (2) Listen to the dialogue. (3) Match the lines in the dialogue with the **manga** frames by writing the frame number next to the person's name.

デパートで

STUDENT

きょうは　石田さんの　たんじょうび (birthday) です。
アリスさんは　デパートに　いきました。

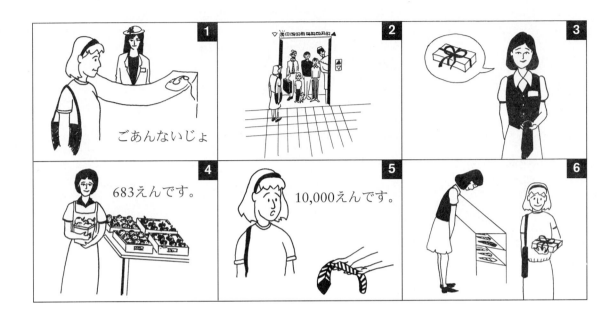

____ アリス：　　　　　　すみません。しょくひんうりばは
　　　　　　　　　　　　どこに　ありますか。

____ あんないがかり：しょくひんうりばは　地下一階に
　　　(Clerk at　　　　　ございます。
　　　information desk)

アリスさんは　しょくひんうりばに　いきました。

____ てんいん (Salesperson): いらっしゃいませ。

____ アリス：　　　　　　あのう、この　りんごを　みっつ
　　　　　　　　　　　　下さい。それから　その
　　　　　　　　　　　　オレンジを　いつつ　下さい。

____ てんいん：　　　　　はい。　りんごを　みっつと
　　　　　　　　　　　　オレンジ　いつつですね。
　　　　　　　　　　　　ぜんぶで　８４０円　いただきます。

アリスさんは　エレベーターの　中に　います。

_____　エレベーターガール：たいへん　おまたせいたしま

(Elevator operator)　　　　　　した。このエレベーターは　三階、

五階、九階に　とまります。

つぎは　三階で　ございます。

_____　アリス：　　　　　あのう、しんしふくうりばは
なんかいに　ありますか。

_____　エレベーターガール：しんしふくうりばは　三階に
ございます。

アリスさんは　しんしふくうりばに　います。

_____　てんいん：いらっしゃいませ。

_____　アリス：　あのう、　その　ネクタイを　みせて
下さい。

_____　てんいん：これですか。　どうぞ。

_____　アリス：　いくらですか。

_____　てんいん：一万円です。

_____　アリス：　そうですか。もう　すこし　やすいのは
ありませんか。

_____　てんいん：じゃ、こちらは　いかがでしょうか。

_____　アリス：　これは　いくらですか。

_____　てんいん：これは　五千円です。

_____　アリス：　いいですね。じゃあ、これ　下さい。

_____　てんいん：しょうひぜいが　２５０円で　ございます

から、５、２５０円　いただきます。
おくりもので　ございますか。

_____　アリス：　　はい、そうです。

てんいんは　ネクタイを　はこに　いれます。　そして、はこを
つつみます。

_____　てんいん：７５０円の　おかえしで　ございます。
どうも、ありがとうございました。

わかりましたか

A. If the following statement is true, circle はい; and if it is false, circle いいえ.

はい いいえ 1. アリスさんは　オレンジを　みっつ
　　　　　　　　 かいました。

はい いいえ 2. しんしふくうりばは　三階（さんかい/がい）に　あります。

はい いいえ 3. アリスさんは　一万円（いちまんえん）の　ネクタイを
　　　　　　　　 かいました。

はい いいえ 4. しょくひんうりばは　地下（ちか）に　あります。

B. Complete the following passage by writing the appropriate words in each blank.

アリスさんは ＿＿＿＿＿ に　いきました。 ＿＿＿＿＿ で　りんごと
＿＿＿＿＿ を　かいました。　そして、 ＿＿＿＿＿ で ＿＿＿＿＿ を
かいました。 ＿＿＿＿＿ 円（えん）でした。

にほんの　ぶんか

- *Japanese department stores. What did you learn about the floor directory of a Japanese department store from the dialogue?*

  Although the floor directories of individual stores in Japan differ, the following directory gives the general layout of a full-scale department store. To find where something is sold, add the phrase うりば to the item you are looking for. For example, food is しょくひん, so the food department is しょくひんうりば. Throughout this chapter, you will be using the names of the departments in Japanese, which you will find in the following floor directory.

Floor directory of a Japanese department store

屋上 (R)	ゆうえんち (amusement center)　ビアガーデン (beer garden)
八 階 (8F)	レストラン
七階 (7F)	ぶんぼうぐ　ほん　レコード　CD　おもちゃ (toys)
六階 (6F)	かていでんき (home appliances)
五階 (5F)	かぐ (furniture) しょっき (tableware) だいど ころようひん (kitchenware)
四階 (4F)	こうげいひん (traditional crafts and gifts)　きもの (kimono)
三 階 (3F)	ふじんふく
二階 (2F)	しんしふく
一階 (1F)	ほうせき (jewelry) くつ　ネクタイ　かばん　アクセサリー けしょうひん (cosmetics)
地下一階 (B1)	しょくひん

- *Customer service. Using the information in the dialogue, how are Japanese department stores similar to the ones in your area? How are they different?*

As in other countries, customer service is very important in Japan. In many major department stores, copies of the floor directory are provided in Japanese and English. Several stores have English-speaking staff. Japanese and foreign customers expect to be treated with courtesy. Uniformed elevator operators announce each floor and special events, such as sales. Salespeople wear special uniforms and are always at hand to assist customers. They speak very polite Japanese. Phrases commonly used by salespeople follow:

いらっしゃいませ。
Welcome.

なにか　おさがしでしょうか。
May I help you (literally: Are you looking for something)?

なん〜／いくつ　さしあげましょうか。
How many 〜 should I give you?

～は　いかがですか。(polite form of ～は　どうですか)

この　セーターは　いかがですか。

How about this sweater?

～で　ございます。(polite form of ～です)

この　コートは　一万円で　ございます。
いちまんえん

This coat is 10,000 yen.

はい　かしこまりました。 Kashikomarimashita

Yes, I understand. (very polite form of はい　わかりました)

しょうしょう　おまち下さい。
くだ

Please wait a moment.

- *Methods of payment. What is your usual form of payment?*

  Cash is still the most frequently used method of payment. The use of credit cards is increasing but it is not as common as in the United States. In addition, personal checks are nonexistent. Loans are used for car and house down payments. Monthly bills, such as utilities and telephones, are usually paid by automatic withdrawals from one's checking or savings account.

LANGUAGE

I.　Making a request, using the て-form of a verb +下さい

			Verb て-form	
その	とけい	を	みせて	下さい。

Please show me that watch.

Irregular verbs

Drop ますfrom the polite form and add て.

Dictionary form	Polite form	て-form
する (to do)	します	して
くる (to come)	きます	きて

る-verbs

Drop る from the dictionary form and add て.

Dictionary form	て-form
いれる (to put in)	いれて
みる (to look at)	みて
たべる (to eat)	たべて
いる (to exist, be)	いて

う-verbs

The て-forms of う-verbs differ depending on the verb ending.

Dictionary form	て-form
かく (to write)	かいて
きく (to listen)	きいて
あるく (to walk)	あるいて
およぐ (to swim)	およいで
はなす (to talk)	はなして
だす (to turn in/bring out)	だして
のむ (to drink)	のんで
よむ (to read)	よんで
つつむ (to wrap)	つつんで
あそぶ (to play)	あそんで
かえる (to return)	かえって
はいる (to enter)	はいって
とる (to take)	とって
かう (to buy)	かって
もつ (to hold)	もって
Exception　いく (to go)	いって

くいぐい pattern
If a dictionary form ends in く (or ぐ), the て-form has いて (or いで).

すし pattern
If a dictionary form ends in す, the て-form has して.

むんぶん pattern
If a dictionary form ends in む or ぶ, the て-form has んで.

るうつ pattern
If a dictionary form ends in る, う, or つ, the て-form has って.

てんいん： いらっしゃいませ。
   Welcome.

きむら： あのう、すみませんが、あの　ジャケットを
   みせて下さい。
   Excuse me, but would you show me that jacket over there?

てんいん： はい、かしこまりました。
   Yes, I understand.

きむら： それから、その　コートも　みせて下さい。
   And then, would you please show me that coat, too.

てんいん： はい、どうぞ。
   Yes, here you are.

- The word 下さい means *please give me* by itself, so you can use it to make
   simple requests by saying 〜を　下さい.

   この　オレンジを　下さい。

   Please give me/ I'd like this orange.

はなして　みましょう

A. Make a request using the て-form and the words given.

> **Example**
>
> もう　一度　いう　　もう　一度　いって下さい

1. ゆっくり／はなす
2. くるま／くる　　　　kite
3. この　かんじ／よむ
4. もう　一度／きく
5. こくばん／みる
6. ゆうびんきょく／いく
7. バス／くる
8. あたらしい　くつ／かう
9. ネクタイ／はこ／いれる

B. Work with a partner. Think of five things that you want your partner to do and have your partner act them out.

Example

私の　デーパックを　もって下さい。

Your partner picks up and holds your backpack.

C. Alice is shopping at a department store. Each of the following pictures shows her making a request. Determine the request she is making by using the Verb て + 下さい。

Example

この　ネックレスを　みせて下さい。

1. misete
2. tote
3. 24 cm ookii moo sukoshi
4. tsutsunde
5.

D. Work with a partner. Pretend you are in a department store and your partner is the salesperson. Make requests based on each drawing in exercise C. Place the appropriate word in the blank.

Example

A: いらっしゃいませ。

B: あのう、すみませんが、＿＿＿＿＿下さい。

A: はい、かしこまりました。

E. Work with a partner. Pretend you are in a department store and your partner is a salesperson. You would like to buy some clothes for yourself and a present for a friend. Create your own dialogue based on this situation.

Example

A: いらっしゃいませ。

B: あのう、すみませんが、＿＿＿＿＿＿ 下さい。

A: はい。どうぞ。

B: ああ、いいですね。じゃあ、＿＿＿＿＿＿ を 下さい。

A: はい、かしこまりました。あのう、おくりものですか。

B: ええ、すみませんが、＿＿＿＿＿＿ 下さい。

or いいえ、ちがいます。

A: かしこまりました。しょうしょう おまち下さい。

II. Using Chinese origin numbers, 100 and above

Numbers

100	ひゃく	1,000	せん	10,000	いちまん
200	にひゃく	2,000	にせん	20,000	にまん
300	※さんびゃく	3,000	※さんぜん	30,000	さんまん
400	よんひゃく	4,000	よんせん	40,000	よんまん
500	ごひゃく	5,000	ごせん	50,000	ごまん
600	※ろっぴゃく	6,000	ろくせん	60,000	ろくまん
700	ななひゃく	7,000	ななせん	70,000	ななまん
800	※はっぴゃく	8,000	※はっせん	80,000	はちまん
900	きゅうひゃく	9,000	きゅうせん	90,000	きゅうまん

- The pronunciation of ふん (*minute*), ひゃく (*hundred*), and せん (*thousand*) changes when they are combined with some numbers. The symbol ※ indicates that the pronunciation has changed.

- Numbers like *346*, *995*, and *6,126* are formed by combining the words for the thousands, hundreds, tens, and ones.

  346　さんびゃくよんじゅうろく

  995　きゅうひゃくきゅうじゅうご

  6,126　ろくせんひゃくにじゅうろく

- For numbers 10,000 or larger, まん becomes the base unit.

10,000	いちまん	350,000	さんじゅうごまん
20,000	にまん	1,000,000	ひゃくまん
35,000	さんまんごせん	2,000,000	にひゃくまん
100,000	じゅうまん	3,500,000	さんびゃく
200,000	にじゅうまん		ごじゅうまん

はなして　みましょう

A. Write out the number your instructor says.

Example

Your instructor says 100. You write ひゃく.

B. Say the following numbers in Japanese.

Example

100　　　ひゃく

1. 200
2. 300
3. 400
4. 500
5. 600
6. 700
7. 800
8. 900
9. 1,000
10. 2,100
11. 3,333
12. 20,600
13. 88,666
14. 142,918
15. 153,000

C. Write the following mathematical problems in Japanese. The plus sign (+) is pronounced たす, and the minus sign (–) is pronounced ひく. The topic marker は is used for the equals sign (=).

Example

100 + 200 = 300　　ひゃく　たす　にひゃくは　さんびゃくです。

1. 300 + 9,500 =
2. 660 – 40 =
3. 12,350 + 45 =
4. 3,900 + 700 =
5. 45,000 – 450 =
6. 3,210 + 28 =
7. 7,600 – 228 =

D. Working with a partner, have your partner "write" a 4-digit number on your back with a finger. Say which number it is.

Example

Your partner writes 1,000 on your back.
You say せん.

E. Working in groups of three or four, have each member of your group write a 5-digit number on a card. Show the card to the other members of the group and have them read it aloud as quickly as they can. The first person to finish answering is the winner.

III. Referring to quantities with numbers and counters, using まい, 本, ひき, さつ, and Japanese origin numbers

A. Referring to quantities of thin, flat objects with まい

		Number	Counter	
セーター	を	一 いち	まい	下さい。 くだ

Please give me a sweater.

あの　Tシャツを　三まい　下さい。

Please give me those three t-shirts.

B. Referring to quantities of bound objects with さつ

		Number	Counter	
ざっし	を	二 に	さつ	よみました。

I read two magazines.

田中：　としょかんには　日本語の　本が　たくさん
　　　　　ありますか。

Are there a lot of Japanese books in the library?

スミス：ええ、四千さつぐらい　あります。

Yes, there are about four thousand.

C. Referring to quantities of long, cylindrical objects with 本

		Number	Counter	
ビール	を	二	本	のみました。

I drank two bottles of beer.

アリス：はこの　中に　えんぴつが　何本　ありますか。
How many pencils are in the box?

みちこ：六本　あります。
There are six.

D. Referring to quantities of fish and small four-legged animals with ひき

		Number	Counter	
その　さかな	を	一	ぴき	下さい。

Please give me one fish.

スミス：ねこが　なんびき　いますか。
How many cats are there?

石田：二ひき　います。
There are two.

E. Referring to quantities of round, discrete objects, using Japanese origin numbers

		Japanese origin number	
オレンジ	を	とお	下さい。

Please give me ten oranges.

アリス：きのう　りんごを　いくつ　たべましたか。
How many apples did you eat yesterday?

鈴木：みっつ　たべました。
I ate three.

- You learned something about counters in Chapter 6. In this chapter, you will learn more about them and how they work. When you count things, including people, you must attach a counter to the number. The English equivalent would be *two cups of coffee* or *three sheets of paper*. Japanese uses different counters determined by the kind, shape, and size of the object.

まい	thin, flat objects	sheets of paper, T-shirts, CDs, records
ひき	fish, small four-legged animals	dogs, cats, mice
ほん 本	long, cylindrical objects	pencils, pens, bottles, cans, belts, ties, trousers
さつ	bound objects	books, dictionaries, magazines
つ	round discrete objects	oranges, apples, balls

- To say *how many* 〜 or *how much* 〜, use なん + counter.

セーターは　なんまい　ありますか。

How many sweaters are there?

ベルトを　なん^{ぼん}本　かいますか。

How many belts will you buy?

本は　なんさつ　ありますか。

How many books are there?

オレンジは　いくつ　ありますか。

How many oranges are there?

- Counter expressions come immediately after the object and its particle.

じしょを　^{いっ}一さつ　かいました。

I bought a dictionary.

いぬが　^{さん}三びき　ここに　います。

There are three dogs here.

- As you have seen in ふん, ひゃく, and せん, the pronunciation of counters and of numbers associated with them varies. In the following chart, the expressions preceded by the ※ symbol are examples of these changes. The change of pronunciation for counters and numbers is basically the same for ほん and ひき.

Counters	Thin, flat objects まい 枚	Long, cylindrical objects ほん（本）	Fish, small four-legged animals ひき 匹	Bound objects さつ 冊	Round, discrete objects つ
1（一）	いちまい	※いっぽん	※いっぴき	※いっさつ	ひとつ *hitotsu*
2（二）	にまい	にほん	にひき	にさつ	ふたつ *futatsu*
3（三）	さんまい	※さんぼん	※さんびき	さんさつ	みっつ *mittsu*
4（四）	よんまい	よんほん	よんひき	よんさつ	よっつ *yo'tsu*
5（五）	ごまい	ごほん	ごひき	ごさつ	いつつ *yitsusu*
6（六）	ろくまい	※ろっぽん	※ろっぴき	ろくさつ	むっつ *mu'tsu*
7（七）	ななまい	ななほん	ななひき	ななさつ	ななつ *nanatsu*
8（八）	はちまい	※はっぽん	※はっぴき	※はっさつ	やっつ *ya'tsu*
9（九）	きゅうまい	きゅうほん	きゅうひき	きゅうさつ	ここのつ *kokono*
10（十）	じゅうまい	※じゅっぽん	※じゅっぴき	※じゅっさつ	とお *tō*

- When you need to count objects that do not fit in any of the other four categories, you can use Japanese origin numbers, also used for round, discrete objects. The question word is いくつ.

アリス： オレンジは　いくつ　ありますか。
　　　　　How many oranges are there?

<ruby>鈴木<rt>すずき</rt></ruby>： みっつ　あります。
　　　　There are three.

- Japanese origin numbers go up to only 10. For numbers larger than 10, Chinese origin numbers are used.

1	ひとつ	5	いつつ	9	ここのつ
2	ふたつ	6	むっつ	10	とお
3	みっつ	7	ななつ	11	じゅういち
4	よっつ	8	やっつ	12	じゅうに
				⋮	⋮

田中： たまごは　いくつ　ありますか。
　　　How many eggs are there?
スミス： じゅうに　あります。
　　　There are twelve.

はなして みましょう

A. Request the following items in Japanese.

Example

ネクタイ (1)　　　ネクタイを　一本（いっぽん）下（くだ）さい。

1. シャツ (7)
2. ビール (5)
3. オレンジ (10)
4. えんぴつ (3)
5. いぬ (1)
6. ほん (4)
7. かばん (2)
8. ネックレス (1)
9. たまご (8)
10. ＣＤ (6)

B. Work in groups of three or four. Ask members of your group how many of the following items they own. Find out who owns the most of each item. Use the phrase もっています, which means *to own*.

Example

A: えんぴつを　何本（なんぼん）もっていますか。

B: 二本（にほん）もっています。

1. えんぴつ
2. けしゴム
3. セーター
4. かさ
5. じしょ
6. ハンドバッグ

C. Work with a partner. Pretend you are going shopping and that your partner is a salesperson in each of the stores listed in the table on the next page. Make a shopping list of what you need to buy at each store. Then go to each store and ask the sales associate for the items on your list. Your partner will write down what you ask for in each store. See whether your list and that of your partner match.

Example

A: いらっしゃいませ。

B: あのう、りんごを　下（くだ）さい。

A: いくつ　さしあげましょうか。

B: ひとつ　下（くだ）さい。

スーパー	デパート	ほんや

D. Work with a different partner. Describe to your partner what you have bought in Exercise C, and compare your purchases with his or hers.

Example

私は　本屋で　ざっしを　二さつ　かいました。
～さんは　ざっしを　二さつ　かいました。

IV. Referring to prices and floor levels, using 円 and かい

A. Referring to prices, using 円

Question				Answer		
	Question Word			Number	Counter	
これは	いくら	です	か。	三千	円	です。

How much is this?　　　　　　　　　　It's three thousand yen.

B. Referring to floor levels, using かい

		Question Word	Suffix			
アクセサリーうりば	は	なん	かい	に	あります	か。

On which floor is the accessory department?

Number	Suffix		
いっ	かい	に	あります。

It's on the first floor.

スミス：　すみません。ぶんぼうぐうりばは　どこに　あります
　　　　か。
　　　　Excuse me. Where is the stationery department?

てんいん：六^{ろっ}かいに　ございます。

> It's on the sixth floor.

スミス：　あのう、この　かさは　いくらですか。

> Excuse me. How much is this umbrella?

てんいん：それは　２、５００円^{にせんごひゃくえん}で　ございます。

> That is two thousand five hundred yen.

- Numbers before 円^{えん} are pronounced the same way as in the counter まい, except that four yen becomes よえん.

- Numbers before かい are pronounced the same way as in the counter 本^{ほん}. Both さんかい (*third floor*) and なんかい (*which floor*) can be pronounced さんがい and なんがい, respectively. Use 地下^{ちか}〜 (*underground*) to refer to basement floors.

1. いっかい		6. ろっかい	
2. にかい		7. ななかい	
3. さんかい／さんがい		8. はちかい／はっかい	
4. よんかい		9. きゅうかい	
5. ごかい		10. じゅっかい	

はなして　みましょう

A. Look at the following pictures of Japanese currency. Name the value of each bill and coin.

Example

一円^{いちえん}

B. Look at the following items. How much do they cost?

Example

えんぴつは　にじゅうごえんです。

¥ 780	¥ 50	¥ 1,700	¥ 2,300

¥ 19,800	¥ 4,600	¥ 290	¥ 3,400

C. Work with a partner. Your budget is 20,000 yen. You want to buy the items in the following chart. Ask your partner, the salesperson, how much each item costs and decide whether will you buy it or not.

Example

A: すみません、この　〜は　いくらですか。

B: ＿＿＿＿＿＿＿　えんです。

A: (buying)じゃ、これを　下(くだ)さい。
(not buying)　そうですか。じゃ、また　きます。（また ＝ *again, some other time*)

くつした	スカート	ジーンズ	ハンドバック	ジャケット

D. Look at the floor directory and answer the following questions using 〜かい.

Example

くつうりばは　なんかいに　ありますか。
一階(いっかい)に　あります。

Floor directory of a Japanese department store

屋上 おくじょう	(R)	*yuuenchi* ゆうえんち (amusement center)　*biagaden* ビアガーデン (beer garden)
八 階 はち／はっかい	(8F)	*resutoran* レストラン
七階 ななかい	(7F)	*bun boogu*　*hon*　*rekodo*　*omochya* ぶんぼうぐ　ほん　レコード　おもちゃ (toys)
六階 ろっかい	(6F)	でんかせいひん (electrical appliances)
五階 ごかい	(5F)	*kagu*　　　　*shyo'ki* かぐ (furniture) しょっき (tableware) だいどころようひん (kitchenware) *dai dokoro yoohin*
四階 よんかい	(4F)	こうげいひん (traditional crafts and gifts) きもの (kimono)
三 階 さんかい／がい	(3F)	ふじんふく　*women*
二階 にかい	(2F)	*Shinshifuku* しんしふく　*men*
一階 いっかい	(1F)	ほうせき (jewelry)　くつ　ネクタイ　かばん アクセサリー　けしょうひん (cosmetics)
地下一階 ち　かいっかい	(B1)	*Shyokuhin* しょくひん　*store (food)*

uriba / dept.

1. レストランは　なんかいに　ありますか。
2. どこで　つくえを　かいますか。
3. どこで　ズボンを　かいますか。
4. レコードうりばは　どこに　ありますか。
5. どこで　スカートを　かいますか。
6. なんかいで　にくを　かいますか。

E.　Work with a partner. Pretend you are a customer and your partner works at the information booth on the first floor of a department store. Ask where the following departments or facilities are and write the information in the chart on the next page.

Example

A:　いらっしゃいませ。

B:　すみませんが、かばんうりばは　どこですか。

A:　かばんうりばは　一階に　ございます。
　　　　　　　　　　いっかい

B:　一階ですね。どうも　ありがとう。
　　いっかい

doko de　hooseki を kaimasuka
nankai

	7F	
かばんうりば	6F	
おてあらい	5F	
レコードうりば	4F	
レストラン	3F	
ふじんふくうりば	2F	
しんしふくうりば	1F	
しょくひんうりば	B1F	

V. Abbreviating verbal expressions, using です

Question			Answer	
	Verb			**Copula**
きのう　なにを	かいました	か。	えんぴつ	です。

What did you buy yesterday?　　　　　　　　I bought a pencil (literally: It's a pencil).

田中：　アリスさんは　なにを　かいますか。
　　　　What are you going to buy, Alice?

アリス：ベルトです。
　　　　I am going to buy a belt (literally: It's a belt).

- です acts as a substitute for a verb previously mentioned. In colloquial language, substitution with です is very common when answering a question asking for information.

- です can be used even when the previously mentioned verb is in the past tense, as in the key sentence.

- The particles が, で, を, and に associated with regular verbs are deleted before です, but から, まで, and と may stay.

アリス：田中さんは　どこに　いますか。

田中：　　ゆうびんきょくです。

アリス：なんで　きましたか。

田中：　　くるまです。

アリス：だれが　きましたか。

田中：　　山田さんです。

アリス：　どこから　きましたか。

田中：　　カナダ（から）です。

アリス：　なんじまで　ねましたか。

田中：　　十時<ruby>十時<rt>じゅうじ</rt></ruby>（まで）です。

アリス：　だれと　はなしましたか。

田中：　　スミスさん（と）です。

- It is impolite to use です for every question asking for information. If you overuse it when talking to the same person, you might sound indifferent or cold.

はなして　みましょう

A. Edit the following conversation, using です.

Example

A: どこに　いきますか。
B: とうきょうに~~いきます~~。　　です。

1. A: いつ　日本に　いきますか。

   B: こんしゅうの　土曜日<ruby>土曜日<rt>どようび</rt></ruby>に　いきます。

2. A: どこで　その　ふくを　かいましたか。

   B: あそこの　デパートで　かいました。

3. A: なんじから　じゅぎょうが　はじまりますか。

   B: 八時<ruby>八時<rt>はちじ</rt></ruby>から　はじまります。

4. A: だれが　でんわを　かけましたか。

   B: アリスさんが　かけました。

5. A: なんじまで　べんきょうしましたか。

   B: 十二時<ruby>十二時<rt>じゅうにじ</rt></ruby>まで　しました。

B. Work with a partner. Take turns asking each other how you spent last weekend. Use です and regular verbs to answer questions asking for information.

Example

A: せんしゅうの　しゅうまつに　なにを　しましたか。
B: ドライブに　いきました。
A: どこまで　いきましたか。
B: シカゴ（まで）です。

Using **kanji** for numbers

Although you can write any number in **kanji**, you don't normally see numbers written in a long string of **kanji** such as 六万三千五百二十二円 (¥63,522). In such cases, arabic numerals are used. In general, simple numerical expressions are written in **kanji**, while long expressions are written in arabic numerals. The following are examples of common uses:

- prices with simple numbers such as 100, 1000, 2000, etc.:　ひゃくえん　せんえん
  百円　千円
  にせんえん
  二千円

- counter expressions with single or double-digit numbers:　さんぼん　よん
  三本　四まい
  はち／はっ
  八　かい

- dates:　ろくがつにじゅうごにち　じゅうにがつさんじゅういちにち
  六月二十五日　十二月三十一日

- time:　いちじ　さんじにじゅっぷん
  一時　三時二十分

Variations in the pronunciation of **kanji**

The pronunciation of **kanji** varies slightly depending on usage. For example, 一 (いち) is pronounced いっ when it is used in the word 一本 (いっぽん), and 本 (ほん) is pronounced ぽん.

　えんぴつを　一本　ください。

When you read a sentence, you don't see any markings indicating such changes. Likewise, you don't add any markings when you write them. (Note that small **hiragana** on new **kanji** is instructional help.)

あたらしい　よみかた　(New readings)

本 (ほん)	いっぽん 一本	さんぼん 三本	ろっぽん 六本	はっぽん 八本
下 (した)	ちか 地下	くだ 〜下さい		

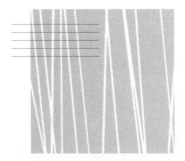

one

イチ

ひと（つ）

いちじ
一時
いっぽん
一本

two

ニ

ふた（つ）

にじ
二時
にひゃく
二百
にせん
二千

three

サン

み、みっ（つ）

さんじ
三時
さんびゃく
三百
さんぜん
三千

four

シ

よ、よん、よっ（つ）

よじ
四時
よんひゃく
四百
よんせん
四千

five

ゴ

いつ（つ）

ごじ
五時
ごひゃく
五百
ごせん
五千

six

ロク

むっ（つ）

ろくじ
六時
ろっぴゃく
六百
ろくせん
六千

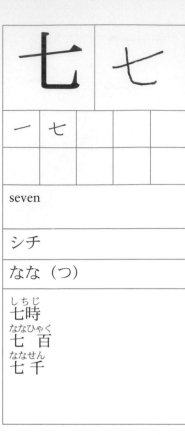

一	七		

seven

シチ

なな（つ）

しちじ
七時
ななひゃく
七 百
ななせん
七千

ノ	八		

eight

ハチ、ハッ

やっ（つ）

はちじ
八時
はっぴゃく
八 百
はっせん
八千

て	九		

nine

キュウ、ク

ここの（つ）

くじ
九時
きゅうひゃく
九 百
きゅうせん
九千

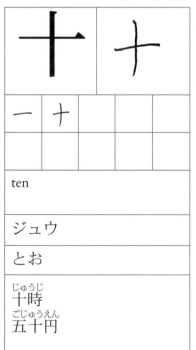

一	十		

ten

ジュウ

とお

じゅうじ
十時
ごじゅうえん
五十円

一	一	丆	石	百
百				

hundred

ヒャク、ビャク、ピャク

ひゃく
百
さんびゃく
三 百
ろっぴゃく
六 百

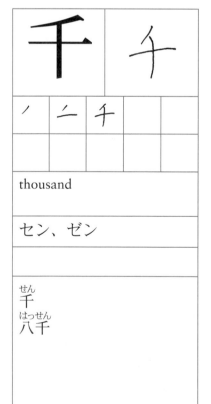

ノ	二	千		

thousand

セン、ゼン

せん
千
はっせん
八千

万	万		
一	フ	万	

ten thousand

マン

いちまん
一万
じゅうまん
十万
ひゃくまん
百万

円	円		
丶	冂	冂	円

yen (Japanese currency)

エン

じゅうえん
十円
にまんさんぜんえん
二万三千円

Read the following sentences with **kanji.**

1. 田中さんは十一時三十分に学生会館にきます。
2. としょかんには日本の本が四千五百さつぐらいあります。
3. 山川さんのつくえの上に二万八千円あります。
4. 私は六時にごはんをたべます。そして、七時に大学にいきます。

じょうずな　よみかた

Scanning

You do not always need to read the whole text when you are looking for specific information. For example, if you want to find which floor sells food in a Japanese department store, you would not read the entire store directory. Rather, you would look for a specific indicator, such as the **kanji** 食 (*eat*). By doing this you can find the information you are seeking more quickly.

The same is true when you read a text. You can skip through the text to find the information you need. This is called *scanning*.

よむまえに

Read the following advertisements and find out what is being sold in each ad.

近所のスーパー　(Neighborhood supermarket)

ことばの　リスト
タオル　towel
スリッパ　slippers
石けん　soap
お酒　liquor

　私の家の近くに大きいスーパーがあります。そのスーパーの
地下一階には食品売り場があります。でも、お酒はありません。
私はそこでよく野菜や魚を買います。二階は日用品売り場です。
安いタオルやスリッパや石けんがあります。三階には本や
文房具が　あります。きのう、私はこのスーパーでノートを
三冊と鉛筆を五本買いました。

わかりましたか

A. Answer the following questions in Japanese.

1. この人は　このスーパーで　なにを　よく　かいますか。

2. このスーパーの　地下に　なにが　ありますか。

3. 二かいに　なにが　ありますか。

4. おさけは　なんかいに　ありますか。

5. にちようひんって　なんですか。

6. きのう　この人は　なにを　かいましたか。それは　どこに　ありましたか。

B. Write a short passage in Japanese about a department store in your area. Use the following questions to guide you as to which information to include.

1. デパートは　どこに　ありますか。

2. デパートは　大きいですか。小さいですか。

3. いい　デパートですか。

4. デパートに　どんな　うりばが　ありますか。

6. いりぐち (entrance) の　ちかくに　なにが　ありますか。

7. そのデパートで　なにを　よく　かいますか。どうしてですか。

じょうずな　ききかた

Recognizing the characteristics of speech

Awareness of the characteristics of spoken language will help you understand it better. Spoken language is highly redundant; that is, it repeats the same information more than once. It also contains hesitations, false starts, incomplete sentences, and interruptions. These are all integral parts of speech.

Listen to the following conversation and write, in English, whether the customer is willing to buy the items. Also, write which expressions indicate the customer's willingness to buy.

1. _____

2. _____

You will hear three conversations. Listen to each and list, in English, the items and the quantity of each item the customer bought. Then, write the total amount the customer paid.

1. Items and quantities: _____

   Total cost: _____

2. Items and quantities: _____

   Total cost: _____

3. Items and quantities: _____

   Total cost: _____

 DICT-A-CONVERSATION

You, Smith-san, are in a department store and are looking for a shirt. You talk first with the staff person at the information desk, and then with a salesperson in the men's apparel department.

デパートで

　あんないがかり (Clerk at the information desk)：いらっしゃいませ。

　スミス：_____

　あんないがかり：_____

しんしふくうりばで

　てんいん：いらっしゃいませ。

　スミス：_____

　てんいん：_____

　スミス：_____

　てんいん：_____

　スミス：_____

　てんいん：_____

　スミス：_____

　てんいん：はい、かしこまりました。

きき じょうず　はなし じょうず

Asking someone to repeat or reword a phrase

So far, you have learned some strategies to provide feedback and to indicate you are listening to the speaker and understand what is being said. For example, you nod your head, or you say はい and ええ. However, at times you will be in situations where you don't understand what the speaker is saying and can't respond, because you don't know the words or didn't hear what the person said. In these cases, it is important for you to know how to ask for repetition or a paraphrase and how to ask someone to speak more loudly or slowly. The following is a list of some useful expressions you can use in these situations.

Asking for repetition:	もう　いちど　いって下さい。
	(Please say it again.)
Asking for paraphrasing:	やさしい　ことばで　いって下さい。
	(Please say it in easier words.)
Asking someone to speak slowly:	ゆっくり　いって下さい。
	ゆっくり　はなして下さい。
	(Please say it/speak slowly.)
Asking someone to speak loudly:	おおきい　こえで　いって下さい。
	おおきい　こえで　はなして下さい。
	(Please say it/speak more loudly.)

Also remember that it is a good strategy to add conversation fillers and phrases like あのう and すみませんが before making a request. These phrases not only soften a request—an important part of communicating in Japanese—but also give you time to think of the next phrases.

Work with a partner. Imagine that you are a salesperson. Find polite expressions used by a salesperson in this chapter. Say those expressions to your partner and have your partner respond with the expressions above.

そうごうれんしゅう

デパートのうりば　(Departments in a department store)

The following is the floor directory of a full-scale department store in Tokyo. Work together with a partner to describe which items are available on the different floors as much as possible. Try to guess the meanings of some words written in カタカナ. Next, your instructor will give you a list of specific items to purchase. Determine where you can find each item.

本館							南館	
8 家電製品 インテリア用品	ブライダルサロン 貸衣装 家電製品 ヘルシーコーナー	カーテン・カーペット クレジットセンター キャッシュコーナー（クレジット系）	「エミリオロバ」 クチュールフラワー 手芸用品 ペット用品	園芸用品	連絡通路	金魚・熱帯魚	屋上遊園 ゲームコーナー プレイランド	**R**
7 きもの 家具	カトレヤルーム レストラン 釜サロン（洋食）	きものと帯 和装用品 特選きものサロン クエレコーナー	外商お得意さまサロン 和洋家具			めがね 美術品・画廊	ファミリーレストラン お好み食堂（和食） レストラン 美術品	**7**
6 催し場		大催事場			連絡通路	かばん・旅行用品 スポーツ用品	事務用品・文具 おもちゃ 歯科室 おもちゃ・文具 スポーツ用品	**6**
5 リビング用品 寝装品	タオル　寝具 バス・トイレタリー用品 石けん　表札	ギフトセンター 調理・日用品	和洋陶器・漆器 和洋食器 シャンブル・ド・リュックス			こども服 こども洋品	ベビーウェア ベビー用品 マタニティウェア ベビー体操室 こども服 ベビー用品	**5**
4 婦人服 プレタポルテブティック	フォーマルサロン 喫茶 カフェ・ド・パリ	特選プレタポルテ プレタポルテ プレタカジュアル	キャリアカジュアル		連絡通路	ヤングカジュアル ヤングトラッド キャリアエレガンス	キャリアパーツショップ 婦人服 ヤング＆キャリア	**4**
3 婦人服 エレガンス＆カジュアル	カジュアルウェア 喫茶 カフェ・キャビン	ブリティッシュトラッド ミッシー・ミセスカジュアル	セーター・ブラウス スカート・パンツ ドレス・スーツ・コート			大きい（L）サイズの婦人服 小さい（S）サイズの婦人服 ランジェリー ナイトウェア・エプロン	毛皮サロン 婦人服オーダーサロン 婦人イージーオーダー服 イタリア料理 キャンティ 婦人服 サイズ＆インナー	**3**
2 紳士服 紳士靴	紳士服オーダーサロン 紳士イージーオーダー服	キングサイズコーナー 紳士スーツ・コート 紳士フォーマルウェア	紳士カジュアルウェア 紳士靴			特選サロン 宝飾品・時計	ゴルフ用品 ゴルフウェア 宝飾品 特選服飾品	**2**
M2 "F-WAY"	紳士肌着・ナイトウェア オーダーワイシャツ ジーンズショップ 学生服 キャッシュコーナー（生保系）	サンリオプラザ カメラ モノショップ 旅行センター チケットぴあ	フォトスタジオ シバヤマ美容室 ウイッグ 婦人帽子 喫茶 ヴィド・フランス			店内ご案内所 カステルバジャックスポーツ ファッションウオッチ「ゲス」	ミスターミニット 商品券 免税カウンター ハンドバッグ 婦人靴	**1**
1 婦人・紳士洋品 化粧品	店内ご案内所 キャッシュコーナー（クレジット系）	ハンカチーフ 婦人靴下 婦人アクセサリー 化粧品	ワイシャツ　たばこ 紳士靴下 ネクタイ・紳士洋品 紳士セーター			婦人靴・革 ハンドバッグ・さいふ		
B1 食品 マツザカヤ食楽館	くだもの のり・茶・かつおぶし	味とのれんの名店街 和・洋菓子 缶詰・調味料	ベーカリーショップ 乳製品 和洋酒 できたて屋＆イートイン小路	食品催事場		和・洋・中華惣菜 鮮魚・精肉・野菜・デイリーフーズ	食品 マツザカヤ食楽館	**B1**
B2	コインロッカー フラワーショップ 地下鉄連絡口					お忘れ物承り所 薬品・介護用品 クリーニング 日洋舎 健康食品 お客様相談コーナー 書籍 宅急便・海外発送承カウンター	中国料理 赤坂飯店 そば処 加茂 甘味処 みはし 喫茶 松栄 喫茶 コロンバン 寿司処 たこ八 レストラン 喫茶・書籍	**B2**

至浅草 ◄——— 地下鉄銀座線 上野広小路駅 ———► 至渋谷

ロールプレイ

1. Work in a group of six. You and one other person are customers in a department store and each have 50,000 yen to spend. The other members of the group are salespeople in different departments. Your instructor will give them a price list of items available in their departments. Go to as many departments as you can and make one or more purchases. Before leaving each department, note what you have bought and how much you have paid. Try to spend all your money, and buy at least four different items. The student who spends closest to 50,000 yen is the winner.

Examples

Sales staff: いらっしゃいませ。

Customer: あのう、　ハンドバッグを　下さい。
（それから、　ベルト　も　下さい。）
or その　あかい　ハンドバッグ　を
みせて下さい。

Sales staff: はい、どうぞ。

Sales staff:	いらっしゃいませ。
Customer:	<u>スタンド</u> を 下さい。
Sales staff:	<u>これ</u> は いかがですか。
Customer:	いいですね。／
	<u>大きい</u> ですね。もっと <u>小さいの</u>は
	ありますか。／<u>もう すこし やすい</u> のは
	ありますか。

2. You have run out of vegetables and fruit. Go to a market and buy the following items.

レタス	1	りんご	8
トマト	3	オレンジ	6
にんじん	5	バナナ	6

たんご (ESSENTIAL VOCABULARY)

Nouns

Tシャツ T-shirt
アクセサリー accessories アクセサリーうりば（アクセサリー売り場）accessory department
うりば（売り場）department
かさ（傘）umbrella
くつ（靴）shoes
くつした（靴下）socks
コート coat
ジャケット jacket
シャツ shirt
ジーンズ jeans
しょくひん（食品）food しょくひんうりば（食品売り場）food department
しんしふく（紳士服）menswear しんしふくうりば（紳士服売り場）menswear department
スカート skirt
ズボン trousers, pants
セーター sweater

ちか（地下）basement ちかいっかい（地下一階）B 1
ネクタイ tie
ネックレス necklace
はこ（箱）box
パンツ shorts, briefs
ハンドバッグ handbag
ふく（服）clothing
ふじんふく（婦人服）women's clothing ふじんふくうりば（婦人服売り場）women's clothing department
ぶんぼうぐ（文房具）stationery ぶんぼうぐうりば（文房具売り場）stationery department
ベルト belt
レコード record レコードうりば（レコード売り場）music department
(Although the store may not carry records, the term refers to a department of the store (レコードや).)

る -verbs

いれる（入れる）(to) put in
みせる（見せる）(to) show
もっている（持っている）(to) have, (to) own

う -verbs

だす（出す）(to) bring out
つつむ（包む）(to) wrap
とる（取る）(to) take, (to) get
もつ（持つ）(to) hold

い -adjectives

たかい（高い）expensive
やすい（安い）inexpensive, cheap

Adverbs

たくさん　a lot, many, much
もう　another, an additional 〜　もう　すこし（もう少し）a little more
もっと　more

Question Words

いくつ　How many 〜 ?
いくら　How much (money) 〜 ?

Counters

〜えん（〜円）〜 yen (Japanese currency)
〜かい（〜階）〜 floor/s of a building
〜さつ（〜冊）counter for bound objects
　（e.g., books, magazines）
〜つ　general counter (Japanese origin number)
〜ひき（〜匹）counter for fish and small
　four-legged animals

〜ほん（〜本）counter for long, cylindrical
　objects (e.g., pens, pencils, bottles)
〜まい（〜枚）counter for thin, flat objects
　（e.g., paper, shirts, plates）

～は　ありませんか。　　Do you have ～ ? / Do you carry ～　(literally: Isn't there ～)?

～を　ください（～を　下さい）Please give me ～.

やさしい　ことばで　いってください。（やさしい言葉で言って下さい。）Please say it simply.

Passive Vocabulary

Nouns

エレベーターガール　elevator operator

おかえし　change (of money) (おかえし refers only to cash received back after an amount was tendered.)

おくりもの（贈り物）gift

おつり　change (the same as おかえし) おかえし is more polite.

しょうひぜい（消費税）sales tax

しょっき（食器）tableware

せっけん（石鹸）soap

タオル　towel

たんじょうび（誕生日）birthday

つぎ（次）next

にちようひん（日用品）daily goods

プレゼント　present

う -verbs

とまる（止まる）(to) stop

Adverbs

また　again

Counter

～ドル　～ dollar/s

Expressions

いらっしゃいませ。　Welcome.

しょうしょう　おまちください。（少々 お待ち下さい。）Please wait a moment. (polite)

ぜんぶで（全部で）altogether

たいへん　おまたせいたしました。 Thank you for waiting.

～で　ございます　～ is/are　(polite form of ～です)

なにか　おさがしでしょうか。（何かお
　　さがしでしょうか。）May I help you (lit-
　　erally: Are you looking for something)?
なにを　さしあげましょうか。（何を差
　　し上げましょうか。）Can I help you (lit-
　　erally: What shall I give you)?
なん〜／いくつ　さしあげましょうか。
　　（何〜／いくつ差し上げましょうか。）
　　How many 〜 shall I give you?

〜は　いかがでしょうか。　　How about
　　〜?/ How is 〜? (polite form of 〜はどうで
　　すか?)
はい　かしこまりました。　　I see./ I will
　　do it./ I understand it. (Polite)

Supplementary Vocabulary

Clothing

イヤリング　earring
うでどけい（腕時計）wrist watch
サンダル　sandal
したぎ（下着）underwear
スカーフ　scarf
スニーカー　sneaker
スリッパ　slippers
ドレス　dress

ハンカチ　handkerchief
ブレスレット　bracelets
ぼうし（帽子）hat, cap
ゆびわ（指輪）ring
ワイシャツ　man's dress shirt (ワイ is
　　believed to come from *white*. However, colored
　　shirts are now called ワイシャツ as well.)

Fabrics

もめん（木綿）cotton
シルク　silk
ウール　wool

A Japanese meal

レストランとしょうたい

RESTAURANTS AND INVITATIONS

Functions	Inviting people; Ordering food and beverages in a restaurant
New Vocabulary	Things to order; Dishes from around the world; Ordering food and inviting people
Dialogue	いっしょに　いきませんか。(Won't you go with me?)
Culture	Japanese eating habits; Restaurants in Japan
Language	I. Deciding on something, using 〜に　します, and making a request, using 〜を　おねがいします
	II. Inviting and responding, using 〜ませんか, 〜ましょうか, and 〜ましょう
	III. Expressing purpose, using the verb stem 〜に　いきます／きます／かえります
	IV. Using a question word + か + (particle)
	V. Talking about activities and events, using 〜で　〜が　あります
Kanji	Writing **kanji**; *Kanji* made from pictures and symbols 2
Reading	Understanding the format of a postcard
Listening	Using context
Communication	Making and receiving telephone calls

あたらしい　ことば

A. ちゅうもんする　もの (Things to order).

(お)すし
sushi

(お)さしみ
sashimi

てんぷら
tempura

うどん
white noodles

そば
buckwheat noodles

ラーメン
Chinese noodles

チャーハン
Chinese fried rice

カレーライス
curried rice

スパゲティ
spaghetti

サラダ
salad

ピザ
pizza

ステーキ
steak

ハンバーガー
hamburger

スープ
soup

サンドイッチ
sandwich

Aランチ
A-Lunch (Western-style)

デザート
dessert

ケーキ
cake

アイスクリーム
ice cream

ミルク
milk

ジュース
juice

おちゃ
green tea

みず
water

日本語で　こたえて下さい。

1. レストランで　何を　よく　ちゅうもんしますか。
2. きっさてんで　何を　よく　ちゅうもんしますか。
3. うちで　何を　よく　たべますか。何を　よく　のみますか。
4. どんな　日本の　りょうりが　すきですか。
5. どんな　りょうりを　つくりますか。

B. せかいの　りょうり (Dishes from around the world). Group the dishes in section A, according to the following kinds of food.

りょうり		りょうり
わしょく／日本りょうり	Japanese food	
ちゅうかりょうり	Chinese food	
イタリアりょうり	Italian food	
フランスりょうり	French food	
ほか	Other	

C. しょうたいの　ことば (Ordering food and inviting people).

一緒に　　together

ともだちに　あう　　(to) meet friends

誕生日パーティーに　ともだちを　よぶ　　(to) invite friends to a birthday party

パーティーに　先生を　しょうたいする　　(to) invite a teacher to a party

ようじが　ある　　(to) have to run an errand.

ええ、ぜひ。　　Yes, I would love to.

つごうが　わるい　　it is not convenient

どうぞ　おかまいなく。　　Please don't go out of your way.

いいえ、けっこうです。　　No, thank you.

何も　いりません。　　I don't need anything.

日本語で　こたえて下さい。

1. 誕生日パーティーに　だれを　よびますか。
2. たいてい　どこで　パーティーを　しますか。
3. ともだちと　一緒に　よく　どこへ　いきますか。
4. どこで　クラスメートに　あいますか。
5. If you are invited to a party and you cannot attend, what would you say?

6. If you are offered a cup of tea but have to decline, what would you say?

7. What would you say to accept an invitation?

ダイアローグ

はじめに

A. 日本語で　こたえて下さい。
1. 週末に　どこに　いきますか。
2. ともだちと　よく　何を　しますか。
3. レストランで　よく　何を　たべますか。

B. How do you identify yourself when you make a phone call? How do you respond to the caller? Call your partner on the phone and invite him/her to do something.

C. Remember the three steps in the dialogue: (1) Look at the **manga.** (2) Listen to the dialogue on the tape. (3) Match the dialogue and the **manga,** writing the appropriate number in each blank.

いっしょに　いきませんか。(Won't you go with me?)

石田さんが　アリスさんに　でんわを　かけます。

リン　リン

____　石田：　もしもし、すずきさんの　おたくですか。

____　アリス：はい、そうです。　otaku

_____ 石田： ぼく　石田ですが、アリスさんは
　　　　　　　いらっしゃいますか。

_____ アリス： はい、私ですが。

_____ 石田： ああ、アリスさん。あのう、今週の
　　　　　　　土曜日は　いそがしいですか。

_____ アリス： いいえ。

_____ 石田： じゃあ、一緒に　えいがを　みに
　　　　　　　いきませんか。

_____ アリス： ええ、いいですよ。何時ごろ
　　　　　　　いきましょうか。

_____ 石田： そうですね。一時ごろは　どうですか。

_____ アリス： いいですね。

_____ 石田： じゃあ　一時に　アリスさんの　うちに
　　　　　　　いきますよ。

_____ アリス： そうですか。　ありがとう。　じゃあ　一時に。

きょうは　土曜日です。　アリスさんと　石田さんは　えいがの
あと (after the movie) レストランに　いきます。

_____ ウェイター： ごちゅうもんは。

_____ 石田： アリスさん、何に　しますか。

_____ アリス： そうですね。ピザを　おねがいします。

_____ 石田： じゃあ、ぼくは　カレーに　します。

_____ ウェイター： ピザを　おひとつと　カレーを　おひとつ
　　　　　　　　　ですね。かしこまりました。

わかりましたか

A. If the following statement is true, circle はい; if it is false, circle いいえ.

はい　いいえ　1. アリスさんは　石田さんに　でんわを
　　　　　　　　　かけました。

はい　いいえ　2. 石田さんは　アリスさんと　えいがを
　　　　　　　　　みました。

はい　いいえ　3. 石田さんは　アリスさんに　石田さんの
　　　　　　　　　うちで　あいました。

はい　いいえ　4. 石田さんは　カレーを　ちゅうもんしました。

はい　いいえ　5. アリスさんも　カレーを　たべました。

B. Complete the following passage by filling in each blank with the appropriate article.

石田さん _____ アリスさんは 土曜日 _____
えいが _____ みました。そして、 レストラン _____
ごはん _____ たべました。

日本の文化

● 日本人の たべものの しゅうかん (*Japanese eating habits*).
What do you eat for breakfast, lunch, and dinner?

Rice is probably the most important food in Japan. Most Japanese probably do not go a day without eating rice. In fact, many eat it at every meal. The importance of rice can be seen in the fact that many industries use the price of rice as an index to determine the prices of other commodities.

A traditional Japanese breakfast consists of a bowl of rice, miso soup, a raw egg with some soy sauce, seaweed, pickles, and fish. However, due to Western influence, a growing number of Japanese eat a Western style breakfast—buttered toast, an egg, salad, and coffee or tea. The Japanese prefer not to eat sweet food like pancakes and waffles for breakfast. Sweet foods are eaten as a snack after lunch. Adult males tend to avoid eating sweets, like cakes, because they tend to think it is not manly to eat sweets. Although many people eat breakfast at home, special breakfast meals are offered in many restaurants and cafes for commuters. They are called モーニング サービス or モーニング セット and can be Japanese- or Western-style.

At lunchtime, most Japanese businesspeople and students eat at the company or university cafeteria or at restaurants and cafes. Some companies order box lunches (おべんとう) for their employees, whereas some people bring their own box lunches. Most primary schools provide lunch to the children but students at secondary schools usually bring their own box lunches.

Many restaurants have daily specials called 日替わりランチ that consist of a soup, pickles or a salad, rice or bread, and a main dish. Other popular lunch dishes are noodles and a variety of rice dishes (curried rice, fried rice, or rice topped with beef stew, pork cutlet and eggs, or tempura).

For most people in Japan, dinner is the largest meal of the day. Dinner is at about the same time as in the United States. A wide range of dishes such as tempura, sashimi, grilled fish, sukiyaki, as well as foreign dishes are cooked at home. Many local food shops offer various prepared dishes for working mothers and businesspeople. Small, local restaurants usually deliver sushi, noodles, and Chinese dishes at no charge.

The most popular foreign dishes are Chinese, Italian, and French. Korean barbecue and Indian curry dishes are also popular. With American fast-food franchises, like McDonald's, hamburgers, pizza, and fried chicken are gaining popularity among young people. However, there are no American dishes per se in Japan. Mexican food is not as common in Japan as in the United States.

Before a meal, the Japanese say いただきます (literally: *I humbly receive this*), and after the meal they say ごちそうさまでした (literally: *It was a feast*). Both are expressions of gratitude directed toward the people and things that made the meal possible, such as farmers, fishermen, cooks, and natural phenomena, like the rain.

● *Restaurants in Japan. What are the similarities and differences between restaurants in Japan and those in your country?*

You will find a wide variety of restaurants in Japan. Many restaurants display realistic-looking models of food in the window so that the customer can see what kinds of food the restaurant serves, and at what prices, before deciding to eat at a particular place.

At many moderately priced restaurants in Japan, you can seat yourself. As soon as you are seated, a waiter or waitress will often bring a steaming hot towel, called おしぼり, to wipe your hands and face. Because the service charge is included in the bill, it is customary not to tip.

If someone treats you to a meal, it is customary for you to thank the person after the meal (ごちそうさまでした) and again also the next time you see him or her by saying, for example, きのう／せんじつは　どうも　ごちそうさまでした (*Thank you for the feast yesterday/the other day*). You do not have to send a thank-you note except for special occasions. If possible, return the invitation. Returning invitations and other favors plays a vital role in relationships among the Japanese.

LANGUAGE

I. Deciding on something, using 〜に　します, and making a request, using 〜を　おねがいします

A. Deciding on something, using 〜に　します

Question				Answer		
Topic	Noun	Particle		Noun	Particle	
のみものは	何^{なに}	に	しますか。	ミルク	に	します。

What will you drink
(literally: As for drinks, what will you decide on)?

I will have some milk
(literally: I decide on milk).

B. Making a request, using 〜を　おねがいします

Question		Answer		
		Noun	Particle	
ごちゅうもん	は。	コーヒー	を	おねがいします。

Your order, please?

I will have some coffee (literally: I request coffee).

鈴木：　何を　のみますか。
What would you like to drink (literally: What will you drink)?

スミス：ええ、と...
Well . . .

鈴木：　ビールは　どうですか。
How about a beer?

スミス：いいですね。　じゃ、私は　ビールに　します。
That would be nice. I will have a beer.

鈴木：　じゃ、私も　ビールに　します。
Well then, I will have a beer, too.

スミス：(To the waiter) すみません。ビールを　二本　おねがいします。
Excuse me. We will have two bottles of beer (literally: we request two bottles of beer).

● When ordering something in a restaurant, you may say 〜に　します or 〜を　おねがいします as well as 〜を　下さい (in Chapter 8). します in the 〜に　します construction does not mean *do* but something like *decide on* 〜. It may also be used in other contexts, as in トヨタに　します (decide on a Toyota).

● You can use a number of quantity expressions with 〜を　おねがいします and 〜を　下さい depending on what it is you are asking. Use 〜つ (Japanese origin number) to order dishes and drinks and 〜本 for bottles. The quantity expression directly follows the particle を. When two or more items are listed, the sentence takes the form of "X を Quantity Expression と Y を Quantity Expression . . ." おねがいします.

コーヒーを　ひとつ　下さい。

Please bring one coffee.

ビールを　一本　おねがいします。

Please bring a bottle of beer.

ビールを　一本と　コーラを　二本　おねがいします。

Please bring a bottle of beer and two bottles of cola.

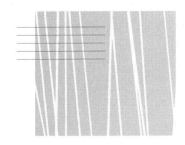

はなしてみましょう

A. Place an order, using 〜を　おねがいします. Use すみません to get your waiter's attention.

Example

そば／1
すみません。そばを　ひとつ　おねがいします。

1. コーラ／1
2. サンドイッチ／2
3. こうちゃ／1
4. ハンバーガー／3
5. ラーメン／5
6. Aランチ／1
7. おさしみ／4
8. うどん／2

B. Work with a partner. Pretend you are going to a restaurant. Circle one item that you would like to have in each category. Ask your partner to which restaurant he/she would like to go and what he/she is going to order. Find out if you and your partner have similar tastes in food and drinks.

Example

A: どの　レストランに　しますか。

B: 日本りょうりの　レストランに　します。

A: のみものは　何に　しますか。

B: ミルクに　します。

レストラン	日本りょうり　ちゅうかりょうり　イタリアりょうり　フランスりょうり
のみもの	ミルク　オレンジジュース　おちゃ　みず　ワイン　ビール　コーヒー
たべもの 1	スープ　サンドイッチ　ハンバーガー　サラダ　スパゲティ　ピザ
たべもの 2	おすし　おさしみ　てんぷら　チャーハン　カレーライス　ステーキ
デザート	ケーキ　アイスクリーム

C. Work in groups of three. Pretend you are at a restaurant. One person plays the waiter/waitress, and hands out the menu. The other members of the group are the customers. The waiter/waitress says ごちゅうもんは (*Your order, sir/madam?*). Choose a dish from the menu and place your orders. The waiter/waitress should confirm the order by saying X と　Y ですね。かしこまりました。Change roles and repeat the role play.

レストランで
ウェイター：ごちゅうもんは。
A:　　　　　のみものは　どうですか。
B:　　　　　ぼくは　ビールに　します。
A:　　　　　私は　オレンジジュースに　します。じゃあ、
　　　　　　ビールを　一本と　オレンジジュースを
　　　　　　一本　おねがいします。
ウェイター：ビールを　一本と　ジュースを　一本ですね。
　　　　　　かしこまりました。

メニュー

オードブル		スパゲティ	
オードブル取り合わせ	¥800	スパゲティ・イタリアン	¥900
スモークサーモン	¥1000	スパゲティ・ナポリタン	¥900
チキンレバーソテー	¥900	スパゲティ・ミートソース	¥1,000
スープ		**サラダ**	
コンソメスープ	¥400	レタスサラダ	¥500
ポタージュスープ	¥400	トマトサラダ	¥500
オニオングラタンスープ	¥600	カニサラダ	¥800
		チキンサラダ	¥700
魚料理		**米飯料理**	
エビフライ・タルタルソース添	¥1,200	カレーライス	¥800
エビマカロニグラタン	¥1,200	オムライス	¥900
カニコロッケ	¥1,000	エビピラフ	¥800
		カニピラフ	¥1,000
肉料理		**サンドイッチ**	
サーロインステーキ	¥3,500	ビーフサンド	¥900
ヒレステーキ	¥3,500	ハムサンド	¥600
ビーフシチュー	¥3,000	タマゴサンド	¥500
タンシチュー	¥3,500	野菜サンド	¥500
ハンバーグステーキ	¥1,000	ミックスサンド	¥600
ポークソテー	¥1,200		
ポークカツレツ	¥1,200		
鳥料理			
ローストチキン	¥1,200		
チキンソテー	¥1,000		
チキンコロッケ	¥1,000		

II. Inviting and responding, using 〜ませんか, 〜ましょうか, and 〜ましょう

A. Inviting, using 〜ませんか

			Verb stem + ませんか
わしょく	に	し	ませんか。

Why don't we have Japanese food (literally: Why don't we decide on Japanese food)?

B. Eliciting and stating agreement, using 〜ましょうか　and 〜ましょう

			Verb stem + ましょうか
わしょく	を	たべ	ましょうか。

			Verb stem +ましょう
わしょく	を	たべ	ましょう。

Shall we have Japanese food?　　　　　　　　Let's have Japanese food.

山田：　アリスさん、　今週の　金曜日に　一緒に
　　　　コンサートに　いきませんか。

Alice, why don't we go to a concert together this Friday?

アリス：ええ、ぜひ。　じゃあ、　何時に　あいましょうか。

Yes, I would love to. Well, at what time shall we meet?

山田：　そうですね。　三時ごろは　どうですか。

Let's see. How about around three o'clock?

アリス：いいですね。　じゃあ、三時に　えきの　まえで
　　　　あいましょう。

That would be fine. Let's meet in front of the station at three o'clock.

- The negative question form with a verb ending in 〜ませんか is often used for invitations. It is the equivalent of *won't you* 〜 or *why don't we*〜 in English.

- いっしょに means *together* and is often used with invitation phrases.

- Some common expressions for accepting an invitation are:

    ええ、ぜひ。 Yes, I'd love to (literally: Yes, by all means).

    ええ、〜ましょう。 Yes, let's do 〜.

    ええ、いいですよ。 Yes, that would be fine.

• When you decline an invitation, you usually apologize and give a reason for not being able to accept the invitation. If you don't want to give a specific reason, use one of the following phrases:

あのう、すみません。ちょっと　つごうが　わるいんです（が）。

Sorry, I'm a little busy (literally: Sorry, it's a little inconvenient).

あのう、すみません。ちょっと　ようじが　あるんです（が）。

Sorry, I have some errands/business to attend to.

はなしてみましょう

A. Work with a partner. Extend an invitation by rephrasing the following sentences with the ～ませんか form. Your partner will accept your invitation, saying ええ、～ましょう. Reverse roles.

Example

あした　テニスを　する
A: ～さん、あした　テニスを　しませんか。
B: ええ、しましょう。

1. 木曜日（もくようび）に　一緒（いっしょ）に　えいがを　みる
2. きっさてんで　アイスクリームを　たべる
3. 来週（らいしゅう）　一緒（いっしょ）に　しょくじを　する
4. うちで　コーヒーを　のむ
5. あの　きっさてんに　はいる
6. 週末（しゅうまつ）に　一緒（いっしょ）に　かいものに　いく
7. パーティーに　くる

B. On the next page, write down three activities you would like to do this weekend. Then invite at least one of your classmates for each activity. If you are invited by one of your classmates for an activity that you are not interested in, politely decline the invitation.

Example

You have written えいがを　みる for 金曜日（きんようび）.
A: 金曜日（きんようび）に　えいがを　みませんか。

B: ええ、いいですよ。

or すみません。ちょっと　つごうが　わるいんです。
　　ちょっと　ようじが　あるんです。

～曜日	すること (Activities to invite for)	なまえ (Person who has agreed)
きんようび 金曜日		
どようび 土曜日		
にちようび 日曜日		

C. Work with a partner. Invite your partner to do the following activities.
Decide on a time and place.

A: かいものに　いきませんか。
B: ええ、いいですね。いつ　いきましょうか。
A: あした　いきませんか。
B: いいですね。どこに　いきましょうか。
A: ～に　いきませんか。
B: ええ、いいですよ。じゃあ、～に　いきましょう。

	いつ	どこ
かいものに　いく		
コンサートに　いく		
いっしょに　しゅくだいを　する		
ちゅうかりょうりを　たべる		
えいがを　みる		

D. Pretend you want to go away for the holidays. Think of where you would
like to travel. Invite a few people to join you, and discuss the details, such as
when to meet, where to go, what to do, and so on. こんどの　やすみに
means *the next vacation*.

Example

たぐち
田口：　木村さん、スミスさん、こんどの　やすみに
ハワイに　いきませんか。

きむら
木村：　ええ、いいですね。

スミス：　ええ、いきましょう。

きむら
木村：　いつ　いきましょうか。
どこで　あいましょうか。
なに
何を　しましょうか。

III. Expressing purpose, using the verb stem 〜に　いきます／きます／かえります

	Verb Stem	Particle	Verb of Movement
先生に	あい	に	いきます。

I will go and see my professor.

Noun (place)	Particle		Verb Stem	Particle	Verb of Movement
レストラン	に	ごはんを	たべ	に	いきます。

I will go to a restaurant to have a meal.

田中：　　あした　何^{なに}を　しますか。

What are you doing tomorrow?

アリス：デパートに　くつを　かいに　いきます。

I'll go buy shoes in a department store.

田中：　　そうですか。

Is that right?

- The verb stem is the part of the verb that comes before ます. Thus, たべ is the stem of the verb たべます, and のみ is the stem of the verb のみます.

- The verb stem + に expresses a specific purpose when used with the verb for coming, going, or returning.

- The place can be stated either before or after the purpose. The particle に must be used for the place of destination because it modifies the main verb, and not the verb expressing the purpose.

こうえんに　あそびに　いきます。

I go to the park to play.

本を　よみに　としょかんに　いきます。

I go to the library to read books.

- に is also used for some nouns that indicate activities.

かいものに　いきます。

I'll go shopping.

りょこうに　いきます。

I'll go traveling.

はなしてみましょう

A. Based on each situation, make a sentence stating a purpose, using the verb
stem + に　いきます／きます／かえります.

Example

ちゅうかりょうりが　すきですから、そのレストランに
いきました。
ちゅうかりょうりを　たべに　そのレストランに
いきました。

1. ミルクが　ありませんから、スーパーに　いきます。
2. およぐのが　すきですから、ハワイに　いきます。
3. しゅくだいが　ありますから、うちに　かえります。
4. 日本に　ともだちが　いますから、日本に　いきます。
5. しゃしんを　とるのが　すきですから、この　山に　きま
した。

B. Work with a partner. One person asks the questions and the other gives as
many answers as possible.

Example

とうきょう

A: とうきょうに　何を　しに　いくんですか。

B: 日本語を　べんきょう　しに　いくんですよ。
or　しごとを　しに　いくんですよ。

まち／くに	もくてき (Purpose)
ニューヨーク	
ワシントン DC	
イギリス	
フランス	
日本	
中国	
オーストラリア	

C. Work with a partner. Ask your partner where he/she nomally goes on weekends or during vacations and what he/she does there. Report to the class the
place and purpose of your partner's activity.

A: 週末に　よく　どんな　ところに　いきますか。
B: イタリアりょうりの　レストランに　いきますね。
A: ああ、そうですか。どんな　りょうりを
　　たべるんですか。
B: スパゲティを　よく　たべますね。
　　<u>アリスさんは　週末に　よく　スパゲティを　たべに
　　イタリアりょうりの　レストランに　いきます。</u>

しゅうまつ	
やすみ (vacation)	

D. Work with a partner. You want to become friends with him/her. Think of a place and an activity, and then extend an invitation. If he/she says yes, discuss the details such as a time and a place to meet. If he/she says no, suggest another place and activity.

Example

A: 〜さん、私の　うちに　あそびに　きませんか。
B: ええ、いいですよ。いつ　いきましょうか。
A: そうですね。あしたは　どうですか。

IV. Using a question word + か + (particle)

Question			Answer		
Question Word + か	**Verb**				
何か	たべません	か。	ええ、	いいです	よ。

Why don't we eat something?　　　　　　　　Sure (literally: Yes, that would be fine).

Question					
Question Word + か	**Particle**			**Verb**	
どこ　か	に	いい　イタリアりょうりの　レストランが		あります	か。

Is there a good Italian restaurant somewhere?

Yes, there is.

小川 : 何<small>なに</small>か　のみませんか。
Why don't we drink something?

ジョンソン : ええ、いいですよ。
Sure (literally: Yes, that would be fine).

小川 : 何<small>なに</small>を　のみますか。
What will you have?

ジョンソン : 私は　ジュースを　のみます。
I will have some juice.

- Indefinite expressions, such as *something, someone,* and *somewhere,* are formed by adding か after a question word.

何<small>なに</small> + か = 何<small>なに</small>か　　　something　　どこ + か = どこか　　somewhere

だれ + か = だれか　　someone　　いつ + か = いつか　　someday

- The particles は, も, and に for time are not used with indefinite expressions. The particles が and を are usually deleted when they are used with indefinite expressions. The other particles are added after か.

だれか　きました。　　　　Someone came.

何<small>なに</small>か　たべます。　　I'll eat something.

いつか　かえります。　　　He'll come back sometime.

どこか<u>に</u>　いきました。　　She went somewhere.

どこか<u>で</u>　あいました。　　They met somewhere.

何<small>なに</small>か<u>に</u>　いれます。I'll put it in something.

- A question with question word + か + (particle) is a はい／いいえ question, although it looks like a question asking for information.

鈴木<small>すずき</small> : 何<small>なに</small>か　のみますか。
Are you going to drink something?

ブラウン : いいえ、どうぞ　おかまいなく。 *okamainaku*
No, please <u>don't bother</u>.

ジョーンズ : 何<small>なに</small>を　のみますか。
What are you going to drink?

山田 : コーヒーを　のみます。
I will drink coffee.

- To decline an offer, such as for food and drinks, use the following phrases.

いいえ、今(いま)は　いいです。　　　No, I'm fine for now.　　*ima wa iidesu.*

いいえ、何(なに)も　いりません。　　No, I don't need anything.　*nanimo irimasen.*

いいえ、どうぞ　おかまいなく。　　No, please don't bother.　*doozo okamainaku.*

いいえ、けっこうです。　　　　　　No, thank you.　　　*Kekkoo desu.*

はなしてみましょう

A. Answer the following questions.

Examples

今日(きょう)　何(なに)か　たべましたか。
ええ、たべました。 or いいえ、たべませんでした。
今日(きょう)　何(なに)を　たべましたか。
サンドイッチを　たべました。

1. いつか　日本に　いきますか。　*itsu(ka) when or sometime*
2. よく　どこで　ビールを　のみますか。*doko where ..*
3. いつ　うちに　かえりますか。
4. 今日(きょう)　だれかに　あいますか。　*dare (ka) who or someone*
5. 来週(らいしゅう)　どこかに　いきますか。
6. よく　だれに　でんわを　かけますか。

B. Ask a question for each of the following answers.

Example

ええ、のみます。コーヒーを　おねがいします。
何(なに)か　のみますか。

1. ええ、たべました。おいしい　フランスりょうりを
　たべました。
2. せんたくを　しました。　*sentaku = laundry.*
3. ざっしを　かいました。
4. いいえ、うちに　いました。
5. ええ。田中さんに　あいました。
6. 日本語(ご)の　本を　よみました。
7. ええ、みました。つくえの　下で　みました。

C. Ask your classmates whether they have had anything to eat or drink today. If they have, find out what it was. Also, find out how many people had nothing to eat or drink.

Example

A: スミスさん、今日 何か たべましたか。
B: いいえ、たべませんでした。
A: 何か のみましたか。
B: ええ、コーヒーを のみました。

なまえ	たべもの	のみもの
スミス	——	コーヒー

D. Work with a partner. Extend an invitation to your partner for drinks, food, a place to go, and something to do.

Example

A: 何か のみませんか。
B: いいですね。／ええ、いいですよ。
A: 何を のみましょうか。
B: ジュースは どうですか。／ジュースを のみましょう。

	Items/Places/Things
のみもの	
たべもの	
いく ところ (place to go)	
する こと (thing to do)	

V. Talking about activities and events, using ～で ～が あります

Noun (place)	Particle	Noun (activity)	Particle	Verb		but/and		
りょう	で	パーティ	が	ある	んです	が、	きません	か。

There is a party in the dormitory, so won't you come?

大川： たいいくかんで　ロックコンサートが　あるんですが、
一緒（いっしょ）に　いきませんか。
There is a rock concert in the gym, won't you go with me (literally: together)?

アリス： ええ、いいですよ。
Yes, that will be nice.

リー： 先生、しけんは　どこで　あるんですか。
Professor, where will the exam be?

先生： この　きょうしつで　あります。
It will be in this classroom.

- When the subject of ある is an activity, such as a concert or a party, ある roughly means *to be held* or *to take place*.
- The place at which an event is held is indicated by the particle で, instead of に, because に is used to indicate the location of an object.
- ～んです is often used to introduce a topic, indicating that the reason is being given for the subsequent statement or question.
- が at the end of the introductory phrase is called a "weak" *but*. It simply introduces a topic of conversation and implies *and*. It does not introduce negation.

はなしてみましょう

A. Ask questions about the place of an activity or an event using the particles で or に.

___ **Example**

コンサート
コンサートは　どこで　ありますか。

1. テスト
2. いぬ
3. パーティ
4. 本屋（や）

5. テニスの　しあい (game)
6. じゅぎょう
7. くつ
8. えいが

B. Work with a partner. Think about major events at your high school, college campus, hometown, and country. Describe them to your partner.

私の　こうこうでは　大きい　シニアプロム (*senior prom*) が
ありました。
パーティは　こうこうの　たいいくかんで　ありました。

	できごと (**event**) と　ところ
こうこう	
大学	
まち	
くに	

C. Work with a new partner. Report one of the events that your previous partner described. Compare it to one of the events you described to your previous partner.

～さんの　こうこうでは　大きい　シニアプロム (*senior prom*) が　ありました。ぼくの　こうこうでも
シニアプロム が　ありました。～さんの　こうこうの
パーティは　こうこうの　たいいくかんで　ありましたが、
ぼくの　こうこうのパーティは　ホテルで　ありました。

漢字

Kanji made from pictures and symbols 2

moon, month

fire

water

(squeezing a river to get water)

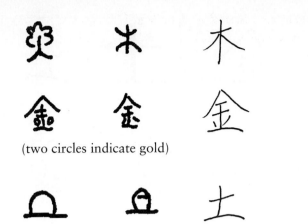

木　tree

金　gold, money, metal

(two circles indicate gold)

土　ground, earth, soil

(a pile of earth)

分　divide, minute

(a sword to cut)

あたらしい　よみかた　(New Readings)

<ruby>誕<rt>たんじょうび</rt></ruby> 生日　　<ruby>山本<rt>やまもと</rt></ruby>

月	月		
丿	刀	月	月

moon, month

ゲツ、ガツ

つき

<ruby>月曜日<rt>げつようび</rt></ruby>
<ruby>一月<rt>いちがつ</rt></ruby>
<ruby>先月<rt>せんげつ</rt></ruby>

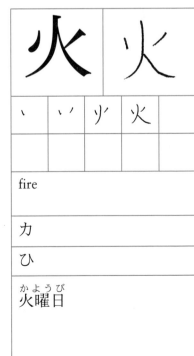

火	火		
丶	丷	少	火

fire

カ

ひ

<ruby>火曜日<rt>かようび</rt></ruby>

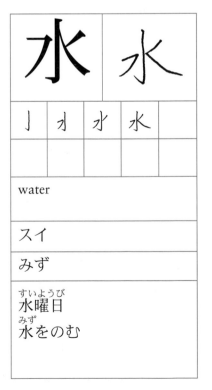

水	水		
丿	가	가	水

water

スイ

みず

<ruby>水曜日<rt>すいようび</rt></ruby>
<ruby>水<rt>みず</rt></ruby>をのむ

| 一 | 十 | オ | 木 | |
| | | | | |

tree

モク

き

<ruby>木曜日<rt>もくようび</rt></ruby>
<ruby>木の上<rt>き うえ</rt></ruby>

| ノ | 入 | 人 | 合 | 全 |
| 全 | 金 | 金 | | |

gold, money

キン

かね

<ruby>金曜日<rt>きんようび</rt></ruby>
<ruby>お金<rt>かね</rt></ruby>

| 一 | 十 | 土 | |
| | | | |

soil

ド

つち

<ruby>土曜日<rt>どようび</rt></ruby>

| 日 | 日ㇵ | 日ㇵㇵ | 曜 | 曜 |
| 曜 | 曜 | 曜 | 曜 | 曜 |

day of the week

ヨウ

<ruby>月曜日<rt>げつようび</rt></ruby>
<ruby>日曜日<rt>にちようび</rt></ruby>
<ruby>水曜日<rt>すいようび</rt></ruby>

| ノ | 𠂉 | 乇 | 午 | 年 |
| 年 | | | | |

year

ネン

とし

<ruby>一年<rt>いちねん</rt></ruby> <ruby>来年<rt>らいねん</rt></ruby>
<ruby>今年<rt>ことし</rt></ruby>
<ruby>三年生<rt>さんねんせい</rt></ruby>
1995<ruby>年<rt>ねん</rt></ruby>

| l | 冂 | 日 | 日 | 日ㇵ |
| 旷 | 旷 | 旷 | 時 | 時 |

time, hour

ジ

とき

<ruby>四時<rt>よ じ</rt></ruby>
<ruby>三時間<rt>さんじかん</rt></ruby>

こどもの <ruby>時<rt>とき</rt></ruby>

間	間

丨	冂	冂	冃	冃
門	門	門	間	

interval, duration

カン

あいだ

いっしゅうかん
一週間
はちじかん
八時間

週	週

丿	刀	月	冑	用
周	周	淍	调	週

week

シュウ

せんしゅう
先週
にしゅうかん
二週間

何	何

丿	亻	仁	仃	何
何	何			

what

なに、なん

なんじ
何時ですか。
なに
何を　しますか。
なんぼん
何本　ありますか。

半	半

丶	丷	丷	三	半

half

ハン

ごじはん
五時半に　きます。
じゅうじはん
十時半に　ねます。

分	分

丿	八	分	分	

to divide, to understand, minute

フン、ブン、プン

わ（ける）、わ（かる）

さんじじゅうごふん
三時十五分です。
くじじゅっぷん
九時十分です。
わ
分かりません。

今	今

丿	八	今	今	

now

コン

いま

こんしゅう
今週
いま　い
今　行きます。

Read the following sentences written in **hiragana**, **katakana**, and **kanji**.

1. 私は七月にハワイにいきます。
2. 先週の木曜日と火曜日はじゅぎょうがありませんでした。
3. 本田さんの誕生日は月曜日です。
4. 水曜日の七時半にきます。
5. こうこうの時、よく何をしましたか。
6. アメリカに一年います。
7. 今四時二十三分です。
8. 土曜日と日曜日には十時間ぐらいねました。

上手な読み方

Understanding the format of a postcard

Japanese postcards (はがき) are usually written vertically: that is, text is read from right to left. The stamp is located at the upper left corner of the front of the card. The sender's name and address are written under the stamp. Write the sender's ZIP code in the small boxes on the lower left corner. The addressee's address should be written on the right side, with the ZIP code, in the boxes at the top of the card, and his/her name should be in the center of the card. Use さま (様), a formal version of さん, after the addressee's name.

It is not necessary to write the names of the sender and addressee on the back of the card. The card usually contains a short greeting phrase, a body, a short closing phrase, and a date.

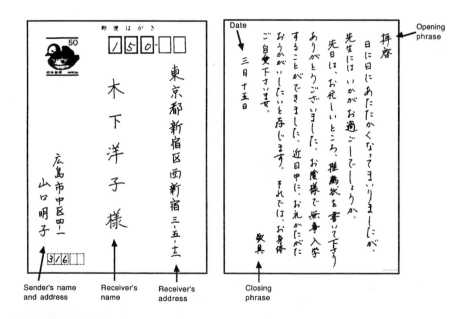

A New Year's card (ねんがじょう) is probably the most important greeting card in Japan. New Year's cards are exchanged not only among friends and relatives, but also among business people, neighbors, students, and teachers. Look at the following New Year's card and identify the names, addresses, and ZIP codes of the sender and the addressee. Then identify the greeting phrases.

読む前に

A postcard can be used to send an invitation. For which occasions have you sent invitations? Talk in Japanese about such occasions.

Read the following postcard to answer the questions below.

山川さんの　はがき　(Yamakawa-san's postcard)

ことばの　リスト

前略　*opening phrase*

草々　*closing phrase*

（お）ひさしぶり　It's been a long time.　o hisashiburi

よかったら　If it is all right . . .　yokatara

いろいろ　various　iroiro

山川さんが　ともだちに　はがきを　かきました。

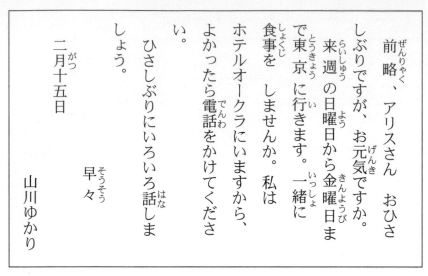

前略、アリスさん　おひさ
しぶりですが、お元気ですか。
来週の日曜日から金曜日ま
で東京に行きます。一緒に
食事を　しませんか。私は
ホテルオークラにいますから、
よかったら電話をかけてくださ
い。
ひさしぶりにいろいろ話しま
しょう。

二月十五日

早々

山川ゆかり

わかりましたか

A. 日本語で　こたえて下さい。

1. この　はがきは　だれに　かきましたか。
2. その　人は　どこに　すんでいますか。(residing)　*Sunde imasu*
3. どうして　山川さんは　この　はがきを　かきましたか。
4. この　人は　来週　何を　しますか。

B. Write a postcard to a friend you haven't seen for a while. Invite him/her to your graduation (そつぎょうしき).

上手な聞き方
<ruby>上<rt>じょう</rt></ruby><ruby>手<rt>ず</rt></ruby>な<ruby>聞<rt>き</rt></ruby>き<ruby>方<rt>かた</rt></ruby>

Using context

You do not need to understand every word to comprehend what is being said in a conversation. If you can get the general idea or pick up key words, you can probably guess the words that you missed. The context provides many clues that will help you fill in the words you don't completely understand.

A. You are talking on the phone to Chin-san, who tells you about his vacation in Florida. However, the connection is not very good, and there is some static on the line. Write down the words you couldn't hear but that you guessed from the context of the conversation.

ことばの　リスト

フロリダ　Florida

オーランド　Orlando

マイアミ　Miami

1. _____

2. _____

3. _____

B. レストランの　かいわ (Conversations in a Restaurant). Listen to each conversation and fill in the blanks with the appropriate words.

1. この　レストランは　_____　りょうりの　レストランです。
   この　人は　_____　を　たべます。

2. この　レストランは　_____　りょうりの　レストランです。
   おとこの　人は　<ruby>今日<rt>きょう</rt></ruby>　_____　を　たべます。
   おんなの　人は　_____　を　ちゅうもんします。

3. この　レストランは　_____　りょうりの　レストランです。
   おんなの　人は　_____　を　ちゅうもんします。
   おさしみは　_____　円です。
   おとこの　人は　_____　を　ちゅうもんします。

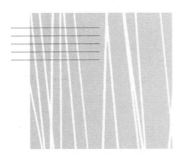

You, Smith-san, have been studying with Yamamoto-san all morning. It is now noon, and you are both getting hungry.

山本 :＿＿＿＿＿＿＿＿＿＿＿＿＿＿＿＿＿＿＿＿＿

スミス :＿＿＿＿＿＿＿＿＿＿＿＿＿＿＿＿＿＿＿

山本 :＿＿＿＿＿＿＿＿＿＿＿＿＿＿＿＿＿＿＿＿

スミス :＿＿＿＿＿＿＿＿＿＿＿＿＿＿＿＿＿＿＿

山本 :＿＿＿＿＿＿＿＿＿＿＿＿＿＿＿＿＿＿＿＿

ウェイトレス : ごちゅうもんは。

山本 :＿＿＿＿＿＿＿＿＿＿＿＿＿＿＿＿＿＿＿＿

スミス :＿＿＿＿＿＿＿＿＿＿＿＿＿＿＿＿＿＿＿

山本 :＿＿＿＿＿＿＿＿＿＿＿＿＿＿＿＿＿＿＿＿

聞き上手　話し上手

Making and receiving telephone calls

Every language has specific ways to initiate and answer phone calls and to start a conversation. The following list of expressions should help you make a phone call. You should use formal language at first, and it is customary to identify yourself by your last name.

A. How to make a telephone call

Situation: You, Smith-san, are making a phone call to Alice-san. You do not know who will answer the phone.

Variation 1: Somebody in the Suzuki family answers the phone.

スミス :　もしもし。<u>すずきさんの　おたくですか。</u>　　　*otaku / desuka)*
　　　　　Hello. Is this the Suzuki residence?

Person:　はい、そうです。
　　　　　Yes, it is.

スミス :　<u>スミス</u>と　もうしますが、<u>アリスさん</u>(は)　　　*— to mooshimasu ga,*
　　　　　いらっしゃいますか。　　　　　　　　　　　　　　*— san wa iraíshyaimasuka?*
　　　　　My name is Smith. Is Alice home?

Person:　はい、います。ちょっと　まって下さい。　　*chotto matte kudasái.*
　　　　　Yes, she is. Please wait a moment.

アリス： もしもし。アリスです。
Hello. This is Alice.

Variation 2: This time, Alice happens to answer the phone, but you don't know
it is she.

スミス： もしもし、<u>すずきさんの</u> おたくですか。 ー San no otaku desu ka?
Hello, is this the Suzuki residence?

アリス： はい、そうです。
Yes, it is.

スミス： <u>スミス</u>ですが、<u>アリスさん</u>（は） いらっしゃいますか。
My name is Smith. Is Alice home?

アリス： はい、私です。
This is she.

スミス： ああ、<u>アリスさん</u>。
Hi, Alice.

B. How to receive a phone call

リン　リン

スミス： はい、（もしもし。）<u>スミス</u>です。
Hello. This is Smith.

Voice: ああ、<u>スミスさん</u>。<u>アリス</u>です。
Hi, Mr. Smith. This is Alice.

スミス： ああ、<u>アリスさん</u>。
Hi, Alice.

C. What to do when you reach a wrong number

Situation: You are making a phone call to Alice, but you reach a wrong number.

スミス： もしもし。<u>すずきさんの</u> おたくですか。
Hello. Is this the Suzuki residence?

Person: いいえ、ちがいます。 Chigaimasu.
No, it isn't.

スミス： あっ、<u>どうも</u> すみません。ばんごうは <u>３２３４の</u>
<u>５４３２</u>ですか。
Oh, excuse me. Is this 3234-5432?

Person: いいえ、<u>３２３４の ５３４２</u>です。
No, it is 3234-5342.

スミス： どうも すみません。
I'm sorry.

- もしもし functions very much like *hello* in English but is used only in a telephone conversation.

- When you answer the phone, the best phrase is simply はい、*your last name*です although you may use もしもし as well.

- Don't panic when you realize that you have reached a wrong number. Simply ask what phone number you have reached to determine whether you have the wrong number.

- Japanese people tend to say ええ and はい more often than Americans say *Uh uh* or *OK*. This has two implications: (1) An American may feel pressure if he/she often hears ええ or はい. (2) A Japanese person may feel unsure about whether the other party is still on the line if he/she does not receive enough signals. The Japanese person may start saying もしもし, which in this case is equivalent to *Are you there?*

A. Look at the examples on pages 308 and 309. Work with a partner. Practice making phone calls. Two situations are provided. When you are done, reverse roles with your partner.

   1. You call Ms. Hiroko Suzuki (or Mr. Hiroshi Suzuki). Your partner plays the role of Suzuki-san's parent, who answers the phone.

   2. You call Ms. Hiroko Suzuki (or Mr. Hiroshi Suzuki). Your partner plays the role of Ms. Suzuki (or Mr. Suzuki), who answers the phone.

B. Refer to the examples on page 309. With your partner, practice how to handle the situation when you have reached a wrong number. When you are done, reverse roles with your partner.

そうごうれんしゅう

Your instructor will give you a card with a day of the week written on it. This is the day on which you are free and don't have classes. On the card, write the name of an activity for which you want to invite someone. Then your instructor will divide the class into two groups: one group extends invitations, and the other receives them. One person in the first group must find someone in the second group who has the same free day and who wants to do the same activity. Then negotiate the details, such as where to go, what time and where to meet, and so on.

You are free on :	すいようび Wednesday
Activity :	えいがを みる (to) go to a movie

ロールプレイ

1. You are at a Japanese department store with your friend and have decided to get something to eat. You go to the eighth floor, which has a variety of restaurants (めいてんがい); you select a restaurant (わしょく、ようしょく、ちゅうかりょうり, etc).

2. You have gone to a restaurant with your friend. Order what you want. Ask how long your order will take. If an order takes more than 15 minutes, order something else.

たんご (ESSENTIAL VOCABULARY)

Nouns

Aランチ   A-Lunch (Western-style)

アイスクリーム   ice cream

イタリア   Italy
   イタリアりょうり   Italian food

うどん   Japanese wheat noodles *udon*

おちゃ（お茶）green tea   *ochya*

カレーライス   curry and rice dish
   An abbreviated form is カレー.

ケーキ   cake

(お)さしみ（(御)刺身）   sashimi (filet of fresh raw fish, such as tuna) (usually used with お at the beginning)

サラダ   salad   *sarada*

サンドイッチ   sandwich

ジュース   juice   オレンジジュース orange juice   *jyusu*

(お)すし（(御)寿司）   sushi (usually used with お at the beginning)

ステーキ   beefsteak

スープ   soup

スパゲティ spaghetti   *supagetei*

そば（蕎麦）Japanese buckwheat noodles

たんじょうび（誕生日）birthday *tanjyoobi*

チャーハン   Chinese-style fried rice

ちゅうかりょうり（中華料理）Chinese food   *chyuka ryori*

デザート   dessert

てんぷら（天麩羅）tempura (fish, shrimp, and vegetables battered and deep-fried)

はがき（葉書）postcard   *hagaki*

ばんごう（番号）number
   でんわばんごう（電話番号）telephone number

ハンバーガー   hamburger

ピザ   pizza

みず（水）water

ミルク   milk

ようじ（用事）errand   *yooji*

ラーメン   ramen (Chinese noodles in soup)

わしょく（和食）Japanese food   にほんりょうり（日本料理）

Irregular Verbs

ちゅうもんする（注文する）(to) order

う -verbs

あう（会う）(to) meet   *ainasu*
よぶ（呼ぶ）(to) invite; to call   *yobu*

Adverbs

いっしょに（一緒に）together   *yi'shyo (ni)*
ちょっと　a little bit   *chyotto*

Prefixes

ご〜（御〜）(polite)　ごちゅうもん

Expressions

いいえ、けっこうです。No, thank you. *kekko* どうぞ　おかまいなく。Please don't *ogamainaku*
〜さんの　おたくですか。（〜さんの *otaku* bother.
　お宅ですか。）Is this the 〜 residence?　　なにも　いりません。（何も　いりませ
ちょっと　つごうが　わるいんです。　　　　ん。）I don't need anything. *nanimo irimasen*
　（ちょっと都合が悪いんです。）*tsugoo(ga)* に　します　decide/s on 〜.
　It's not really convenient./I already have plans. *waruin(desu)* もしもし　Hello (on the phone).
ちょっと　ようじが　あるんです。　　　　〜を　おねがいします。（〜を　お願い
　（ちょっと　用事が　あるんです。）*yooji* します。）I would like to have 〜.
　I have some errands to do.
〜ですが、〜さんは　いらっしゃいます *ira'shyaimasuka*
　か。My name is 〜. Is 〜 home?

Passive Vocabulary

Nouns

そつぎょうしき（卒業式）graduation ceremony　*sotsugyoo*
　そつぎょう（卒業）graduation　しき（式）ceremony　*shiki*
ねんがじょう（年賀状）New Year's card　*nengajyoo*

Expressions

（お）げんきですか。（（お）元気ですか。）
   How have you been (literally: Are you well/healthy)?

（お）ひさしぶり（（お）久しぶり） It's been a long time since we last met. *Ohisashyoburi*

かしこまりました。 Certainly.
   (Polite language used by waiters, clerks, etc.)

ごちゅうもんは。（御注文は。） What would you like to order?

ぜんりゃく（前略） opening phrase of a letter *zenryaku*

そうそう（草々） closing phrase of a letter *soo soo*

とくに　よていは　ありません。（特に　予定は　ありません。） I don't have any particular plans. *toku ni yotei wa arimasen*

〜の　あと（〜の　後） after 〜
   えいがの　あと（映画の　後） after the movie

よかったら　If it's all right . . . *yo kata ra*

Supplementary Vocabulary

Foods

インドりょうり（インド料理） Indian food

えびフライ　*ebi* shrimp, breaded and deep-fried

かんこくりょうり（韓国料理） Korean food

すきやき　Japanese dish consisting of beef slices and vegetables cooked together *suki yaki*

スペインりょうり（スペイン料理）
   Spanish food

チキンかつ　chicken cutlet, breaded and deep-fried

ていしょく（定食） (lunch, dinner) set
   てんぷらていしょく（てんぷら定食）
   tempura dinner

とんかつ（豚かつ） pork cutlet, breaded and deep-fried *donkatsu = paigu*

パイ　pie

パスタ　pasta

ハンバーグ　hamburger steak

ホットドッグ　hotdog

メキシコりょうり（メキシコ料理）
   Mexican food

ロシアりょうり（ロシア料理） Russian food

— to mooshi masu ga —
This is

chotto waruyin desu
It's not convenient

zehi – by all means
（ぜひ）

A traditional family

私の家族
かぞく

MY FAMILY

Functions	Describing people; Addressing family members
New Vocabulary	Kinship terms; The body; Physical appearance; Verbs used with clothes; Verbs of resultant state; Personality and ability
Dialogue	私の家族は　五人家族です。(There are five people in my family.) かぞく　　　ごにんかぞく
Culture	The Japanese family
Language	I. Counting people, using 人; Counting age, using さい; Expressing the にん order within a family, using 番(目) ばんめ
	II. Describing a resultant state, using the verb て-form＋いる
	III. Describing physical appearance and skills, using 〜は 〜が
	IV. Connecting phrases, using the verb and the adjective て-forms
	V. Describing people and things, using nouns and modifying clauses
Kanji	Pictographs and kinship terms
Reading	Transforming textual information into charts and figures
Listening	Using one's background knowledge about a person
Communication	Being modest

A. 家族 (Kinship terms). Japanese has two sets of kinship terms. One is used to refer to one's own family, and the other is used to refer to someone else's family.

	Your own family (humble form)	Someone else's family (polite form)
Family	家族	ご家族
Father	父	お父さん
Mother	母	お母さん
Parents	りょうしん	ごりょうしん
Elder brother	兄	お兄さん
Elder sister	姉	お姉さん
Younger brother	弟	弟さん
Younger sister	妹	妹さん
Siblings	兄弟	ご兄弟
Grandfather	そふ	おじいさん
Grandmother	そぼ	おばあさん
Husband	主人／おっと	ご主人
Wife	かない／つま	おくさん
Child/children	子供	お子さん

● 子供, 兄弟, 家族 and りょうしん are generic terms as well as terms used for one's own family.

日本の子供は　よく　あそびます。

Japanese children play a lot.

ハワイには　日本人の　家族が　たくさん　います。

There are many Japanese families in Hawaii.

● 男の子 means a *boy*. 女の子 means a *girl*.

Look at the following family trees. Note that each family member is represented by a letter. Form groups of three students. One will write the letters from A through T at random on a piece of paper. Then, you will read aloud each letter on your list, and the other two will compete to say a kinship term that corresponds to each letter. Remember to say 私の〜 or

山田さんの～. The person who says the correct term first gets a point. The person with the most points wins. Take turns reading the letters.

Example

The dealer says H. Player 1 says 私の 妹（いもうと）first. Player 1 gets a point.

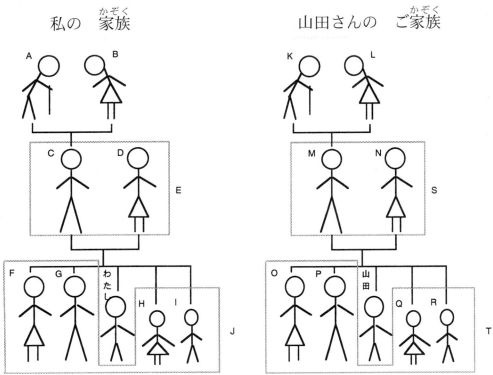

私の 家族（かぞく）　　　　　　　山田さんの ご家族（かぞく）

B. からだ (The body). Write the following Japanese words in the appropriate places in the picture.

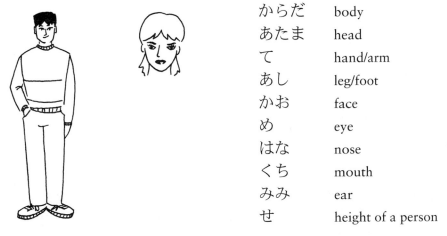

からだ	body
あたま	head
て	hand/arm
あし	leg/foot
かお	face
め	eye
はな	nose
くち	mouth
みみ	ear
せ	height of a person

Work with a partner. Name a body part in Japanese. Your partner will point out on a picture the part of the body that you named. Reverse rolls.

C. かお　と　からだを　あらわすことば (Physical appearance).

せが　たかい　　tall (height)

せが　ひくい　　short (height)

はなが　たかい　　with a big nose

はなが　ひくい　　with a flat nose

ながい　　long (length)

みじかい　　short (length)

まるい　　round

しかくい　　square

ほそながい　　narrow and long

日本語で　こたえて下さい。

1. How would you describe yourself? _____

2. Choose adjectives to describe your . . .

かお _____　はな _____

あし _____　て _____

D. きるものに　つかうことば (Verbs used with clothing). Look at the picture and learn the verbs used in connection with the following articles of clothing and accessories. Then fill in the blanks below with the correct verbs.

ぼうしを　かぶる　(to) put on a hat

めがねを　かける　(to) put on glasses

イヤリングを　する　(to) put on earrings

とけいを　する　(to) put on a wristwatch

シャツを　きる　(to) put on a shirt

スカートを　はく　(to) put on a skirt

くつを　はく　(to) put on shoes

セーター	ズボン	ベルト	ネックレス
———	———	———	———
スーツ	めがね	ぼうし	とけい
———	———	———	———

E. Verbs of resultant state.

ふとる　(to) gain weight

やせる　(to) lose weight

けっこんする　(to) marry

～に　すむ　(to) reside

かいしゃに　つとめる　(to) become employed at a company

ふとっている　(to) be chubby

やせている　(to) be thin

けっこんしている　(to) be married

～にすんでいる　(to) live

かいしゃに　つとめている　(to) be employed at a company

日本語で　こたえて下さい。

1. けっこんしていますか。いつ　けっこんしますか。

2. どこに　すんでいますか。

3. どんな　ところに　すむのが　すきですか。

4. さいきん (recently) やせましたか。ふとりましたか。

5. お父さんは／お母さんは　やせていますか。ふとっていますか。

6. お父さんは／お母さんは　どこかに　つとめていますか。

F.　せいかくと　のうりょく (Personality and ability).

げんき（な）lively

しんせつ（な）kind

やさしい　　gentle

あかるい　　cheerful

かわいい　　cute, adorable

あたまが　いい　　smart, intelligent

日本語が　わかる　(to) understand Japanese

りょうりが　上手（な）good at cooking

日本語で　こたえて下さい。

1. お父さんは　どんな人ですか。

2. お母さんは　どんな人ですか。

3. どんな　人が　すきですか。

4. 一ばん　いい　ともだちは　どんな人ですか。

ダイアローグ

はじめに

A. 日本語で こたえて下さい。
　1. 何人家族ですか。
　2. お兄さんが いますか。お姉さんは？
　3. 妹 さんが いますか。弟 さんは？

まんがを みて下さい。そして、ダイアローグを きいて下さい。

私の家族は 五人家族です。(There are five people in my family.)

アリスさんのともだちの 川口さんが アリスさんのうちに あ
そびに きました。アリスさんと 川口さんは 今 アリスさん
のへやに います。

_____ 川口： あ、あの　つくえの　しゃしん、アリスさんの
　　　　　　ご家族ですか。

アリスさんは　川口さんに　しゃしんを　みせます。

_____ アリス： ええ、そうです。これが　父で　これが
　　　　　　母です。

_____ 川口： お父さんも　お母さんも　とても　すてきな
　　　　　　かたですね。

_____ アリス： ありがとう。父も　母も　今　四十五さい　です。
　　　　　　父は　コンピュータの　かいしゃに
　　　　　　つとめています。母は　こうこうの　先生です。

stomei)

_____ 川口： そうですか。　この　ぼうしを
　　　　　　かぶっている　男の子は　弟　さんですか。

_____ アリス： ええ、そうです。　なまえは　デービッドで、
　　　　　　今　小学校の　三年生です。

_____ 川口： かわいいですね。じゃあ、この人は
　　　　　　おねえさんですか。

_____ アリス： いいえ、それは　妹　の　パムです。パムは
　　　　　　まだ　十七さいなんですが、　パムの
　　　　　　ほうが　私より　せがたかくて　大きいので、
　　　　　　よく　年上に　みられるんですよ。

まだ mada
还還

_____ 川口： そうですか。

わかりましたか

1. Look at the picture of a family tree on page 317. Use it as an example to draw Alice's family tree.

2. Complete the following paragraph using appropriate words and phrases.

　　　アリスさんの　家族は　五人家族です。お父さんと
お母さんと　_____ が　います。アリスさんの　_____ は
四十五さいで、　コンピュータの　かいしゃに　つとめています。
アリスさんの　_____ も　四十五さいです。_____ は
こうこうの　先生です。アリスさんの　_____ の

なまえは ＿＿＿＿＿ です。＿＿＿＿＿は 高校生<ruby>高校</ruby>ですが、せが とても　たかいです。アリスさんの　＿＿＿＿＿の　なまえは デービッドで、小学校<ruby>小学校</ruby>の　＿＿＿＿＿ です。とても　かわいいです。

日本の文化

日本の家族. *How would you describe your family to your friends?*

In Japan, the wife traditionally takes care of the children and house while the husband supports the family financially. Even when the wife has a job, she is expected to do housework. The oldest son and his wife are expected to take care of his elderly parents. About fifteen percent of all households are so-called three-generation families. Only about ten percent of the elderly live alone.

Since the end of World War II, the number of children in a family has rapidly decreased. It now averages 1.7. (In the United States it is 2.1.) Some of the reasons for this decline are economic; others are social, such as the growing reluctance among young women to marry early.

The Japanese rarely praise members of their own family when they talk to someone outside the family. They are very conscious of the distinction between in-groups (うち) and out-groups (そと). It is very important to be polite to those who are not in one's in-group, and praising members of your own family, the primary in-group, is considered impolite. Thus, you often hear a Japanese man complaining that his wife is not a good cook when in fact she is an excellent cook, or you may hear a woman say that her husband is impractical and inept at household matters. Similarly, boasting about yourself is considered socially inappropriate.

Within one's own family, お父さん, お母さん, お兄さん, お姉さん and similar terms are used to address senior members. First names are used only toward younger members. Thus, a daughter or son would call their mother お母さん or お母ちゃん (the more familiar form), an older brother お兄さん or お兄ちゃん, and a younger sister みち子ちゃん. Senior family members tend to use a kinship term to refer to themselves when talking to younger family members. Instead of using their first names, parents usually call each other お父さん or お母さん. in urban areas, パパ and ママ are often used instead of お父さん and お母さん. The Japanese do not distinguish between biological parents and step-parents when addressing parents.

I. Counting people, using 人 (にん); Counting age, using さい; Expressing the order within a family, using 番(目) (ばん め)

A. Counting people, using 人 (にん).

	Noun (Kinship Term)		Number Counter	
私は	弟 (おとうと)	が	二人 (ふたり)	います。

I have two younger brothers.

私は	兄弟 (きょうだい)	が	四人 (よにん)	います。

I have four siblings.

B. Counting age, using さい

Question		
Kinship Term		
お父さん (とう)	は	おいくつですか。

How old is your father?

Answer				
Kinship Term		**Number**	**Counter**	
父	は	四十五	さい	です。

My father is 45 years old.

C. Expressing the order within a family, using 番（目）

Question			
	Question Word	**Counter**	
石田さんは	何	番目	です	か。

Where do you fit in your family/among your siblings, Ishida-san?

Answer				
Noun	**Particle**	**Number**	**Counter**	
上	から	二	番目	です。

I am the second oldest (literally: second from the top).

田中 : 私の家族は　五人家族です。

My family consists of five people (literally: My family is a five-people family).

モネ : ゆみ子さんは　何番目ですか。

Where do you fit in your family, Yumiko?

田中 : 私は　一番上です。

I am the oldest (literally: the highest).

モネ : そうですか。一番下は　どの人ですか。

I see. Who is the youngest (literally: the lowest)?

田中 : 妹　の　きみ子です。きみ子は　今　１５さいです。

My younger sister, Kimiko. She is fifteen years old now.

● The pronunciation of a number depends on the counter.

	～人 (～ people)		～さい （～years old)		～番（目） (ordinal, ～th)	
何	なんにん	何人	なんさい	何さい	なんばん(め)	何番（目）
一	※ひとり	一人	※いっさい	一さい	いちばん(め)	一番（目）
二	※ふたり	二人	にさい	二さい	にばん(め)	二番（目）
三	さんにん	三人	さんさい	三さい	さんばん(め)	三番（目）
四	※よにん	四人	よんさい	四さい	よんばん(め)	四番（目）
五	ごにん	五人	ごさい	五さい	ごばん(め)	五番（目）
六	ろくにん	六人	ろくさい	六さい	ろくばん(め)	六番（目）
七	しちにん	七人	ななさい	七さい	ななばん(め)	七番（目）
八	はちにん	八人	※はっさい	八さい	はちばん(め)	八番（目）
九	きゅうにん	九人	きゅうさい	九さい	きゅうばん(め)	九番（目）
十	じゅうにん	十人	※じゅっさい／十さい ※じっさい		じゅうばん(め)	十番（目）
百	ひゃくにん	百人	ひゃくさい	百さい	ひゃくばん(め)	百番（目）
千	せんにん	千人				
一万	いちまんにん	一万人				

● The symbol ※ indicates that the pronunciation of the cardinal number has changed.

● いくつ or おいくつ (polite form of いくつ) is often used instead of 何さい as in Key Sentence B.

● 番（目） converts cardinal numbers into ordinal numbers, and it is used to describe one's order within the family, as in:

一番上　　　　　　the oldest (literally: the first from the top, the highest)

上から　二番目　　the second oldest (literally: the second from the top, the second highest)

まん中　　　　　　the right in the middle

下から　二番目　　the second youngest (literally: the second from the bottom, the second lowest)

一番下　　　　　　the youngest (literally: the first from the bottom, the lowest)

- ～は　～が　ある／いる is used to express one's ownership.
  ～を　もっている in Chapter 8 also indicates ownership. However, もっている is used for concrete inanimate objects such as a car or a bag. ～は～が　ある／いる can be used for people, animals, or abstract things.

私は　くるまを　もっています。

I have a car.

私は　弟<ruby>弟<rt>おとうと</rt></ruby>が　一人<ruby>一人<rt>ひとり</rt></ruby>　います。

I have a younger brother.

私は　じゅぎょうが　あります。

I have class.

話<ruby>話<rt>はな</rt></ruby>してみましょう

A. Listen to your instructor's directions and, as quickly as possible, form groups accordingly.

Example

三人<ruby>三人<rt>さんにん</rt></ruby>の　グループを　つくって下さい。

B. Write three numbers on a piece of paper. Your instructor will say an age. Cross out each number on your list that corresponds to the age that has been said. The person who crosses out all the numbers first is the winner.

C. Work in groups of five or six. Write one number on a piece of paper and put it on the back of a member of your group. The number on your back represents your age. Take turns asking one another what your age is and form a line from the youngest to the oldest.

D. Take turns asking your classmates how many people are in their family. Compare the results. Whose family is the largest or the smallest? Discuss whether it is better to come from a large family or a small family.

Example

A: ～さんの　ご家族<ruby>家族<rt>かぞく</rt></ruby>は　何人家族<ruby>何人家族<rt>にんかぞく</rt></ruby>ですか。
B: 三人家族<ruby>人家族<rt>にんかぞく</rt></ruby>です
or 母<ruby>母<rt>はは</rt></ruby>と　私の　二人<ruby>二人<rt>ふたり</rt></ruby>です。

E. Work in groups of four or five. Take turns asking your classmates how many siblings they have and their order in the family. Compare the results. Who is the oldest or the youngest in their family? Discuss whether it is better to be a younger or older member of the family.

Example

A: ～さんは　ご兄弟_{きょうだい}が　いますか。

B: はい、二人_{ふたり}　います。

A: ～さんは　何番目_{ばんめ}ですか。

B: 私は　一番上_{ばんうえ}です。

F. Work with a partner. Take turns describing the members of your family by name and age. Fill in the following chart with information about your partner's family.

Example

私は　兄_{あに}が　一人_{ひとり}　います。なまえは　トーマスです。
二十五さいです。父_{ちち}の　なまえは　ジョンです。今
五十二さいです。

ご兄弟	おなまえ	～さい

ごりょうしん	おなまえ	～さい

(handwritten) Kanai + to kodomo

II. Describing a resultant state, using the verb て-form ＋ いる

		Verb て-form	
アリスさんは	スカートを	はいて	います。

Alice-san is wearing a skirt.

ワット：田中さんは　めがねを　かけていますか。

Does Tanaka-san wear glasses?

木村：　いいえ、めがねは　かけていません。でも　ぼうしを
　　　　よく　かぶっています。

No, he doesn't. But he often wears a hat.

Plain Present	Present	
Affirmative	Affirmative	Negative
かけている	かけています	かけていません

wearing　　　　　is wearing　　　　　is not wearing

Past	
Affirmative	Negative
かけていました	かけていませんでした

was wearing　　　　　was not wearing

● The verb て-form + いる describes a current state resulting from a past
action. For example, めがねを　かける means to put on glasses, and
めがねを　かけている means that as the result of putting them on, the
person is now wearing glasses. The following are two more examples to
illustrate this point.

Action:　けっこんする
　　　　（to get married）

Resultant state:　けっこんしている
　　　　（to be married）

Action: ふとる　　　　　　Resultant state: ふとっている
    (to gain weight)　　　　　　　　　(to be chubby)

- The verb in the past indicates an action:

たくさん　たべて　ふとりました。

I ate a lot and gained some weight.

Whereas the past verb て-form + いました describes a resultant state at a specified time in the past:

私は　子供の時　ふとっていました。

I was fat when I was a child.

- The verb て-form + いる can be used to describe what a person habitually wears.

田中さんは　よく　めがねを　かけています。

Tanaka-san often wears glasses.

山田さんは　いつも　ネクタイを　しています。

Yamada-san always wears a tie.

- The verbs すむ and つとめる are usually used with the verb て-form + いる. The particle に is used to refer to a location, a company, or an organization.

私は　とうきょうに　すんでいます。

I live in Tokyo.

山田さんは　アパートに　すんでいました。

Yamada-san used to live (was living) in an apartment.

ぼくは　じょうとう大学に　つとめています。

I work for Joto University. (or: I am employed by Joto University.)

話してみましょう

A. Describe what each person is wearing, using the verb て-form + いる.

Example

木村さんは　スーツを　きています。そして、ネクタイを
しています。

さとうさん　　山口さん　　こんどうさん　　木村さん

B. Work with a partner. Pick a classmate and have your partner guess who it is
by asking what the person is wearing. Use はい／いいえ questions.

Example

A:　その　人は　ぼうしを　かぶっていますか。
B:　いいえ、かぶっていません。
A:　その　人は　スカートを　はいていますか。
B:　はい、はいています。

C. The instructor will tell the class to walk around the classroom and observe
what others are wearing. When he/she tells the class to stop, each student
will stand back to back with the person who is closest and describe his/her
clothing. How many items can you describe correctly?

Example

〜さんは　あかい　セーターを　きています。
そして、ジーンズを　はいています。

D. Work in groups of four or five. Take turns finding out where your class-mates lived ten years ago (十年まえ). Who in your group lived the closest to each other? Who lived the farthest apart?

Example

A: ～さんは　十年まえ　どこに　すんでいましたか。
B: 私は　ニューヨークの　マンハッタンに　すんでいました。

III. Describing physical appearance and skills, using ～は ～が

A. Describing physical appearance

Topic	Particle	Noun	Particle	Adjective
石田さん	は	目	が	きれいです。

Ishida-san has beautiful eyes (literally: As for Ishida-san, his eyes are beautiful).

B. Describing skills and ability

Topic	Particle	Noun	Particle	Adjective
スミスさん	は	テニス	が	上手です。

Smith-san is good at tennis. *skilled.*

Topic	Particle	Noun	Particle		Verb
みち子さん	は	えいご	が	すこし	わかります。

Michiko understands English a little.

A: あの人は　足が　とても　ながいですね。
That person has long legs!

B: そうですね。それに、かみが　とても　きれいですね。
Yes. Also, he has beautiful hair.

A: チョーさんは　日本語が　わかりますか。
Do you understand Japanese, Cho-san?

B: ええ、わかります。でも、あまり　上手じゃありません。
Yes, I do. But I'm not very good at it.

- A sentence describing a skill/ability or physical appearance ends with the adjective 上手（じょうず） or the intransitive verb わかる. Unlike a transitive verb, an intransitive verb does not take a direct object or the direct object marker を. Instead, the particle が is used.

  山田さんは　フランスごが　わかります。

  Yamada-san understands French.

  石田（いしだ）さんは　えいごが　上手（じょうず）です。

  Ishida-san is good at English.

- Like すき and きらい, the plain present affirmative form of a verb + の can be used with 上手（じょうず）.

  田中さんは　うたを　うたうのが　上手（じょうず）です。

  Tanaka-san is good at singing songs.

話（はな）してみましょう

A. Using the following chart that lists various physical characteristics, describe each person in the list on the next page.

Example

私　→　私は　せが　ひくいです。そして、手（て）と　足（あし）が
　　　　ながいです。
　　　　私は　かおが　まるいです。そして、かみが
　　　　ながいです。　目（め）も　はなも　口（くち）も　小さいです。

からだ					
せ	たかい	ひくい			
手	ながい	みじかい	きれい		
足（あし）	ながい	みじかい	きれい		
かお	まるい	しかくい	ほそながい	きれい	
かみ	ながい	みじかい	くろい	ちゃいろい	きんぱつ
目（め）	大きい	小さい	あおい	ちゃいろい	くろい	みどり
はな	大きい	小さい	たかい	ひくい	
口（くち）	大きい	小さい			

1. 私
2. 父（ちち）
3. 母（はは）

4. 一番（ばん） いい ともだち
5. Other members of your family

B. Work with a partner. Pick one of the faces below and describe it to your partner. Have him/her identify the face by the letter.

Example

この 人は かおが まるいです。
この 人は 目（め）が 大きいです。

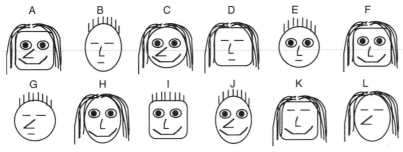

C. Work with a partner. Draw a person's face, then describe the face to your partner. Your partner will try to draw the face according to your description. Compare the two faces.

D. Find out which languages your classmates can speak, who knows the most languages, and any other talents they may have. List the information you obtain in the following chart.

Example

1. A: 〜さんは 何語（ご）が わかりますか。
   B: 日本語（ご）が わかります。
2. A: 〜さんは 何が 上手（じょうず）ですか。
   B: かんじを かくのが 上手（じょうず）です。

クラスメートの なまえ	ことば (Languages)	上手（じょうず）な こと

IV. Connecting phrases, using the verb and the adjective て-forms

A. Using the adjective て-form

		Adjective て-form		
兄は	目が	大きくて、	せが	たかいです。

My older brother has large eyes and is tall.

い-adjectives

Dictionary form　　大きい

て-form　　　　　大きく＋て　＝　大きくて

田中さんは　せが　たかくて　きれいです。

Tanaka-san is tall and pretty.

田中さんは　せが　たかくて　きれいな　人です。

Tanaka-san is a tall and pretty person.

田中さんは　あたまが　よくて　しんせつです。

Tanaka-san is intelligent and kind.

Negative form ない

Plain negative form　大きくない／きれいじゃない

て-form　　　　　大きくなく＋て＝大きくなくて
　　　　　　　　きれいじゃなく＋て＝きれいじゃなくて

きのうの　えいがは　あまり　おもしろくなくて　よくなかったです。

Yesterday's movie was neither very interesting nor good.

な-adjectives

Dictionary form　　きれい

て-form　　　　　きれい＋で　＝　きれいで

アリスさんは　げんきで　きれいです。

Alice is lively and pretty.

アリスさんは　げんきで　きれいな　人です。

Alice is a lively and pretty person.

Copula verb です

Present affirmative form　先生です

て-form　　　　　　　　先生＋で　＝　先生で

田中さんの　妹<ruby>妹<rt>いもうと</rt></ruby>さんは　大学の　先生で　今　アメリカに
すんでいます。

Tanaka-san's younger sister is a professor and now lives in the United
States.

B. Using the verb て-form

		Verb (て-form of いる)		
ジョンソンさん	は	やせていて	とても せがたかい	です。

Johnson-san is slim and very tall.

山田さんは　めがねを　かけていて、ぼうしを　かぶっています。

Yamada-san has glasses and a hat on.

この　大学には　ゆうめいな　としょかんが　あって、
大きい　たいいくかんも　あります。

This college has a famous library, and it also has a large athletic center.

- The て-form of いい is よくて.
- The て-form is used to connect two or more adjectival and verb phrases.
  When used in this manner, it means *and*. Both adjectival and verb て-forms
  can be used in a sentence. For example,

山田さんは　スポーツが　できて、あたまもよくて　しんせつ　です。

Yamada-san plays sports and is intelligent and kind.

- The particles と and や connect only noun phrases. They cannot be used to
  connect adjectives, verb phrases, or clauses.

話<ruby>話<rt>はな</rt></ruby>してみましょう

A. Connect each pair of sentences using the て-form.

Example

母<ruby>母<rt>はは</rt></ruby>は　きれいです。　母<ruby>母<rt>はは</rt></ruby>は　りょうりが　上手<ruby>上手<rt>じょうず</rt></ruby>です。
母<ruby>母<rt>はは</rt></ruby>は　きれいで　りょうりが　上手<ruby>上手<rt>じょうず</rt></ruby>です。

1. みち子さんの　お父<ruby>父<rt>とう</rt></ruby>さんは　やさしいです。みち子さんの
   お父<ruby>父<rt>とう</rt></ruby>さんは　しんせつです。

2. 山田さんの　ご主人<ruby>主人<rt>しゅじん</rt></ruby>は　かおが　まるいです。山田さんの
   ご主人<ruby>主人<rt>しゅじん</rt></ruby>は　目<ruby>目<rt>め</rt></ruby>が　大きいです。

3. 田中さんの 弟さんは えいごが わかります。

田中さんの 弟さんは フランスごが わかります。

4. 先生の おくさんは 日本人です。先生の おくさんは
こうこうの 先生です。

5. 先生の お子さんは やせています。先生の お子さんは
とても 小さいです。

6. 山田さんは テニスが 上手です

山田さんは やきゅうが 上手です。

B. Work with a partner. You are an employment agency representative, and
your partner is looking for people to fill the positions listed below. Ask your
partner what type of person he/she needs to fill each position.

Example

A: どんな 人が いいですか。
B (looking for an editor): あたまが よくて、かくのが
じょうずな 人が いいです。

へんしゅうしゃ (editor)	あたまが いい人、 かくのが じょうずな 人
モデル (model)	
日本語の先生	
ひしょ (secretary)	
バスケットボールの せんしゅ (player)	

C. Work with a new partner. Your instructor will have a stack of cards with
pictures of famous people. Without looking, pick a card and describe the
person's (この 人) physical appearance, clothes, residence, and occupation (if you know it). Have your partner guess who it is. Your partner can
also ask questions.

Example

A: この人は せが たかくて、つよい 人です。
B: その人は どこに すんでいますか。
A: シカゴに すんでいます。
B: そして、何が 上手ですか。
A: バスケットボールが 上手です。
B: マイケルジョーダン (*Michael Jordan*) ですか。
A: はい、そうです。

D. Work with a partner. Have him/her ask you questions about the physical appearance, clothes, residence, and occupation of a member of your family.

Example

A: 〜さんの　お父さんは　めがねを　かけていますか。
B: はい、かけています。
A: そうですか。せが　たかいですか。
B: いいえ、たかくありません。ひくいです。
A: 〜さんの　お父さんは　どこに　すんでいますか。
B: ニューヨークに　すんでいます。
A: どんな　かいしゃに　つとめていますか。
continue . . .

V. Describing people and things, using nouns and modifying clauses

Topic			Comment
Noun Modifying Clause (plain form)	Noun	Particle	
しろい　ふくを　きている	人	は	田中さんです。

The person who is wearing white is Tanaka-san.

木村：田中さんの　お母さんは　どの　かたですか。
　　　Which person is Tanaka-san's mother?

山本：あそこに　いる　人です。かみが　ながくて　せが
　　　とても　たかい　人です。
　　　(She is) the person who is over there. The person who has long hair and is very tall.

木村：ああ、あの　かたですか。とても　きれいな　かたですね。
　　　Oh, that person. She's a very beautiful person.

山本：そうですね。
　　　I think so, too.

- A noun may be modified by another noun, an adjective, or a modifying clause. The modifier always comes before the noun. In a noun-modifying clause, the verb must be in the plain form. The negative forms of adjectives and the copula verb must be in the plain form as well.

私の　ともだち　　　　　　　my friend
きれいな　うち　　　　　　　a clean house
きれいじゃない　うち　　　　a house which is not clean
小さい　人　　　　　　　　　a small person

小さくない　人	a person who is not small
かみが　ながい　人	a person who has long hair
かみが　ながくない　人	a person who does not have long hair
けっこんしている　人	a person who is married
けっこんしていない　人	a person who is not married

話してみましょう

A. Look at the drawings and answer the questions using a noun-modifying clause whenever appropriate.

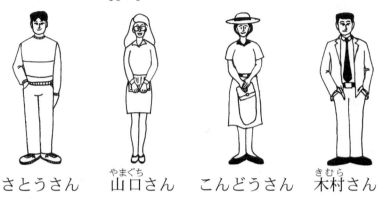

さとうさん　　山口さん　　こんどうさん　　木村さん

Example

木村さんは　どの　人ですか。
スーツを　きている　人です。

1. さとうさんは　どの　人ですか。
2. こんどうさんは　どの　人ですか。
3. 木村さんは　どの　人ですか。
4. 山口さんは　どの　人ですか。
5. ジーンズを　はいている　人は　木村さんですか。
6. ぼうしを　かぶっている　人は　どの人ですか。
7. めがねを　かけている　人は　こんどうさんですか。

B. Make a circle with all the students' chairs and remove one chair. The person without a chair stands in the center of the circle and, in order to find a chair, describes a physical trait that applies to at least one other person in the group. Everybody fitting the description must get up and find another chair. The person without a chair stands in the center.

Example

The person in the center says: めがねを　かけている　人。
People who wear glasses must move to another seat.

C. Find out how many people in the class fall into the categories listed in the
   chart below. Check your facts with a classmate. Note that 私の　データで
   は means according to my data.

Examples

1. A: ～さんは　けっこんしていますか。
   B: いいえ、　していません。
2. A: けっこんしている　人は　何人（にん）　いますか。
   B: 二人（ふたり）　います。
   A: そうですか。　私のデータ では　一人（ひとり）です。

	はい	いいえ
けっこんしています		
お姉（ねえ）さんが　います		
妹（いもうと）が　います		
兄弟（きょうだい）が　いません		
りょうに　すんでいません		
スポーツが　上手（じょうず）です		
スペイン語（ご）が　わかります		

D. Work with a partner. Ask him/her what kind of person they would like to
   date. Have them describe the person's physical appearance, personality,
   interests, and talents using noun modifiers. Take turns. Take detailed notes
   of the information that your partner gives you. Note that せいかく means
   personality.

Example

A: ～さんは　どんな　人が　すきですか。
B: 目（め）が　大きくて　かみが　ながい　人が　すきです。
   そして　テニスが　できる　人が　すきです。
   りょうりが　すきな　人も　いいですね。
A: どんな　せいかくの　人が　いいですか。
B: そうですね。やさしくて　かわいい　人が　いいですね。

E. You are a dating consultant. Ask another classmate what kind of person his/her partner in exercise D described as the ideal date. Then ask your classmate to describe his/her partner in exercise D. Agree or disagree about whether the two people described are a match. Switch roles.

Example

A: どの　人の　データ (*data*) を　もっていますか。

B: スミスさんの　データを　もっています。

A: スミスさんは　どんな　人が　すきなんですか。

B: 目が　大きくて　かみが　ながい　人が　すきです。
そして　やさしくて　かわいい　人が　すきです。

<ruby>漢字<rt>かんじ</rt></ruby>

Pictographs and kinship terms

(A rice field and a strong arm → "male.")

(女, "female," with breasts → "mother.")

(An axe and a strong hand → "father")

(A person with a big head → "older brother")

(A pig under a roof → "house." Pigs were important livestock.)

男	男

丨　冂　冊　甲　田

甼　男

male, man

ダン

おとこ

おとこ　　　ひと
男　の　人
おとこ　　　こ
男　の　子
だんし
（男子）

女	女

く　女　女

female, woman

ジョ

おんな

おんな　　　ひと
女　の　人
おんな　　　こ
女　の　子
じょし
（女子）

子	子

了　了　子

child

シ

こ

おとこ　　　こ
男　の　子こ子
おんな
女　の　子
こ
子ども

目	目

丨　冂　冊　目　目

eye

モク

め

め　　　おお
目が　大きい
め　　　ちい
目が　小さい

耳	耳

一　丁　下　下　耳

耳

ear

ジ

みみ

みみ　　　おお
耳が　大きい

口	口

丨　冂　口

mouth

コウ

くち

くち　　　おお
口が　大きい

足	足

丶 口 口 尸 尸

尸 足

foot, leg

ソク

あし

足が　ながい
足が　はやい

手	手

ノ 二 三 手

hand

シュ

て

手が　大きい
手の　中
スポーツが上手です。

父	父

ノ ハ 父 父

father

フ

ちち、とう

私の　父
〜さんの　お父さん

母	母

乚 口 口 母 母

mother

ボ

はは、かあ

私の　母
〜さんの　お母さん

兄	兄

丶 口 口 尸 兄

older brother

ケイ、キョウ

あに、にい

私の　兄
〜さんの　お兄さん
兄弟

姉	姉

乚 乚 女 女 女

女 女 姉

older sister

シ

あね、ねえ

私の　姉
〜さんの　お姉さん

弟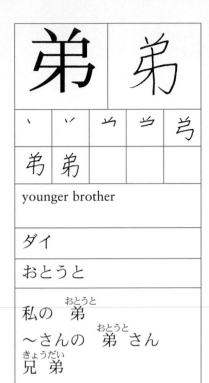

丶 ゛ ⺍ 弚 弟

弚 弟

younger brother

ダイ

おとうと

私の 弟（おとうと）
〜さんの 弟（おとうと） さん
兄弟（きょうだい）

妹

く く 女 如 妒

奸 妔 妹

younger sister

マイ

いもうと

私の 妹（いもうと）
〜さんの 妹（いもうと） さん

家

丶 宀 宀 宀 宀

宀 宊 宊 家 家

house

カ

いえ、（うち）

大（おお）きい 家（いえ）
私の 家族（かぞく）
家（うち）の 人（ひと）

族 族

亠 方 方 方 方

方 方 扩 族 族

tribe

ゾク

家族（かぞく）

Read the following sentences written in **hiragana, katakana,** and **kanji.**

1. 私の父は先週の月曜日に川につりにいきました。母は家に
   いました。
2. 中山さんのお父さんは目が大きいですね。耳も大きいです
   ね。
3. 妹は小学生で、弟は中学一年生です。
4. ご兄弟は何人いますか。
5. 姉はもうけっこんしていますが、兄はまだけっこんしてい
   ません。
6. 四人家族です。
7. 田中さんのお子さんは目が大きくて、口が小さくて、とて
   もかわいいですよ。
8. 川口<ruby>口<rt>かわぐち</rt></ruby>さんのお母さんは手と足がながいです。

上手な<ruby>読<rt>よ</rt></ruby>み<ruby>方<rt>かた</rt></ruby>

Transforming textual information into charts and figures

People usually read with a specific purpose in mind. It may be to gather specific
information or to skim for main ideas. When reading an assignment, you might
jot down only the information that is of interest to you. If you organize your
notes systematically, you may understand the assignment better and retain the
information longer. One way to organize material is to make charts or tables.

<ruby>読<rt>よ</rt></ruby>む<ruby>前<rt>まえ</rt></ruby>に

Read the dialogue on page 321 and complete the following table.

アリスさんの　家族	なまえ	しごと	Physical appearance

アリスさんの家族

The following passage was written by Alice, but some of the information is different from the information in the dialogue on page 321. Find the discrepancies.

　私の家族は五人家族です。父は四十五歳で、銀行に勤めているサラリーマンです。父は目があまりよくありませんから、たいていめがねをかけています。ゴルフが大好きで、日曜日によくゴルフに行きます。母は四十三歳です。大学で文学を教えています。背があまり高くありませんから、たいていハイヒールの靴を履いています。母はとても優しい人です。弟のトムは十五歳で、中学生です。背が高くて、目がとても大きいです。スポーツは好きですが、勉強は嫌いです。そして、妹のパムは高校一年生です。パムは背が高くありませんが、とてもかわいいです。頭がよくて、勉強もとても好きです。

わかりましたか

A. Underline sentence and clause connectors in the reading.

B. Describe your ideal family (りそうの家族). Use the following questions as cues.

1. 何人家族ですか。
2. 子供が　いますか。男の子ですか。女の子ですか。
3. どんな　子供ですか。
4. お父さんと　お母さんは　どんな　人ですか。
5. どんな　ところに　すんでいますか。
6. お父さんは／お母さんは　しごとを　していますか。どんなしごとですか。

上手な聞き方

Using one's background knowledge about a person

Besides visual cues, background knowledge about a person such as his/her age, gender, and occupation can help you to understand better what is being said or asked.

A. Look at the following picture. Listen to the questions and circle the letter you think is correct. The questions will be repeated.

1.　　a　　　b　　　c　　　d
2.　　a　　　b　　　c　　　d
3.　　a　　　b　　　c　　　d

B. 私たちの家族 (Our family). Listen to each family description. There are two activities for each description. First, draw the family tree (かけいず). Then, read the statements and circle はい or いいえ.

1. 中山よしこさんの　家族
　　かけいず

はい　　いいえ　　　中山さんは　お兄さんが　います。

はい　　いいえ　　　中山さんの　弟さんは　せが　たかい
　　　　　　　　　　です。

はい　　いいえ　　　中山さんの　お母さんは　びょういんに
　　　　　　　　　　つとめています。

はい　　いいえ　　　中山さんの　お姉さんは　大学生
　　　　　　　　　　です。

2. 吉田^{よしだ}けいこさんの　家族
　　かけいず

はい　　いいえ　　　吉田^{よしだ}さんは　兄弟が　いません。

はい　　いいえ　　　吉田^{よしだ}さんの　家に　おじいさんが
　　　　　　　　　　います。

はい　　いいえ　　　吉田^{よしだ}さんの　お父さんは　ふとって
　　　　　　　　　　います。

はい　　いいえ　　　吉田^{よしだ}さんの　おばあさんは
　　　　　　　　　　七十五さいで　やせています。

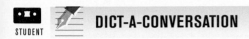
Your friend Ogawa-san is asking you, Smith-san, questions about your family.

ともだち：_____

スミス：_____

ともだち：_____

スミス：_____

ともだち：_____

スミス：_____

ともだち：_____

スミス：_____

聞き上手、話し上手

Being modest

As noted earlier in this chapter, the Japanese generally refrain from praising or boasting about their families. If someone else praises a member of their own family, they usually deny it. For example, when someone says to a Japanese person that his/her mother is beautiful, he/she will say something like *No, she isn't.* or *Do you really think so?* This may seem strange to people from cultures where a compliment is received in a straightforward manner, but while in Japan, it is better to follow the local custom. Some commonly used phrases when complimented are:

いいえ、それほどじゃありません。

No, not to that extent.

いいえ、そんな　ことは　ありません。

No, that isn't the case.

いいえ、まだまだです。

No, I still have a long way to go.

Work with a partner. Respond to each compliment appropriately. Ask your instructor to check your manner of delivery.

1. ～さんは　テニスが　上手ですね。
2. ～さんの　お母さんは　とても　きれいな　かたですね。

3. ～さんの　お兄さんは　あたまが　いいですね。
4. ～さんは　足が　ながくて、　かっこいいですね。
5. ～さんは　日本語が　上手ですね。
6. ～さんの　家は　大きくて　りっぱな家ですね。

総合練習
そうごうれんしゅう

Your instructor will give you a card like the one in the example with a description of two people, A and B. You are A. You are looking for B. Go around the class and ask your classmates questions using B's description. After you find B, check his/her identity card with your information.

Example

Features	A Your identity	B The person you are looking for
かみ	ながい	くろい
目	あおい	みどり
すんでいる	とうきょう	ニューヨーク
上手	日本語	えいご

A: その　人は　かみが　くろいですか。
B: はい、くろいです。
A: その　人は　目が　あおいですか。
B: いいえ、あおくありません。
A: そうですか。それじゃあ、また。
(Go to a different person.)

ロールプレイ

1. You are introducing a member of your family to your instructor. Your instructor praises the person. Respond accordingly.

2. You are looking for a new roommate. Tell your partner what type of person you are looking for and ask for his/her help.

たんご　(ESSENTIAL VOCABULARY)

Nouns

あし（足）leg, foot

あたま（頭）head　あたまが　いい（頭
　が　いい）smart, intelligent

あに（兄）(the speaker's) brother

あね（姉）(the speaker's) older sister

いもうと（妹）(the speaker's) younger sister

いもうとさん（妹さん）(someone else's)
　younger sister

イヤリング　earring

おかあさん（お母さん）(someone else's)
　mother

おくさん　　（奥さん）(someone else's) wife

おじいさん（お祖父さん）(someone else's)
　grandfather

おとうさん（お父さん）(someone else's)
　father

おとうと（弟）(the speaker's) younger
　brother

おとうとさん（弟さん）(someone else's)
　younger brother

おにいさん（お兄さん）(someone else's)
　older brother

おねえさん（お姉さん）(someone else's)
　older sister

おばあさん（お祖母さん）(someone else's)
　grandmother

かいしゃ（会社）company

かお（顔）face

かぞく（家族）family, (the speaker's) family

かた（方）person (polite version of 人)
　(must be preceded by a modifier as in
　その　かたは　田中さんの
　お母さんですか。)

かない（家内）(the speaker's) wife

かみ（髪）hair

からだ（体）body

きょうだい（兄弟）siblings

くち（口）mouth

ごかぞく（ご家族）(someone else's) family

ごきょうだい（ご兄弟）(someone else's)
　siblings

ごしゅじん（ご主人）(someone else's) hus-
　band

しゅじん（主人）(the speaker's) husband

スーツ　suit (clothing)

せ（背）back (body part); height of a person

せいかく（性格）personality

そふ（祖父）(the speaker's) grandfather

そぼ（祖母）(the speaker's) grandmother

ちち（父）(the speaker's) father

て（手）hand

はな（鼻）nose

はは（母）(the speaker's) mother

ぼうし（帽子）hat, cap

みみ（耳）ear

め（目）eye

めがね（眼鏡）glasses

Irregular Verbs

けっこんする（結婚する）(to) marry

田中さんと　けっこんしている（田中さんと　結婚している）is married to Tanaka-san

する　(to) have, (to) wear　イヤリングを　している　is wearing earrings

る -verbs

かける　(to) put on (glasses)
　めがねを　かけている　is wearing
　glasses
きる（着る）(to) put on (a sweater, a shirt, a
　jacket)
　セーターを　きている
　（セーターを着ている）is wearing
　a sweater

つとめる（勤める）(to) become employed
　つとめている（勤めている）is
　employed at, works for
　かいしゃに　つとめている（会社に勤
　めている）employed at a company
やせる　(to) lose weight　やせている　is thin

う -verbs

かぶる　(to) put on (a hat, a cap)　ぼうしを
　かぶっている　has a hat on
すむ（住む）(to) live, reside
　すんでいる（住んでいる）lives　アパ
　ートに　すんでいる（アパートに住ん
　でいる）(to) live in an apartment
はく　(to) put on (skirt, pants, socks)
　スカートを　はいている　has on a skirt

ふとる（太る）(to) gain weight
　ふとっている（太っている）is fat
わかる（分かる）(to) understand
　にほんごが　わかる（日本語が分か
　る）(to) understand Japanese

Auxiliary Verbs

〜ている　resultant state

な-adjectives

げんき（な）（元気（な））healthy
じょうず（な）（上手（な））good at, skillful
しんせつ（な）（親切（な））kind

い-adjectives

あかるい（明るい）cheerful
　(see Chapter 3 for あかるい, bright)
かわいい　cute, adorable
しかくい（四角い）square
ながい（長い）long
ひくい（低い）low, short (height)

ほそながい（細長い）long, elongated
まるい（丸い）round
みじかい（短い）short (length)
やさしい（優しい）gentle

Question Words

いくつ　How old 〜?
　おいくつ　polite form of いくつ

Counters

〜さい（〜歳）〜 years old
〜にん（〜人）〜 people
　exceptions ひとり（一人）one person　ふたり（二人）two people
〜ばんめ（〜番目）〜th (ordinal)

Expressions

いいえ、それほどじゃありません。No, not to that extent.
いいえ、そんな　ことは　ありません。No, that's not the case.
いいえ、まだまだです。No, I still have a long way to go.

Passive Vocabulary

Nouns

こうこうせい（高校生）senior high school
　student
しょうがっこう（小学校）elementary
　school
せんしゅ（選手）player (on a sports team)

としうえ（年上）older person
へんしゅうしゃ（編集者）editor
モデル　(fashion) model

Expressions

ごめんなさい。（御免なさい。）Sorry. (Colloquial)
としうえに　みられる。（年上に　みられる。）look/s older than (one's) age.

Supplementary Vocabulary

Occupations

いしゃ（医者）doctor
エンジニア　engineer

かいしゃいん（会社員）businessman, company man

きょういん（教員）teacher; instructor
サラリーマン　white-collar worker (*salary man* in Japanese)
じえいぎょう（自営業）self-employed
しょうがくせい（小学生）elementary-school student

ちゅうがくせい（中学生）junior high-school student
はいしゃ（歯医者）dentist
べんごし（弁護士）lawyer
マネージャー　manager

Kinship Terms

いとこ　(the speaker's) cousin
（お）いとこさん　(someone else's) cousin
おい（甥）(the speaker's) nephew
おいごさん（甥子さん）(someone else's) nephew
おじ（叔父／伯父）(the speaker's) uncle
おじさん（叔父さん／伯父さん）(someone else's) uncle
おっと（夫）(the speaker's) husband (used also as a legal term)
おば（叔母／伯母）(the speaker's) aunt
おばさん（叔母さん／伯母さん）(someone else's) aunt

おまごさん（お孫さん）(someone else's) grandchild
ごしんせき（ご親戚）(someone else's) relatives
しんせき（親戚）(the speaker's) relatives
つま（妻）(the speaker's) wife (used also as a legal term)
まご（孫）(the speaker's) grandchild
めい（姪）(the speaker's) niece
めいごさん（姪子さん）(someone else's) niece

The Body

あご（顎）chin
うで（腕）arm
おしり（お尻）buttocks
おなか（お腹）belly
くちびる（唇）lip
くび（首）neck
こし（腰）lower back; hip
せなか（背中）back, upper back

つめ（爪）nail
のど（咽）throat
は（歯）tooth
ひげ（髭）mustache, beard
ほっぺた　cheek
まつげ（睫）eyelash
まゆ（眉）eyebrow
ゆび（指）finger

A Japanese summer festival

おもいで

MEMORIES

Functions	Describing past events
New Vocabulary	Seasons and months; Days of the month; Other time expressions; Past experience
Dialogue	子供の　時の　アリスさん　(Alice as a child) こども
Culture	National holidays and yearly events
Language	I. Talking about time, using noun/adjective + 時, 〜月, 〜日, 〜か月, and duration + まえ(に) がつ　にち　げつ
	II. Talking about past experiences, using verb た + ことがある; listing representative activities, using verb たり verb たり　する
	III. Expressing reasons, using the plain past form of verbs and adjectives + んです and the plain form of verbs and adjectives + からです
	IV. Expressing hearsay, using the plain form of verbs/adjectives/the copula + そうです
	V. Using noun-modifying clauses in the past and present
Kanji	Writing verbs in **kanji**
Reading	Understanding the format of a letter
Listening	Taking turns in a conversation
Communication	Conversation fillers

A. 日本の　きせつと　月 (Seasons and months).　日本には
きせつが　よっつ　あります。　はると　なつと　あきと
ふゆです。大学の　スケジュールを　見て下さい。どの
月が　いちばんいそがしいですか。そして、どの　月が
いそがしく　ありませんか。

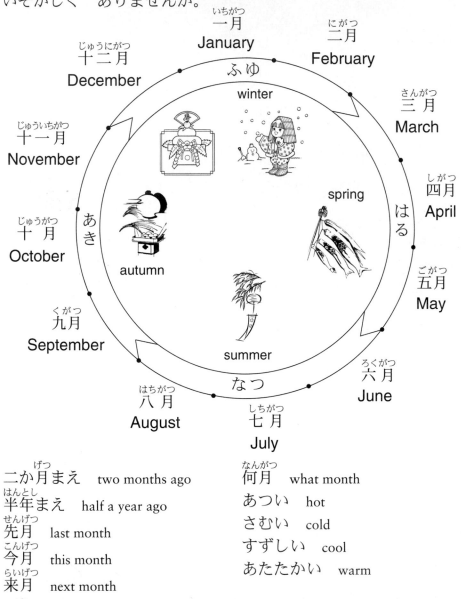

一月　January
二月　February
三月　March
四月　April
五月　May
六月　June
七月　July
八月　August
九月　September
十月　October
十一月　November
十二月　December

ふゆ winter
はる spring
なつ summer
あき autumn

二か月まえ　two months ago
半年まえ　half a year ago
先月　last month
今月　this month
来月　next month

何月　what month
あつい　hot
さむい　cold
すずしい　cool
あたたかい　warm

日本語で　こたえて下さい。

1. 今月は　何月ですか？　先月は？　来月は？
2. 二か月まえは　何月でしたか。　五か月まえは？

3. どの　きせつが　いちばん　すきですか。きらいな
   きせつは　いつですか。

4. アメリカで　一番ばん　さむい　しゅう (state) は　どこですか。

5. アメリカで　一番ばん　あつい　しゅう (state) は　どこですか。

6. ～さんの　まちでは　何月なんがつから　何月なんがつまで　あたたかい
   ですか。

7. ～さんの　まちでは　何月なんがつが　すずしいですか。

B. ひにち (Days of the month). ひにちを　読よんで下さい。そして、
   しつもんに　こたえて下さい。

日	月	火	水	木	金	土
		一日 ついたち*	二日 ふつか	三日 みっか	四日 よっか	五日 いつか
六日 むいか	七日 なのか	八日 ようか	九日 ここのか	十日 とおか	十一日 じゅういち にち	十二日 じゅうに にち
十三日 じゅう さんにち	十四日 じゅう よっか	十五日 じゅうご にち	十六日 じゅうろく にち	十七日 じゅうしち にち	十八日 じゅうはち にち	十九日 じゅうく にち
二十日 はつか	二十一日 にじゅう いちにち	二十二日 にじゅう ににち	二十三日 にじゅう さんにち	二十四日 にじゅう よっか	二十五日 にじゅう ごにち	二十六日 にじゅう ろくにち
二十七日 にじゅう しちにち	二十八日 にじゅう はちにち	二十九日 にじゅう くにち	三十日 さんじゅう にち	三十一日 さんじゅう いちにち		

*いちにち means *one day;* ついたち means *the first of the month.*

1. レーバーデーは　いつですか。
2. ハロウィーンは　いつですか。
3. サンクスギビングは　いつですか。
4. バレンタインデーは　いつですか。
5. アメリカの　どくりつきねんび (*Independence Day*) は　いつ
   ですか。
6. メモリアルデーは　いつですか。
7. がんたん (*New Year's Day*) は　いつですか。
8. クリスマスは　いつですか。
9. エイプリルフールは　いつですか。

What are important days in your country?

C. ほかの　時間の　言い方 (Other time expressions). Fill in the blanks with the age, year, or date that corresponds to each of the expressions.

おととし　　year before last year 　　　　　　　＿＿＿＿＿＿さい

去年　last year 　　　　　　　　　　　　　　　＿＿＿＿＿＿さい

今年　this year 　　　　　　　　　　　　　　　＿＿＿＿＿＿さい

十さいの　時　when I was 10 years old 　　　＿＿＿＿＿＿年

小さい　時　when I was small 　　　　　　　＿＿さいから＿＿さいまで

子供の　時　when I was a child 　　　　　　　＿＿さいから＿＿さいまで

小学校の　時　when I was in elementary school 　＿＿さいから＿＿さいまで

中学の　時　when I was in junior high school 　　＿＿さいから＿＿さいまで

やすみ　break, vacation

はるやすみ　spring vacation 　　　　　　　　＿＿さいから＿＿さいまで

なつやすみ　summer vacation 　　　　　　　　＿＿さいから＿＿さいまで

ふゆやすみ　winter vacation 　　　　　　　　＿＿さいから＿＿さいまで

日本語で　こたえて下さい。

うれしい時　when (I am) happy

さびしい時　when (I am) lonely

かなしい時　when (I am) sad

1. 今度の　やすみは　いつですか。

2. やすみの　日に何をしますか。

3. どんな　時に　ともだちに　でんわを　かけますか。

4. どんな　時に　ごりょうしん (parents)と　話を　しますか。

5. どんな　時に　パーティを　しますか。

D. かこのけいけん (Past experience). Work in groups of three or four. One person acts out the activity in the list while the rest of the group tries to guess what that activity is.

なく　(to) cry

わらう　(to) laugh

こうつうじこにあう　(to) get involved in/have a traffic accident

お金が　ある　(to) have money

ゆうえんちに　行く　(to) go to an amusement park

どうぶつえんに 行く　(to) go to the zoo

はくぶつかんに 行く　(to) go to a museum

教会に 行く　(to) go to church

おてらや じんじゃを 見る　(to) see Buddhist temples and Shinto shrines

山に のぼる　(to) climb a mountain

きものを きる　(to) wear a kimono

うみで およぐ　(to) swim in the sea

キャンプを する　(to) camp

つりを する　(to) fish

ひこうきに のる　(to) get on a plane

たばこを すう　(to) smoke a cigarette

へんな ものを 食べる　(to) eat strange food

デートを する　(to) have a date

日本語で こたえて下さい。

1. 子供の 時 どんな ことを よく しましたか。
   しませんでしたか。

2. 子供の 時 どんな ところに よく 行きましたか。
   行きませんでしたか。

3. 今 どんな ことを よく しますか。
   あまり しませんか。

4. 何さいの 時 はじめて デートを しましたか。

5. たばこを すう 人を しっていますか (do you know?)。

6. 今 お金が たくさん ありますか。ありませんか。
   小さい 時は どうでしたか。

ダイアローグ

はじめに

A. 小さい 時 何を よく しましたか。どんな 子供でしたか。

B. まんがを 見て、会話 (dialogue) を 聞いて下さい。

子供の時のアリスさん　(Alice as a child)

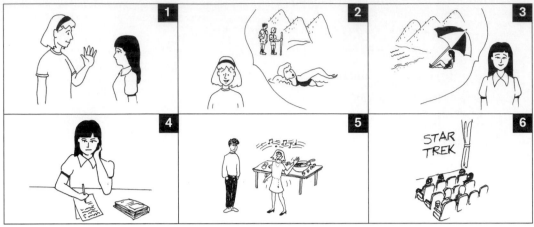

アリスさんと　道子さんは　子供の　時の　話を　しています。

＿＿＿　道子：　アリスさんは　子供の　時　どんな
　　　　　　　　子供でしたか。

＿＿＿　アリス：　そうですね。父や　母に　よると　とても
　　　　　　　　げんきで　よく　わらう　子供だった
　　　　　　　　そうです。よく　山に　のぼったり　うみで
　　　　　　　　およいだりしました。

＿＿＿　道子：　そうですか。

＿＿＿　アリス：　道子さんは　どんな　子供だったんですか。

＿＿＿　道子：　私も　小さい　時は　りょうしんと　よく
　　　　　　　　山や　うみに　あそびに　行きました。でも、
　　　　　　　　中学や　高校の　時は　あまり　あそびません
　　　　　　　　でしたね。

＿＿＿　アリス：　どうしてですか。

＿＿＿　道子：　じゅけんべんきょうが　いそがしかった
　　　　　　　　からです。

＿＿＿　アリス：　たいへんですね。私は　中学や　高校の　時は
　　　　　　　　よく　パーティに　行ったり　ともだちと
　　　　　　　　えいがを　見たりしました。べんきょうは
　　　　　　　　あまりしなかったんですよ。

＿＿＿　道子：　いいですね。

わかりましたか

Complete the chart with information about Alice's and Michiko's childhoods.

	どんな 子供でしたか。	何を よく しましたか。
アリス		
道子		

日本の 文化

National holidays and yearly events. How many national holidays do you have in your country? What do you do on these holidays?

There are fourteen national holidays in Japan.

1月1日	がんたん	New Year's Day
1月15日	成人の 日	Coming-of-Age Day honors young people who turn twenty that year. The age of twenty is considered the beginning of adulthood in Japan.
2月11日	けんこく きねんの 日	National Foundation Day commemorates the founding of Japan by Jinmu, the putative first emperor around the fifth century B.C. Neither the emperor nor the date has any historical basis.
3月20日	春分の 日	Vernal Equinox Day
4月29日	みどりの 日	Green Day, formerly observed as Emperor Showa's (Hirohito; 1901–1989) birthday, is now the day for trees and plants in memory of the emperor who was a dedicated biologist.
5月3日	けんぽう記念日	Constitution Day commemorates the day the present constitution took effect in 1947.

５月５日	子供の　日 （こども）　（ひ）	Children's Day, formerly known as Boys' Day, is a day to wish for children to grow up to be healthy and strong.
７月２０日	うみの　日	Ocean Day celebrates the sea and its resources.
９月１５日	けいろうの　日	Day of the Elderly, a day to thank and appreciate senior citizens
９月２３日	秋分の　日 （しゅうぶん）	Autumnal Equinox Day
１０月１０日	たいいくの　日	Health and Sports Day promotes physical fitness with sports events throughout the country.
１１月３日	文化の　日 （ぶんか）	Culture Day, formerly observed as Emperor Meiji's (1852–1912) birthday
１１月２３日	きんろう かんしゃの　日	Labor and Harvest Day honors workers and is a time to give thanks for a good harvest. It has no connection with Thanksgiving Day in the United States.
１２月２３日	てんのう誕生日 （たんじょうび）	Emperor's Birthday celebrates the birthday of the present Emperor, Akihito.

Besides national holidays, the Japanese traditionally celebrate the following days:

２月３日	せつぶん	First day of spring, according to the old lunar calendar
３月３日	ひなまつり	Girls' Day features displays of dolls handed down in the family. It is a day to wish for daughters to grow up to be gentle, beautiful women.
７月７日	たなばた	According to Chinese mythology, the day when two star-crossed lovers, separated by the Milky Way, meet once a year
８月１３〜１５日	おぼん	**Bon** is a Buddhist festival in honor of deceased relatives and ancestors.

More recently, especially in urban areas, the Japanese have begun to celebrate days like Valentine's Day, April Fools' Day, and Christmas. The latter is completely nonreligious, except for a small minority of Christians.

- *Major holiday seasons. When is the biggest holiday season in your country? What do people do during this time?*

Japan has three major holiday seasons: お正月 (しょうがつ) (the New Year's Day), おぼん (Buddhist festival in honor of deceased relatives and ancestors, August 13-15) and ゴールデンウイーク (the week between April 29, Green Day, and May 5, Children's Day).

LANGUAGE

I. Talking about time, using noun/adjective + 時, 〜月 (がつ), 〜日 (にち), 〜か月 (げつ), and duration + まえ (に)

A. Noun/adjective + 時

		Noun	**Particle**	**Noun**	
石田さん (いしだ)	は	子供 (こども)	の	時	よく　あそびました。

Ishida-san played a lot/often when he was a child.

な-adjective (Prenominal)		**Noun**	
ひまな		時 （に）	よく　つりを　します。

I often go fishing when I am free/I have free time.

B. 年 (とし) (Year)

	Number	**Counter**		**Number**	**Counter**	
へいせい	三	年	は	1 9 9 1 (せんきゅうひゃくきゅうじゅういち)	年	です。

The third year of the Heisei period is 1991. (Heisei refers to the reign name of the present emperor.)

C. ひにち (Date)

	Number	**Counter**	**Number**	**Counter**	
私の　誕生日は (たんじょうび)	一	月 (がつ)	十五	日 (にち)	です。

My birthday is January 15.

D. ～か月 Month (duration)

	Number	Counter	
日本に	三	か月	いました。

I was in Japan for three months.

(handwritten, right side) E. 二週間 まえ (に) 日本に 行きました。

	～年 (year)		～か月 (month for duration)	
1	いちねん	一年	※いっかげつ	一か月
2	にねん	二年	にかげつ	二か月
3	さんねん	三年	さんかげつ	三か月
4	※よねん	四年	よんかげつ	四か月
5	ごねん	五年	ごかげつ	五か月
6	ろくねん	六年	※ろっかげつ	六か月 (はんとし 半年)
7	ななねん／しちねん	七年	ななかげつ	七か月
8	はちねん	八年	※はちかげつ／はっかげつ	八か月
9	きゅうねん	九年	きゅうかげつ	九か月
10	じゅうねん	十年	※じゅっかげつ／じっかげつ	十か月
11	じゅういちねん	十一年	※じゅういっかげつ	十一か月
12	じゅうにねん	十二年	じゅうにかげつ	十二か月
20	にじゅうねん	二十年		

※ indicates irregular reading.

スミス：いつアメリカに来ましたか。

When did you come to the United States?

山田： 六年まえの八月です。高校の時でした。

It was in August six years ago. It was when I was in high school.

スミス： そうですか。ながいですね。じゃあ、今度は　いつ

　　　　　日本に　帰りますか。

　　　　　I see. That's a long time ago, isn't it? When will you go back to
　　　　　Japan?

山田：　来月の　十日に　帰ります。

　　　　　I will go back on the tenth, next month.

- 時 is a noun meaning *time*. It is translated as *when* if preceded by the

  prenominal form of an adjective such as ひまな　時 (when I have some

  free time), or by a noun followed by the particle の such as 高校の　時

  (when I was in high school).

いそがしい時	busy time
たいへんな時	tough time
うれしい時	happy time
〜さいの　時	when one is/was 〜 year(s) old
かなしい時	sad time

- The particle に for a time expression can be used or omitted after 〜時.

  いそがしい　時（に）when I am busy

- 〜年 and 〜日 can also be used to indicate duration:

  私は　日本に　一年　いました。

  I was in Japan for one year.

  ここから　シカゴまで　三日　かかります。

  It takes three days from here to Chicago.

- 〜月, however, cannot be used for duration.　〜か月 is used instead.

  私は　とうきょうに　二か月　いました。

  I was in Tokyo for two months.

- Duration + まえ(に) is the equivalent of *ago* or *before* in English.

  三年まえに　日本に　行きました。

  I went to Japan three years ago.

  一か月まえに　けっこんしました。

  I got married a month ago.

- Instead of the Western (Gregorian) calendar, the Japanese frequently use the current emperor's reign name to refer to a certain year. For example,

へいせい十年 is 1998. The more recent reign names are めいじ (1868–1912), たいしょう (1912–1926), しょうわ (1926–1989), and へいせい (1989–). The first New Year's Day after the crowning of an emperor is the beginning of year 2 of his reign. So January 1990 is へいせい二年。

話してみましょう

A. Look at the list of national holidays on pages 359 and 360, and say the dates in Japanese.

Example

一月一日　がんたん
がんたんは　一月一日です。

B. Work in groups of four or five. Ask the others when their birthdays are and form a line from the youngest to the oldest as quickly as possible. The group that finishes first is the winner.

Example

A: ～さんの　誕生日は　いつですか。
B: １９６８年の　四月九日です。

C. Work with a partner. Ask what he/she does on each of the following occasions.

Example

A: ひまな　時に　何を　しますか。
B: うちで　テレビを　見ます。
A: ～さんは　ひまな　時に　何を　しますか。
B: たいてい　ともだちと　電話で　話します。

	すること
ひまな　時	
あつい　時	
さむい　時	
うれしい　時	
かなしい　時	
さびしい　時	

D. Work with a partner. Ask your partner about places that he/she has visited in the past six months and for how long he/she was there.

Example

A: どんな　ところに　行きましたか。

B: シカゴに　行きました。

A: いつ　行きましたか。

B: 三週間まえです。

A: 何日ぐらい　シカゴに　いましたか。

B: 二日　いました。

どこ	いつ	どのくらい

II. Talking about past experiences, using verb た　ことが　ある; listing representative activities, using verb たり verb たり　する

A. Talking about past experiences, using verb たことが　ある

Question					Answer	
Verb (plain past)	Noun	Particle (subject)			Yes	
たばこを　すった	こと	が	あります	か。	はい、	あります。

Have you ever smoked?

Yes, I have.

No	
いいえ、	ありません。

No, I haven't.

Question						
Question Word		Verb (plain past affirmative)	Noun	Particle (subject)		
どんな	日本の　食べ物を	食べた	こと	が	あります	か。

What kinds of Japanese food have you eaten?

Answer				
	Verb (plain past affirmative)	Noun	Particle (subject)	
おすしや　てんぷらを	食<ruby>た</ruby>べた	こと	が	あります。

I have eaten sushi and tempura.

B. Listing representative activities, using verb たり verb たりする

Topic	Verb (plain past) たり	Verb (plain past) たり	Verb (する)
やすみの　日<ruby>ひ</ruby>には	家で　テレビを　見<ruby>み</ruby>たり	本を　読<ruby>よ</ruby>んだり	します。

I do things like watching television and reading books on a holiday.

The plain past affirmative form of verbs

Take the て-form of a verb and replace it with た (or だ).

	Plain Present Affirmative		て-form		Plain Past Affirmative
Irregular verb	する	→	して	→	した
	来<ruby>く</ruby>る	→	来<ruby>き</ruby>て	→	来<ruby>き</ruby>た
る-verb	見<ruby>み</ruby>る	→	見<ruby>み</ruby>て	→	見<ruby>み</ruby>た
	食<ruby>た</ruby>べる	→	食<ruby>た</ruby>べて	→	食<ruby>た</ruby>べた
う-verb	書<ruby>か</ruby>く	→	書<ruby>か</ruby>いて	→	書<ruby>か</ruby>いた
	読<ruby>よ</ruby>む	→	読んで	→	読んだ

川口：　てんぷらを　食<ruby>た</ruby>べた　ことが　ありますか。
Have you ever eaten tempura?

ワット：ええ、あります。
Yes, I have.

川口：　じゃあ、おすしは　どうですか。
Then, how about sushi?

ワット：ざんねんですが、おすしは　食<ruby>た</ruby>べた　ことが　ありません。
Unfortunately, I have never eaten sushi.

川口： 子供の　時　どんな　ことを　よく　しましたか。

What kinds of things did you do when you were a child?

ワット： そうですね。　やきゅうを　したり　ゆうえんちに
行ったり　しました。

Well, I did things like playing baseball and going to an amusement park.

● Verb た　ことが　ある is used to express a past experience. In contrast, verb ました simply expresses a past action. The absence of any past experience is expressed by verb た　ことが／は　ない。

私は　こうつうじこに　あった　ことが　あります。

I have had a traffic accident.

私は　こうつうじこに　あった　ことが　ありません。

I have never had a traffic accident.

私は　こうつうじこに　あいました。

I had a traffic accident.

● Verb た　ことが　ある is usually used to talk about experience in the not-so-recent past, not about something that took place very recently, such as きのう or おととい.

私は　五年まえに　中国に　行った　ことが　あります。

I went to China five years ago.

● Verb たり...verb たり　する is used to list representative activities. It is similar to や (Chapter 7), which is used to list nouns and noun phrases.

新聞や　ざっしを　読みます。
新聞を　読んだり　ざっしを　見たり　します。

話してみましょう

A. Look at the drawings and form questions asking whether someone has ever done what is pictured.

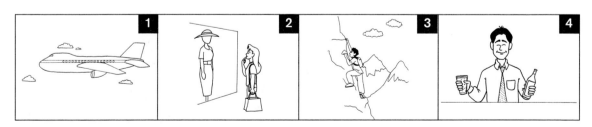

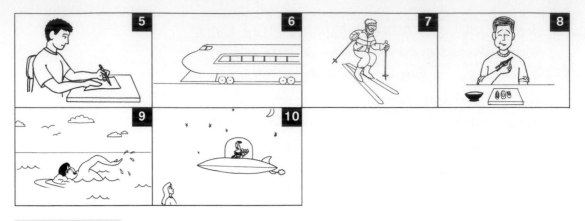

Example

Picture 1

<u>ひこうきに　のった　ことが　ありますか。</u>

B. Ask your classmates whether they have done the things in the following bingo chart. Write the name of the person when he/she answers yes. The first one to complete a row or column with all different names wins.

へんな　ものを 食べる	ゴルフを　する	日本に　行く	ゆうめいな　スター (*movie star*) に　会う
_____	_____	_____	_____
おてらを　見る	日本の　ざっしを 読む	たばこを　すう	日本人と 日本語で　話す
_____	_____	_____	_____
きものを　きる	スペイン語を べんきょうする	キャンプに 行く	ふとんで　ねる
_____	_____	_____	_____
はくぶつかんに 行く	くるまを　買う	つりを　する	こうつうじこに あう
_____	_____	_____	_____

C. Work with a partner. Ask your partner what kinds of places he/she has been on vacation, when he/she went, and what he/she did.

Example

A: ～さんは　どんな　ところに　あそびに　行った　ことが
ありますか。

B: ボストンに　行った　ことが　あります。

A: そうでずか。いつ　行きましたか。

B: 去年　行きました。

A: ボストンで　どんな　ことを　しましたか。

B: はくぶつかんに　行ったり　ふるい　教会を　見たり
しました。

D. Look at Watt-san's personal history and make sentences that express the kinds of activities he did at different stages in his life.

Example

ワットさんは　小学校の　時　よく　どうぶつえんに　行ったり、
こうえんで　あそんだり　しました。

	よくしたこと
1980 12/3　誕生日	
1986～1991　小学校	どうぶつえんに　行く　やきゅうを　する こうえんで　あそぶ　はくぶつかんに　行く
1991～1994　中学	としょかんに　行く　べんきょうする 山に　のぼる　キャンプに　行く
1994～1997　高校	ともだちと　電話で　話す アルバイトを　する　うみに　あそびに　行く デートを　する　本や　ざっしを　読む
1997～今　大学	べんきょうする　パーティに　行く アルバイトを　する　ドライブに　行く

E. Work with a partner. Ask what kinds of activities he/she did at different times in his/her life.

___ **Example**

A: 小学校の　時　よく　どんな　ことを　しましたか。

B: そうですね。ともだちの　家に　あそびに　行ったり、父と　ゆうえんちに　行ったり　しました。

	よく　した　こと／よく　する　こと
小学校	
中学	
高校	
今	

F. Work in groups of three or four. Think about a place, such as a park, department store, supermarket, and so on. Describe to the rest of the group what people do at that place and make them guess each place.

___ **Example**

A: ここで　およいだり　バスケットボールを　したり　します。

B: たいいくかんですか。

A: はい、そうです。

III. Expressing reasons, using the plain past form of verbs and adjectives + んです and the plain form of verbs and adjectives + からです

A. **Using the plain past form of verbs/adjectives + んです**

Question					
		Verb (plain past)			
どうして	きのう	来なかった	ん	です	か。

Why didn't you come yesterday?

Answer				
		Verb (plain past)		
アルバイト	が	あった	ん	です。

I had a part-time job.

	Adjective (plain past)		
とても	いそがしかった	ん	です。

I was very busy.

B. Using the plain form of verbs/adjectives + からです

Question					
		Verb (plain present)			
どうして	ビールを	飲まない	ん	です	か。

Why don't you drink beer?

Answer				
		Adjective (plain present)		
ビール	は	きらいだ	から	です。

Because I don't like beer.

Question					
			Verb (plain past)		
どうして	シカゴ	に	行った	ん	です	か。

Why did you go to Chicago?

Answer						
				Adjective (plain past)		
ともだち	が	日本	から	来た	から	です。

Because a friend arrived from Japan.

Formation of plain forms

Plain present affirmative form of な-adjectives and noun + copula

	Plain Present Affirmative		Polite Present Affirmative		Plain Present Affirmative
な-adjective	すき	→	すき<u>です</u>	→	すき<u>だ</u>
	げんき	→	げんき<u>です</u>	→	げんき<u>だ</u>
Noun + copula	学生	→	学生<u>です</u>	→	学生<u>だ</u>

	Plain Present Affirmative		Polite Past Affirmative		Plain Past Affirmative
な-adjective	すき	→	すき<u>でした</u>	→	すき<u>だった</u>
	げんき	→	げんき<u>でした</u>	→	げんき<u>だった</u>
Noun + copula	学生	→	学生<u>でした</u>	→	学生<u>だった</u>

Plain past affirmative form of い-adjectives

	Plain Present Affirmative		Polite Past Affirmative		Plain Past Affirmative
い-adjective	あつい	→	あつ<u>かったです</u>	→	あつ<u>かった</u>
	いい	→	<u>よかったです</u>	→	<u>よかった</u>

Plain past negative form of adjectives and verbs of all types: Replace the plain present negative ending ない with なかった.

	Plain Present Affirmative		Plain Present Negative		Plain Past Negative
な-adjective	げんき	→	げんきじゃ<u>ない</u>	→	げんきじゃ<u>なかった</u>
い-adjective	さむい	→	さむく<u>ない</u>	→	さむく<u>なかった</u>
	いい	→	<u>よくない</u>	→	<u>よくなかった</u>
Irregular verb	する	→	<u>し</u><u>ない</u>	→	<u>し</u><u>なかった</u>
	来る	→	来<u>ない</u>	→	来<u>なかった</u>
る-verb	おきる	→	おき<u>ない</u>	→	おき<u>なかった</u>
	食べる	→	食べ<u>ない</u>	→	食べ<u>なかった</u>
う-verb	行く	→	行か<u>ない</u>	→	行か<u>なかった</u>
	飲む	→	飲ま<u>ない</u>	→	飲ま<u>なかった</u>
	ある	→	<u>ない</u>	→	<u>なかった</u>

山田：　高校の　時、よく　アルバイトを　しましたか。
Did you work part time often when you were in high school?

木村：　ええ。一週間に　二十時間ぐらい　しました。お金が
なかったんです。
Yes, I worked about twenty hours a week. I didn't have money.

アリス：きのう　どうして　ないたんですか。
Why did you cry yesterday?

モネ：　とても　うれしかったからです。
I was very happy.

- The plain form + からです explicitly states a reason, whereas 〜んです does it more implicitly. 〜からです is used only when a reason is asked for explicitly.

- Both からです and んです take the plain form of adjectives and verbs. からです requires the plain present affirmative form of な-adjective and noun + copula, such as しずかだからです and 学生だからです. In contrast, んです requires the prenominal form of な-adjective and noun + な, such as しずかなんです and 学生なんです.

	な-adjective + からです／んです		Noun + Copula + からです／んです	
Present affirmative	すきだ すきな	からです or んです	学生だ 学生な	からです or んです
Present negative	すきじゃない		学生じゃない	
Past affirmative	すきだった		学生だった	
Past negative	すきじゃなかった		学生じゃなかった	

	い-adjective + からです／んです		いい + からです／んです	
Present affirmative	あつい	からです or んです	いい	からです or んです
Present negative	あつくない		よくない	
Past affirmative	あつかった		よかった	
Past negative	あつくなかった		よくなかった	

	する + からです／んです		来る + からです／んです	
Present affirmative	する	からです	来る	からです
Present negative	しない	or	来ない	or
Past affirmative	した	んです	来た	んです
Past negative	しなかった		来なかった	

	る-verb + からです／んです		う-verb + からです／んです	
Present affirmative	見る	からです	のぼる	からです
Present negative	見ない	or	のぼらない	or
Past affirmative	見た	んです	のぼった	んです
Past negative	見なかった		のぼらなかった	

- In *clause 1* から, *clause 2*, the verb in clause 1 can be in the plain form. It makes the sentence less formal although the level of speech is still polite.

  あした　しけんが　あるから、べんきょうします。
  あした　しけんが　ありますから、べんきょうします。

  I have an exam tomorrow, so I will study.

話してみましょう

A. Change the following adjectives and verbs into the plain present negative, plain past affirmative, and plain past negative. Pay attention to the types of adjectives and verbs.

Example

おいしい
おいしくない　おいしかった　おいしくなかった

1. さむい
2. すずしい
3. すき
4. ひま
5. あつい
6. いい

7. にぎやか
8. たのしい
9. たいへん
10. げんき
11. そうじを　する
12. なく

13. わらう
14. しゅくだいを　だす
15. ごはんを　つくる
16. ねる

17. ふとる
18. あそぶ
19. シャワーを　あびる
20. おきる

B. Draw a line between the sentences that express a cause and its effect. Then construct a dialogue that asks for a reason.

Example

A: どうして　サラダを　食べないんですか。
B: レタスが　きらいだからです。

サラダを　食べません———————レタスが　きらいです

いそがしかったです　　　　　　きのうは　さむかったです

おふろに　はいります　　　　　ひこうきは　きらいです

よく　うみに　行きます　　　　かなしかったです

でんしゃに　のります　　　　　アルバイトが　ありました

ふとっていました　　　　　　　あまり　うんどうを　しませんでした

日本語が　上手です　　　　　　お金が　ありませんでした

なきました　　　　　　　　　　日本に　すんでいました

アルバイトを　しました　　　　つりを　するのが　すきです

C. Work with a partner. Make a list of activities that you have never done. Your partner will ask you why you didn't do those activities. Take turns asking.

Example

A: 小学校の　時、あまり　ともだちと　あそびませんでした。

B: どうして　あそばなかったんですか。

A: 本を　読むのが　すきだったんです。

D. Work with a new partner. Ask him/her what activities he/she did or didn't often do in elementary, junior high, or senior high school and why.

Example

A: 小学校の　時　よく　何を　しましたか。

B: そうですね。やきゅうが　すきだったから、よく　やきゅうを　しました。

A: そうですか。じゃあ　どんな　ことは　あまり
　　しなかったんですか。

B: そうですね。家の　ことは　しませんでしたね。

A: どうしてですか。

B: 母が　したからです。

IV. Expressing hearsay, using the plain form of verbs/adjectives/the copula + そうです

				Verb (plain present)		
ジョンソンさん	は	来年	日本	に	行く	そう	です。

I heard that Johnson-san will go to Japan next year.

			Verb (plain past)		
山田さん	は	日本	に	帰った	そう	です。

I heard that Yamada-san went back to Japan.

山下：　　小学校の　時　日本に　すんでいたそうですね。
　　　　　You lived in Japan when you were in elementary school, right?

ジョーンズ：ええ。二年生の　時から　三年生の　時まで　すんで
　　　　　　いました。
　　　　　　Yes. I lived (there) from the second grade until the third grade.

山下：　　どうして　日本に　行ったんですか。
　　　　　Why did you go to Japan?

ジョーンズ：父が　日本の　大学に　つとめていたからです。
　　　　　　My father was employed at a Japanese university.

● 〜そうです expresses hearsay meaning *I heard* or *I have heard*. It is often used with 〜によると, which means *according to* 〜.

　　田中さんに　よると　キムさんは　けっこんしているそうです。

　　According to Tanaka-san, (I heard that) Kim-san is married.

● The verb or adjective that precedes 〜そうです must be in the plain form.

　　リーさんは　大学生だそうです。

　　I heard Lee-san is a college student.

リーさんは　大学生じゃないそうです。

I heard Lee-san is not a college student.

リーさんの　アパートは　せまいそうです。

I heard Lee-san's apartment is small.

パーティは　あまり　おもしろくなかったそうです。

I heard the party was not very interesting.

話してみましょう

A. You have heard something about Tanaka-san. Make a sentence that reports what you have heard.

Example

田中さんは　子供の　時　よく　ねる　子供でした。
<u>田中さんは　子供の　時　よく　ねる　子供だったそうです。</u>

1. 田中さんは　大学院の　学生です。
2. 田中さんは　中学の　時　よく　山に　のぼりました。
3. 田中さんは　しゃしんを　とるのが　すきです。
4. 田中さんは　こうつうじこに　あった　ことが　あります。
5. 田中さんは　先週　キャンプに　行きました。
6. 田中さんの　へやは　とても　さむかったです。

B. Work in groups of four or five. The instructor will say something to one member of each team, who will return to his/her respective team, tell what he/she heard to the next person in the team, who will tell the next person, and so on. The last person in each team will go to the blackboard and write down what he/she heard.

Example

きょうは　テストが　ありません。
<u>きょうは　テストが　ないそうです。</u>

C. Work with a partner. Choose one person from the list (or think of someone) and pretend you are that person. Your partner will interview you and take detailed notes. Then reverse your roles.

Example

A: クリントンさんは　今　どこに　すんでいますか。
B: ホワイトハウスに　すんでいます。

ゆうめいな　人の　リスト

クリントン　　　　　　　リンカーン
マドンナ　　　　　　　　エリザベスじょおう(Queen Elizabeth)
マイケル　ジャクソン　　タイガー　ウッズ
コロンブス (Columbus)　　マリリン　モンロー
スーパーマン　　　　　　マジック　ジョンソン
バットマン　　　　　　　マイケル　ジョーダン
ジョージ　ワシントン

D. Work in groups of three or four. Recite your interview notes from exercise C to the group without revealing the name of the interviewee. The rest of the group will try to guess who the interviewee is.

Example

この　人は　アメリカ人じゃないそうです。そして、旅行が
とても　すきだったそうです。

V. Using noun-modifying clauses in the past and present

A. Using the plain present form of verbs

			Modifying Clause				
			Verb (plain present)	Noun			
兄	が	よく	行く	きっさてん	は	あそこ	です。

The coffee shop that my older brother often goes to is over there.

B. Using the plain present or past form of adjectives and verbs

			Modifying Clause		
			Adjective (plain past)	Noun	
これ	は	母	が	すきだった	本	です。

This is the book that my mother liked.

Modifying clause								
			Verb (plain past)	Noun				
兄	が	きのう	行った	きっさてん	は	あそこ	です。	

The coffee shop that my older brother went to yesterday is over there.

● As explained in Chapter 10, in Japanese the modifying clause immediately precedes the noun to be modified. The modifying clause can be in the past or the present tense, but the verb must be in the plain form.

● The topic marker は does not appear in a modifying clause. Thus, the subject of the verb in a modifying clause is marked by が.

弟<u>が</u>　よく　行く　レストラン

the restaurant that my younger brother goes to often

山田さん<u>が</u>　きのう　行った　レストラン

the restaurant that Yamada-san went to yesterday

母<u>が</u>　すきだった　ふく

the clothes that my mother liked

母<u>が</u>　すきな　おんがく

the music that my mother likes

● The subject marker が is often substituted by the particle の when a modifying clause is very short.

父<u>が／の</u>　すきだった　家

the house that my father liked

父<u>が</u>　子供の　時に　すきだった　家

the house that my father liked when he was a child

弟<u>が／の</u>　見た　えいが

the movie that my younger brother watched

弟<u>が</u>　山田さんと　見た　えいが

the movie that my younger brother watched with Yamada-san

● Use the present tense when a modifying clause describes a characteristic of a person or thing even though the sentence is in the past tense.

私は　よく　食べる　子供でした。

I was a child who ate a lot.

山田さんは　せが　たかい　人でした。

Yamada-san was the tall person.

A. Read each statement and form a question that asks for the underlined thing, place, or person.

Example

田中さんは　きのう　<u>どこかに</u>　<ruby>行<rt>い</rt></ruby>きました。

<u>田中さんが　きのう　<ruby>行<rt>い</rt></ruby>った　ところは　どこですか。</u>

1. 田中さんは　きのう　<u>何か</u>　<ruby>食<rt>た</rt></ruby>べました。
2. 田中さんは　きのう　<u>だれかに</u>　<ruby>電話<rt>でんわ</rt></ruby>を　かけました。
3. 田中さんは　きのう　<u>だれかと</u>　デートを　しました。
4. 田中さんは　きのう　<u>どこかで</u>　本を　<ruby>買<rt>か</rt></ruby>いました。
5. 田中さんは　きのう　<u>何か</u>　<ruby>飲<rt>の</rt></ruby>みました。
6. 田中さんのねこは　<u>どこかに</u>　います。
7. 田中さんは　<u>だれかに</u>　<ruby>会<rt>あ</rt></ruby>います。
8. 田中さんは　<u>何か</u>　つくります。

B. Work with a partner. Ask him/her which activities he/she has done, using the given verbs. Then ask how it was.

Example

A: どんな　ものを　<ruby>食<rt>た</rt></ruby>べた　ことが　ありますか。

B: おすしを　<ruby>食<rt>た</rt></ruby>べた　ことが　あります。

A: どうでしたか。

B: あまり　おいしくありませんでした。

	もの／ところ	どうでしたか。
<ruby>食<rt>た</rt></ruby>べる		
<ruby>飲<rt>の</rt></ruby>む		
<ruby>行<rt>い</rt></ruby>く		
<ruby>見<rt>み</rt></ruby>る		
<ruby>聞<rt>き</rt></ruby>く		

C. Work with a new partner. From the information you gathered in Exercise B, tell your new partner about the activities your former partner did and how they were. Use noun-modifying clauses.

Example

～さんが　食べた　ものは　おすしです。

～さんが　食べた　おすしは　あまり　おいしくなかったそうです。

D. Work in groups of three or four. One person will define an item in the table, while the others try to guess what the item is. The person who guesses the most items is the winner.

Example

A: 先生と　べんきょうする　へやです。

B: きょうしつですか。

A: はい、そうです。

としょかん　　　先生　　　学生　　　子供　　　お母さん　　　やきゅう

ファミコン　　　デパート　　　スーパー　　　レストラン

ゆうびんきょく　　　えんぴつ　　　ノート　　　ゆうえんち

小学校　　　デーパック

E. Ask each other what kind of child you were.

Example

A: キムさんは　どんな　子供でしたか。

B: よく　あそんで、よく　食べる　子供でした。

なまえ	どんな子供

Writing verbs in kanji

When you write a verb in **kanji**, you need to write the stem or part of the stem in **kanji** and the inflectional ending in **hiragana**. **Hiragana** indicating inflectional endings is called **okurigana** (おくりがな). When you learn the **kanji** for a new verb, you need to know how much of the verb should be written in **kanji** and how much in **okurigana**. For example, in the case of 飲む(のむ), 飲 is used for の, and its **okurigana** is む. In 食べる, 食 is read as た, and べる is the **okurigana**.

The **kanji** pronunciation in a verb is usually stable, but some **kanji** change their pronunciation depending on the inflection. For example, 来る is pronounced く, き or こ in different forms of the verb:

来る 来ます 来ない

Because a Japanese person knows the correct reading from **okurigana**, the **kanji** is not marked with any superscript.

Learning tips

行　This **kanji** came from a picture of an intersection,

見　This **kanji** is the combination of an eye and legs.

聞　This **kanji** is the combination of a gate and an ear (listening through a gate).

出　This **kanji** came from a picture of a foot stepping over a line.

買　This **kanji** is the combination of a net (at the top) and merchandise. (貝 came from a picture of shellfish, which had a standard trading value.)

話　This **kanji** is the combination of 言 (to say) and 舌 (tongue). (舌 came from a picture of something sticking out of a mouth.)

読　This **kanji** is the combination of 言 (to say) and 売 (to sell). It came from the idea of *shouting to sell,* which later came to mean *reading aloud.*

飲　The left-hand side of this **kanji** is derived from 食, indicating that its meaning, *drinking,* is related to eating.

あたら　　よ
新しい読みかた

しょうがっこう　ちゅうがく
小学校　中学
いちがつ　にがつ　　　　いっ　げつ　に　げつ　　　　　せんげつ　こんげつ　らいげつ　ことし　らいねん
一月　二月...　一か月　二か月...　　先月　今月　来月　今年　来年
らいしゅう　ついたち　ふつか　みっか　よっか　いつか　むいか　なのか　ようか　ここのか　とおか
来週　一日　二日　三日　四日　五日　六日　七日　八日　九日　十日
じゅういちにち　じゅうよっか　はつか　にじゅうよっか　　　　ひ　　　かね
十一日　十四日　二十日　二十四日　やすみの　日　お金

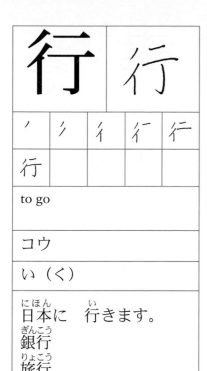

行 行

ノ｜ク｜イ｜イ｜行

行

to go

コウ

い（く）

日本に　行きます。
銀行
旅行

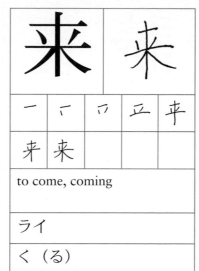

来 来

一｜ㄷ｜ㅁ｜屸｜平

来 来

to come, coming

ライ

く（る）

山田さんが　来た。
山口さんが　来ない。
来週　来年

帰 帰

丨｜リ｜リﾌ｜リﾖ｜リﾖ

リﾖﾟ｜帰｜帰｜帰｜帰

to return, to go home

キ

かえ（る）

アパートに　帰る。
帰りました。
帰った。

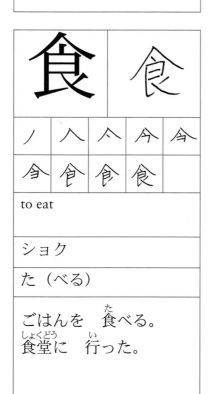

食 食

ノ｜入｜入｜今｜今

今｜食｜食｜食

to eat

ショク

た（べる）

ごはんを　食べる。
食堂に　行った。

飲 飲

ノ｜月｜月｜食｜食

食｜飲｜飲｜飲

to drink

イン

の（む）

コーラを　飲む。
ビールを　飲まない。

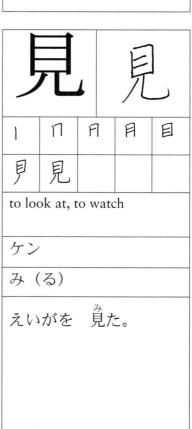

見 見

丨｜冂｜月｜月｜目

貝｜見

to look at, to watch

ケン

み（る）

えいがを　見た。

聞	聞	一	「	ｦ	戸	門
		門	門	問	閒	聞

to hear, to listen

ブン

き（く）

おんがくを　聞くのが
　　すきです。
新聞を　読む。

読	読	二	言	言	訂	計
		計	誌	誌	読	読

to read

ドク

よ（む）

本を　読む。

書	書	フ	ラ	ヲ	聿	聿
		聿	聿	書	書	書

to write

ショ

か（く）

手紙を
　　書いて下さい。

話	話	二	言	言	訂	訮
		訮	話	話	話	

to talk, to speak

ワ

はな（す）

電話で　先生と
　　話します。

高	高	丶	亠	亠	古	古
		古	高	高	高	高

high, expensive

コウ

たか（い）

高校の　時
高い　山
高い　セーター

校	校	一	十	才	才	术
		杧	杧	栌	栌	校

school

コウ

学校に　来る。
小学校の　時

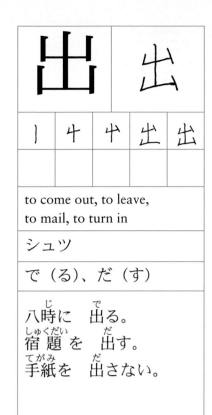

一	十	屮	出	出

to come out, to leave,
to mail, to turn in

シュツ

で（る）、だ（す）

八時に　出る。
宿題を　出す。
手紙を　出さない。

ノ	人	𠆢	今	会
会				

to meet, to see

カイ

あ（う）

会社で　友達と
　会った。
教会に　行く。

丶	冖	皿	四	罒
罒	胃	罒	買	買

to buy

バイ

か（う）

車を　買った。

Read the following sentences.

1. チェンさんは子供の時、本をたくさん読みました。

2. 父はお茶をよく飲みますが、コーヒーはぜんぜん飲みません。

3. 母は高校の時友達に会いにアメリカに行きました。

4. 山田さんのお姉さんは先月高いステレオを買いましたから、今はお金がありません。

5. 妹は五時に出かけました。そして、よる九時ごろ家に帰りました。

6. 毎日何時ごろねますか。

7. きのうは音楽を聞いたり、手紙を書いたりしました。

8. ばんごはんを食べに家に来てください。

上手な読み方

Understanding the format of a letter

The format of Japanese letter writing is relatively fixed and the following example shows the order and layout of the various parts of a letter. Letters can be written either vertically or horizontally. In vertical writing, a letter starts with an opening word. Knowing the format of a letter will help you read letters more efficiently.

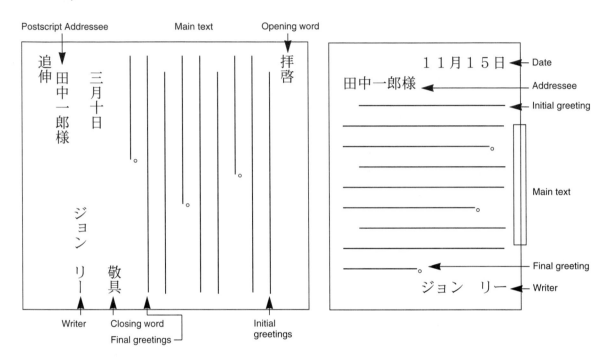

Both opening words and closing words are fixed expressions.

Opening words: 拝啓 (はいけい) greetings 前略 (ぜんりゃく) short greetings

Closing words: 敬具 (けいぐ) yours faithfully かしこ yours faithfully (used by females only)

A. In the letter on page 387, identify the following:

1. Initial greetings
2. Closing word
3. Name of the writer
4. Name of the addressee
5. Location of the main text
6. Date

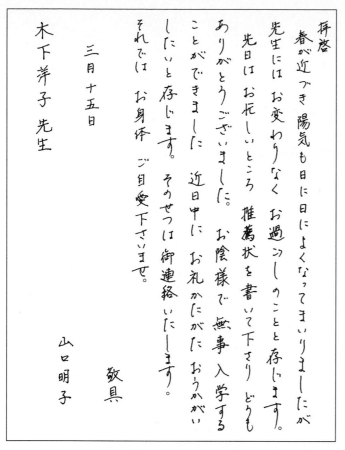

拝啓

春が近づき　陽気も日に日によくなってまいりましたが
先生には　お変わりなく　お過ごしのことと存じます。
先日は　お忙しいところ　推薦状を書いて下さり　どうも
ありがとうございました。　お陰様で　無事　入学する
ことができました。　近日中に　お礼かたがた　おうかがい
したいと存じます。　そのせつは　御連絡いたします。
それでは　お身体　ご自愛下さいませ。

敬具

三月　十五日

山口　明子

木下　洋子　先生

B. Like letters, envelopes can be addressed vertically or horizontally. Look at
the following envelopes and identify the following:

1. the name and address of the sender

2. the name and address of the receiver

150-□□

東京都　新宿区　西新宿　三・五・十二

木下　洋子　様

316 □□

広島市中区　四・一

山口　明子

150
東京都新宿区西新宿 3-5-12

木下　洋子　様

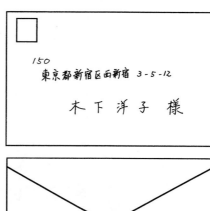

316　広島市中区 4-1

山口　明子

アリスさんの手紙

読む前に

1. Work with a partner. Tell your partner when you went on vacation. Say what you did, and how much you enjoyed it.

2. Write about your partner's vacation in three sentences.

言葉のリスト

(お)まつり　festival

祇園まつり　Gion Festival

山車　float

お体を　大切に　Please take care of yourself.

前略

毎日あついですが、お元気ですか。私はとても元気です。

先月の十五日から二十日まで道子さんと京都に行きました。京都には行ったことがなかったから、とてもうれしかったです。有名なお寺や神社を見たり、京都料理を食べたりしました。私が行ったレストランはとても高かったですが、料理はとてもきれいでおいしかったです。

七月十六日と十七日は祇園まつりでした。祇園まつりは日本で一番古いおまつりだそうです。大川さんは見たことがありますか。大きい出車やきれいな着物を着た人がたくさんいて、とても立派なおまつりでした。夏休みにはまたどこかへ旅行に行きます。

また手紙を書きますね。お体を大切に。それでは、また。

かしこ

有坂アリス

八月二日

大川さなえ様

日本語と　えいごで　こたえて下さい。

1. この手紙は　だれに　書きましたか。
2. アリスさんは　どうして　この　手紙を　書きましたか。
3. アリスさんは　いつ　きょうとに　行きましたか。
4. アリスさんは　だれと　きょうとに　行きましたか。
5. きょうとに　何日　いましたか。
6. アリスさんは　きょうとで　何を　しましたか。
7. アリスさんは　ぎおんまつりを　見た　ことが
　　ありましたか。
8. ぎおんまつりは　どんな　まつりですか。
9. ぎおんまつりは　どうでしたか。

わかりましたか

大川さんに　手紙を　書いて下さい。

～さんの　やすみの　ことを　書いて　下さい。(Write about your vacation)

上手な聞き方

Taking turns in a conversation

An important rule in conversation is taking turns, or allowing only one person to speak at a time. Body language, introductory remarks, and silence are some ways to signal who should speak next. Of course, not everyone waits for their turn to speak. In fact, you may often hear two or more conversations going on at the same time in one group.

A. Listen to the conversations and make a check mark next to the conversation that breaks the rule of taking turns.

Conversation 1 _____   Conversation 2 _____

B. 日本の　おもいで　(Memories of Japan)
　　言葉の　リスト

　　ほっかいどう　Hokkaido
　　ゆきまつり　Snow Festival
　　よこはま　Yokohama City

These students are talking about their experiences in Japan. Listen to their descriptions and complete the following chart in English. You may not understand every detail, but try to get the general idea.

	When did they go to Japan?	What happened? / What did they do?
チョンさん		
モリルさん		
クリシュナさん		

DICT-A-CONVERSATION

You, Smith-san, are talking to your friend, Yamada-san, about her last vacation.

スミス：<u>山田さん、やすみに　どこかに　行きましたか。</u>

山田：＿＿＿＿＿＿＿＿＿＿＿＿＿＿＿＿＿＿＿＿＿

スミス：＿＿＿＿＿＿＿＿＿＿＿＿＿＿＿＿＿＿＿＿

山田：＿＿＿＿＿＿＿＿＿＿＿＿＿＿＿＿＿＿＿＿＿

スミス：＿＿＿＿＿＿＿＿＿＿＿＿＿＿＿＿＿＿＿＿

山田：＿＿＿＿＿＿＿＿＿＿＿＿＿＿＿＿＿＿＿＿＿

スミス：＿＿＿＿＿＿＿＿＿＿＿＿＿＿＿＿＿＿＿＿

山田：＿＿＿＿＿＿＿＿＿＿＿＿＿＿＿＿＿＿＿＿＿

聞き上手、話し上手

Conversation fillers

Speaking always involves false starts, paraphrases, and pauses. Even native speakers do not speak in fluent and complete sentences all the time. In English one often says *um, uh, let's see,* or *well* to fill in pauses. In Japanese, expressions like あのう, えーっと, and そうですね serve as conversation fillers. This usage of あのう differs from that of あのう、すみません, which is used to get someone's attention. However, one should be careful not to overuse fillers.

A: やすみに　よく　どんな　ことを　しますか。

B: <u>そうですね</u>。テニスを　したり、およぎに　行ったり、それから、<u>えーっと</u>、えいがを　見たりしますね。

Work with a partner. Ask your him/her a question that requires a long answer such as a description of his/her apartment, friend, or past experience. Practice using conversation fillers.

総合練習
そうごうれんしゅう

私は　だれですか。

1. Work in a group of three or four. Complete the following paragraph with your own information, as in the example, and then interview one another taking detailed notes.

Example

私のなまえはスーザン　ロスです。私はシカゴから来ました。誕生日は六月二十五日です。私は子供の時しずかな子供でした。よく本を読んだり、おんがくを聞いたりしました。私はフランスに行ったことがあります。十五さいの時でした。フランスにともだちがいたからです。

私のなまえは＿＿＿＿＿ です。私は＿＿＿＿＿ から来ました。誕生日は＿＿＿＿＿ です。私は子供の時＿＿＿＿＿ 子供でした。＿＿＿＿＿ たり、＿＿＿＿＿ たりしました。＿＿＿＿＿ ことがあります。＿＿＿＿＿ 時でした。＿＿＿＿＿ からです。

Sample interview questions

Q: どこから　来ましたか。
Q: 子供の　時、どんな　子供でしたか。
Q: 子供の　時、どんな　ことを　しましたか。
Q: どんな　ことを　した　ことが　ありますか。何さいの　時でしたか。どうして　したんですか。

2. Each group will choose a person and describe that person, except for the name, to the entire class by using そうです for hearsay. The class will try to figure out which member of the group is being described.

Member 1: この　人は　子供(こども)の　時、しずかな　子供(こども)だった
そうです。

Member 2: この　人は　フランスに　行った　ことが
あるそうです。

Member 3: この　人は　十五さいの　時に　フランスに
行った　ことが　あるそうです。

Member 4: この　人は　子供(こども)の　時、本を　読んだり、
おんがくを　聞いたり　したそうです。

Note that the person chosen to be described must still use そうです,
although he/she will be talking about himself/herself.

ロールプレイ

1. You are talking with your Japanese friend about your childhood. Describe
   what kinds of things you did or didn't do.

2. Talk about the best vacation you ever had. What happened? Why was it so special?

3. You are attending a college reunion. Talk about what kinds of things you
   did in college.

たんご　(ESSENTIAL VOCABULARY)

Nouns

あき（秋）fall

うみ（海）ocean, sea

おととし　the year before last, two years ago

（お）かね（（お）金）money

きせつ（季節）season

きもの（着物）traditional Japanese clothes,
　kimono

キャンプ　camping

きょうかい（教会）church

きょねん（去年）last year

こうつうじこ（交通事故）traffic accident
　こうつうじこに　あう（交通事故に
　あう）　have a traffic accident

こと（事）thing, matter (intangible, often
　refers to activities and happenings)

ことし（今年）this year

しょうがっこう（小学校）elementary
　school

じんじゃ（神社）Shinto shrine

せんげつ（先月）last month

タバコ／たばこ　tobacco

ちゅうがく（中学）junior high school
　(shortened form of 中学校(ちゅうがっこう))

つり（釣り）fishing

デート　dating　デートする (to) go out on a
　date

（お）てら（（お）寺）Buddhist temple

どうぶつえん（動物園）zoo

とき（時）when, at the time of ～　こども
　　の　とき（子供の　時）when I was a
　　child
なつ（夏）summer
なつやすみ（夏休み）summer vacation
はくぶつかん（博物館）museum
はる（春）spring
はるやすみ（春休み）spring vacation

ひこうき（飛行機）airplane
ふゆ（冬）winter
ふゆやすみ（冬休み）winter vacation
もの（物）thing (tangible)　おいしい　もの
　　（おいしい物）delicious thing/food
やすみ（休み）vacation, holiday
ゆうえんち（遊園地）amusement park
らいげつ（来月）next month

る-verb

のる（乗る）(to) get on, (to) ride
　　ひこうきに　のる（飛行機に　乗る）(to) get on a plane

う-verbs

すう（吸う）(to) inhale, smoke　たばこを
　　すう（たばこを　吸う）smoke a cigarette
なく（泣く）(to) cry

のぼる（登る）(to) climb　やまに　のぼ
　　る（山に　のぼる）(to) climb a mountain
わらう（笑う）(to) laugh, smile

な-adjective

へん(な)（変（な））strange

い-adjectives

あたたかい（暖かい／温かい）warm
あつい（暑い／熱い）hot
うれしい（嬉しい）happy, joyful
かなしい（悲しい）sad

さびしい（寂しい）lonely
さむい（寒い）cold
すずしい（涼しい）cool

Adverbs

こんど（今度）this time, next time
はじめて（初めて）for the first time

はんとし（半年）a half year

Suffixes

～かげつ（～か月）～month/s (duration)
～がつ（～月）specific month（一月,
　　January）
～にち（～日）～day/s (duration); specific
　　day（十一日, the 11th）

～ねん（～年）specific year（１９９６年)
～まえ（～前）～ago
　　二年まえ（二年前）two years ago

えーっと　Well, let's see. . .

Passive Vocabulary

Nouns

エイプリルフール　April Fools' Day
おもいで（思い出）memories
ぎおんまつり（祇園祭り）Gion Festival
けいぐ（敬具）closing for a letter (similar to *Sincerely, Best wishes,* etc.)
けいけん（経験）experience
サンクスギビング　Thanksgiving
じゅけんべんきょう（受験勉強）study for an entrance examination
（お）しょうがつ（（お）正月）New Year's Day
しょうわ（昭和）the Showa Era (1926–1989)
ぜんりゃく（前略）abbreviated opening phrase of a letter
たいしょう（大正）the Taisho Era (1912–1925)

だし（山車）float
どくりつきねんび（独立記念日）Independence Day
はいけい（拝啓）opening phrase of a letter
バレンタインデー　St. Valentine's Day
ハロウィーン　Halloween
ひにち（日にち）date
へいせい（平成）name of the current reign (started in 1989)
ほっかいどう（北海道）Hokkaido (northernmost main island of Japan)
（お）まつり（（お）祭り）festival
めいじ（明治）the Meiji Era (1868–1911)
ゆきまつり（雪祭り）the snow festival in Sapporo
よこはま（横浜）Yokohama City
レーバーデー　Labor Day

Expressions

おからだを　たいせつに（お体を　大切に）Take good care of yourself.

Supplementary Vocabulary

Expressions

がいこくに　すむ（外国に　住む）
　(to) live in a foreign country
キスを　する　(to) kiss
けんかを　する　(to) have a fight
こいを　する（恋を　する）
　(to) fall in love

すもうを　みる（すもうを　見る）
　(to) watch sumo wrestling
びょうきに　なる（病気に　なる）
　(to) become sick

CHAPTER 12

第<ruby>十<rt>だい</rt></ruby>二<ruby>課<rt>か</rt></ruby>

A hospital waiting-room

<ruby>健<rt>けん</rt></ruby><ruby>康<rt>こう</rt></ruby>

HEALTH

Functions	Describing physical conditions and illnesses; Asking for help; Making polite requests; Giving suggestions
New Vocabulary	Physical symptoms; Health; Things one does and doesn't do when he/she is sick; Describing degrees of sickness or injury and expressing concern
Dialogue	ねつがあるんです。(I have a fever.)
Culture	Japanese hospitals; Medical insurance; Medical terms
Language	I. Expressing capability, using the potential forms of verbs
	II. Expressing cause and effect, using the て-form of adjectives, verbs, and the copula です
	III. Expressing desire, using verb stem + ～たい and ～たがる
	IV. Giving suggestions, using ～たら どうですか and ～ほうが いいです
	V. Asking for and giving permission, using verb ても いいですか
Kanji	Radicals in kanji
Reading	Using knowledge of the real world
Listening	Using the setting
Communication	Talking to a doctor

A. しょうじょう (Physical symptoms). Work with a partner. Your partner will act out the following symptoms. Guess the symptoms.

気分が わるい (to) feel sick (literally: one's feelings are bad)

かおいろが わるい pale (literally: one's face color is bad)

のどが いたい (to) have a sore throat (literally: one's throat is painful)

はが いたい (to) have a toothache

ねつが ある (to) have a fever

おなかが いたい (to) have a stomachache

こしが いたい (to) have lower back pain

はなが つまる (to) have sinus congestion

かゆい itchy

せきが 出る (to) cough

B. けんこう (Health). Write, in Japanese, two sentences for each of the following physical conditions.

病気に なる (to) become sick

ゆびを きる (to) cut one's finger

かぜを ひく (to) catch a cold

体が よわい (to) be weak (literally: one's body is weak)

けんこうな healthy

けがを する (to) have an injury

つかれている (to) be tired

体の調子が いい one's physical condition is good

アレルギーが ある (to) have an allergy

C. 病気の 時に する こと、しない こと (Things one does and doesn't do when he/she is sick). Write, in Japanese, the physical condition for which the following actions may apply:

薬を のむ (to) take (drink) medicine

薬を つける (to) apply medicine

いしゃに 行く (to) go to a doctor

ねつを はかる (to) take one's temperature

学校を 休む (to) be absent from school

入院する　(to) be hospitalized

むりを　する　(to) overstrain

おさけを　のむ　(to) drink an alcoholic beverage

あるく　(to) walk

D. 病気や　けがの　時に　つかう　ことば (Describing degrees of sickness or injury and expressing concern).

かるい　病気　slight illness

おもい　病気　serious illness

だいじょうぶ（な）　all right

こまる　(to) be troubled; (to) be annoyed; (to) suffer

かるい　けが　slight injury

ひどい　けが　serious injury

どうしたんですか／どうしましたか　What happened?

お大事に。　Take good care of yourself.

どうしたらいいですか。　What should I do?

しつもんに　こたえて下さい。

1. どんな　病気に　なった　ことが　ありますか。病気は　おもかったですか。

2. とても　こまった　ことが　ありますか。　どうして　こまったんですか。

3. けがを　した　ことが　ありますか。どんな　けがでしたか。

4. What expression would you use to show concern for someone who looks sick?

ダイアローグ

はじめに

A. 日本語で　こたえて下さい。

1. 病気の　時　何を　しますか。

2. かぜの　しょうじょうは　どんな　しょうじょうですか。

ねつが あるんです。 (I have a fever.)

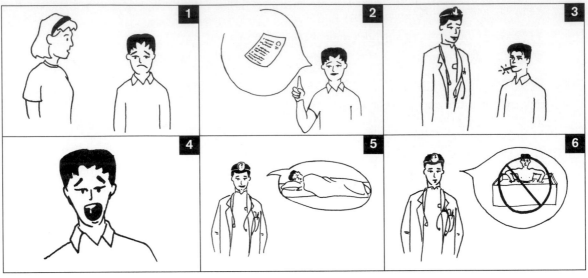

アリスさんは　石田さんに　大学で　会いました。

____　アリス：　石田さん、どうしたんですか。かおいろが

　　　　　　　　わるいですね。

____　石田：　　ええ、ちょっと　気分が　わるいんです。

____　アリス：　病院に　行ったら　どうですか。

____　石田：　　そうですね。でも　きょうは　しけんが　あるから、

　　　　　　　　あまり　休みたくないんです。

____　アリス：　でも、むりを　しない　ほうが　いいですよ。

____　石田：　　そうですね。じゃあ、そうします。

石田さんは　病院に　来ました。

____　いしゃ：　どうしましたか。

____　石田：　　気分が　わるいんです。

____　いしゃ：　そうですか。じゃあ、ちょっと　ねつを

　　　　　　　　はかりましょう。

おいしゃさんは　石田さんの　ねつを　はかります。

____　いしゃ：　八度五分　ありますね。ほかに　どんな

　　　　　　　　しょうじょうが　ありますか。

____　石田：　　せきは　出ないんですが、のどが　いたくて、

　　　　　　　　ごはんが　食べられないんです。

_____ いしゃ： そうですか。じゃあ、ちょっと　口を　あけて
　　　　　　　　下さい。

_____ 石田： はい。

_____ いしゃ： ちょっと　あかいですね。たぶん　かぜ
　　　　　　　　でしょう。　薬を　飲んで、二、三日　休んだ
　　　　　　　　ほうが　いいですね。

_____ 石田： あのう、先生。おふろに　入っても　いいで
　　　　　　　　しょうか。

_____ いしゃ： おふろですか。入らない　ほうが　いいですね。
　　　　　　　　シャワーは　いいですよ。

_____ 石田： はい、わかりました。どうも　ありがとう
　　　　　　　　ございました。

_____ いしゃ： いいえ、それじゃあ　お大事に。

わかりましたか

1. 石田さんは　どうして　病院に　行ったんですか。
2. どんな　しょうじょうでしたか。
3. 石田さんは　どんな　病気に　なりましたか。
4. 石田さんは　おふろに　入れますか。

日本の　文化

Japanese hospitals. Do you go to the hospital when you're sick? Do you have a family doctor?

Apart from the dentist's office, most Japanese hospitals do not operate by appointment, and because patients are treated on a first-come-first-served basis, one often has to wait a long time.

The two types of hospitals in Japan are general hospitals and private clinics. General hospitals handle a full range of medical problems and are equipped with the latest medical technology and complete hospitalization facilities. However, a patient cannot choose a certain doctor or expect to see the same doctor each time. Also, general hospitals tend to be very crowded.

Private clinics are usually run by one or two doctors. The doctor usually treats patients in his/her area of specialization and handles routine illnesses and less complicated surgeries. More complicated procedures are referred to specialists at general hospitals. With a smaller clientele, the doctor sees a patient on a long-term basis and is also available for informal consultations. Doctors in private clinics play a role similar to that of a family doctor in the United States. The following is a list of major specialty areas.

内科 internal medicine 　　産婦人科 gynecology

外科 surgery 　　泌尿器科 urology

小児科 pediatrics 　　精神科 psychiatry

歯科 dentistry 　　耳鼻咽喉科 otorhinolaryngology

眼科 ophthalmology 　　整形外科 orthopedics, cosmetic surgery

皮膚科 dermatology

- *Medical insurance. Do you have medical insurance? What kind of insurance is it?*

  Virtually all Japanese people are covered by medical insurance. The national health insurance provided by the government is available for both Japanese people and foreigners who plan to stay in Japan for more than a year. Application forms are available at the local ward or municipal office. Those who plan to stay in Japan for less than a year should apply for private insurance. National health insurance covers approximately 70 percent of all medical expenses.

  If you work for a company in Japan, the company most likely will provide medical insurance.

- *Medical terms*

  Many Japanese doctors do not speak English, although some can understand it or write medical terms in English. Check with your school, embassy, or consulate for lists of hospitals or clinics with personnel who speak your native language. The following are some common medical terms:

心臓病 heart disease 　　花粉症 hay fever

エイズ AIDS 　　食中毒 food poisoning

癌 cancer 　　骨折 fracture

高血圧 high blood pressure 　　抗生物質 antibiotics

糖尿病 diabetes 　　コレステロール cholesterol

はしか measles

- *Terminal disease. If a doctor discovers that a patient has a terminal disease, how does he/she handle it in your country?*

  In Japan, when a patient is diagnosed as having a terminal disease, the doctor does not tell him/her about it without first consulting the patient's family. Traditionally, it has been considered cruel for a doctor to tell a patient the truth, so it is left up to the family to decide whether to tell the patient.

- *Addressing a doctor. How do you address your doctor in your country?*

  In Japan, a medical doctor is addressed as 先生. The term 先生 can be used for any figure of authority, whether he/she is a schoolteacher, master craftsman, clergyman, political leader, or instructor in general. It is not used in a company. Instead, rank titles, such as section head or department chief, are used.

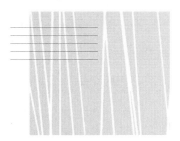

LANGUAGE

I. Expressing capability, using the potential forms of verbs

								Verb Potential Form
日本語	を	八か月	べんきょうした	から、	すこし	かんじ	が	読めます。

Since I studied Japanese for eight months, I can read **kanji** a little.

Question				Answer			
	Verb Potential Form						Verb Potential Form (negative)
来週	来られます	か。		いいえ、	来週	は	来られません。

Can you come next week?　　　　No, I cannot come next week.

Irregular verbs

Dictionary Form	Potential Forms			
	Plain Present		Polite Present	
	Affirmative	Negative	Affirmative	Negative
する	できる	できない	できます	できません
来る	来られる	来られない	来られます	来られません

る-verbs

Take the dictionary form:　食べる

食べ ＋られる ＝ 食べられる

Dictionary Form	Potential Forms			
	Plain Present		Polite Present Form	
	Affirmative	Negative	Affirmative	Negative
食べる	食べられる	食べられない	食べられます	食べられません
ねる	ねられる	ねられない	ねられます	ねられません
おきる	おきられる	おきられない	おきられます	おきられません
いる	いられる	いられない	いられます	いられません

アリス：どうしたんですか。
　　　　What's wrong?

山川：　はが　いたくて　ねられなかったんです。
　　　　I had a toothache, so I couldn't sleep.

アリス：そうですか。それは　大変ですね。
　　　　Is that so? I'm sorry to hear that. (literally: That is awful/terrible,
　　　　isn't it?)

う-verbs

Take the dictionary form: 飲む
飲め +る ＝ 飲める

Dictionary Form	Potential Forms			
	Plain Present		Polite Present	
	Affirmative	Negative	Affirmative	Negative
飲む	飲める	飲めない	飲めます	飲めません
あるく	あるける	あるけない	あるけます	あるけません
はしる	はしれる	はしれない	はしれます	はしれません
話す	話せる	話せない	話せます	話せません
会う	会える	会えない	会えます	会えません

- When the verb is in the potential form, the direct object of the verb takes either が, or を, except for できる, which takes only が.

  にくを　食べます。　　I eat meat.

  にくが／を　食べられます。　　I can eat meat.

  あたらしい　くるまを　買います。　　I will buy a new car.

  あたらしい　くるまが／を　買えます。　　I can buy a new car.

  テニスを　します。　　I play tennis.

  テニスが　出来ます。　　I can play tennis.

- The younger generation now drops the ら out of ～られる in -る verb potential forms, as in たべれる and ねれる, in colloquial speech.

- The potential forms of all verbs conjugate as る-verbs.

Dictionary Form	Potential Forms				
	Present		Past		て-form
	Affirmative	Negative	Affirmative	Negative	
する (Irreg. verb)	出来る	出来ない	出来た	出来なかった	出来て
ねる (る-verb)	ねられる	ねられない	ねられた	ねられなかった	ねられて
飲む (う-verb)	飲める	飲めない	飲めた	飲めなかった	飲めて

話してみましょう

A. Make a sentence describing what each person is able to do. Be sure to choose the correct verb from the box and use が to make the direct object.

Example

ジョンソン　　おすし

ジョンソンさんは　おすしが　たべられます。

おきる　食べる　する　書く　話す　飲む　つくる

1. ハモンド　　　　　　日本語の手紙
2. クラーク　　　　　　あさ五時
3. きむら　　　　　　　テニス
4. ジョーンズ　　　　　スペイン語
5. キム　　　　　　　　フランスりょうり
6. スペンサー　　　　　ビール

B. Using the following sentences as reasons, make statements about what one is not able to do as a result.

Example

かぜを　ひいたんです。

かぜを　ひいたから、学校に　行けないんです。

1. のどが　いたいんです。　　5. はが　いたいんです。
2. ねつが　あるんです。　　　6. ゆびを　きったんです。
3. アレルギーが　あるんです。　7. つかれているんです。
4. おなかが　いたいんです。

C. Work in groups of three or four. Think about a place, then describe what a person can or cannot do there. The members of your group will try to guess the place.

Example

A: ここでは　やすい　コーヒーが　飲めます。やすい
　　食べものも　食べられます。
B: 食堂ですか。
A: はい、そうです。

D. What kinds of special talents do your classmates have? Ask them what they can do, and find out who has the most interesting talent.

Example

A: ～さんは　どんな　ことが　出来ますか。

B: そうですね。私は　ピザを　十まい　食べられます。

A: すごいですね。(That's great/impressive.)　～さんは　どんな　ことが　できますか。

B: 私は　一人で　きものが　きられます。

II. Expressing cause and effect, using the て-form of adjectives, verbs, and the copula です

Cause			Effect		
		Adjective て-form			
は	が	いたくて	ねられない	ん	です。

I have a toothache, so I cannot sleep.

Cause			Effect				
		Verb て-form					
本	を	たくさん	読んで、	あたま	が	いたい	ん	です。

I read a lot, so I have a headache (literally: my head hurts).

Cause		Effect			
	Copula て-form				
きのう	病気で、	学校	に	行けません	でした。

I was sick yesterday, so I was not able to go to school/college.

すずき：どうしたんですか。　かおいろが　わるいですね。
　　　　What's happened? You look pale.

モネ：　かぜを　ひいて、ねつが　あるんです。
　　　　I caught a cold, so I have a fever.

- The て-form of verbs, adjectives, and the copula has several uses. It can be used to indicate a reason or a cause. In contrast to から, the result or effect is usually spontaneous, obvious, or inevitable.

アレルギーが　あるから、薬<ruby>薬<rt>くすり</rt></ruby>を　<ruby>飲<rt>の</rt></ruby>みます。

I'm going to take some medicine because I have an allergy.

あたまが　いたくて、ねられません。

I have a headache, so I cannot sleep.

- To show concern when someone expresses a physical problem, you can say:

それは　<ruby>大変<rt>たいへん</rt></ruby>ですね。／<ruby>大変<rt>たいへん</rt></ruby>でしたね。

That's a lot of trouble, isn't it?/That was a lot of trouble, wasn't it?

それは　こまりますね。／こまりましたね。

That is/was a nuisance, isn't/wasn't it?

話してみましょう

A. Each of the following sentences describes an effect or result. Using the て-form, make a sentence describing a cause and an effect.

Example

ねられないんです。
こしが　いたくて　ねられないんです。

1. あるけないんです。
2. ケーキが　食べられないんです。
3. べんきょうが　できないんです。
4. はなが　つまるんです。
5. 目が　かゆいんです。
6. せきが　<ruby>出<rt>で</rt></ruby>るんです。
7. チーズや　たまごが　食べられないんです。

B. Work in groups of three or four. Construct a sentence with the て-form for cause by combining a reason and a result given in the chart. Then act it out. The rest of your group will try to guess what your sentence is.

Example

A: (Act to show that you cannot fall asleep because of a headache.)
B: あたまが　いたくて、ねられないんですか。
A: ええ、そうです。

りゆう (Reason)	あたまが　いたいです。のどが　いたいです。　　アレルギーが　あります。 かぜを　ひきました。こしが　いたいです。　　足を　けがしました。 はが　いたいです。　　ゆびを　きりました。
けっか (Result)	ねられません。　　　　話せません。　　　　　　　書けません。 はなが　つまります。　ごはんが　食べられません。　おき　られません。 目が　かゆいです。　　あるけません。

C. Work with a partner. Think of a physical problem. Your partner will ask what happened to you. Tell your partner your problem. He/she will try to show concern.

Example

A: どうしたんですか。
B: はが　いたくて、ぜんぜん　ねられなかったんです。
A: それは　<ruby>大変<rt>たいへん</rt></ruby>でしたね。／こまりましたね。

D. Find out if any of your classmates are not feeling well or have a minor injury, then ask the reasons. Your classmates will give you explanations, using the て-form. Write the name of the person and the condition in the following chart.

Example

1. A: <ruby>体<rt>からだ</rt></ruby>の　<ruby>調子<rt>ちょうし</rt></ruby>は　どうですか。
   B: ええ、とても　いいですよ。
   A: そうですか。それは　よかったですね。じゃあ　また。
   B: じゃあ、また。
2. A: <ruby>体<rt>からだ</rt></ruby>の　<ruby>調子<rt>ちょうし</rt></ruby>は　どうですか。
   B: きょうは　あまりよくありませんね。
   A: どうしたんですか。
   B: かぜを　ひいて、はなが　つまっているんですよ。
   A: そうですか。それは　こまりましたね。

なまえ	びょうき
Bさん	かぜを　ひいて、はなが　つまっている。

III. Expressing desire, using verb stem + 〜たい and 〜たがる

A. Speaker's desire

		Direct object	Particle	Verb stem＋たい	
私	は	コーヒー	が／を	飲みたい	です。

I want to drink coffee.

			Noun (place)	Particle	Verb stem＋たい	
私	は	来年	日本	に	行きたい	です。

I want to go to Japan next year.

B. Someone else's desire

		Direct object		Particle	Verb stem＋たがっている
山田さん	は	あたらしい	くるま	を	買いたがっています。

Yamada-san wants to buy a new car.

山本： どうしたんですか。あまり　食べませんね。
> What's the matter? You are not eating much.

アリス：食べたいんですが、はが　いたくて、食べられないんです。
> I want to eat, but I have a toothache, so I cannot eat.

山本： そうですか。それは　こまりましたね。
> Is that so? That's an annoyance.

● *Want to do* 〜 is expressed by verb stem + たいです and verb stem + たがっています. The first form is used when the speaker is referring to himself or herself or to the listener in a question. The second form is used when the speaker is referring to a third person. 〜たがっています literally means *is showing (repeatedly) the sign of wanting to do* 〜. This distinction is based on the notion that in Japanese one does not presume to know what another person wants or desires.

● Instead of 〜たがっています, endings such as 〜そうです (hearsay) can be used with 〜たい to express a third person's desire because these endings merely convey the speaker's knowledge, not a presumption, about someone else's desire.

ジョンソンさんは　日本に　行きたいそうです。
> I heard that Johnson-san wants to go to Japan.

- Verb stem + たいです is conjugated like an い-adjective. 食べたい — 食べたくありません — 食べたかったです — 食べたくありませんでした, and so on.
- With 〜たいです, the direct object marker を can be replaced with が. Other particles remain unchanged. With 〜たがっています, however, use を to indicate the direct object.

私は　ごはんを　食べたいです。

I want to eat a meal.

私は　ごはんが　食べたいです。

I want to eat a meal.

私は　ここに　いたいです。

I want to stay here.

田中さんは　ごはんを　食べたがっています。

Tanaka-san wants to eat a meal.

- It is considered impolite to use 〜たいですか to one's superior to find out whether he/she wants to do something. Use 〜ますか or 〜ませんか instead.

ごはんを　食べますか。

(literally: Will you eat a meal?)

ごはんを　食べませんか。

(literally: Won't you eat a meal?)

話してみましょう

A. Change the verbs into 〜たいです and 〜たがっています.

Example

家に帰る

私は　家に　帰りたいです。スミスさんは　家に　帰りたがっています。

1. 旅行に　行く
2. あたらしい　ふくを　買う
3. 水を　飲む
4. えいがを　見る
5. ファミコンを　する
6. 大学院に　入る
7. 富士山に　のぼる

B. Work with a partner. Think of three things that you want to do but can't.
Tell your partner what they are and why you can't do them.

Example

A: 私は　日本に　行きたいんですが、行けません。

B: どうしてですか。

A: お金が　ないからです。

B: そうですか。それは　ざんねんですね。

C. Work with a new partner. Tell your new partner about your previous partner's wishes.

Example

A: 〜さんは　日本に　行きたがっています。
　　でも、お金が　ないから、行けないそうです。

B: そうですか。

D. You are thinking about going on a trip. Look at the following chart and
make your own travel wish list by circling one in each category (destination,
transportation, accommodation, and activity). Ask your classmates about
their plans. Try to find a person who has the same (or similar) wish.

Example

A: 〜さんは　どこに　行きたいですか。

B: 私は　ニューヨークに　行きたいです。

A: そうですか。私は　とうきょうに　行きたいんです。
　　それじゃ、また。

　　　or

A: 私も　ニューヨークに　行きたいんです。

B: どんな　ところに　とまりたいですか (stay at)。

A: いい　ホテル (hotel) に　とまりたいです。

行く　ところ	ニューヨーク	とうきょう	ハワイ	シドニー
のる　もの	くるま	ひこうき	バス	でんしゃ
とまる　ところ	いい　ホテル (hotel)	ともだちの　家	やすい　ホテル (hotel)	YMCA
する　こと	およぐ	買いものを　する	えいがを　見る	しゃしんを　とる

IV. Giving suggestions, using verb たら　どうですか and ほうが　いいです

A. Using Verb たら　どうですか

		Verb (plain affirmative past)					
薬<ruby>くすり</ruby>	を	飲んだ	ら	どう	です	か。

How about taking some medicine?

B. Using Verb た　ほうが　いいです／Verb ない　ほうが　いいです

		Verb (plain past affirmative)				
病院<ruby>びょういん</ruby>	に	行った	ほう	が	いいです	よ。

You should go to a hospital.

		Verb (plain present negative)				
おさけ	を	のまない	ほう	が	いいです	よ。

You should not drink alcohol.

山上：　どうしたんですか。　かおいろが　わるいですね。
　　　　What's the matter? You look pale.

ロペス：ええ、ちょっと　ねつが　あるんです。
　　　　Yeah. I have a slight fever.

山上：　家に　帰って　ねたら　どうですか。
　　　　Why don't you go home and go to bed. /How about going home and
　　　　going to bed?

ロペス：でも　しごとが　ありますから。
　　　　But I have some work to do.

山上：　でも、むりを　しない　ほうが　いいですよ。　よく
　　　　休んだ　ほうが　いいですよ。
　　　　But you shouldn't overstrain/overwork. You should rest well.

● Both verb たら　どうですか and verb ほうが　いいです are used
to provide advice or suggestions.

Verb ほうが　いいです (*it's better to* ～, *you should* ～) is stronger
than verb たら　どうですか (*how about doing* ～, *why don't you* ～).

- Use the plain past affirmative or plain present negative of a verb with 〜ほうが　いいです.

  <u>食べた</u>　ほうが　いいです。

  It's better to eat. (You should eat.)

  <u>食べない</u>　ほうが　いいです。

  It's better not to eat. (You shouldn't eat.)

- Verb たら　どうですか is formed by adding ら to the plain past affirmative form of a verb. Verb たら is called the conditional form of a verb and has many functions which you will learn in later chapters.

  <u>食べたら</u>　どうですか。

  Why don't you eat (literally: How would it be if you ate)?

- To ask for a suggestion, use どうしたら　いいですか／いいでしょうか (What should I do?).

山田：　しゅくだいが　おわらなかったんです。どうしたら
　　　　いいでしょうか。

　　　I did not finish my homework. What should I do?

ワット：先生に　話したら　どうですか。

　　　Why don't you ask the instructor?

話してみましょう

A. Change each of the following into a suggestion using verb たら　どうですか.

Example

ごはんを　食べる

ごはんを　食べたら　どうですか。

1. 薬（くすり）を　飲む
2. いしゃに　行く
3. 電話（でんわ）を　かける
4. 薬（くすり）を　つける
5. 入院（にゅういん）する
6. ともだちと　話す
7. よく　ねる
8. 学校を　休（やす）む

B. Think of a physical condition such as having a cold or not being able to sleep. Get suggestions from your classmates and report them to the class.

Example

A: かぜを　ひいて、ねつが　あるんですが。

B: そうですか。じゃ、家に　帰って　休んだら　どうですか。

A: そうですね。

C. Make suggestions for each of the following conditions, using the list in the box. Make both positive and negative suggestions.

Example

おなかが　いたい　時
薬を　飲んだ　ほうが　いいですよ。それから、たくさん
食べない　ほうが　いいですよ。

薬を　飲む	薬を　つける	いしゃに　行く	あるく
ともだちと　あそぶ	べんきょうする	むりを　する	家で　ねる
うたを　うたう	うんどうを　する		

1. のどが　いたい　時
2. こしが　いたい　時
3. 目が　いたい　時
4. 気分が　わるい　時
5. アレルギーの　時
6. かぜの　時
7. けがを　した　時
8. ねつが　ある　時

D. Work in groups of four. One person will name a problem, and the other members will suggest what he/she should or shouldn't do. Then create a dialogue based on the suggestions. Use both verb stem + た　ほうが　いいです and verb stem + ない　ほうが　いいです.

Example

A: かぜを　ひいたんです。どうしたら　いいでしょうか。

B: 学校を　休んだ　ほうが　いいですよ。

C: セーターを　きたほうが　いいですよ。

D: きょうは　出かけない　ほうが　いいですよ。

A: どうしたんですか。

B: ちょっと　かぜを　ひいたんです。

A: ねつが　あるんですか。

B: ええ。

A: じゃあ、出かけない　ほうが　いいですよ。

V. Asking for and giving permission, using verb stem + てもいいですか

Question				Answer
	Verb て-form	Particle		
たばこを	すって	も	いいですか。／ いいでしょうか。／ かまいませんか。	はい、　どうぞ。

May I smoke a cigarette?　　　　　　　　　　　　　Yes, please (go ahead).

Answer
すみませんが、ちょっと。

I am sorry, but . . .

チョー：　先生、じゅぎょうを　休んでも　いいでしょうか。
　　　　　Professor, may I be absent from the class?

先生：　　どうしてですか。
　　　　　Why?

チョー：　ちょっと　ねつが　あるんです。
　　　　　I have a slight fever.

先生：　　ああ、そうですか。いいですよ。
　　　　　Oh, is that so. That's fine./You may.

● The following are common ways to respond positively to a request for permission.

はい／ええ、どうぞ。

Yes, please go ahead.

はい／ええ、かまいません。

That's fine. I don't care.

ええ、もちろん。

Yes, of course.

Although はい、いいです is grammatically correct, it would be used only when a superior is granting permission to someone hierarchically inferior.

- Answering negatively can be awkward. (Think of how you would deny a request in your own language.) As in other countries, the Japanese tend to avoid direct prohibition such as "No, you may not" and use instead phrases such as the following:

すみませんが、ちょっと。

I am sorry, but . . .

ええっと、それは　ちょっと。

Well, that would be a bit . . .

すみません、それは　ちょっと　こまるんですが。

I am sorry. That would be a little troublesome.

In such a situation, the word ちょっと serves to deflect whatever tension may arise from withholding permission. It also saves the respondent from spelling out his/her reasons for denying permission.

- 〜ても　いいでしょうか is more tentative and thus more polite than 〜ても　いいですか, but it can also be used toward someone in one's peer group. 〜ても　かまいませんか is as polite as 〜ても　いいでしょうか. Although it ends with a negative, the way you answer is the same as 〜ても　いいでしょうか.

話してみましょう

A. Change each sentence to a question asking for permission, using 〜たい and 〜ても　いいですか／いいでしょうか／かまいませんか.

Example

一緒に　行く
一緒に　行きたいんですが、行っても　いいですか。／いいでしょうか。／　かまいませんか。

1. 家に　帰る
2. この　ケーキを　食べる
3. たばこを　すう
4. おふろに　入る
5. じゅぎょうを　休む
6. 電話を　かける
7. えんぴつで　書く
8. ジャケットを　買う

B. Work with a partner. Choose a physical problem from the list in the box.
Your partner will try to figure out what you have chosen by asking
questions with 〜ても　いいですか／いいでしょうか.／
かまいませんか.

Example

A: おふろに　入^{はい}っても　いいですか。

B: いいえ、入^{はい}らない　ほうが　いいですね。

A: じゃあ、しごとを　しても　いいですか。

B: いいえ、しない　ほうが　いいですね。

つかれている	おなかが　いたい	耳が　いたい	足を　けがした
のどが　いたい	ゆびを　きる	はが　いたい	

C. Work with a partner. Think of three places and write in the boxes labeled 1,
2, and 3. Your partner will do the same. Then, you and your partner will try
to figure out what each of the three places is by asking questions with 〜て
も　いいですか／いいでしょうか／かまいませんか. You may
only ask one question and make one guess at a time. The first one to reach
ゴール (goal) wins.

Example

A: ここで　たばこを　すっても　いいですか。

B: いいえ、すわない　ほうが　いいですよ。

A: 学校ですか。

B: いいえ、そうじゃありません。

パートナー 1 → 2 → 3 →　ゴール！

D. Work with a partner. In the chart, the left column indicates your partner's
role and the middle column indicates what you want to do. Ask your partner for permission to do what you want to do. You partner will not give
you permission right away, so you must convince him/her why you need to
do so. Write はい in the right column of the chart if you get permission.

Example

A: しゅくだいを　あした　出^だしても　いいでしょうか。

B: どうしてですか。

A: ねつが　あるんです。

B: いしゃに　行きましたか。

A: はい。

B: じゃ、いしゃの　手紙（てがみ）を　見せて下さい。

A: はい。

B: そうですか。じゃあ、あした　出（だ）しても　いいですよ。

パートナーは　〜です	したいこと	はい
先生	しゅくだいを　あした　出す	
いしゃ	出かける	
ともだち	あそびに　行く	
先生	水曜日（ようび）に　じゅぎょうを　休（やす）む	
会社のじょうし(boss)	きょう　しごとを　休（やす）む	

漢字（かんじ）

Radicals in kanji

Some **kanji** share the same components. For example, 話 (はなす talk), 読 (よむ read), and 語 (〜ご language) share the identical component on the left-hand side, which is 言. This is a radical that identifies the general area of the meaning of **kanji.** The radical 言 signals that the meaning of the **kanji** is related to *language and word*. If you encounter a new **kanji** that contains 言, you can more or less assume that the meaning of the **kanji** has something to do with *language*. Traditionally, **kanji** are classified by radicals. There are a little over two hundred radicals, and they appear in different parts of **kanji.** 亻, 阝, 夂, and 艹 are common radicals. Some of the radicals found in the **kanji** you have learned so far are the following:

人	person, people	亻	休	体
食	eating	𩙿	飲	
日	time, date	日	時	曜
女	female	女	妹	姉
	grass	艹	薬 (herbal medicine)	

元 元	気 気	入 入
一 二 テ 元	ノ ケ ニ 气 気 気	ノ 入
origin, former	spirit, energy, mind	to enter, go in
ゲン	キ	ニュウ
モト		はい（る）、いれ（る）
元気です げんき 元気じゃない げんき	元気な　人 げんき 病気な　人 びょうき 気分が　わるい／いい きぶん	大学に　入る だいがく　はい 入院する にゅういん

薬 薬	休 休	体 体
一 艹 艾 苩 苺 莁 莁 荳 萆 薬	ノ イ 仁 什 休 休	ノ イ 仁 什 休 休 体
medicine, drugs	to rest	body
ヤク	キュウ	タイ、テイ
くすり	やす（む）、やす（み）	からだ
薬を　飲む くすり	休みの　日は　いつで やす 　すか。 しごとを　休みます。 やす	体が　大きい からだ 体が　よわい からだ

病 病	院 院	住 住
ヽ 亠 广 广 广 疒 疒 病 病 病	フ ３ ３ ３ ３ 阝 阝 阡 院 院	ノ イ イ 仁 什 住 住
sickness, illness	institution	to dwell, live
ビョウ	イン	ジュウ
やま（い）		す（む）
びょういん 病院に　行く びょうき 病気に　なる	びょういん 病院の　まえに　ある だいがくいん　　はい 大学院に　入る	アパートに　住む とうきょう　　　す 東京に　住んでいます

所 所	語 語	好 好
一 ３ ヨ 戸 戸 戸 所 所	` ２ ３ 言 言 訂 評 語 語 語	く く 女 女 好 好
place	language, word	like, love
ショ	ゴ	コウ
ところ	かた（る）	す（き）
きのう　行った　所 ところ しずかな　所 ところ じゅうしょ 住所	日本語が　話せる ご フランス語 ご	だいす 大好きな　人 す 好きでした

毎	回	度
毎	回	度
ノ　ト　亇　每　毎	丨　冂　冂　回　回	丶　亠　广　庐　庐
毎	回	庐　庐　庐　度
every 〜	times, frequency	degree, frequency
マイ	カイ	ド
	まわ（る）	
まいにち 毎日 　べんきょうします。 まいしゅう 毎週　行く	いちにち　さんかい 一日に　三回　飲んで 　下さい。	いちにち　さんど 一日に　三度　飲む こんど　　にちようび 今度の　日曜日に 　行きましょう 　　　　　ど　　ぶ 三十八度五分

Read the following sentences aloud.

1. 田中さんはねつが三十八度あったので、家で休みました。
2. 学校を休んで、病院に行きました。
3. 私は一日三回この薬を飲みます。
4. 体がとてもつかれていて、元気が出ませんでした。
5. 母は病気で入院しています。
6. 山田さんはしずかな所にあるアパートに住んでいます。
　いぬがとても好きです。
7. ジョンソンさんは毎日日本語をべんきょうします。

上手な読み方 <small>かた</small>

Using knowledge of the real world

As mentioned earlier, you should always look at the title, subtitles, pictures, and captions to determine what they are referring to before you start reading. Then, think about what you know about that particular topic. This chapter is about illnesses and medical care, so you should try to remember what you know or have experienced concerning illnesses and hospitals in your country and then apply your knowledge.

読む　前<ruby>に<rt>まえ</rt></ruby>

Most Japanese clinics and hospitals have their own pharmacies. A prescription drug is usually put in a small packet with the drug's name and instructions for use. Now look at the following pictures and try to guess which one is a drug packet.

診　察　申　込　書

◎ 保険証を添えて窓口へお出し下さい。
◎ 太枠だけご記入下さい。

申込日	年	月	日

診療科	10 内 科	20 外 科	30 産 婦 人 科	40 消 化 器 科	50 整 形 外 科	60 耳 鼻 咽 喉 科	70 眼 科	80 放 射 線 科	21 皮 膚 科	22 形 成 外 科	健 康 診 断	交 通 事 故
受付時間	＊平日は、午前8時 ～ 午前11時30分まで							月・水・金 午後1～3：30	院内掲示をご覧ください		
氏 名	フリガナ						男・女	明大昭平	年　月　日　歳		
住所	〒							☎ (　　　)			
勤務先名	☎ (　　　)										

保険区分	負担率	保険者名	記号	番号
公費負担番号	受給者番号		取得年月日	被保険者名　続柄

030-04Z001

診察券

阿部眼科
Abe Eye Clinic
〒798　宇和島市堀端町1-4
TEL（0895）22-0217

No. □□□□ － □□□□

様

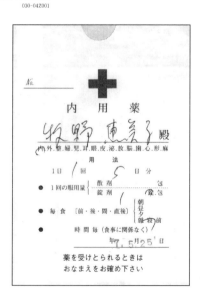

父の　病気

読む　前<ruby>に<rt>まえ</rt></ruby>

● どんな　人が　よく　病気に　なりますか。
● <ruby>子供<rt>こども</rt></ruby>は　よく　どんな　病気に　なりますか。
● おとな (adults) は　よく　どんな　病気に　なりますか。

<ruby>言葉<rt>ことば</rt></ruby>の　リスト
<ruby>心配<rt>しんぱい</rt></ruby>です worried

Read the following passage and try to identify the type of sickness referred to.

私の父はたばこが大好きで一日二十本ぐらいすいます。そして、仕事のあとでよくお酒を飲みに行って、毎晩十二時ごろまで家に帰りません。ですから、このごろとても顔色が悪くて、ごはんもあまり食べません。父は仕事が大好きで、家にいるのはあまり好きじゃありません。ですから、病気で会社を休んだことはありません。でも、私も母もとても心配です。一週間ぐらいまえに、父と話しましたが、父は仕事は休みたくないそうです。どうしたらいいでしょうか。

わかりましたか

1. お父さんは　病気ですか。
2. お父さんは　何を　するのが　すきですか。
3. お父さんは　どのぐらい　たばこを　すいますか。
4. お父さんは　何が　きらいですか。
5. お父さんは　しごとを　休みたがっていますか。
6. この人 (author) に　アドバイス (advise) を　して下さい。

上手な聞き方

Using the setting

What you know about the setting gives you many clues about the type of speech you hear. For example, the content of a conversation will be very different if your are in a doctor's office, at school, or in a restaurant. Also, you will use different phrases and words, even with the same topic, if you are at school or at home. The setting gives you clues about the content of a conversation, choice of words and phrases, and much more. The setting includes not only the places but also the time of day. Conversations in the morning may be very different from those in the afternoon in context and in effectiveness, even if you are talking to the same person.

STUDENT
いつ　どこで　何が　ありましたか。
(What happened, where, and when)

Listen to each conversation and try to identify where it took place. Circle the place name, then write what happened in the blank.

1. 学校　　　病院　　　　デパート　　　家

   _____

2. 病院　　　デパート　　　学校　　　　レストラン

   _____

3. 病院　　　レストラン　　学校　　　　デパート

   _____

DICT-A-CONVERSATION

スミスさんは　山本さんに　会いました。山本さんは　すこし
かおいろが　わるいです。

スミス：_____

山本：_____

スミス：_____

山本：_____

スミス：_____

山本：_____

スミス：_____

山本：_____

聞き上手、話し上手

Talking to a doctor

Talking to a doctor can be stressful, especially when you are not familiar with
the language. Even for the Japanese, medical terms are difficult to understand,
so it is important to ask for clarification. Some useful phrases are the following:

はじめてなんですが。

I'm a new patient (literally: This is my first time).

(日本語が)　よくわからないんです。

I don't understand (Japanese) well.

もうすこし　やさしい　ことばで　いって　下さいませんか。

Please say it with easier words.

これは　何の　薬ですか。

What is this medicine for?

一日に　何回　飲みますか。

How many times a day shall I take it?

A. Your instructor will be the doctor or a receptionist at a hospital. He/she will ask you questions or make requests. Respond accordingly.

B. Look at the pictures on page 421. Your instructor will be the nurse. Ask question about the pictured items.

<ruby>総合練習<rt>そうごうれんしゅう</rt></ruby>

けんこうですか

Work with a partner, who should not look at the following flow chart. Ask him/her about various habits and follow the flow chart according to the answers given. Then, if his/her physical condition is not perfect, make suggestions.

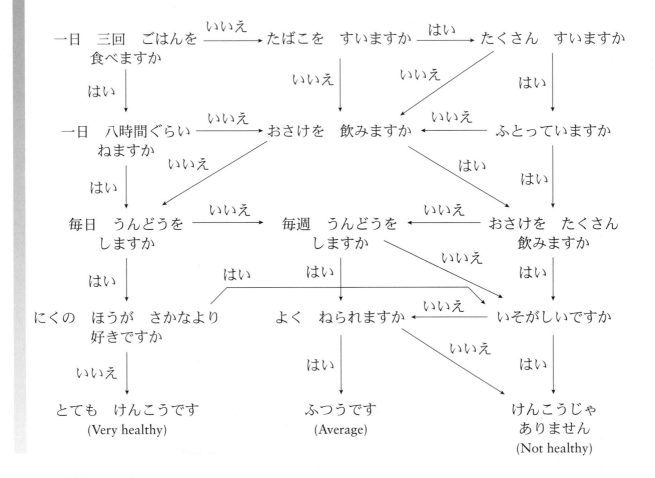

A: 一日　三回（かい）　ごはんを　食べますか。
B: いいえ。
A: ～さんは　あまり　けんこうじゃありませんね。
B: そうですか。
A: うんどうを　した　ほうが　いいですよ。
　　それから、たばこは　すわない　ほうが　いいですね。

ロールプレイ

1. You go to a hospital, where you are a new patient and need to tell the staff at the reception desk what kind of problem you have.

2. You started feeling sick in the middle of a class. Ask your instructor whether you can excuse yourself.

3. Your friend looks sick. Ask what is wrong and give several suggestions.

4. You are going on a trip tomorrow, but you feel sick. Tell a doctor what you want to do during the trip and ask for advice.

単語（たんご）　(ESSENTIAL VOCABULARY)

Nouns

アレルギー　allergy
いしゃ（医者）doctor
（お）さけ（（お）酒）alcoholic beverages; Japanese sake
おなか（お腹）belly, stomach
かおいろ（顔色）facial tone with respect to one's health
かぜ（風邪）cold
きぶん（気分）feeling　　きぶんが　わるい（気分が　悪い）feeling sick
くすり（薬）medicine, drug
けが（怪我）injury

こし（腰）lower back; waist
しょうじょう（症状）symptom
せき（咳）cough
ちょうし（調子）condition
ねつ（熱）fever, temperature
のど（咽）throat
は（歯）tooth
びょうき（病気）sickness
むり（無理）overwork, overstrain　　むりを　する（無理を　する）overwork
ゆび（指）finger

Irregular Verb

にゅういんする（入院する）(to) be hospitalized

る-verbs

つかれる（疲れる）(to) become tired
　つかれている（疲れている）(to) be tired
つける（付ける）(to) attach, (to) apply
　(medicine)

でる（出る）(to) come out　せきが
　でる（咳が　出る）(to) cough　ねつが
　でる（熱が　出る）(to) run a fever

う-verbs

あるく（歩く）(to) walk
きる（切る）(to) cut
こまる（困る）(to) be troubled by, (to) be
　annoyed; (to) suffer
つまる（詰まる）(to) stuff　はなが
　つまる（鼻が　詰まる）(to) have a
　stuffy nose

なる（成る）(to) become
はかる（計る）(to) measure
ひく　(to) catch　　かぜを　ひく
　（風邪を　ひく）(to) catch a cold
やすむ（休む）(to) rest

な-adjectives

けんこう（な）（健康（な））healthy
だいじょうぶ（な）（大丈夫（な））all right

い-adjectives

いたい（痛い）hurting, painful
おもい（重い）heavy; serious (sickness)
かゆい（痒い）itchy
かるい（軽い）light (weight)

ひどい　serious (injury)
よわい（弱い）weak
わるい（悪い）bad

Particle

を　from　　じゅぎょうをやすむ（授業を　休む）(to) be absent from a class

Expressions

ええっと／すみません。それは　ちょっ
　と（こまるんですが）。Well, that is a
　little bit (troublesome).
おだいじに（お大事に）Take good care of
　yourself.

〜ても　いいですか／いいでしょうか／
　かまいませんか　May I do 〜? Is it OK to
　do 〜?
どうしたら　いいですか。What should I do?
どうしましたか。／どうしたんですか。
　What happened?

はい／ええ、かまいません。　No, I don't mind. (Yes, please.)

はい／ええ、どうぞ。　Yes, please (go ahead).

はい／ええ、もちろん。　Yes, of course. / Yes, sure.

はじめてなんですが。　This is my first time . . .

Passive Vocabulary

Nouns

エイズ　AIDS
おとな（大人）adult
かふんびょう（花粉病）hay fever
がん（癌）cancer
がんか（眼科）ophthalmology
げか（外科）surgery
こうけつあつ（高血圧）high blood pressure
こうせいぶっしつ（抗生物質）antibiotic
こっせつ（骨折）fracture
コレステロール　cholesterol
さんふじんか（産婦人科）gynecology
しか（歯科）dentistry
じびいんこうか（耳鼻咽喉科）otorhinolaryngology

しょうにか（小児科）pediatrics
しょくちゅうどく（食中毒）food poisoning
しんぞうびょう（心臓病）heart disease
せいけいげか（整形外科）orthopedics; reconstructive surgery
せいしんか（精神科）psychiatry
とうにょうびょう（糖尿病）diabetes
ないか（内科）internal medicine
はしか　measles
ひにょうきか（泌尿器科）urology
ひふか（皮膚科）dermatology
ホテル　hotel
ほけんしょう（保険証）health insurance card

る-verbs

あける（開ける）(to) open

い-adjective

すごい　great, impressive, splendid

Conjunction

ほかに　other than 〜

Expressions

しんぱいです（心配です）be worried

たぶん　〜でしょう　It's probably 〜　たぶん　かぜでしょう。（たぶん　風邪でしょう。）
It is probably a cold.

Supplementary Vocabulary

Medical Conditions

あせを　かく（汗をかく）(to) sweat

かたが　こる（肩が凝る）(to) have a stiff shoulder

あたまが　がんがんする（頭が　がんがんする）(to) have a pounding headache

きりきりする　(to) have a sharp pain

きもちが　わるい（気持ちが　悪い）(to) feel nauseated

きを　うしなう（気を　失う）(to) lose consciousness

けいれんする（痙攣する）(to) convulse

げりを　する（下痢を　する）(to) have diarrhea

さむけが　する（寒気が　する）(to) have chills

しょくよくが　ない（食欲が　ない）(to) have no appetite

ずきずきする　(to) have a festering pain

ちが　でる（血が　出る）(to) bleed

ねんざする（捻挫する）(to) sprain

はきけが　する（吐き気が　する）(to) have nausea

ひりひりする　(to) have a burning pain

ふるえる（震える）(to) tremble

ほねを　おる（骨を　折る）(to) break a bone

めまいが　する　(to) feel dizzy

やけどを　する（火傷を　する）(to) have a burn

The Body

あしくび（足首）ankle

い（胃）stomach

うで（腕）arm

かた（肩）shoulder

ちょう（腸）intestine

てくび（手首）wrist

Expressions Used by Doctors and Nurses

あおむけに　なってください。（仰向けに　なって下さい。）Please lie on your back.

いきを　とめてください。（息を　止めて下さい。）Please hold your breath.

いきを　はいてください。（息を　吐いて下さい。）Please exhale.

上だけ　ぬいでください。（上だけ　脱いで下さい。）Please take off your top (shirt, blouse, etc.).

うしろを　むいてください。（後ろを　向いて下さい。）Please turn around.

うつぶせに　なってください。（うつ伏せに　なって下さい。）Please lie face down.

大きく　いきを　すってください。（大
きく　息を　吸って下さい。）Please
take a deep breath.

口を　大きく　あけてください。（口を
大きく　開けて下さい。）Please open
your mouth wide.

ここは　どうですか。How does it feel here?

よこに　なってください。（横に　なっ
て下さい。）Please lie down.

Other Expressions

〜ても　よろしいですか。／よろしいでしょうか。（〜ても　宜しいですか。／宜しい
でしょうか。）May I do 〜?, Is it OK to do 〜?

English Translation of Dialogues

NOTE: IN THE DIALOGUE TRANSLATIONS, SOME IDIOMATIC EXPRESSIONS ARE GIVEN ENGLISH EQUIVALENTS RATHER THAN WORD-FOR-WORD TRANSLATIONS.

CHAPTER 2
How do you do?

Lee: Excuse me, what is your name?
Alice: I am Alice Arisaka.
Lee: I see. You are Ms. Arisaka. How do you do? My name is Lee. It's nice to meet you.
Alice: It's nice to meet you, too.
Lee: I'm from Taiwan. Where are you from, Ms. Arisaka?
Alice: I'm from Chicago. I'm a junior at Westside University.
Lee: I see. I'm a junior, too. My major is Japanese literature. What is your major?
Alice: Economics.

A staff member of the International Student Center and a Japanese man approach them.

Staff member: Are you Ms. Arisaka?
Alice: Yes, I am.
Staff member: Mr. Suzuki, this is Ms. Alice Arisaka. Ms. Arisaka, this is your host parent, Mr. Suzuki.
Alice: How do you do? I'm Alice Arisaka. I'm pleased to meet you.
Suzuki: I'm Mr. Suzuki. Pleased to meet you.

CHAPTER 3
Suzuki-san's house

Mr. Suzuki, Michiko, and Alice arrive at the Suzukis' house.

Mr. Suzuki: Well, Alice, here we are. (*Mr. Suzuki opens the door.*) I'm home!

Mrs. Suzuki: Oh, welcome home.
Mr. Suzuki: Dear (LITERALLY, MOTHER), this is Alice. Alice, this is my wife and my son, Ken'ichi.
Alice: How do you do? I'm Alice. Pleased to meet you.
Mrs. Suzuki: How do you do? Please come in. (LITERALLY, PLEASE STEP UP.)
Alice: Thank you. (LITERALLY, I'LL INTRUDE.)

After some conversation and tea, Mrs. Suzuki takes Alice to her room.

Mrs. Suzuki: Alice, here are the bathroom and the toilet.
Alice: Yes.
Mrs. Suzuki: And this is your room.
Alice: Oh, it's a nice room, isn't it?
Mrs. Suzuki: The futons are inside that closet. Let's unfold them together later.
Alice: Thank you very much. And . . .
Mrs. Suzuki: Yes?
Alice: Whose room is that?
Mrs. Suzuki: It's Michiko's room.

CHAPTER 4
What is that over there?

Alice and Michiko are on the campus of Joto University.

Alice: There is a big building over there.
Michiko: Yes.
Alice: What is that?
Michiko: Oh, that's the library.
Alice: It's a gorgeous building, isn't it?
Michiko: Yes, Joto University's library is very famous.
Alice: Is that so. That's great. Say, which building is the student union?

Michiko: It's that white one.
Alice: Oh, I see. It's not very big, is it?
Michiko: No.
Alice: And, which is the Economics building?
Michiko: It's here.
Alice: Here? And where is the business office?
Michiko: There is a brown door to your right.
Alice: Yes?
Michiko: It's over there.
Alice: Oh, I see.

CHAPTER 5
I have class.

Alice and Mr. Lee run into each other on campus.

Alice: Hi, Mr. Lee.
Lee: Oh, hi, Alice. Do you have class now?
Alice: Yes, I have economics class. How about you, Mr. Lee?
Lee: I don't have class today.
Alice: Oh really. That's nice!
Lee: What time does your economics class end?
Alice: It ends at 2:30.
Lee: I see. Do you have a class after that, too?
Alice: No, but I have a test tomorrow, so I am going to study in the library for about an hour.

The bell rings.

Lee: Oh, it's time for your class.
Alice: Yes. Well, see you later.
Lee: See you later.

CHAPTER 6
I saw a movie on Sunday.

Alice and Mr. Lee are talking about what they did last weekend.

Alice: Mr. Lee, what did you do last weekend?

Mr. Lee: I cleaned my apartment and did laundry on Saturday. But on Sunday I watched a movie.

Alice: Is that right? How was the movie?

Mr. Lee: It wasn't very interesting.

Alice: Oh, really. That's too bad! Do you often watch movies?

Mr. Lee: Yes, I do. How about you, Alice?

Alice: I do, once in a while. About once every two weeks.

Mr. Lee: Is that so? Did you watch a movie this week too?

Alice: No. Since there was an exam on Monday, I did not go out during the weekend.

Mr. Lee: I see.

CHAPTER 7
What kinds of sports do you like?

Alice and Mr. Ishida are talking about sports.

Alice: What sports do you like, Mr. Ishida?

Mr. Ishida: Let's see. I often play baseball and basketball. How about you, Alice?

Alice: I like to swim. I like basketball, too.

Mr. Ishida: How about baseball?

Alice: Baseball? Unfortunately, I don't really know much about baseball.

Mr. Ishida: I see. How about music?

Alice: Let's see. I like quiet music, especially classical music and jazz.

Mr. Ishida: So, which do you like better, classical music or jazz?

Alice: I like both very much.

CHAPTER 8
At the department store

Today is Mr. Ishida's birthday. Alice went to a department store.

Alice: Excuse me, where is the food department?

Clerk at the information desk: The food department is in the basement.

Salesperson: What can I do for you? (LITERALLY, WELCOME.)

Alice: Please give me three of these apples. And then, please give me five of those oranges.

Salesperson: Three apples and five oranges, right? It will be 840 yen altogether.

Alice is on the elevator.

Elevator operator: Thank you for waiting. This elevator will stop at the third, fifth, and ninth floors. The next is the third.

Alice: Excuse me. Which floor is the men's clothing department on?

Elevator operator: The men's clothing department is on the third floor.

Alice is in the men's clothing department.

Salesperson: Welcome.

Alice: Ah, please show me that tie.

Salesperson: This one? Here you are.

Alice: How much is it?

Salesperson: It's 10,000 yen.

Alice: Is that so? Isn't there one a little cheaper?

Salesperson: Well, how about this?

Alice: It's nice. How much is this?

Salesperson: This one is 5,000 yen.

Alice: Then, I'll take this one.

Salesperson: The sales tax is 250 yen, so the total will be 5,250 yen. Is this a gift?

Alice: Yes, it is.

The salesperson puts the tie into a box and wraps it.

Salesperson: Here is 750 yen for change. Thank you very much.

CHAPTER 9
Won't you go with me?

Mr. Ishida phones Alice.
Ring ring.

Ishida: Hello, is this the Suzuki residence?

Alice: Yes, it is.

Ishida: This is Ishida. Is Alice there?

Alice: This is she.

Ishida: Hi, Alice. Are you busy this Saturday?

Alice: No.

Ishida: Then, would you like to go see a movie?

Alice: Yes, that would be nice. About what time should we go?

Ishida: Let's see. How about around one o'clock?

Alice: That's fine.

Ishida: Then, I will come pick you up at one o'clock.

Alice: All right. Thanks. See you at one o'clock.

Today is Saturday. Alice and Mr. Ishida go to a restaurant after the movie.

Waiter: Your order, please?

Ishida: Alice, what will you have?

Alice: Let's see. I would like pizza, please.

Ishida: And I will have some curried rice.

Waiter: One pizza and one order of curried rice. Certainly, sir.

CHAPTER 10
There are five people in my family.

Alice's friend, Ms. Kawaguchi, has come to visit Alice at her house. They are in Alice's room.

Ms. Kawaguchi: Oh, Is that picture on the desk of your family?

Alice shows the picture to Ms. Kawaguchi.

Alice: Yes. This is my father, and this is my mother.

Ms. Kawaguchi: Your parents are very attractive people.

Alice: Thank you. Both my father and mother are forty-five years old. He is working for a computer company, and she is a high school teacher.

Ms. Kawaguchi: I see. Is the boy wearing a hat your younger brother?

Alice: Yes. His name is David and he is in the third grade now.

Ms. Kawaguchi: He is adorable. And is this your older sister?

Alice: No, that is my younger sister, Pam. She is only seventeen years old, but she is taller and bigger than I am, people often think she is older.

Ms. Kawaguchi: Really?

CHAPTER 11
Alice as a child

Alice and Michiko are talking about their childhood.

Michiko: What kind of child were you when you were young?

Alice: Let's see. According to my father and mother, I was a very active child who laughed a lot. I often climbed mountains and swam in the sea.

Michiko: Is that so?

Alice: What kind of child were you, Michiko?

Michiko: I also went to the mountains and to the sea with my parents when I was small. But, when I was in junior and senior high school, I did not have much free time.

Alice: Why is that?

Michiko: I was busy because of the university entrance exam.

Alice: That's tough, isn't it. When I was in junior high and high school, I often went to parties and watched movies with my friends. I did not study much.

Michiko: That's nice!

CHAPTER 12
I have a fever.

Alice met Mr. Ishida at the university.

Alice: Mr. Ishida, what happened? You look pale.

Ishida: Yes, I am feeling a little sick.

Alice: How about going to a hospital?

Ishida: Yes, but I have a test today, so I don't want to take too much time off.

Alice: But you shouldn't overdo it.

Ishida: Yes, all right, I will go. (LITERALLY, I WILL DO SO.)

Mr. Ishida came to the hospital.

Doctor: What's the problem?

Ishida: I feel a little sick.

Doctor: Is that so? Let's check your temperature.

The doctor takes Mr. Ishida's temperature.

Doctor: It's 38.5 degrees. What other symptoms do you have?

Ishida: I don't cough much, but my throat hurts, so I can't eat.

Doctor: Is that so? In that case, please open your mouth.

Ishida: All right.

Doctor: It's a little red. It's probably a cold. You should take some medicine and rest for two or three days.

Ishida: Well, doctor. Can I take a bath?

Doctor: A bath? Better not. A shower is alright.

Ishida: Understood. Thank you very much.

Doctor: Not at all. Well, take care of yourself.

APPENDIX B

Accent

Whereas English uses stress (or loudness) for accent, Japanese uses two relative pitches: high and low. Standard Japanese has the following rules.

1. The first mora (or syllable) and the second mora must have different pitches. Thus, a word always begin with either a low-high or a high-low combination.
2. Once the pitch goes low, it will never go up within a word.
3. For an N-mora word, there are N + 1 accent patterns. This becomes obvious when a particle follows a noun.

Common patterns

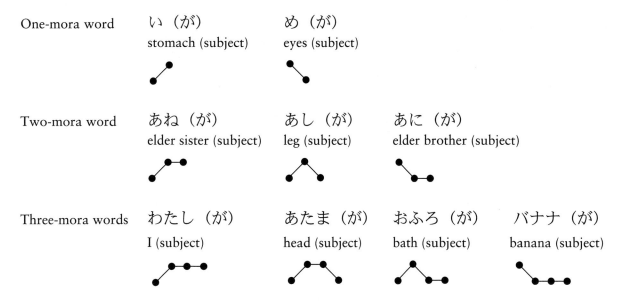

One-mora word

い（が）
stomach (subject)

め（が）
eyes (subject)

Two-mora word

あね（が）
elder sister (subject)

あし（が）
leg (subject)

あに（が）
elder brother (subject)

Three-mora words

わたし（が）
I (subject)

あたま（が）
head (subject)

おふろ（が）
bath (subject)

バナナ（が）
banana (subject)

Verb Conjugation

			Irregular Verb	Irregular Verb	る-verb	う-verb
Dictionary Form			くる (to come)	する (to do)	たべる (to eat)	いく (to go)
Plain	**Present**	**Affirmative**	くる	する	たべる	いく
		Negative	こない	しない	たべない	いかない
	Past	**Affirmative**	きた	した	たべた	いった
		Negative	こなかった	しなかった	たべなかった	いかなかった
Polite	**Present**	**Affirmative**	きます	します	たべます	いきます
		Negative	きません	しません	たべません	いきません
	Past	**Affirmative**	きました	しました	たべました	いきました
		Negative	きません でした	しません でした	たべません でした	いきません でした
Volitional	**Plain**		こよう	しよう	たべよう	いこう
	Polite		きましょう	しましょう	たべましょう	いきましょう
Potential	**Plain**		こられる	できる	たべられる	いける
	Polite		こられます	できます	たべられます	いけます
Conditional			くれば	すれば	たべれば	いけば
て-form			きて	して	たべて	いって

う-verb	う-verb	う-verb	う-verb	う-verb
およぐ (to swim)	かえる (to go home)	かく (to write)	のむ (to drink)	はなす (to talk)
およぐ	かえる	かく	のむ	はなす
およがない	かえらない	かかない	のまない	はなさない
およいだ	かえった	かいた	のんだ	はなした
およがなかった	かえらなかった	かかなかった	のまなかった	はなさなかった
およぎます	かえります	かきます	のみます	はなします
およぎません	かえりません	かきません	のみません	はなしません
およぎました	かえりました	かきました	のみました	はなしました
およぎません でした	かえりません でした	かきません でした	のみません でした	はなしません でした
およごう	かえろう	かこう	のもう	はなそう
およぎましょう	かえりましょう	かきましょう	のみましょう	はなしましょう
およげる	かえれる	かける	のめる	はなせる
およげます	かえれます	かけます	のめます	はなせます
およげば	かえれば	かけば	のめば	はなせば
およいで	かえって	かいて	のんで	はなして

Adjective and Copula Conjugation

			い-adjective おおきい (big)	な-adjective しずか (な) (quiet)	Copula だ／です (be)
Plain	**Present**	**Affirmative**	おおきい	しずかだ	Nだ
		Negative	おおきくない	しずかじゃない	Nじゃない
	Past	**Affirmative**	おおきかった	しずかだった	Nだった
		Negative	おおきくなかった	しずかじゃなかった	Nじゃなかった
Polite	**Present**	**Affirmative**	おおきいです	しずかです	Nです
		Negative	おおきくないです ／ おおきくありません	しずかじゃないです ／ しずかじゃありません	Nじゃないです ／ Nじゃありません
	Past	**Affirmative**	おおきかったです	しずかでした	Nでした
		Negative	おおきくなかったです ／ おおきくありませんでした	しずかじゃなかったです ／ しずかじゃありませんでした	Nじゃなかったです ／ Nじゃありませんでした
Prenominal			おおきい (だいがく)	しずかな (ひと)	Nの
Conditional			おおきければ	しずかなら／しずかだったら	Nなら／Nだったら
て-form			おおきくて	しずかで	Nで
Adverbial			おおきく	しずかに	N/A

Counters and Time Expressions

Common Counters			
	General Counter 〜つ	People 〜にん	Bound Objects (book, magazine, etc.) 〜さつ	Cylindrical Objects (pen, umbrella, etc.) 〜ほん
1	ひとつ	ひとり	いっさつ	いっぽん
2	ふたつ	ふたり	にさつ	にほん
3	みっつ	さんにん	さんさつ	さんぼん
4	よっつ	よにん	よんさつ	よんほん
5	いつつ	ごにん	ごさつ	ごほん
6	むっつ	ろくにん	ろくさつ	ろっぽん
7	ななつ	しちにん	ななさつ	ななほん
8	やっつ	はちにん	はっさつ	はっぽん
9	ここのつ	くにん	きゅうさつ	きゅうほん
10	とお	じゅうにん	じゅっさつ じっさつ	じゅっぽん じっぽん
11	じゅういち	じゅういちにん	じゅういっさつ	じゅういっぽん
12	じゅうに	じゅうににん	じゅうにさつ	じゅうにほん

	Specific Time			
	Month 〜がつ	**Day** 〜にち	**Time (o'clock)** 〜じ	**Time (minute)** 〜ふん
1	いちがつ	ついたち	いちじ	いっぷん
2	にがつ	ふつか	にじ	にふん
3	さんがつ	みっか	さんじ	さんぷん
4	しがつ	よっか	よじ	よんぷん
5	ごがつ	いつか	ごじ	ごふん
6	ろくがつ	むいか	ろくじ	ろっぷん
7	しちがつ	なのか	しちじ	ななふん
8	はちがつ	ようか	はちじ	はっぷん
9	くがつ	ここのか	くじ	きゅうふん
10	じゅうがつ	とおか	じゅうじ	じゅっぷん、 じっぷん
11	じゅういちがつ	じゅういちにち	じゅういちじ	じゅういっぷん
12	じゅうにがつ	じゅうににち	じゅうにじ	じゅうにふん
14		じゅうよっか (14)		
20		はつか (20)		
24		にじゅうよっか (24)		

Extent

	Year ～ねん	Month ～かげつ	Week ～しゅうかん	Day ～にち	Hour ～じかん
1	いちねん	いっかげつ	いっしゅうかん	いちにち	いちじかん
2	にねん	にかげつ	にしゅうかん	ふつか (かん)	にじかん
3	さんねん	さんかげつ	さんしゅうかん	みっか (かん)	さんじかん
4	よねん	よんかげつ	よんしゅうかん	よっか (かん)	よじかん
5	ごねん	ごかげつ	ごしゅうかん	いつか (かん)	ごじかん
6	ろくねん	ろっかげつ	ろくしゅうかん	むいか (かん)	ろくじかん
7	しちねん ななねん	ななかげつ	ななしゅうかん	なのか (かん)	しちじかん
8	はちねん	はちかげつ はっかげつ	はっしゅうかん	ようか (かん)	はちじかん
9	きゅうねん くねん	きゅうかげつ	きゅうしゅうかん	ここのか (かん)	くじかん
10	じゅうねん	じゅっかげつ じっかげつ	じゅっしゅうかん じっしゅうかん	とおか (かん)	じゅうじかん
11	じゅういちねん	じゅういっかげつ	じゅういっしゅうかん	じゅういちにち (かん)	じゅういちじかん
12	じゅうにねん	じゅうにかげつ	じゅうにしゅうかん	じゅうににち (かん)	じゅうにじかん
14				じゅうよっか (かん) (14)	
20				はつか (かん) (20)	
24				にじゅうよっか (かん) (24)	

Demonstrative Words (こそあど)

	こ series	そ series	あ series	ど series
	Close to both speaker and lister	Closer to listener than to speaker; moderately away from both	Away from both speaker and listener	Interrogative
Adjective	この〜 (this 〜)	その〜 (that 〜)	あの〜 (that 〜)	どの〜 (which〜)
Pronoun	これ (this thing)	それ (that thing)	あれ (that thing)	どれ (which thing)
Location	ここ (this place)	そこ (that place)	あそこ (that place)	どこ (where)
Direction	こちら (this way)*	そちら (that way)	あちら (that way)	どちら (which way)
Manner	こう (this way)	そう (that way)	ああ (that way)	どう (how)

---

*こちら can be used for "this person" (polite)

Kanji List

	Kanji	Chapter	Kun-reading	On-reading	Examples
1	山	7	やま	サン	山田さん、山下さん
2	日	7	ひ	ニチ ニ	日本、日曜日
3	田	7	た、だ	デン	田中さん、 山田さん
4	人	7	ひと	ジン ニン	おとこの 人、日本人
5	上	7	うえ	ジョウ	つくえの 上
6	下	7	した	カ ゲ	つくえの 下
7	中	7	なか	チュウ	はこの 中
8	大	7	おお（きい）	ダイ	大きい 人
9	小	7	ちい（さい）	ショウ	小さい くるま
10	本	7	もと	ホン ボン	本、日本
11	学	7	まな（ぶ）	ガク	学生
12	生	7	なま	セイ	学生、先生
13	先	7	さき	セン	先生
14	私	7	わたし	シ	私の 本
15	川	7	かわ	セン	川が あります
1	一	8	ひと（つ）	イチ	一時
2	二	8	ふた（つ）	ニ	二時
3	三	8	みっ（つ）	サン	三時
4	四	8	よっ（つ）	シ ヨン	四時
5	五	8	いつ（つ）	ゴ	五時
6	六	8	むっ（つ）	ロク	六時
7	七	8	なな（つ）	シチ	七時
8	八	8	やっ（つ）	ハチ	八時
9	九	8	ここの（つ）	キュウ ク	九時
10	十	8	とお	ジュウ	十時
11	百	8		ヒャク	百円
12	千	8		セン	千円
13	万	8		マン	一万円
14	円	8		エン	五千円

	Kanji	Chapter	Kun-reading	On-reading	Examples
1	月	9	つき	ゲツ ガツ	一月、月曜日
2	火	9	ひ	カ	火曜日
3	水	9	みず	スイ	水曜日
4	木	9	き	モク	木曜日
5	金	9	かね	キン	金曜日
6	土	9	つち	ド	土曜日
7	曜	9		ヨウ	日曜日
8	年	9	とし	ネン	一年
9	時	9	とき	ジ	三時間
10	間	9	あいだ	カン	八時間
11	週	9		シュウ	一週間
12	何	9	なに		何時
13	今	9	いま	コン	今
14	分	9	わ（かる）	フン	五分
15	半	9		ハン	六時半
1	男	10	おとこ	ダン	男の子、男の人
2	女	10	おんな	ジョ	女の子、女の人
3	子	10	こ	シ	子ども
4	目	10	め	モク	目が　いたい
5	耳	10	みみ	ジ	耳が　わるい
6	口	10	くち	コウ	口が　小さい
7	足	10	あし	ソク	足が　ながい
8	手	10	て	シュ	手が　大きい
9	父	10	ちち　とう	フ	お父さん
10	母	10	はは　かあ	ボ	お母さん
11	兄	10	あに　にい	ケイ キョウ	お兄さん
12	姉	10	あね　ねえ	シ	お姉さん
13	弟	10	おとうと	ダイ	私の　弟
14	妹	10	いもうと	マイ	私の　妹
15	家	10	いえ　うち	カ	私の　家、家族
16	族	10		ゾク	家族
1	行	11	い（く）	コウ	銀行に　行く
2	来	11	く（る）	ライ	学校に　来る
3	帰	11	かえ（る）	キ	家に　帰る
4	食	11	た（べる）	ショク	ごはんを　食べる
5	飲	11	の（む）	イン	水を　飲む
6	見	11	み（る）	ケン	テレビを　見る
7	聞	11	き（く）	ブン	おんがくを　聞く

	Kanji	Chapter	Kun-reading	On-reading	Examples
8	読	11	よ（む）	ドク	本を　読む
9	書	11	か（く）	ショ	手紙を　書く
10	話	11	はな（す）	ワ	電話で　話す
11	高	11	たか（い）	コウ	高校、高い
12	校	11	で（る）or だ（す）	コウ	高校
13	出	11		シュツ	手紙を出す
14	会	11	あ（う）	カイ	会社で　会う
15	買	11	か（う）	バイ	くるまを　買う
1	元	12	もと	ゲン	元気です
2	気	12		キ	元気な　人、病気
3	入	12	はい（る）	ニュウ	大学に　入る、入院する
4	薬	12	くすり	ヤク	薬を　飲む
5	休	12	やす（む）	キュウ	休みの日、しごとを　休みます
6	体	12	からだ	タイ	体が　大きい
7	病	12	やま（い）	ビョウ	病気、病院
8	院	12		イン	病院、入院する
9	住	12	す（む）	ジュウ	アパートに　住む、住所
10	所	12	ところ	ショ	きれいな　所、住所
11	語	12		ゴ	日本語
12	好	12	す（き）	コウ	好きな　人
13	毎	12		マイ	毎日、毎年、毎週
14	回	12	まわ（る）	カイ	三回　飲む
15	度	12		ド	三度、今度

Japanese-English Glossary

This glossary contains all Japanese words that appear in the vocabulary list of each chapter. They are listed according to **gojuuon-jun** (Japanese alphabetical order). Each entry follows this format: word written in **kana**, word written in **kanji**, part of speech, English meaning, and chapter number where the word first appears. If the chapter number is followed by the letter P, the word is designated as passive vocabulary. If the chapter number is followed by letter S, the word is designated as supplementary vocabulary. Other abbreviations are identical to the labels used in each chapter's vocabulary list.

adv.	adverb	*conj.*	conjunction	*q. word*	question word
な-*adj.*	な-adjective	*interj.*	interjection	*pref.*	prefix
い-*adj.*	い-adjective	*count.*	counter	*suf.*	suffix
う-*v.*	う-verb	*n.*	noun	*part.*	particle
る-*v.*	る-verb	*loc. n.*	location noun	*pron.*	pronoun
ir. v.	irregular verb	*exp.*	expression		
cop.	copula	*demo.*	demonstrative		

Ａランチ　*n.* lunch set A (Western style), 9

Ｔシャツ　*n.* T-shirt, 8

あ

ああ　*exp.* oh, 3

アイスクリーム　*n.* ice cream, 9

あいだ（間）*loc. n.* between, 3S

あう（会う）う-*v.* to meet, 9

あお（青）*n.* the color blue, 7P

あおい（青い）い-*adj.* blue, 1P, 4

あおむけに　なってください。*exp.* Please lie on your back., 12S

あか（赤）*n.* the color red, 7P

あかい（赤い）い-*adj.* red, 1P, 4

あがってください。*exp.* Please come in., 3

あかるい（明るい）い-*adj.* bright; cheerful, 3, 10

あき（秋）*n.* fall, 11

アクセサリー　*n.* accessories, 8

アクセサリーうりば（アクセサリー売り場）*n.* accessory department, 8

あける（開ける）る-*v.* to open, 12P

あご（顎）*n.* chin, 10S

あさ（朝）*n.* morning, 1P, 5

あさごはん（朝御飯）*n.* breakfast, 5

あし（足/脚）*n.* leg; foot, 1P, 10

アジアけんきゅう（アジア研究）*n.* Asian Studies, 2

あしくび（足首）*n.* ankle, 12S

あした（明日）*n.* tomorrow, 6

あしたテストが　ありますから，*exp.* I have a test tomorrow, so . . . , 5P

あせをかく（汗をかく）*exp.* to sweat, 12S

あそこ　*demo.* over there, that place, 3

あそぶ（遊ぶ）う-*v.* to play; have fun, 7

あたたかい（暖かい／温かい）い-*adj.* warm, 11

あたま（頭）*n.* head, 1P, 10

あたまが　いい（頭が　いい）*exp.* smart, intelligent, 10

あたまが　がんがんする（頭が　がんがんする）*exp.* to have a pounding headache, 12S

あたらしい（新しい）い-*adj.* new, 3

あつい（暑い／熱い）い-*adj.* hot, 11

あなた（貴方）*pron.* you, 2P

あに（兄）*n.* (the speaker's) brother, 10

あね（姉）*n.* (the speaker's) older sister, 10

あの　*demo.* that + noun over there, 3

アパート　*n.* apartment, 3

アパートにすんでいる（アパートに住んでいる）*exp.* (to) live in an apartment, 10

あびます（浴びます）る-*v.* take/s (a shower), 5

あびる（浴びる）る-*v.* to take (a shower), 5

あまり　*adv.* very, 3

あめ（雨）*n.* rain, 1P

アメリカ　*n.* America; United States, 2

アメリカじん（アメリカ人）*n.* American, 2

あらいます（洗います）う-*v.* to wash, 6

ありがとうございます。*exp.* Thank you, 1

あります　う-*v.* is/are, exist/s, 3

ある　う-*v.* (to) be; (to) exist, 3

あるいて（歩いて）*adv.* on foot, 6

あるく（歩く）う-*v.* to walk, 12

アルバイト　*n.* part-time job, 5P 6

あれ　*demo.* that, that one over there, 4

あれは　にほんごで　なんと　いいますか。（あれは　日本語で　何と　言いますか。）*exp.* What do you call that (over there) in Japanese?, 1

アレルギー　*n.* allergy, 12

アンケートちょうさ（アンケート調査）*n.* survey, 6P

い

い（胃）*n.* stomach, 12S

いい　い-*adj.* good, 3

いいえ　*adv.* no, 2

いいえ、けっこうです。*exp.* No, thank you., 9

いいえ、そうじゃありません。*exp.* No, that's not so., 2

いいえ、それほどじゃありません。*exp.* No, not to that extent., 10

いいえ、そんなことは　ありません。*exp.* No, that's not the case., 10

いいえ、まだまだです。*exp.* No, I still have a long way to go., 10

いがく　*n.* medical science, 2S

いきます（行きます）う-*v.* go/es, 5

イギリス　*n.* England, 2S

いきを　とめてください。*exp.* Please hold your breath., 12S

いきを　はいてください。*exp.* Please exhale., 12S

いく（行く）う-*v.* to go, 5

いくつ　*q. word* How many〜?; How old 〜?, 8, 10

いくら　*q. word* How much〜 (money)〜?, 8

いけ（池）*n.* pond, 1P

いけばな（生け花）*n.* flower arrangement, 3S

いけばなをする（生け花をする）*exp.* to arrange flowers, 7S

いしゃ（医者）*n.* doctor, 1P, 10S, 12

いす（椅子）*n.* chair, 1P, 3

いそがしい（忙しい）い-*adj.* busy, 6

いたい（痛い）い-*adj.* hurting, painful, 12

イタリア　*n.* Italy, 2S, 9

イタリアりょうり（料理）*n.* Italian food, 9

いちがつ（一月）*n.* January, 5S

いちご（苺）*n.* strawberry, 7S

いちねん（一年）*n.* first year, 2

いちねんせい（一年生）*n.* freshman; first-year student, 2

いちばん（一番）*adv.* most, best, 4P

いつ　*q. word* when, 5

いつか（五日）*n.* the fifth day, 5S

いっしょに　*adv.* together, 9

いって　ください。*exp.* Please say it.; Repeat after me., 1

いつも　*adv.* always, 5

いとこ　*n.* (the speaker's) cousin, 10S

いとこさん　*n.* (someone else's) cousin, 10S

いぬ（犬）*n.* dog, 1P, 3

いま（今）*n.* now, 2P 5
いま（居間）*n.* family room, 3S
います　る-*v.* is/are, 3
いまから　*exp.* from now on, 5P
いもうと（妹）*n.* (the speaker's) younger sister, 1P, 10
いもうとさん（妹さん）*n.* (someone else's) younger sister, 10
イヤリング　*n.* earring, 8S, 10
イヤリングをしている　*ir. v.* (to) be wearing earrings, 10
いらっしゃいませ。*exp.* Welcome., 8P
いらっしゃいます　う-*v.* come/s (polite), 2P
いる　る-*v.* (to) be; (to) exist, 3
いれる（入れる）る-*v.* (to) put in, 8
いろ（色）*n.* color, 4
インドりょうり（インド料理）*n.* Indian food, 9S

う

ウール　*n.* wool, 8S
うえ（上）*loc. n.* on; above; over, 3
うえだけ　ぬいでください。（上だけぬいでください。）*exp.* Please take off your top (shirt, blouse, etc.)., 12S
うしろ（後ろ）*loc. n.* behind; back of, 3
うしろを　むいてください。（後ろを向いて下さい。）*exp.* Please turn around., 12S
うた（歌）*n.* song, 7
うたう（歌う）う-*v.* to sing, 7
うち（家）*n.* house; home, 1P, 3
うつぶせに　なってください。（うつ伏せになって下さい。）*exp.* Please lie face down., 12S
うで（腕）*n.* arm, 1P, 10S, 12S
うでどけい（腕時計）*n.* wrist watch, 8S
うどん　*n.* Japanese wheat noodles, 9
うま　*n.* horse, 1P
うみ（海）*n.* ocean, sea, 11
うりば（売り場）*n.* department; section, 8
うれしい（嬉しい）い-*adj.* happy, joyful, 11
うんどう（運動）*n.* (physical) exercises, 6

え

え（絵）*n.* picture, 1P, 3
エアロビクス　*n.* aerobics, 7
えいが（映画）*n.* movie, 5
えいがのあと（映画の後）*exp.* after the movie, 9P
えいご（英語）*n.* English, 2
エイズ　*n.* AIDS, 12P
エイプリルフール　*n.* April Fools' Day, 11P
ええ　*interj.* yes, 2
えーっと　*exp.* Well, let's see . . ., 11
ええっと／すみません、それは　ちょっと（こまるんですが）。*exp.* Well, that is a little bit (troublesome), 12
えき（駅）*n.* station, 1P, 4
えび（海老）*n.* shrimp, 7S
えびフライ　*n.* shrimp, breaded and deep-fried, 9S
エレベーターガール　*n.* elevator operator, 8P
～えん（～円）*count.* ～ yen (Japanese currency), 8
エンジニア　*n.* engineer, 10S
えんぴつ（鉛筆）*n.* pencil, 1P, 4

お

お～（御～）*pref.* polite prefix, 2P, 5
おい（甥）*n.* (the speaker's) nephew, 10S
おいくつ　*q. word* polite form of いくつ, 10
おいごさん（甥子さん）*n.* (someone else's) nephew, 10S
おいしい　い-*adj.* delicious, tasty, good, 7
おいしいもの（おいしい物）*exp.* delicious thing/food, 11
（お）いとこさん　*n.* (someone else's) cousin, 10S
おおきい（大きい）い-*adj.* big, large, 1P, 3
おおきい　こえで　はなして　ください。（大きい声で話して下さい）*exp.* Please speak loudly., 1
おおきく　いきを　すってください。（大きく息を吸って下さい。）*exp.* Please take a deep breath., 12S
オーストラリア *n.* Australia, 2
オーストラリアじん　*n.* Australian, 2

おかあさん（お母さん）*n.* (someone else's) mother, 1P, 10

おかえし　*n.* change (of money), 8P

おかえりなさい。*exp.* Welcome back., Welcome home., 3

おかし　*n.* candy, confection, 1P

おからだをたいせつに（お体を大切に）*exp.* Take good care of yourself., 11P

おきます（起きます）る-*v.* get/s up; wake/s up, 5

おきる（起きる）る-*v.* (to) get up; (to) wake up, 5

おく（奥）*loc. n.* inner part of a house or a room, 3S, 4P

おくさん（奥さん）*n.* (someone else's) wife, 3P, 10

おくりもの（贈り物）*n.* gift, 8P

おさけ（お酒）*n.* alcoholic beverages; Japanese sake, 12

おじ（叔父／伯父）*n.* (the speaker's) uncle, 10S

おじいさん（お祖父さん）*n.* (someone else's) grandfather, 1P, 10

おしいれ（押し入れ）*n.* Japanese-style closet; storage space, 3

おじさん（叔父さん／伯父さん）*n.* (someone else's) uncle, 1P, 10S

おじゃまします。*exp.* Thank you (for allowing me to come in), 3

おしり（お尻）*n.* buttocks, 10S

おだいじに（お大事に）*exp.* Take good care of yourself, 12

おちゃ（お茶）*n.* green tea, 7S, 9

おっと（夫）*n.* (the speaker's) husband, 10S

おつり　*n.* change (the same as おかえし), 8P

おてあらい（お手洗）*n.* rest room, 3P

おてあらいに　いきます。（お手洗いに　行きます。）*exp.* go/es to the restroom, 6S

おとうさん（お父さん）*n.* (someone else's) father, 1P, 10

おとうと（弟）*n.* (the speaker's) younger brother, 1P, 10

おとうとさん（弟さん）*n.* (someone else's) younger brother, 10

おとこ（男）*n.* male, 2

おとこのひと（男の人）*n.* man, 2

おととし　*n.* the year before last, two years ago, 11

おとな　*n.* adult, 12P

おなか（お腹）*n.* belly, stomach, 1P, 10S, 12

おなまえ（お名まえ）*n.* polite form of なまえ（名まえ）*n.* name, 2P

おにいさん（お兄さん）*n.* (someone else's) older brother, 1P, 10

おねえさん　*n.* (someone else's) older sister, 1P, 10

おねがいします。（お願いします。）*exp.* Excuse me (to get the attention of a salesperson)., 4

おば（叔母／伯母）*n.* (the speaker's) aunt, 10S

おばあさん（お祖母さん）*n.* (someone else's) grandmother, 1P, 10

おばさん（叔母さん／伯母さん）*n.* (someone else's) aunt, 10S

おはよう　ございます。*exp.* Good morning.; Hello., 1

おふろ（お風呂）*n.* bathroom; bathtub, 3P

おふろにはいります。*exp.* I take a bath., 5

おまごさん（お孫さん）*n.* (someone else's) grandchild, 10S

おもい（重い）い-*adj.* heavy; serious (sickness), 12

おもいで（思い出）*n.* memories, 11P

おもしろい（面白い）い-*adj.* interesting, 5

およぐ（泳ぐ）う-*v.* (to) swim, 7

オレンジ　*n.* orange, 4S, 7

オレンジジュース　*n.* orange juice, 9

おわります（終わります）う-*v.* end/s, is/are over, 5

おわる（終わる）う-*v.* to end; be over, 5

おんがく（音楽）*n.* music, 2S, 6

おんな（女）*n.* female, 2

おんなのひと（女の人）*n.* woman, 2

か

か　*part.* question marker, 2

が　*part.* subject marker, 4

カーテン, *n.* curtain, 3S

〜かい（〜回）*count.* times (frequency), 6

～かい（～階）*count.* floor/s of a building, 8

がいこくに　すむ　*exp.* (to) live in a foreign country, 11S

かいしゃ（会社）*n.* company, 10

かいしゃいん（会社員）*n.* businessman, company man, 10S

かいしゃにつとめている（会社に勤めている）*exp.* (to) be employed at a company, 10

かいて ください。（書いて下さい。）*exp.* Please write., 1

かいます（買います）う-*v.* buy/s, 6

かいもの（買物）*n.* shopping, 6

かう（買う）う-*v.* (to) buy, 6

かえります（帰ります）う-*v.* return/s, go/es home, 5

かえる（帰る）う-*v.* (to) return, go home, 5

かお（顔）*n.* face, 1P, 10

かおいろ（顔色）*n.* facial tone, 12

かおを　あらいます。（顔を洗います。）*exp.* wash/es (one's) face., 6S

かがく（化学）*n.* chemistry, 2S

かぎ　*n.* key, 1P

かきます（書きます）う-*v.* write/s, 6

かく（書く）う-*v.* (to) write, 6

～がく（～学）*suf.* study of ～, 2

がくせい（学生）*n.* student, 1P, 2

がくせいかいかん（学生会館）*n.* student union, 4

がくせいしょくどう（学生食堂）*n.* School cafeteria (often shortened to がくしょく), 4S

～がくぶ（～学部）*suf.* school of ～, 4

～かげつ（～か月）*count.* month(s) (duration), 6, 11

かけます　る-*v.* make/s a telephone call, 6

かける　る-*v.* (to) make (a telephone call), 6

かける　る-*v.* put on (glasses), 10

かさ（傘）*n.* umbrella, 8

かしこまりました。*exp.* Certainly. (Polite language used by waiters, clerks, etc.), 9P

かじを　します。（家事をします。）*exp.* do/es household work, 6S

～がすきです（～が好きです）*exp.* (to) like, be fond of, 4P

かぜ（風邪）*n.* cold, 12

かぜ（風）*n.* wind, 1P

かぜをひく（風邪をひく）*exp.* catch a cold, 12

かぞく（家族）*n.* family; the speaker's family, 10

かた（方）*n.* person (polite version of ひと), 10

かた（肩）*n.* shoulder, 12S

かたがこる（肩が凝る）*exp.* (to) have a stiff shoulder, 12S

～がつ（～月）*count.* suffix for months, 11

がっき　*n.* musical instrument, 1P

がっこう（学校）*n.* school, 1P, 4

かていきょうし　*n.* private tutor, 5P

かない（家内）*n.* (the speaker's) wife, 3P, 10

かなしい（悲しい）い-*adj.* sad, 11

カナダ　*n.* Canada, 2

カナダじん（カナダ人）*n.* Canadian, 2

（お）かね（（お）金）*n.* money, 11P

かばん（鞄）*n.* bag, briefcase, 1P, 4

かぶる　う-*v.* (to) put on (a hat, a cap), 10

かふんびょう（花粉病）*n.* hay fever, 12P

かみ（髪）*n.* hair, 10

かゆい（痒い）い-*adj.* itchy, 12

かようび（火曜日）*n.* Tuesday, 5

から　*part.* from, 2P, 6

～から　いらっしゃいました。*exp.* ～ came from ～ (polite)., 2

～から　きました。*exp.* ～ came from ～ (casual), 2

カラオケで　うたう（カラオケで歌う）*exp.* (to) sing with karaoke, 7S

からし　*n.* mustard, 1P

からだ（体）*n.* body, 1P, 10

からて（空手）*n.* karate, 7S

かるい（軽い）い-*adj.* light (weight), 12

カレーライス　*n.* curry and rice dish, 9

ガレージ　*n.* garage, 3S

かわ（川）*n.* river, 1P

かわいい　い-*adj.* cute; adorable, 10

がん（癌）*n.* cancer, 12P

がんか（眼科）*n.* ophthalmology, 12P

かんこく（韓国）*n.* South Korea, 2

かんこくじん（韓国人）*n.* Korean, 2

かんこくりょうり（韓国料理）*n.* Korean food, 9S

き

き（木）*n.* tree, 1P

きいて ください。（聞いて下さい。）*exp.* Please listen., 1

きいろい（黄色い）い-*adj.* yellow, 4

ぎおんまつり（祇園祭り）*n.* Gion Festival, 11P

ききます（聞きます）う-*v.* listen/s, 6

きく（聞く）う-*v.* (to) listen, 6

きく（菊）*n.* chrysanthemum, 1P

キスを する *exp.* (to) kiss, 11S

きせつ（季節）*n.* season, 11

きたない（汚い）い-*adj.* dirty, 3S

きっさてん（喫茶店）*n.* coffee shop, 4

きって（切手）*n.* stamp, 1P

きってを あつめる（切手を集める）*exp.* (to) collect stamps, 7S

きっぷ（切符）*n.* ticket, 1P

きのう（昨日）*n.* yesterday, 6

きぶん（気分）*n.* feeling, 12

きぶんがわるい（気分が悪い）*exp.* feeling sick, 12

きます（来ます）*ir. v.* come, 2P, 5

きみどり（黄緑）*n.* light green, 4S

きもちがわるい（気持ちが悪い）*exp.* nauseous, 12S

きもの（着物）*n.* traditional Japanese clothes, kimono, 11

キャッチボール *n.* playing catch, 7S

キャベツ *n.* cabbage, 7S

キャンパス *n.* campus, 4

キャンプ *n.* camping, 11

ぎゅうにく（牛肉）*n.* beef, 7S

ぎゅうにゅう *n.* milk, 1P

きゅうり *n.* cucumber, 1P, 7S

きょう（今日）*n.* today, 1P, 5

きょういくがく（教育学）*n.* education, 2S

きょういん（教員）*n.* teacher, instructor, professor, 10S

きょうかい（教会）*n.* church, 11

きょうかしょ（教科書）*n.* textbook, 4

きょうしつ（教室）*n.* classroom, 4

きょうだい（兄弟）*n.* siblings, 10

きょうようがくぶ（教養学部）*n.* school of liberal arts, 4

きょねん（去年）*n.* last year, 11

きらい（な）（嫌いな）な-*adj.* disliked, hated, 7

きりきりする *exp.* (to) have a sharp pain, 12S

きる（着る）る-*v.* (to) put on (a sweater, a shirt, a jacket), 10

きる（切る）う-*v.* (to) cut, 12

きれい（な）な-*adj.* clean, neat; pretty, 3

きをうしなう（気を失う）*exp.* (to) lose consciousness, 12S

ぎんこう（銀行）*n.* bank, 4

きんじょ *n.* neighborhood, 1P

きんぱつ（金髪）*n.* blond, 10

きんようび（金曜日）*n.* Friday, 5

く

くがつ（九月）*n.* September, 5S

くすり（薬）*n.* medicine; drug, 1P, 12

くち（口）*n.* mouth, 1P, 10

くちびる（唇）*n.* lip, 10S

くちを おおきく あけてください。（口を大きく開けてください。）*exp.* Please open your mouth wide., 12S

くつ（靴）*n.* shoes, 8

くつした（靴下）*n.* socks, 8

くに（国）*n.* country, 2

くび（首）*n.* neck, 10S

くも *n.* cloud, 1P

くらい（暗い）い-*adj.* dark, 3S

クラシック *n.* classical music, 7

クラス *n.* class, 6

クラスメート *n.* classmate, 6

クリームいろ（クリーム色）*n.* cream, off-white, 4S

くる（来る）*ir. v.* to come, 5

くるま（車）*n.* automobile, car, 6

グレー *n.* gray, 4S

くろい（黒い）い-*adj.* black, 1P, 4

クローゼット *n.* Western-style closet, 3S

け

けいえいがく（経営学）*n.* business administration, 2

けいぐ（敬具）*n.* closing of a letter (similar to *Sincerely, Best wishes,* etc.) 11P

けいけん（経験）*n.* experience, 11P

けいざいがく（経済学）*n.* economics, 2

けいざいがくぶ（経済学部）*n.* school of economics, 4

けいじばん（掲示板）*n.* bulletin board, 4S

けいれんする（痙攣する）*exp.* (to) convulse, 12S

ケーキ　*n.* cake, 9

ゲームを　する　*exp.* (to) play a game, 7S

けが（怪我）*n.* injury, 12

げか（外科）*n.* surgery, 12P

けしゴム（消しゴム）*n.* eraser, 4

げたばこ（下駄箱）*n.* shelf for putting shoes, 3S

けっこんする（結婚する）*ir. v.* (to) marry, 10

げつようび（月曜日）*n.* Monday, 5

げりをする（下痢をする）*exp.* (to) have diarrhea, 12S

けんかを　する　*exp.* (to) have a fight, 11S

げんかん（玄関）*n.* front entrance, 3S

げんき（な）（元気）な-*adj.* healthy, 10

（お）げんきですか。（お元気ですか。）*exp.* How have you been (literally: Are you well/healthy)?, 9P

けんきゅうしつ（研究室）*n.* professor's office, research room, 4

けんこう（な）（健康）な-*adj.* healthy, 12

けんちくがく　*n.* architecture, 2S

けんどう（剣道）*n.* kendo (Japanese style fencing), 7S

こ

〜ご（〜語）*suf.* language, 2

ご〜（御〜）*pref.* polite prefix, 9

こいを　する（恋をする）*exp.* (to) fall in love, 11S

こうえん（公園）*n.* park, 4

こうがく（工学）*n.* engineering, 2

こうがくぶ（工学部）*n.* school of engineering, 4

こうけつあつ（高血圧）*n.* high blood pressure, 12P

こうこう（高校）*n.* senior high school, 1P, 2

こうこうせい（高校生）*n.* senior high school student, 9P

こうこうのとき　*exp.* when I was in high school, 6

こうせいぶっしつ（抗生物質）*n.* antibiotic, 12P

こうちゃ（紅茶）*n.* black tea, 1P, 7

こうつうじこ（交通事故）*n.* traffic accident, 11

こうつうじこにあう（交通事故にあう）*exp.* (to) have a traffic accident, 11

こうどう（講堂）*n.* auditorium, 4S

こうばん（交番）*n.* police box, 4

コート　*n.* coat, 8

コーヒー　*n.* coffee, 5

コーラ　*n.* cola, 7

こおり（氷）*n.* ice, 1P

ごかぞく（ご家族）*n.* (someone else's) family, 10

ごがつ（五月）*n.* May, 5S

ごきょうだい　*n.* (someone else's) siblings, 10

こくばん（黒板）*n.* blackboard, 4

ここ　*demo.* here, this place, 2

ここのか（九日）*n.* the ninth (day), 5S

ここは　どうですか。*exp.* How does it feel here?, 12S

こし（腰）*n.* lower back; hip, 10S, 12

ごしゅじん（ご主人）*n.* (someone else's) husband, 10

ごしんせき（ご親戚）*n.* (someone else's) relatives, 10S

ごちゅうもんは。（御注文は。）*exp.* What would you like to order?, 9P

こちら　*demo.* this person; this way, 2

こちらこそ。*exp.* It is I who should be saying that; Thank you, 2

こっき　*n.* national flag, 1P

こっせつ（骨折）*n.* fracture, 12P

こと（事）*n.* thing; matter (intangible, often refers to activities and happenings), 11

ことし（今年）*n.* this year, 11
こどものとき（子供の時）*exp.* when I was a child, 11
こどもべや（子供部屋）*n.* child's room, 3S
この　*demo.* this + noun, 3
こまる（困る）う-*v.* (to) be annoyed; (to) suffer, 12
ゴミを　すてます（ゴミを捨てます）*exp.* discard/s the trash, 6S
ゴミを　だします（ゴミを出します）*exp.* take/s out the trash, 6S
ごめんなさい。（御免なさい。）*exp.* Sorry. (Colloquial), 10P
ごりょうしん（御両親）*n.* (someone else's) parents, 6
ゴルフ　*n.* golf, 7
これ　*demo.* this, this one, 4
コレステロール　*n.* cholesterol, 12P
これは　にほんごで　なんと　いいますか。*exp.* What do you call this in Japanese?, 1
こんしゅう（今週）*n.* this week, 6
こんど（今度）*adv.* this time; next time, 11
こんにちは。*exp.* Good afternoon.; Hello., 1
こんばん（今晩）*n.* tonight, 5
こんばんは。*exp.* Good evening.; Hello., 1
コンピュータ　*n.* computer, 3S, 4
コンピュータサイエンス　*n.* computer science, 2S

さ

～さい（～歳）*count.* ～ year(s) old, 10
サイクリングに　いく（サイクリングに行く）*exp.* (to) go biking, 7S
さかな（魚）*n.* fish, 7
さかなや（魚屋）*n.* fish market, 4
さき（先）*loc. n.* ahead, 3S
さけ　*n.* sake, 1P
（お）さしみ（御刺身）*n.* sashimi (filet of fresh raw fish, such as tuna), 9
～さつ（～冊）*count.* counter for bound objects, 8
さっか　*n.* writer, 1P
サッカー　*n.* soccer, 7S
ざっし（雑誌）*n.* magazine, 1P, 6

さとう　*n.* sugar, 1P
さびしい（寂しい）い-*adj.* lonely, 11
ざぶとん（座布団）*n.* cushion for sitting on tatami floor, 3S
さむい（寒い）い-*adj.* cold, 11
さむけがする（寒気がする）*exp.* (to) have chills, 12S
さようなら。*exp.* Good-bye, 1
サラダ　*n.* salad, 9
サラリーマン　*n.* white collar worker, 10S
～さん　*suf.* Mr./Mrs./Miss/Ms. ～, 1
さんがつ（三月）*n.* March, 5S
サンクスギビング　*n.* Thanksgiving, 11P
さんじゅういちにち（三十一日）*n.* the thirty-first (day), 5S
さんじゅうにち（三十日）*n.* the thirtieth (day), 5S
サンダル　*n.* sandal, 8S
サンドイッチ　*n.* sandwich, 9
ざんねん（な）（残念な）な-*adj.* unfortunate, sorry, 6
さんねんせい（三年生）*n.* junior; third-year student, 2
～さんの　おたくですか。（～さんのお宅ですか。）*exp.* Is this the ～ residence?, 9
さんびゃく（三百）*n.* three hundred, 1P
さんふじんか（産婦人科）*n.* gynecology, 12P
さんぽを　します（散歩をします）*exp.* go/es for a walk, 6S

し

～じ（～時）*count.* ～ o'clock, 5
～じはん（～時半）*count.* half past ～, 5
ジーンズ　*n.* jeans, 8
じえいぎょう（自営業）*n.* self-employed, 10S
しお　*n.* salt, 1P
しか（歯科）*n.* dentistry, 12P
しかくい（四角い）い-*adj.* square, 10
しがつ（四月）*n.* April, 5S
～じかん（～時間）*count.* ～ hour(s), 5
しき（式）*n.* ceremony, 9
しけん（試験）*n.* examination; test, 6
しごと（仕事）*n.* work; permanent job, 6

じしょ（辞書）*n.* dictionary, 4
しずか（な）（静かな）*な-adj.* quiet, 3
した（下）*loc. n.* under; beneath, 3
したぎ（下着）*n.* underwear, 8S
しちがつ（七月）*n.* July, 5S
しっぽ　*n.* tail, 1P
しつれいします。*exp.* Goodbye, 1
しつれいですが（失礼ですが）*exp.*
　Excuse me, but . . . (used before asking a
　personal question), 4
じてんしゃ（自転車）*n.* bicycle, 6
〜じはん（〜時半）*count.* half past 〜, 5
じびいんこうか（耳鼻咽喉科）*n.*
　otorhinolaryngology, 12P
しまい（姉妹）*n.* (the speaker's) sisters, 10
します　*ir. v.* do/es, 5
じむしつ（事務室）*n.* business office, 4
じゃあ、また。*exp.* See you later., 1
しゃかいがく　*n.* sociology, 2S
ジャケット　*n.* jacket, 8
しゃしん（写真）*n.* photograph, 1P, 3
しゃしんをとる（写真をとる）*exp.* (to)
　take a picture, 7
しゃっくり　*n.* hiccup, 1P
ジャズ　*n.* jazz, 7
シャツ　*n.* shirt, 8
シャワー　*n.* shower, 3S, 5
シャワをあびます　*exp.* take/s a shower, 5
しゅう（州）*n.* state in the United States,
　Canada, and Australia), 7P
じゅういちがつ（十一月）*n.* November,
　5S
じゅういちにち（十一日）*n.* the eleventh
　(day), 5S
じゅうがつ（十月）*n.* October, 5S
〜しゅうかん（〜週間）*count.* 〜 week/s
　(duration), 6
じゅうくにち（十九日）*n.* the nineteenth
　(day), 5S
じゅうごにち（十五日）*n.* the fifteenth
　(day), 5S
じゅうさんにち（十三日）*n.* the thirteenth
　(day), 5S
じゅうしちにち（十七日）*n.* the
　seventeenth (day), 5S

ジュース　*n.* juice, 7S, 9
じゅうたん　*n.* carpet, 3S
じゅうどう（柔道）*n.* judo, 7S
じゅうにがつ（十二月）*n.* December, 5S
じゅうににち（十二日）*n.* the twelfth
　(day), 5S
じゅうはちにち（十八日）*n.* the eighteenth
　(day), 5S
しゅうまつ（週末）*n.* weekend, 6
じゅうよっか（十四日）*n.* the fourteenth
　(day), 5S
じゅうろくにち（十六日）*n.* the sixteenth
　(day), 5S
じゅぎょう（授業）*n.* class, course, 5
じゅぎょうをやすむ（授業を休む）*exp.*
　(to) be absent from class, 12
しゅくだい（宿題）*n.* homework, 5
しゅくだいを　だします。（宿題を出し
　ます。）*exp.* turn/s in homework, 6S
じゅけんべんきょう（受験勉強）*n.* study
　for entrance examination, 11P
しゅじゅつ（手術）*n.* surgical operation, 7P
しゅじん（主人）*n.* (the speaker's) husband,
　10
しゅっぱつ　*n.* departure, 1P
しゅみ（趣味）*n.* hobby, 7
しょうがくせい（小学生）*n.* elementary
　school student, 10S
（お）しょうがつ（（お）正月）*n.* New
　Year's Day, 1P, 11P
しょうがっこう（小学校）*n.* elementary
　school, 10P, 11
しょうじ（障子）*n.* paper sliding door, 3S
しょうじょう（症状）*n.* symptom, 12
しょうしょう　おまちください。*exp.*
　Please wait a moment. (Polite), 8P
じょうず（な）（上手な）*な-adj.* good at,
　skillful, 10
しょうにか（小児科）*n.* pediatrics, 12P
しょうひぜい（消費税）*n.* sales tax, 8P
しょうわ（昭和）*n.* the Showa era
　(1926–1989), 10P
ジョギング　*n.* jogging, 5P, 7
しょくじ（食事）*n.* dining, 7

しょくじをする（食事をする）*exp.* (to) dine, 7

しょくちゅうどく（食中毒）*n.* food poisoning, 12P

しょくどう（食堂）*n.* dining room/hall, cafeteria, 4

しょくひん（食品）*n.* food, 8

しょくひんうりば（食品売り場）*n.* food department, 8

しょくよくがない（食欲がない）*exp.* (to) have no appetite, 12S

しょっき（食器）*n.* tableware, 1P, 8P

しょっきを　あらいます（食器を洗います）*exp.* do/es the dishes, 6S

シルク　*n.* silk, 8S

しろ（白）*n.* the color white, 7P

しろい（白い）い-*adj.* white, 1P, 4

～じん（～人）*suf.* nationality, 2

しんしつ（寝室）*n.* bedroom, 3S

しんしふく（紳士服）*n.* menswear, 8

しんしふくうりば（紳士服売場）*n.* menswear department, 8

じんじゃ（神社）*n.* Shinto shrine, 11

しんせき（親戚）*n.* (the speaker's) relatives, 10S

しんせつ（な）（親切な）な-*adj.* kind, 10

しんぞうびょう（心臓病）*n.* heart disease, 12P

しんぱいです（心配です）*exp.* (to) be worried, 6P, 12P

しんぶん（新聞）*n.* newspaper, 6

しんりがく（心理学）*n.* psychology, 2S

じんるいがく（人類学）*n.* anthropology, 2S

す

すいえい（水泳）*n.* swimming, 7S

スイッチ　*n.* switch, 3S

ずいぶん　*adv.* quite, 4P

すいようび（水曜日）*n.* Wednesday, 5

すう（吸う）う-*v.* (to) inhale, smoke, 11

すうがく　*n.* mathematics, 2S

スーツ　*n.* suit (clothing), 10

スーパー　*n.* supermarket, 4

スープ　*n.* soup, 9

スカート　*n.* skirt, 8

スカートをはいている　*exp.* (to) be wearing a skirt, 10

スカーフ　*n.* scarf, 8S

すき（な）（好きな）な-*adj.* liked, 4P, 7

スキー　*n.* skiing, 7

ずきずきする　*exp.* (to) have a festering pain, 12S

すきやき　*n.* Japanese dish consisting of beef slices and vegetables cooked together, 9S

スケート　*n.* skating, 7S

すごい　い-*adj.* great, impressive, splendid, 12P

すこし（少し）*adv.* a little, a few, 7

（お）すし（御寿司）*n.* sushi, 9

すずしい（涼しい）い-*adj.* cool, 11

ずっと　*adv.* much more, by far, 7

スタンド　*n.* lamp, 3

ステーキ　*n.* beefsteak, 9

すてき（な）（素敵な）な-*adj.* attractive, nice, 3

ステレオ　*n.* stereo, 3

スニーカー　*n.* sneaker, 8S

スパゲティ　*n.* spaghetti, 9

スペイン　*n.* Spain, 2

スペインご　*n.* Spanish language, 2

スペインりょうり（スペイン料理）*n.* Spanish food, 9S

スポーツ　*n.* sports, 7

ズボン　*n.* trousers, pants, 8

（あのう、）すみません。　*exp.* (Er,) Excuse me., 1

すみません。　*exp.* I am sorry., 1

すむ（住む）う-*v.* (to) live, reside, 10

すもうを　みる　*exp.* (to) watch sumo wrestling, 11S

スリッパ　*n.* slippers, 8S

する　*ir. v.* (to) do, 5

する, *ir. v.* (to) have, (to) wear , 10

すんでいます（住んでいます）る-*v.* am/is/are living; residing, 3P

せ

せ（背）*n.* back (body part); height of a person, 10

〜せい（〜生）*suf.* student, 2

せいかく（性格）*n.* personality, 10

せいかつ（生活）*n.* daily life, daily routine, daily activities, 5

せいけいげか（整形外科）*n.* orthopedics; reconstructive surgery, 12P

せいじがく（政治学）*n.* political science, 2S

せいしんか（精神科）*n.* psychiatry, 12P

せいもん（正門）*n.* main entrance, 4S

セーター *n.* sweater, 8

セーターをきている（セーターを着ている）*exp.* (to) be wearing a sweater, 10

せかい *n.* world, 1P

せき（咳）*n.* cough, 12

せきがでる（咳が出る）(to) cough, 12

せっけん（石鹸）*n.* soap, 1P, 3S, 8P

せなか（背中）*n.* back, upper back, 10S

せまい（狭い）い-*adj.* cramped; narrow, 3

せんげつ（先月）*n.* last month, 11

せんこう（専攻）*n.* major, 2

せんしゅ（選手）*n.* player (on a sports team), 10P

せんしゅう（先週）*n.* last week, 6

せんせい（先生）*n.* teacher, professor, 1P, 2

〜せんせい（〜先生）*suf.* Professor 〜, 1

ぜんぜん（全然）*adv.* not at all (used with the negative form of verbs), 5

センター *n.* center, 2P

せんたく（洗濯）*n.* laundry, 6

せんたくき（洗濯機）*n.* washing machine, 3S

ぜんぶで（全部で）*exp.* altogether, 8P

せんめんじょ（洗面所）*n.* washbowl area, 3S

ぜんりゃく（前略）*exp.* abbreviated opening phrase of a letter, 9P, 11P

そ

そう *pron.* so, 2

そうじ（掃除）*n.* cleaning, 6

そうそう（草々）*exp.* closing phrase of a letter, 9P

そうですか。 *exp.* I see. Is that so. Really?, 2P

そこ *demo.* there, that place, 3

そこ *n.* bottom, 1P

そして *conj.* and, 2, 7

そつぎょう（卒業）*n.* graduation, 9

そつぎょうしき（卒業式）*n.* graduation ceremony, 9P

そと（外）*loc. n.* outside, 3

その *demo.* that + noun, 3

そのあとも, *exp.* after that, too, 5P

そば（蕎麦）*n.* Japanese buckwheat noodles, 9

そふ（祖父）*n.* (the speaker's) grandfather, 10

ソファ *n.* sofa, 3

ソフトボール *n.* softball, 7S

そぼ（祖母）*n.* (the speaker's) grandmother, 10

それ *demo.* that, that one nearby, 4

それから *conj.* and, in addition, also, 7

それは にほんごで なんと いいますか。 *exp.* What do you call that in Japanese?, 1

た

たいいくかん（体育館）*n.* gym, 4

だいがく（大学）*n.* college, university, 2

だいがくいん（大学院）*n.* graduate school, 2

だいがくいんせい（大学院生）*n.* graduate student, 2

だいがくせい（大学生）*n.* college student, 2

たいしょう（大正）*n.* Taishoo Era (1912–1925), 11P

だいじょうぶ（な）（大丈夫な）な-*adj.* all right, 12

だいすき（な）（大好きな）な-*adj.* like very much, 7

たいそう（体操）*n.* calisthenics, gymnastics, 7S

たいてい, *adv.* usually, 5

だいどころ（台所）*n.* kitchen, 3P

ダイニングキッチン　*n.* dining kitchen, 3S

たいへん　おまたせいたしました。*exp.* Thank you for waiting., 8P

たいへん（な）（大変な）な-*adj.* tough, hectic, hard, 6

たいわん（台湾）*n.* Taiwan, 2P

タオル　*n.* towel, 8P

たかい（高い）い-*adj.* high; expensive; tall, 1P, 3, 8

たき　*n.* waterfall, 1P

たくさん，*adv.* many, much, a lot, 4P, 8

だし（山車）*n.* float, 11P

だす（出す）う-*v.* (to) bring out, 8

ただいま。*exp.* I'm back!, 3

たたみ（畳）*n.* tatami mat, 3S

たてもの（建物）*n.* building, 3

たのしい（楽しい）い-*adj.* fun, 6

タバコ／たばこ　*n.* tobacco, 11

たばこをすう（たばこを吸う）*exp.* (to) smoke a cigarette, 11

たぶん　〜でしょう　*exp.* It's probably 〜, 12P

たぶんかぜでしょう（たぶん風邪でしょう）*exp.* It is probably a cold., 12

たべます（食べます）る-*v.* eat(s), 5

たべもの（食べ物）*n.* food, 7

たべる（食べる）る-*v.* (to) eat, 5

たまご（卵）*n.* egg, 7

たまねぎ　*n.* onion, 7S

だれ　*q. word* who, 3

だれの　*q. word* whose + noun, 3

たんじょうび（誕生日）*n.* birthday, 8P, 9

たんす（箪笥）*n.* chest, 3

ち

ちいさい（小さい）い-*adj.* small, 1P, 3

ちか（地下）*n.* basement, 8

ちかいっかい（地下一階）*n.* B1, 3S

ちかしつ（地下室）*n.* basement, 3S

ちかく（近く）*loc. n.* near; vicinity, 3

ちが　でる（血が出る）*exp.* (to) bleed, 12S

チキンかつ　*n.* chicken cutlet, breaded and deep-fried, 9S

ちず　*n.* map, 1P

ちち（父）*n.* (the speaker's) father, 2P, 10

チャーハン　*n.* Chinese-style fried rice, 9

（お）ちゃ（お茶）*n.* green tea, 9

ちゃいろい（茶色い）い-*adj.* brown, 4

ちゅうがく（中学）*n.* junior high school (shortened form of 中学校), 11

ちゅうがくせい（中学生）*n.* junior high school student, 10S

ちゅうかりょうり（中華料理）*n.* Chinese food, 9

ちゅうごく（中国）*n.* China, 2

ちゅうごくじん（中国人）*n.* Chinese, 2

ちゅうしゃじょう（駐車場）*n.* parking lot; parking garage, 4S

ちゅうもんする（注文する）*ir. v.* (to) order, 9

（ご）ちゅうもんは。（ご注文は。）*exp.* What would you like to order? 9P

ちょう（腸）*n.* intestine, 12S

ちょうし（調子）*n.* condition, 12

ちょっかく　*n.* right angle, 1P

ちょっと　*adv.* a little bit, 9

ちょっと　すみませんが（ちょっと　済みませんが）*exp.* Excuse me, but . . . (used to make a request, to ask a question), 4

ちょっと　つごうが　わるいんです。（ちょっと都合が悪いんです。）*exp.* It's not really convenient. I already have plans, 9

ちょっと　ようじが　あるんです。（ちょっと用事があるんです。）*exp.* I have some errands to do., 9

つ

〜つ　*count.* general counter (Japanese origin number), 8

ついたち（一日）*n.* the first (day), 5S

つかれる（疲れる）る-*v.* (to) become tired, 12

つかれている（疲れている）る-*v.* (to) be tired, 12

つき（月）*n.* moon, 1P

つぎ（次）*n.* next, 8P

つくえ（机）*n.* desk, 3

つくります（作ります）う-*v.* make/s, 6

つくる（作る）う-*v.* (to) make, 6

つける（付ける）る-*v.* (to) attach; (to) apply (medicine), 12
つつむ（包む）う-*v.* (to) wrap, 8
〜って　なんですか。*exp.* What does 〜 mean?, 1
つとめる（勤める）る-*v.* (to) become employed, 10
つとめている（勤めている）る-*v.* (to) be employed at, works for, 10
つま（妻）*n.* (the speaker's) wife, 10S
つまる（詰まる）う-*v.* (to) stuff, 12
つめ（爪）*n.* nail, 10S
つり（釣り）*n.* fishing, 7S, 11

で

て（手）*n.* hand, 1P, 6S, 10
で　*part.* at, in, on, 5
で　*part.* with, by means of, 6
〜で　ございます　*exp.* 〜 is/are polite form of 〜です), 8P
テーブル　*n.* table, 3
ていしょく（定食）*n.* (lunch, dinner) set, 9S
〜ている　*aux.* resultant state, 10
デート　*n.* dating, 11
デートする　*exp.* (to) go out on a date, 11
デーパック　*n.* backpack, 4
でかけます（出かけます）る-*v.* go/es out, 6
でかける（出かける）る-*v.* (to) go out, 6
てがみ（手紙）*n.* letter, 6
てくび（手首）*n.* wrist, 12S
デザート　*n.* dessert, 9
です　*cop.* (to) be, 2
〜ですが、〜さんは　いらっしゃいますか。（〜ですが、〜さんはいらっしゃいますか。）*exp.* My name is 〜. Is 〜 home?, 9
ですから　*conj.* so, therefore, 5P
テスト　*n.* test, 6
テニス　*n.* tennis, 7
デーパック　*n.* backpack, 4
デパート　*n.* department store, 4
てまえ（手前）*loc. n.* this side, 3S, 4P
でも　*conj.* but, 7

〜てもいいですか。／いいでしょうか。／かまいませんか。*exp.* May I do 〜?; Is it OK to do 〜?, 12
〜てもよろしいですか。／よろしいでしょうか。*exp.* May I do 〜?; Is it OK to do 〜?, 12S
（お）てら（お寺）*n.* Buddhist temple, 11
でる（出る）る-*v.* (to) come out, 12
テレビ　*n.* television, 3
てを　あらいます（手を洗います）*exp.* wash/es (one's) hands, 6S
てんいん（店員）*n.* sales clerk, 7P
でんき（電気）*n.* light; electricity, 3S
でんしゃ（電車）*n.* (electric) train, 1P, 6
でんしレンジ（電子レンジ）*n.* microwave oven, 3S
てんぷら（天麩羅）*n.* tempura, 1P, 9
てんぷらていしょく（てんぷら定食）*n.* tempura dinner, 9S
でんわ（電話）*n.* telephone, 1P, 3
でんわばんごう（電話番号）*n.* telephone number, 9
でんわをかけます（電話をかけます）*exp.* (to) make a phone call, 6

と

と　*part.* and, 2
と　*part.* with, 6
〜ど（〜度）*count.* times (frequency), 6
ドア　*n.* door, 3
ドイツ　*n.* Germany, 2S
トイレ　*n.* toilet, 3P
どういたしまして。*exp.* You are welcome., 1
どうしたらいいですか。*exp.* What should I do?, 12
どうしましたか。／どうしたんですか。*exp.* What happened?, 12
どうぞ　*adv.* please, 3
どうぞ　あがってください。*exp.* Please come in., 3
どうぞ　おかまいなく。*exp.* Please don't bother., 9
どうぞ　よろしく。*exp.* Pleased to meet you., 1

どうですか。 *exp.* How about 〜?, 7
とうにょうびょう（糖尿病）*n.* diabetes, 12P
どうぶつえん（動物園）*n.* zoo, 11
どうも　*adv.* very, 3
どうもありがとうございます。 *exp.* Thank you very much., 3
とおか（十日）*n.* the tenth (day), 5S
とおり　*n.* street, 1P
とき（時）*n.* when, at the time of 〜, 11
ときどき（時々）*adv.* sometimes, 5
とくに（特に）*conj.* especially, particularly, 7P
とくに　よていは　ありません。（特に予定はありません。）*exp.* I don't have any particular plans., 9P
どくりつきねんび（独立記念日）*n.* Independence Day, 11P
とけい（時計）*n.* clock; watch, 1P, 3
どこ　*q. word* where, 2
とこのま（床の間）*n.* alcove, 3S
ところ（所）*n.* place, 4
としうえ（年上）*n.* older person, 10P
としうえに　みられる（年上にみられる。）*exp.* look/s older than (one's) age, 10P
としょかん（図書館）*n.* library, 4
とだな（戸棚）*n.* cabinet, 3
どちら　*q. word* where (more polite than どこ), which way, 2
とても　*adv.* very, 3
となり（隣り）*loc. n.* next to, 3
どの　*q. word* which + noun, 3
トマト　*n.* tomato, 7
とまる（止まる）う-*v.* stop, 8P
ともだち（友達）*n.* friend, 2
どようび（土曜日）*n.* Saturday, 5
ドライブ　*n.* driving (pleasure driving), 7
とり　*n.* bird, 1P
とりにく（鳥肉）*n.* chicken, 7S
とる（撮る）う-*v.* (to) take (a photograph), 7
とる（取る）う-*v.* (to) take, get, 8
〜ドル　*count.* dollar, 8P
どれ　*q. word* which, which one, 4
ドレス　*n.* dress, 8S

とんかつ（豚かつ）*n.* pork cutlet, breaded and deep-fried, 9S
どんな　*q. word* what kind of + noun, 3

な

ないか（内科）*n.* internal medicine, 12P
なか（中）*loc. n.* in, inside, 3
ながい（長い）い-*adj.* long, 1P, 10
なく（泣く）う-*v.* (to) cry, 11
なつ（夏）*n.* summer, 11
なつやすみ（夏休み）*n.* summer vacation, 11
なに/なん（何）*q. word* what, 2
なにか　おさがしでしょうか。 *exp.* May I help you (literally: Are you looking for something)?, 8P
なにも　いりません。（何もいりません。）*exp.* I don't need anything., 9
なにを　さしあげましょうか。 *exp.* Can I help you(literally: What shall I give you)?, 8P
なのか（七日）*n.* the seventh (day), 5S
なまえ（名前）*n.* name, 2
なる（成る）う-*v.* (to) become, 12
なん〜／いくつ　さしあげましょうか。 *exp.* How many 〜 shall I give you?, 8P
なんですか（何ですか）*q. word* What is it?, 2

に

に　*part.* at, on, in (point in time), 5
に　*part.* to (goal, activity + に), 5
に　*part.* to (indirect object marker, person + に) , 6
に　*part.* time frame, 6
〜に　します　*exp.* decide/s on 〜, 9
にがつ（二月）*n.* February, 5S
にぎやかな（賑やかな）な-*adj.* lively, 3S
にく（肉）*n.* meat, 1P, 7
にじゅういちにち（二十一日）*n.* the 21st (day), 5S
にじゅうくにち（二十九日）*n.* the 29th (day), 5S
にじゅうごにち（二十五日）*n.* the 25th (day), 5S

にじゅうさんにち（二十三日）*n.* the 23rd (day), 5S

にじゅうしちにち（二十七日）*n.* the 27th (day), 5S

にじゅうににち（二十二日）*n.* the 22nd (day), 5S

にじゅうはちにち（二十八日）*n.* the 28th (day), 5S

にじゅうよっか（二十四日）*n.* the 24th (day), 5S

にじゅうろくにち（二十六日）*n.* the 26th (day), 5S

〜にち（〜日）*count.* 〜 days (duration); specific day （十一日, the 11th), 11

にちようび（日曜日）*n.* Sunday, 5

にちようひん（日用品）*n.* daily goods, 8P

にっき　*n.* diary, 1P

にねんせい（二年生）*n.* sophomore; second-year student, 2

にほん（日本）*n.* Japan, 2

にほんご（日本語）*n.* Japanese language, 1P, 2

にほんごがわかる（日本語が分かる）*exp.* (to) understand Japanese, 10

にほんぶんがく（日本文学）*n.* Japanese literature, 2

にほんじん（日本人）*n.* Japanese, 2

にほんりょうり（日本料理）*n.* Japanese food, 9

にゅういんする（入院する）*ir. v.* (to) be hospitalized, 12

ニュージーランド　*n.* New Zealand

にわ（庭）*n.* garden, yard, 3S

〜にん（〜人）*count.* 〜 people, 10

にんぎょう　*n.* doll, 1P

にんじん　*n.* carrot, 7

ね

ね　*part.* isn't it (seeking confirmation), 4

ねぎ　*n.* scallion, 7S

ネクタイ　*n.* tie, 8

ねこ（猫）*n.* cat, 1P, 3

ねつ（熱）*n.* fever, temperature, 12

ねつがでる（熱が出る）*exp.* (to) run a fever, 12

ねっとう　*n.* boiling water, 1P

ネックレス　*n.* necklace, 8

ねます（寝ます）る-*v.* go/es to bed, 5

ねる（寝る）る-*v.* (to) go to bed, 5

〜ねん（〜年）*count.* years (grade in school; duration; specific year), 2, 5S, 6, 11

ねんがじょう（年賀状）*n.* New Year's card, 9P

ねんざする（捻挫する）*exp.* (to) sprain, 12S

の

の　*part.* of, ('s) 2

〜の　あと（〜の後）*exp.* after 〜, 9P

〜の　ことは　しんぱいしていません。（〜のこと心配していません。）*exp.* not worried about 〜, 6P

ノート　*n.* notebook, 4

のど（咽）*n.* throat, 1P, 10S, 12

〜のとき（〜の時）*exp.* at the time when 〜, 6

のぼる（登る）う-*v.* (to) climb, 11

のみます（飲みます）う-*v.* drink/s, 5

のみもの（飲み物）*n.* beverage, drink, 7

のむ（飲む）う-*v.* (to) drink, 5

のる（乗る）う-*v.* (to) get on; (to) ride, 11

は

は（歯）*n.* tooth, 6S, 10S, 12

は　*part.* topic marker, 2

〜は　ありませんか。*exp.* Do you have 〜 Do you carry 〜 (literally: Isn't there〜)?, 8

〜は　いかがでしょうか。*exp.* How about 〜 How is 〜 (Polite form of 〜はどうですか)?, 8P

パーティ　*n.* party, 7

パートナー　*n.* partner, 2P

パイ　*n.* pie, 9S

はい／ええ　*adv.* yes, 2

はい／ええ　かまいません。*exp.* No, I don't mind. (Yes, please.), 12

はい／ええ　どうぞ。*exp.* Yes, please, 12

はい／ええ　もちろん　*exp.* Yes, of course.; Yes, sure., 12

はい（ええ）、そうです。 *exp.* Yes, that's so., 2

はい　かしこまりました。 *exp.* I see.; I will do it.; I understand it. (Polite), 8P

ハイキング　*n.* hiking, 7

ハイキングに　いく（ハイキングに行く） *exp.* (to) go hiking, 7S

はいけい（拝啓）*n.* opening phrase of a letter, 11P

はいしゃ（歯医者）*n.* dentist, 10S

はいります（入ります）う-*v.* enter/s; take/s a bath, 5

はいる（入る）う-*v.* (to) enter, (to) take a bath, 5

はがき（葉書）*n.* postcard, 9

はかる（計る）う-*v.* (to) measure, 12

はきけがする（吐き気がする）*exp.* (to) have nausea, 12S

はく　う-*v.* (to) put on (skirt, pants, socks), 10

はくぶつかん（博物館）*n.* museum, 11

はくぶつかんに　いく（博物館に行く） *n.* (to) go to a museum, 7S

はこ（箱）*n.* box, 8

はし（端）*loc. n.* end, 3S

はしか　*n.* measles, 12P

はじまります（始まります）う-*v.* begin/s, 5

はじまる（始まる）う-*v.* (to) begin, 5

はじめて（初めて）*adv.* for the first time, 11

はじめてなんですが。 *exp.* This is my first time . . . , 12

はじめまして, *exp.* How do you do?, 1

バス　*n.* bus, 6

バスケットボール　*n.* basketball, 7

パスタ　*n.* pasta, 9S

はた（旗）*n.* flag, 2P

はちうえ（鉢植え）*n.* potted plants, 3S

はちがつ（八月）*n.* August, 5S

パチンコを　する　*n.* (to) play pachinko, 7S

はつか（二十日）*n.* the 20th (day), 5S

はっぱ　*n.* leaf, 1P

はな（花）*n.* flower, 1P

はな（鼻）*n.* nose, 1P, 10

はながつまる（鼻が詰まる）*exp.* (to) have a stuffy nose, 12

はなします（話します）う-*v.* talk/s, 6

はなす（話す）う-*v.* talk, 6

バナナ　*n.* banana, 7

〜は　にほんごで　なんと　いいますか。（〜は日本語で何と言いますか。） *exp.* How do you say 〜 in Japanese?, 1

はは（母）*n.* (the speaker's) mother, 2P 10

はる（春）*n.* spring, 11

はるやすみ（春休み）*n.* spring vacation, 11

はれ　*n.* clear weather, 1P

バレーボール　*n.* volleyball, 7S

バレンタインデー　*n.* St. Valentine's Day, 11P

ハロウィーン　*n.* Halloween, 11P

はを　みがきます（歯を磨きます）*exp.* brush/es (one's) teeth, 6S

ばん（晩）*n.* night; evening, 5

〜ばんめ（〜番目）*count.* 〜th (ordinal), 10

ハンカチ　*n.* handkerchief, 8S

ばんごう（番号）*n.* number, 9

ばんごはん（晩御飯）*n.* supper, dinner, 5

パンツ　*n.* shorts, briefs, 8

はんとし（半年）*adv.* half year, 11

ハンドバッグ　*n.* handbag, 8

ハンバーガー　*n.* hamburger, 9

ハンバーグ　*n.* hamburger steak, 9S

ひ

ピアノを　ひく　*exp.* (to) play the piano, 7S

ピーマン　*n.* green pepper, 7S

ビール　*n.* beer, 7

〜ひき（〜匹）*count.* counter for fish and small four-legged animals, 8

ひく　う-*v.* (to) catch (a cold), 12

ひくい（低い）い-*adj.* low; short height), 1P, 3S, 10

ピクニックに　いく（ピクニックに行く） *exp.* (to) go on a picnic, 7S

ひげ（髭）*n.* mustache, beard, 1P, 10S

ひこうき（飛行機）*n.* airplane, 11

ひこうきにのる（飛行機に乗る）*exp.*
　(to) get on a plane, 11
ひざ　*n.* knee, 1P
ピザ　*n.* pizza, 9
（お）ひさしぶり（お久しぶり）*exp.* It's
　been a long time since we last met., 9P
びじゅつ（美術）*n.* fine arts, 2S
ひだりがわ（左側）*loc. n.* to the left; left
　side, 3
ひだりはし（左端）*loc. n.* left end, 3S
ビデオ　*n.* videotape, 6
ビデオを　かります。（ビデオを借りま
　す。）*exp.* rent/s a video, 6S
ひと（人）*n.* person, people, 1P, 2
ひどい　い-*adj.* serious (injury), 12
ひとり（一人）*count.* one person, 10
ひとりで（一人で）*adv.* alone, by oneself, 6
ひにち（日にち）*n.* date, 11P
ひにょうきか（泌尿器科）*n.* urology, 12P
ひふか（皮膚科）*n.* dermatology, 12P
ひま（な）　な-*adj.* free, idling, 6
ひゃく（百）*n.* one hundred, 1P
びょういん（病院）*n.* hospital, 4
びょうき（病気）*n.* sickness, 1P, 12
びょうきに　なる（病気になる）*exp.*
　(to) become sick, 11S
ひりひりする　*exp.* (to) have a burning pain,
　12S
ひる（昼）*n.* afternoon, 1P, 5
ひるごはん（昼御飯）*n.* lunch, 5
ひろい（広い）い-*adj.* spacious, wide, 3
ピンク　*n.* pink, 4S

ふ

ファックス　*n.* fax machine, 3S
ファミコン　*n.* family computer, computer
　game, 7
ふうせん　*n.* balloon, 1P
ふえ　*n.* flute, 1P
ふく（服）*n.* clothing, 8
ふじんふく（婦人服）*n.* women's clothing,
　8
ふじんふくうりば（婦人服売り場）*n.*
　women's clothing department, 8

ぶたにく（豚肉）*n.* pork, 7S
ふたり（二人）*count.* two people, 10
ふつか（二日）*n.* the 2nd (day), 5S
フットボール　*n.* (American) football, 7
ぶつりがく（物理学）*n.* physics, 2S
ぶどう, *n.* grape, 7S
ふとる（太る）う-*v.* (to) gain weight, 10
ふとっている（太っている）*exp.* (to) be
　chubby, 10
ふとん（布団）*n.* futon, 3
ふゆ（冬）*n.* winter, 11
ふゆやすみ（冬休み）*n.* winter vacation, 11
フランス　*n.* France, 2
ふるい（古い）い-*adj.* old, 3
ふるえる（震える）*exp.* (to) tremble, 12S
ブレスレット　*n.* bracelets, 8S
プレゼント　*n.* present, 8P
〜ふん（〜分）*count.* 〜 minute; (for) 〜
　minutes, 5
ぶんがく（文学）*n.* literature, 2
ぶんぼうぐ（文房具）*n.* stationery, 8
ぶんぼうぐうりば（文房具売り場）*n.*
　stationery department, 8

へ

へいせい（平成）*n.* the Heisei Era (1989〜),
　11P
ベージュ　*n.* beige, 4S
ベッド　*n.* bed, 3
ベッドルーム　*n.* bedroom, 3S
へや（部屋）*n.* room, 3, 6S
へやを　かたづけます（部屋を片付けま
　す）*exp.* tidy/tidies up a room, 6S
ベランダ　*n.* verandah, 3S
ベルト　*n.* belt, 8
へん（な）（変な）な-*adj.* strange, 11
べんきょう（勉強）*n.* study, 5
べんごし（弁護士）*n.* lawyer, 10S
へんしゅうしゃ（編集者）*n.* editor, 10P

ほ

ほうがくぶ（法学部）*n.* law school, 4
ぼうし（帽子）*n.* hat, cap, 8S, 10

ぼうしをかぶっている（帽子をかぶって いる）*exp.* (to) have a hat on, 10

ほうれんそう　*n.* spinach, 7S

ボーリング　*n.* bowling, 7

ボールペン　*n.* ballpoint pen, 4

ほかに　*conj.* other than 〜, 12P

ぼく（僕）*pron.* I (normally used by a male), 2

ぼくは　きょうは　じゅぎょうが　あり ません。*exp.* I don't have class today., 5P

ほけんしょう（保険証）*n.* health insurance card, 12P

ほし　*n.* star, 1P

ポスター　*n.* poster, 3S

ホストファミリー　*n.* host family, 2P

ほそながい（細長い）い-*adj.* long/elongated, 10

ほっかいどう（北海道）*n.* Hokkaido (northernmost main island of Japan), 11P

ホットドッグ　*n.* hotdog, 9S

ポップス　*n.* pops (popular music), 7

ほっぺた　*n.* cheek, 10S

ホテル　*n.* hotel, 12P

ほねをおる（骨を折る）*exp.* (to) break a bone, 12S

ほん（本）*n.* book, 3

〜ほん（〜本）*count.* counter for long, cylindrical objects (e.g., pens, pencils, bottles), 8

ほんだな（本棚）*n.* bookshelf, 3

ほんぶ（本部）*n.* administration office, 4S

ほんや（本屋）*n.* bookstore, 4

ま

〜まい（〜枚）*count.* counter for thin, flat objects (e.g., paper, shirts, plates), 8

まい〜（毎〜）*pref.* every〜, 5

まいあさ（毎朝）*n.* every morning, 5

まいにち（毎日）*n.* every day, 5

まいばん（毎晩）*n.* every night, 5

まえ（前）*loc. n.* in front of; in the front, 3

〜まえ（〜前）*suf.* 〜ago, 11

まご（孫）*n.* (the speaker's) grandchild, 10S

また　*adv.* again, 8P

（せんこうは）まだ　わかりません。 *exp.* I don't know (my major) yet., 2P

まち（町）*n.* town, 4

まつげ（睫）*n.* eyelash, 10S

（お）まつり（（お）祭り）*n.* festival, 11P

まで　*part.* until, 6

まど（窓）*n.* window, 3

マネージャー　*n.* manager, 10S

まゆ（眉）*n.* eyebrow, 10S

まるい（丸い）い-*adj.* round, 10

み

みかん　*n.* mandarin orange, 7S

みぎがわ（右側）*loc. n.* to the right; right side, 3

みぎはし（右端）*loc. n.* the right end, 3S

みじかい（短い）い-*adj.* short (length), 1P, 10

みず（水）*n.* water, 9

みずいろ（水色）*n.* light blue, 4S

みせる（見せる）る-*v.* (to) show, 8

みっか（三日）*n.* the 3rd (day), 5S

みて ください。（見て下さい。）*exp.* Please look (at it)., 1

みどり（緑）*n.* green, 4

みます（見ます）る-*v.* see/s, watch/es, 5

みみ（耳）*n.* ear, 1P, 10

みょうじ　*n.* last name, 1P

みる（見る）る-*v.* (to) see; watch, 5

ミルク　*n.* milk, 7S, 9

む

むいか（六日）*n.* the 6th (day), 5S

むかい（向かい）*loc. n.* opposite side; across (the street), 3S

むこう（向こう）*loc. n.* beyond, 3S

むずかしい（難しい）い-*adj.* difficult, 6

むすこ（息子）*n.* son, 3P

むすめ（娘）*n.* (the speaker's) daughter, 1P

むらさき（紫）*n.* purple, 4S

むり（無理）*n.* overwork, overstrain, 12

むりをする（無理をする）*exp.* (to) overstrain, overwork, 12

め

め （目） *n.* eye, 1P, 10

めい （姪） *n.* (the speaker's) niece, 10S

めいごさん （姪子さん） *n.* (someone else's) niece, 10S

めいじ （明治） *n.* the Meiji Era (1868–1911), 11P

めがね （眼鏡） *n.* glasses, 10

めがねをかけている *exp.* (to) be wearing glasses, 10

メキシコ *n.* Mexico, 2

メキシコじん *n.* Mexican, 2

メキシコりょうり （メキシコ料理） *n.* Mexican food, 9S

めまいがする *exp.* (to) feel dizzy, 12S

メロン *n.* melon, 7S

も

も *part.* also, too, 2

もう *adv.* already, 7P

もう *adv.* a little ～ もう すこし a little more, 8

もう いちど いって ください。（もう一度言って下さい。） *exp.* Please say it again., 1

もくようび （木曜日） *n.* Thursday, 5

もしもし *exp.* Hello (on the phone)., 9

もつ （持つ） う-*v.* (to) hold, 8

もっている （持っている） る-*v.* (to) have, own, 8

もっと *adv.* more, 8

モデル *n.* (fashion) model, 10P

もの （物） *n.* thing (tangible), 11

ものおき （物置） *n.* storage, 3S

もめん （木綿） *n.* cotton, 8S

や

やきゅう （野球） *n.* baseball, 7

やけどをする （火傷をする） *exp.* (to) have a burn, 12S

やさい （野菜） *n.* vegetable, 7

やさしい （易しい） い-*adj.* easy, 6

やさしい （優しい） い-*adj.* gentle, 10

やさしい ことばで いってください。 *exp.* Please say it simply., 8

やすい （安い） い-*adj.* inexpensive, cheap, 8

やすみ （休み） *n.* vacation; holiday, 11

やすむ （休む） う-*v.* (to) rest, 12

やせている *exp.* is thin, 10

やせる る-*v.* (to) lose weight, 10

やっつ （八つ） *count.* eight, 6P

やま （山） *n.* mountain, 1P, 7

やまにのぼる （山に登る） *exp.* (to) climb a mountain, 11

ゆ

ゆうえんち （遊園地） *n.* amusement park, 11

ゆうえんちに いく （遊園地にいく） *exp.* (to) go to an amusement park, 7S

ゆうびんきょく （郵便局） *n.* post office, 4

ゆうめい （な） （有名な） な-*adj.* famous, 3

ゆき （雪） *n.* snow, 1P

ゆきまつり （雪祭り） *n.* the snow festival in Sapporo, 11P

ゆっくり いって ください。（ゆっくり言って下さい。） *exp.* Please say it slowly, 1

ゆっくり はなして ください。（ゆっくり話して下さい。） *exp.* Please speak slowly, 1

ゆび （指） *n.* finger, 1P, 10S, 12

ゆびわ （指輪） *n.* ring, 8S

よ

よ *part.* "you know"; emphasis marker, 4

ようか （八日） *n.* the 8th (day), 5S

ようじ （用事） *n.* errand, 9

ようしつ （洋室） *n.* Western-style room, 3S

～ようび （～曜日） *suf.* days of the week, 5

よかったら *exp.* If it's OK . . . , 9P

よく *adv.* often, 5

よこ （横） *loc. n.* next to, at the side of, 3

よこに なってください。 *exp.* Please lie down., 12S

よこはま （横浜） *n.* Yokohama City, 11P

よっか （四日） *n.* the 4th (day), 5S

よねんせい（四年生）*n.* senior; fourth-year student, 2
よぶ（呼ぶ）う*-v.* (to) invite; (to) call, 9
よみます（読みます）う*-v.* read/s, 5
よむ（読む）う*-v.* (to) read, 5
よわい（弱い）い*-adj.* weak, 12
よる　*n.* night, 1P
よんで ください。（読んで下さい。）*exp.* Please read, 1

ら

ラーメン　*n.* ramen (Chinese noodles in soup), 9
らいげつ（来月）*n.* next month, 11
らいしゅう（来週）*n.* next week, 6
ラボ　*n.* laboratory, 4

り

りっぱ（な）（立派な）な*-adj.* fine; splendid, gorgeous, 1P, 3
リビングルーム　*n.* living room, family room, 3S
りゅうがくせい（留学生）*n.* exchange student, 2
りゅうがくせいセンター（留学生センター）*n.* exchange student center, 2P
りょう　*n.* dormitory, 1P, 3
りょうしん（両親）*n.* parents, 6
りょうり（料理）*n.* cooking, food (cuisine), 7
りょうりをする（料理をする）*exp.* (to) cook, 7
りょこう（旅行）*n.* trip, traveling, 1P, 7
りんご　*n.* apple, 7

る

ルームメート　*n.* roommate, 6

れ

れいぞうこ（冷蔵庫）*n.* refrigerator, 3S
レーバーデー　*n.* Labor Day, 11P
れきし　*n.* history, 2S
レコード　*n.* record, 8

レコードうりば（レコード売り場）*n.* music department, 8
レジャー　*n.* leisure, 7
レストラン, *n.* restaurant, 4
レタス　*n.* lettuce, 7
レポート　*n.* report; term paper, 6

ろ

ろうか（廊下）*n.* hallway, 3S
ろくがつ（六月）*n.* June, 5S
ロシア　*n.* Russia, 2S
ロシアりょうり（ロシア料理）*n.* Russian food, 9S
ロック　*n.* rock and roll, 7

わ

ワイシャツ　*n.* man's dress shirt, 8S
ワイン　*n.* wine, 7
わからないんですよ。*exp.* I don't understand., 7P
わかる（分かる）う*-v.* (to) understand, 10
わしつ（和室）*n.* Japanese-style room, 3S
わしょく（和食）*n.* Japanese food（にほんりょうり），9
わたし（私）*pron.* I, 2
わらう（笑う）う*-v.* laugh, smile, 11
わるい（悪い）い*-adj.* bad, 3S, 12

を

を　*part.* (direct object marker), 5
を　*part.* from, 12
〜を　おねがいします。（〜をお願いします。）*exp.* I would like to have 〜., 9
〜を　ください。（〜を下さい。）*exp.* Please give me 〜., 8

English-Japanese Glossary

A

A lunch (Western-Style)　Aランチ　*n.*, 9

above; on; over　うえ（上）*loc. n.*, 3

accessories　アクセサリー　*n.*, 8

accessory department　アクセサリーうりば（アクセサリー売り場）　*n.*, 8

across (the street), opposite side　むかい（向かい）*loc. n.*, 3S

additional, another～　もうすこし（もう少し）a little more

administration office　ほんぶ（本部）*n.*, 4S

adorable, cute　かわいい　*い-adj.*, 10

adult　おとな（大人）*n.*, 12P

aerobics　エアロビクス　*n.*, 7

after ～　～の　あと（～の後）*exp.*, 9P

after that, too　そのあとも　*exp.*, 5P

after the movie　えいがのあと（映画の後）*exp.*, 9P

afternoon　ひる（昼）*n.*, 1P, 5

again　また　*adv.*, 8P

～ ago　～まえ（～前）*suf.*, 11

ahead　さき（先）*loc. n.*, 3S

AIDS　エイズ　*n.*, 12P

airplane　ひこうき（飛行機）*n.*, 11

alcoholic beverages, Japanese sake　（お）さけ（（お）酒）*n.*, 12

alcove　とこのま（床の間）*n.*, 3S

all right　だいじょうぶ（な）（大丈夫な）*な-adj.*, 12

allergy　アレルギー　*n.*, 12

alone, by oneself　ひとりで（一人で）*adv.*, 6

already　もう　*adv.*, 7P

also, and, in addition　それから　*conj.*, 7

altogether　ぜんぶで（全部で）*exp.*, 8P

always　いつも　*adv.*, 5

America; United States　アメリカ　*n.*, 2

amusement park　ゆうえんち（遊園地）*n.*, 11

and　そして　*conj.*, 2, 7

and　と　*part.*, 2

and, in addition, also　それから　*conj.*, 7

ankle　あしくび（足首）*n.*, 12S

another, an additional ～　もう　*adv.*

anthropology　じんるいがく（人類学）*n.*, 2S

antibiotic　こうせいぶっしつ（抗生物質）*n.*, 12P

apartment　アパート　*n.*, 3

apple　りんご　*n.*, 7

(to) apply (medicine); (to) attach　つける（付ける）*る-v.*, 12

April　しがつ（四月）*n.*, 5S

April Fools' Day　エイプリルフール, *n.*, 11P

architecture　けんちくがく　*n.*, 2S

arm　うで（腕）*n.*, 1P, 10S, 12S

Asian studies　アジアけんきゅう（アジア研究）*n.*, 2

at; on; in (point in time)　に　*part.*, 5

at; in; on　で　*part.*, 5

at the time when ～, when　のとき（時）*n.*, 11

(to) attach; (to) apply (medicine)　つける（付ける）*る-v.*, 12

attractive, nice　すてき（な）（素敵な）*な-adj.*, 3

auditorium　こうどう（講堂）*n.*, 4S

August　はちがつ（八月）*n.*, 5S

(someone else's) aunt　おばさん（叔母さん／伯母さん）　*n.*, 10S

(the speaker's) aunt　おば（叔母／伯母）　*n.*, 10S

Australia　オーストラリア　*n.*, 2

Australian　オーストラリア人　*n.*, 2

automobile, car　くるま（車）*n.*, 6

B

back (body part); height of a person　せ（背）*n.*, 10

back, upper back　せなか（背中）*n.*, 10S, 12S

(lower) back, hip　こし　*n.*, 10S, 12

back of; behind　うしろ（後ろ）*loc. n.*, 3

backpack　デーパック　*n.*, 4

bad　わるい（悪い）い-*adj.*, 3S 12

bag, briefcase　かばん（鞄）*n.*, 1P, 4

balloon　ふうせん　*n.*, 1P

ballpoint pen　ボールペン　*n.*, 4

banana　バナナ　*n.*, 7

bank　ぎんこう（銀行）*n.*, 4

baseball　やきゅう（野球）*n.*, 7

basement (of a house)　ちかしつ（地下室）*n.*, 3S

basement　ちか（地下）*n.*, 8

basketball　バスケットボール　*n.*, 7

bathroom, bathtub　おふろ（お風呂）*n.*, 3P

(to) be　です　*cop.*, 1, 2

(to) be annoyed; (to) suffer　こまる（困る）う-*v.*, 12

(to) be over, (to) end　おわる（終わる）う-*v.*, 5

(to) be tired　つかれている（疲れている）る-*v.*, 12

(to) be troubled, be annoyed, suffer　こまる（困る）う-*v.*, 12

(to) be worried　しんぱいです（心配です）*exp.*, 6P, 12

(to) be, (to) exist　いる　る-*v.*, 3 and ある　う-*v.*, 3

beard, mustache　ひげ（髭）*n.*, 1P, 10S

(to) become　なる（成る）う-*v.*, 12

bed　ベッド　*n.*, 3

bedroom　しんしつ（寝室）*n.*, 3S

(Western-style) bedroom　ベッドルーム　*n.*, 3S

beef　ぎゅうにく（牛肉）*n.*, 7S

beefsteak　ステーキ　*n.*, 9

beer　ビール　*n.*, 7

(to) begin　はじまる（始まる）う-*v.*, 5

behind, back of　うしろ（後ろ）*loc. n.*, 3

beige　ベージュ　*n.*, 4S

belly, stomach　おなか（お腹）*n.*, 1P, 10S, 12

belt　ベルト　*n.*, 8

beneath, under　した（下）*loc. n.*, 3

best, most　いちばん（一番）*adv.*, 4P

between　あいだ（間）*loc. n.*, 3S

beverage, drink　のみもの（飲み物）*n.*, 7

beyond　むこう（向こう）*loc. n.*, 3S

bicycle　じてんしゃ（自転車）*n.*, 6

big, large　おおきい（大きい）い-*adj.*, 1P, 3

bird　とり　*n.*, 1P

birthday　たんじょうび（誕生日）*n.*, 8P 9

black　くろい（黒い）い-*adj.*, 1P, 4

blackboard　こくばん（黒板）*n.*, 4

black tea　こうちゃ（紅茶）*n.*, 1P, 7

(to) bleed　ちが　でる（血が出る）*exp.*, 12S

blond　きんぱつ（金髪）*n.*, 10

blue　あおい（青い）い-*adj.*, 1P, 4

body　からだ（体）*n.*, 1P, 10

boiling water　ねっとう　*n.*, 1P

book　ほん（本）*n.*, 3

bookshelf　ほんだな（本棚）*n.*, 3

bookstore　ほんや（本屋）*n.*, 4

bottom　そこ　*n.*, 1P

bowling　ボーリング　*n.*, 7

box　はこ（箱）*n.*, 8

bracelets　ブレスレット　*n.*, 8S

(to) break a bone　ほねをおる（骨を折る）*exp.*, 12S

breakfast　あさごはん（朝御飯）*n.*, 5

briefcase, bag　かばん（鞄）*n.*, 1P, 4

briefs, shorts　パンツ　*n.*, 8

bright, cheerful　あかるい（明るい）い-adj., 3 10

(to) bring out　だす（出す）う-v., 8

(the speaker's) brother　あに（兄）n., 10

brown　ちゃいろい（茶色い）い-adj., 4

brush/es (one's) teeth　はを　みがきます（歯を磨きます）exp., 6S

Buddhist temple　（お）てら（（お）寺）n., 11

building　たてもの（建物）n., 3

bulletin board　けいじばん（掲示板）n., 4S

bus　バス　n., 6

business administration　けいえいがく（経営学）n., 2

business office　じむしつ（事務室）n., 4

businessman, company man　かいしゃいん（会社員）n., 10S

busy　いそがしい（忙しい）い-adj., 6

but　でも　conj., 7

buttocks　おしり（お尻）n., 10S

(to) buy　かう（買う）う-v., 6

by far, much more　ずっと　adv., 7

by means of, with　で　part., 6

by oneself, alone　ひとりで（一人で）adv., 6

C

cabbage　キャベツ　n., 7S

cabinet　とだな（戸棚）n., 3

cafeteria, dining room/hall　しょくどう（食堂）n., 4

cake　ケーキ　n., 9

calisthenics, gymnastics　たいそう（体操）n., 7S

(to) call, (to) invite　よぶ（呼ぶ）う-v., 9

came from 〜 (Polite)　〜から　いらっしゃいました。exp., 2

came from 〜 (Casual)　〜から　きました。（〜から来ました。）exp., 2

camping　キャンプ　n., 11

campus　キャンパス　n., 4

Can I help you?　なにを　さしあげましょうか。exp., 8P

Canada　カナダ　n., 2

Canadian　カナダじん（カナダ人）n., 2

cancer　がん（癌）n., 12P

candy　おかし　n., 1P

cap, hat　ぼうし（帽子）n., 8S

car　くるま（車）n., 6

carpet　じゅうたん　n., 3S

carrot　にんじん　n., 7

cat　ねこ（猫）n., 1P, 3

(to) catch (a cold)　ひく　う-v., 12

center　センター　n., 2P

ceremony　しき（式）n., 9

Certainly. (Polite)　かしこまりました。exp., 9P

chair　いす（椅子）n., 1P, 3

change (of money) (the same as おかえし)　おつり　n., 8P

change (of money)　おかえし　n., 8P

cheap, inexpensive　やすい（安い）い-adj., 8

cheek　ほっぺた　n., 10S

cheerful, bright　あかるい（明るい）い-adj., 3, 10

chemistry　かがく　n., 2S

chest　たんす（箪笥）n., 3

chicken　とりにく（鳥肉）n., 7S

chicken cutlet (breaded and deep-fried)　チキンかつ　n., 9S

child's room　こどもべや（子供部屋）n., 3S

chin　あご（顎）n., 10S

China　ちゅうごく（中国）n., 2

Chinese　ちゅうごくじん（中国人）n., 2

Chinese food　ちゅうかりょうり（中華料理）n., 9

Chinese-style fried rice　チャーハン　n., 9

cholesterol　コレステロール　n., 12P

chrysanthemum　きく　n., 1P

church　きょうかい（教会）n., 11

class　クラス　n., 6

class, course　じゅぎょう（授業）n., 5

classical music　クラシック　n., 7

classmate　クラスメート　n., 6

classroom　きょうしつ（教室）n., 4

tidy/tidies up a room　へやを　かたづけます（部屋を片付けます）exp., 6S

clean, neat; pretty　きれい（な）な-adj., 3

cleaning　そうじ（掃除）n., 6

clear weather　はれ　*n.*, 1P

(to) climb　のぼる（登る）う-*v.*, 11

(to) climb a mountain　やまにのぼる（山に登る）*exp.*, 11

clock; watch　とけい（時計）*n.*, 1P, 3

(Japanese-style) closet　おしいれ（押し入れ）*n.*, 3

(Western-style) closet　クローゼット　*n.*, 3S

closing of a letter (similar to *Sincerely*, *Best wishes*, etc.)　けいぐ（敬具）*n.*, 11P

closing phrase of a letter　そうそう（草々）*exp.*, 9P

clothing　ふく（服）*n.*, 8

cloud　くも　*n.*, 1P

coat　コート　*n.*, 8

coffee　コーヒー　*n.*, 5

coffee shop　きっさてん（喫茶店）*n.*, 4

cola　コーラ　*n.*, 7

cold　かぜ（風邪）*n.*, 12

cold　さむい（寒い）い-*adj.*, 11

(to) collect stamps　きってを　あつめる（切手を集める）*n.*, 7S

college student　だいがくせい（大学生）*n.*, 2

college, university　だいがく（大学）*n.*, 2

color　いろ（色）*n.*, 4

color blue, the　あお（青）*n.*, 7P

color red, the　あか（赤）*n.*, 7P

color white, the　しろ（白）*n.*, 7P

(to) come　くる（来る）*ir. v.*, 5

come/s　きます（来ます）*ir. v.*, 2P, 5

come/s (present tense, polite form)　いらっしゃいます　う-*v.*, 2P

(to) come out　でる（出る）る-*v.*, 12

company　かいしゃ（会社）*n.*, 10

company man, businessman　かいしゃいん（会社員）*n.*, 10S

computer　コンピュータ　*n.*, 3S, 4

computer game, family computer　ファミコン　*n.*, 7

computer science　コンピュータサイエンス　*n.*, 2S

condition　ちょうし（調子）*n.*, 12

confection　おかし（お菓子）*n.*, 1P

(to) convulse　けいれんする（痙攣する）*exp.*, 12S

(to) cook　りょうりをする（料理をする）*exp.*, 7

cooking; food (cuisine)　りょうり（料理）*n.*, 7

cool　すずしい（涼しい）い-*adj.*, 11

cotton　もめん（木綿）*n.*, 8S

cough　せき（咳）*n.*, 12

(to) cough　せきがでる（咳が出る）*exp.*, 12

counter for bound objects　〜さつ（〜冊）*count.*, 8

counter for fish and small four-legged animals　〜ひき（〜匹）*count.*, 8

counter for long cylindrical objects (e.g. pens, pencils, bottles)　〜ほん（〜本）*count.*, 8

counter for thin, flat objects (e.g., paper, shirts, plates)　〜まい（〜枚）*count.*, 8

country　くに（国）*n.*, 2

course, class　じゅぎょう（授業）*n.*, 5

(someone else's) cousin　いとこさん　*n.*, 10S

(the speaker's) cousin　いとこ　*n.*, 10S

cramped, narrow　せまい（狭い）い-*adj.*, 3

cream, off-white　クリームいろ（クリーム色）*n.*, 4S

(to) cry　なく（泣く）う-*v.*, 11

cucumber　きゅうり　*n.*, 1P, 7S

curry and rice dish　カレーライス　*n.*, 9

curtain　カーテン　*n.*, 3S

cushion for sitting on tatami floor　ざぶとん（座布団）*n.*, 3S

(to) cut　きる（切る）う-*v.*, 12

cute, adorable　かわいい　い-*adj.*, 10

(to) cycle　サイクリングに　いく（サイクリングに行く）*exp.*, 7S

D

daily goods　にちようひん（日用品）*n.*, 8P

daily life/activities, routine　せいかつ（生活）*n.*, 5

dark　くらい（暗い）　い-*adj.*, 3S
date　ひにち（日にち）　*n.*, 11P
dating　デート　*n.*, 11
(the speaker's) daughter　むすめ（娘）　*n.*, 2P
〜 day/s　〜にち（〜日）　*count.*, 11
〜 day/s of the week　〜ようび（〜曜日）　*suf.*, 5
December　じゅうにがつ（十二月）　*n.*, 5S
decide/s on 〜　〜に　します　*exp.*, 9
delicious, tasty, good　おいしい　い-*adj.*, 7
delicious thing/food　おいしいもの（おいしい物）　*n.*, 11
dentist　はいしゃ（歯医者）　*n.*, 10S
dentistry　しか（歯科）　*n.*, 12P
department store　デパート　*n.*, 4
department　うりば（売り場）　*n.*, 8
departure　しゅっぱつ　*n.*, 1P
dermatology　ひふか（皮膚科）　*n.*, 12P
desk　つくえ（机）　*n.*, 3
dessert　デザート　*n.*, 9
diabetes　とうにょうびょう（糖尿病）　*n.*, 12P
diary　にっき　*n.*, 1P
dictionary　じしょ（辞書）　*n.*, 4
difficult　むずかしい（難しい）　い-*adj.*, 6
(to) dine　しょくじをする（食事をする）　*ir. v.*, 7
dining　しょくじ（食事）　*n.*, 7
dining room/hall, cafeteria　しょくどう（食堂）　*n.*, 4
dinner, supper　ばんごはん（晩御飯）　*n.*, 5
dinner set　ていしょく（定食）　*n.*, 9S
direct object marker　を　*part.*, 5
dirty　きたない　い-*adj.*, 3S
discard/s trash　ゴミを　すてます（ゴミを捨てます）　*exp.*, 6S
disliked; hated　きらい（な）（嫌いな）　な-*adj.*, 7
dizzy　めまいがする　*exp.*, 12S
(to) do　する　*ir. v.*, 5
do/es the dishes　しょっきを　あらいます（食器を洗います）　*exp.*, 6S

do/es household work　かじを　します（家事をします）　*exp.*, 6S
do/es laundry　せんたくを　します（洗濯をします）　*exp.*, 6
Do you have 〜 ? ; Do you carry 〜 ?（literally, Isn't there 〜 ?）　〜は　ありませんか。　*exp.*, 8
doctor　いしゃ（医者）　*n.*, 1P, 10S, 12
dog　いぬ（犬）　*n.*, 1P, 3
doll　にんぎょう（人形）　*n.*, 1P
dollar/s　〜ドル　*count.*, 8P
door　ドア　*n.*, 3
dormitory　りょう　*n.*, 1P, 3
dress　ドレス　*n.*, 8S
drink, beverage　のみもの（飲み物）　*n.*, 7
(to) drink　のむ（飲む）　う-*v.*, 5
driving (pleasure driving)　ドライブ　*n.*, 7
drug, medicine　くすり（薬）　*n.*, 12

E

ear　みみ（耳）　*n.*, 1P, 10
earring　イヤリング　*n.*, 8S, 10
easy　やさしい（易しい）　い-*adj.*, 6
(to) eat　たべる（食べる）　る-*v.*, 5
eat-in kitchen　ダイニング　キッチン　*n.*, 3S
economics　けいざいがく（経済学）　*n.*, 2
editor　へんしゅうしゃ（編集者）　*n.*, 10P
education　きょういくがく（教育学）　*n.*, 2S
egg　たまご（卵）　*n.*, 7
eighteenth (day), the　じゅうはちにち（十八日）　*n.*, 5S
eighth (day), the　ようか（八日）　*n.*, 5S
(electric) train　でんしゃ（電車）　*n.*, 1P, 6
electricity, light　でんき（電気）　*n.*, 3S
elementary school　しょうがっこう（小学校）　*n.*, 10P, 11
elementary school student　しょうがくせい（小学生）　*n.*, 10S
elevator operator　エレベーターガール　*n.*, 8P
eleventh (day), the　じゅういちにち（十一日）　*n.*, 5S

elongated, long　ほそながい（細長い）
い-adj., 10

(to) become employed　つとめる（勤める）
る-v., 10

(to) be employed at, (to) work for　つとめて
いる（勤めている）る-v., 10

(to be) employed at a company　かいしゃに
つとめている（会社に勤めている）
exp., 10

end　はし（端）loc. n., 3S

(to) end, (to) be over　おわる（終わる）
う-v., 5

engineer　エンジニア　n., 10S

engineering　こうがく（工学）n., 2

England　イギリス　n., 2S

English　えいご（英語）n., 2

(to) enter, (to) take (a bath)　はいる（入る）
う-v., 5

(entrance examination) study　じゅけんべん
きょう（受験勉強）n., 11P

eraser　けしゴム（消しゴム）n., 4

errand　ようじ（用事）n., 9

especially, particularly　とくに（特に）
conj., 7P

evening, night　ばん（晩）n., 5

every ～　まい～（毎～）pref., 5

every day　まいにち（毎日）n., 5

every morning　まいあさ（毎朝）n., 5

every night　まいばん（毎晩）n., 5

examination, test　しけん（試験）n., 6

exchange student　りゅうがくせい（留学
生）n., 2

exchange student center　りゅうがくせいセ
ンター（留学生センター）n., 2P

(Eh,) excuse me　（あのう、）すみません。
exp., 1

Excuse me, but . . .　しつれいですが（失
礼ですが）exp., 4

Excuse me, but . . .　ちょっと　すみませ
んが（ちょっと　済みませんが）exp.,
4

Excuse me. (to get the attention of a
salesperson)　おねがいします（お願い
します）exp., 4

(physical) exercise　うんどう（運動）n., 6

(to) exist, (to) be　いる　る-v., 3 and
ある　う-v., 3

expensive　たかい（高い）い-adj., 1p, 8

experience　けいけん（経験）n., 11P

eye　め（目）n., 1P, 10

eyebrow　まゆ（眉）n., 10S

eyelash　まつげ（睫）n., 10S

F

face　かお（顔）n., 1P, 10

facial tone　かおいろ（顔色）n., 12

fall　あき（秋）n., 11

(to) fall in love　こいを　する（恋をする）
exp., 11S

(someone else's) family　ごかぞく（ご家族）
n., 10

(the speaker's) family　かぞく（家族）n.,
10　Kazoku

family computer, computer game　ファミコ
ン　n., 7

family room (Japanese-style)　いま（居間）
n., 3S

family room (Western-style)　リビングルー
ム　n., 3S

famous　ゆうめい（な）（有名な）な-
adj., 3

(to) be fat　ふとっている（太っている）
う-v., 10

(someone else's) father　おとうさん（お父
さん）n., 1P, 10

(the speaker's) father　ちち（父）n., 2P, 10

fax　ファックス　n., 3S

February　にがつ（二月）n., 5S

(to) feel dizzy　めまいがする　exp., 12S

(to) feel nauseated　きもちがわるい（気持
ちが悪い）exp., 12S

feeling　きぶん（気分）n., 12

feeling sick　きぶんがわるい（気分が悪
い）exp., 12

female　おんな（女）n., 2

festival　（お）まつり（（お）祭り）n., 11P

fever, temperature (body)　ねつ（熱）n., 12

a few; a little　すこし（少し）adv., 7

fifteenth (day), the　じゅうごにち（十五日）
n., 5S

fifth (day), the　いつか（五日）　n., 5S
fine arts　びじゅつ（美術）　n., 2S
fine, splendid　りっぱ（な）（立派な）な-adj., 1P, 3
finger　ゆび（指）　n., 1P, 10S, 12
first (day), the　ついたち（一日）　n., 5S
first year　いちねん（一年）　n., 2
first-year student, freshman　いちねんせい（一年生）　n., 2
fish　さかな（魚）　n., 7
fish market　さかなや（魚屋）　n., 4
fishing　つり（釣り）　n., 7S, 11
flag　はた（旗）　n., 2P
float　だし（山車）　n., 11P
～ floor/s of a building　～かい（～階）　count., 8
flower　はな（花）　n., 1P
flower arrangement (to arrange flowers)　いけばなを　する（生け花をする）　n., 3S, 7S
flute　ふえ（笛）　n., 1P
food　しょくひん（食品）　n., 8
food　たべもの（食べ物）　n., 7
food (cuisine); cooking　りょうり（料理）　n., 7
food department　しょくひんうりば（食品売場）　n., 8
food poisoning　しょくちゅうどく（食中毒）　n., 12P
foot, leg　あし（足/脚）　n., 1P, 10
(American) football　フットボール　n., 7
for the first time　はじめて（初めて）　adv., 11
fourteenth (day), the　じゅうよっか（十四日）　n., 5S
fourth (day), the　よっか（四日）　n., 5S
fourth-year student, senior　よねんせい（四年生）　n., 1
fracture　こっせつ（骨折）　n., 12P
France　フランス　n., 2
free, idling　ひま（な）な-adj., 6
freshman, first-year student　いちねんせい（一年生）　n., 2
Friday　きんようび（金曜日）　n., 5
(fried breaded) shrimp　えびフライ　n., 9S

friend　ともだち（友達）　n., 2
from　から　part., 2P, 5
from　を（as in じゅぎょうを　やすむ be absent from a class）　part., 12
from now on　いまから　exp., 5P
front entrance　げんかん（玄関）　n., 3S
fun　たのしい（楽しい）い-adj., 6
futon　ふとん（布団）　n., 3

G

(to) gain weight　ふとる（太る）う-v., 10
garage　ガレージ　n., 3S
garden, yard　にわ（庭）　n., 3S
general counter (Japanese origin number)　～つ　count., 8
gentle　やさしい（優しい）い-adj., 10
Germany　ドイツ　n., 2S
(to) get, (to) take　とる（取る）う-v., 8
(to) get on, (to) ride　のる（乗る）う-v., 11
(to) get on a plane　ひこうきにのる（飛行機に乗る）　exp., 11
(to) get up; (to) wake up　おきる（起きる）る-v., 5
gift　おくりもの（贈り物）　n., 8P
Gion Festival　ぎおんまつり（祇園祭り）　n., 11P
glasses　めがね（眼鏡）　n., 10
(to) go　いく（行く）う-v., 5
(to) go for a walk, (to) stroll　さんぽをします（散歩をします）　exp., 6S
(to) go hiking　ハイキングに　いく（ハイキングに行く）　exp., 7S
(to) go home, (to) return　かえる（帰る）う-v., 5
(to) go on a picnic　ピクニックに　いく（ピクニックに行く）　exp., 7S
(to) go out　でかける（出かける）る-v., 6
(to) go out on a date　デートをする　exp., 11
(to) go to a museum　はくぶつかんに　いく（博物館に行く）　exp., 7S
(to) go to an amusement park　ゆうえんちに　いく（遊園地にいく）　exp., 7S
(to) go to bed　ねる（寝る）る-v., 5

(to) go to the restroom　おてあらいに　い
きます（お手洗いに行きます）*exp.*,
6S

golf　ゴルフ　*n.*, 7

good　いい　い-*adj.*, 3

good, delicious, tasty　おいしい　い-*adj.*, 7

Good afternoon./Hello.　こんにちは。*exp.*,
1

good at, skillful　じょうず（な）（上手な）
な-*adj.*, 10

Good evening./Hello.　こんばんは。*exp.*, 1

Good morning./Hello.　おはよう　ござい
ます。*exp.*, 1

Good-bye.　さようなら。*exp.*, 1

Good-bye.　しつれいします。*exp.*, 1

gorgeous　りっぱ（な）（立派な）な-*adj.*, 3

graduate school　だいがくいん（大学院）
n., 2

graduate student　だいがくいんせい（大
学院生）*n.*, 2

graduation　そつぎょう（卒業）*n.*, 9

graduation ceremony　そつぎょうしき（卒
業式）*n.*, 9P

(someone else's) grandchild　おまごさん
（お孫さん）*n.*, 10S

(the speaker's) grandchild　まご（孫）*n.*,
10S

(someone else's) grandfather　おじいさん
（お祖父さん）*n.*, 1P, 10

(the speaker's) grandfather　そふ（祖父）*n.*,
10

(someone else's) grandmother　おばあさん
（お祖母さん）*n.*, 1P, 10

(the speaker's) grandmother　そぼ（祖母）
n., 10

grape　ぶどう　*n.*, 7S

gray　グレー　*n.*, 4S

great, impressive, splendid　すごい　い-*adj.*,
12P

green　みどり（緑）*n.*, 4

green pepper　ピーマン　*n.*, 7S

green tea　おちゃ（お茶）*n.*, 7S, 9

gym　たいいくかん（体育館）*n.*, 4

gymnastics, calisthenics　たいそう（体操）
n., 7S

gynecology　さんふじんか（産婦人科）
n., 12P

H

hair　かみ（髪）*n.*, 10

half year　はんとし（半年）*adv.*, 11

hallway　ろうか（廊下）*n.*, 3S

Halloween　ハロウィーン　*n.*, 11P

hamburger steak　ハンバーグ　*n.*, 9S

hamburger　ハンバーガー　*n.*, 9

hand　て（手）*n.*, 1P, 10

handbag　ハンドバッグ　*n.*, 8

handkerchief　ハンカチ　*n.*, 8S

happy, joyful　うれしい（嬉しい）い-*adj.*,
11

hard, tough, hectic　たいへん（な）（大変
な）な-*adj.*, 6

hat, cap　ぼうし（帽子）*n.*, 8S, 10

hated; disliked　きらい（な）（嫌いな）
な-*adj.*, 7

(to) have; (to) own　もっている（持って
いる）る-*v.*, 8

(to) have; (to) wear　する　*ir. v.*, 10

(to) have a burn　やけどをする（火傷を
する）*exp.*, 12S

(to) have a burning pain　ひりひりする
exp., 12S

(to) have a chill　さむけがする（寒気がす
る）*exp.*, 12S

(to) have a festering pain　ずきずきする
exp., 12S

(to) have a fight　けんかを　する　*exp.*,
11S

(to) have a hat on　ぼうしをかぶっている
（帽子をかぶっている）*exp.*, 10

(to) have a pounding headache　あたまが
がんがんする（頭ががんがんする）
exp., 12S

(to) have a sharp pain　きりきりする　*exp.*,
12S

(to) have a stiff shoulder　かたがこる（肩
が凝る）*exp.*, 12S

(to) have a stuffy nose　はながつまる（鼻
がつまる）*exp.*, 12

(to) have a traffic accident　こうつうじこに
あう（交通事故にあう）*exp.*, 11

(to) have diarrhea　げりをする（下痢をす
る）*exp.*, 12S

(to) have fun; (to) play　あそぶ（遊ぶ）う-
v., 7

(to) have nausea　きもちがわるい（気持
が悪い）、はきけがする（吐き気がす
る）*exp.*, 12S

(to) have no appetite　しょくよくがない
（食欲がない）*exp.*, 12S

(to) have on a skirt　スカートを　はいて
いる　る-*v.*, 10

hay fever　かふんびょう（花粉病）*n.*,
12P

head　あたま（頭）*n.*, 1P, 10

health insurance card　ほけんしょ（保険証）
n., 12P

healthy　げんき（な）（元気）な-*adj.*, 10

healthy　けんこう（な）（健康な）な-
adj., 12

heart disease　しんぞうびょう（心臓病）
n., 12P

heavy; serious (sickness)　おもい（重い）
い-*adj.*, 12

hectic, tough, hard　たいへん（な）（大変
な）な-*adj.*, 6

height of a person; back (body part)　せ（背）
n., 10

Heisei era, the (1989～)　へいせい（平成）
n., 11P

Hello (on the phone).　もしもし　*exp.*, 9

here, this place　ここ　*demo.*, 3

hiccup　しゃくり　*n.*, 1P

high, tall　たかい（高い）い-*adj.*, 1P, 3

high blood pressure　こうけつあつ（高血
圧）*n.*, 12P

high school　こうこう（高校）*n.*, 1P, 2

hiking　ハイキング　*n.*, 7

hip, lower back　こし（腰）*n.*, 10S, 12

history　れきし（歴史）*n.*, 2S

hobby　しゅみ（趣味）*n.*, 7

Hokkaidō (northernmost main island of Japan)
ほっかいどう（北海道）*n.*, 11P

(to) hold　もつ（持つ）う-*v.*, 8

holiday, vacation　やすみ（休み）*n.*, 11

home, house　うち（家）*n.*, 1P, 2P, 3

homework　しゅくだい（宿題）*n.*, 5

horse　うま　*n.*, 1P

hospital　びょういん（病院）*n.*, 4

(to) be hospitalized　にゅういんする（入
院する）*ir. v.*, 12

host family　ホストファミリー　*n.*, 2P

hot　あつい（暑い／熱い）い-*adj.*, 11

hot dog　ホットドッグ　*n.*, 9S

hotel　ホテル　*n.*, 12P

～ hour/s (duration)　～じかん（～時間）
count., 5

house, home　うち（家）*n.*, 1P, 2P, 3

How about ～?　どうですか。*exp.*, 7

How about ～?/How is ～? (polite form of ～
はどうですか)　～は　いかがでしょ
うか。*exp.*, 8P

How do you do?　はじめまして　*exp.*, 1

How do you say ～ in Japanese?　～は　に
ほんごで　なんと　いいますか。（～
は日本語で何と言いますか。）*exp.*, 1

How does it feel here?　ここは　どうです
か。*exp.*, 12S

How have you been? (literally, Are you
well/healthy?)　（お）げんきですか。（お
元気ですか。）*exp.*, 9P

How many ～ shall I give you?　なん～／い
くつ　さしあげましょうか。*exp.*, 8P

How many ～?/How old ～?　いくつ　*q.
word*, 8 10

How many ～?/How old ～? (Polite)　おいく
つ　*q. word*, 10

How much (money) ～?　いくら　*q. word*, 8

hundred　ひゃく（百）*n.*, 1P

hurting, painful　いたい（痛い）い-*adj.*, 12

(someone else's) husband　ごしゅじん（ご
主人）*n.*, 10

(the speaker's) husband　しゅじん（主人）
n., 10

(the speaker's) husband　おっと（夫）*n.*,
10S

I

I わたし（私）*pron.*, 2

I (normally used by a male) ぼく（僕） *pron.*, 2

I am sorry. すみません。*exp.*, 1

I am taking eight classes. じゅぎょうを やっつ とっています。*exp.*, 6P

I don't have class today. ぼくは きょう は じゅぎょうが ありません。*exp.*, 5P

I don't have any particular plans. とくに よていは ありません。（特に予定は ありません。）*exp.*, 9P

I don't know (my major) yet. （せんこうは） まだ わかりません。*exp.*, 2P

I don't mind. (Yes, please.) はい／ええ かまいません。*exp.*, 12

I don't need anything. なにも いりません。（何もいりません。）*exp.*, 9

I don't understand. わからないんですよ。*exp.*, 7P

I have a test tomorrow, so . . . あしたテス トが ありますから *exp.*, 5P

I have some errands to do. ちょっと よう じが あるんです。（ちょっと用事が あるんです。）*exp.*, 9

I see./Is that so./Really? そうですか。*exp.*, 2P

I see. /I will do it. /I understand. (Polite) はい かしこまりました。*exp.*, 8P

I would like to have ～. ～を おねがいし ます。（～をお願いします。）*exp.*, 9

I'm back. ただいま。*exp.*, 3

ice こおり *n.*, 1P

ice cream アイスクリーム *n.*, 9

idling, free ひま（な）*な-adj.*, 6

If it's OK . . . . よかったら *exp.*, 9P

impressive, great, splendid すごい *い-adj.*, 12P

in; at (point in time) に *part.*, 5

in addition, and, also それから, *conj.*, 7

in front of, in the front まえ（前）*loc. n.*, 3

in, inside なか（中）*loc. n.*, 3

in; at; on で *part.*, 5

Independence Day どくりつきねんび（独 立記念日）*n.*, 11P

Indian food インドりょうり（インド料 理）*n.*, 9S

inexpensive, cheap やすい（安い）*い-adj.*, 8

(to) inhale, (to) smoke すう（吸う）*う-v.*, 11

injury けが（怪我）*n.*, 12

inner part of (a house or room) おく（奥） *loc. n.*, 3S, 4P

inside, in なか（中）*loc. n.*, 3

intelligent; smart あたまがいい（頭がい い）*exp.*, 10

interesting おもしろい（面白い）*い-adj.*, 6

internal medicine ないか（内科）*n.*, 12P

intestine ちょう（腸）*n.*, 12S

(to) invite, (to) call よぶ（呼ぶ）*う-v.*, 9

Is it okay to do ～?/May I do～? ～てもい いですか／いいでしょうか／かまい ませんか *exp.*, 12

Is it okay to do ～?/May I do～? (Polite) ～てもよろしいですか／よろしいで しょうか *exp.*, 12S

Is this ～ residence? ～さんの おたくで すか。（～さんのお宅ですか。）*exp.*, 9

～ is/are (polite form of ～です) ～で ご ざいます *exp.*, 8P

isn't it (seeking confirmation) ね *part.*, 4

It is I who should be saying that. (Thank you.) こちらこそ。*exp.*, 2

It is probably a cold. たぶんかぜでしょう （たぶん風邪でしょう）*exp.*, 12

It's not really convenient./I already have plans. ちょっと つごうが わるいんです。 （ちょっと都合が悪いんです。）*exp.*, 9

It's been a long time since we last met. （お） ひさしぶり（お久しぶり）*exp.*, 9P

It's probably ～. たぶん ～でしょう。 *exp.*, 12P

Italian food イタリアりょうり（イタリ ア料理）*n.*, 9

Italy イタリア *n.*, 2S, 9

itchy かゆい（痒い）*い-adj.*, 12

J

jacket　ジャケット　*n.*, 8

January　いちがつ（一月）　*n.*, 5S

Japan　にほん（日本）　*n.*, 2

Japanese　にほんじん（日本人）　*n.*, 2

(Japanese buckwheat) noodles　そば（蕎麦）　*n.*, 9

Japanese dish consisting of beef slices and vegetables cooked together　すきやき　*n.*, 9S

Japanese food　にほんりょうり（日本料理）、わしょく（和食）　*n.*, 9

Japanese language　にほんご（日本語）　*n.*, 1P, 2

Japanese literature　にほんぶんがく（日本文学）　*n.*, 2

Japanese sake, alcoholic beverages　おさけ（お酒）　*n.*, 12

(Japanese wheat) noodles　うどん　*n.*, 9

(Japanese-style) closet　おしいれ（押し入れ）　*n.*, 3

(Japanese-style) room　わしつ（和室）　*n.*, 3S

jazz　ジャズ　*n.*, 7

jeans　ジーンズ　*n.*, 8

(permanent) job, work　しごと（仕事）　*n.*, 6

jogging　ジョギング　*n.*, 5P, 7

joyful, happy　うれしい（嬉しい）　い-*adj.*, 11

judo　じゅうどう（柔道）　*n.*, 7S

juice　ジュース　*n.*, 7S, 9

July　しちがつ（七月）　*n.*, 5S

June　ろくがつ（六月）　*n.*, 5S

junior high school (shortened form of ちゅうがっこう中学校)　ちゅうがく（中学）　*n.*, 11

junior high school student　ちゅうがくせい（中学生）　*n.*, 10S

junior, third-year student　さんねんせい（三年生）　*n.*, 2

K

karaoke singing　カラオケでうたう（カラオケで歌う）　*n.*, 7S

karate　からて（空手）　*n.*, 7S

kendo (Japanese-style fencing)　けんどう（剣道）　*n.*, 7S

key　かぎ　*n.*, 1P

kimono; traditional Japanese clothes　きもの（着物）　*n.*, 11

kind　しんせつ（な）（親切な）　な-*adj.*, 10

(to) kiss　キスを　する　*exp.*, 11S

kitchen　だいどころ（台所）　*n.*, 3P

knee　ひざ　*n.*, 1P

Korean cuisine　かんこくりょうり（韓国料理）　*n.*, 9S

L

Labor Day　レーバーデー　*n.*, 11P

laboratory　ラボ　*n.*, 4

lamp　スタンド　*n.*, 3

language　〜ご（〜語）　*suf.*, 2

large, big　おおきい（大きい）　い-*adj.*, 1P, 3

last month　せんげつ（先月）　*n.*, 11

last name　みょうじ　*n.*, 1P

last week　せんしゅう（先週）　*n.*, 6

last year　きょねん（去年）　*n.*, 11

(to) laugh; (to) smile　わらう（笑う）　う-*v.*, 11

laundry　せんたく（洗濯）　*n.*, 6

law school　ほうがくぶ（法学部）　*n.*, 4

lawyer　べんごし（弁護士）　*n.*, 10S

left end　ひだりはし（左端）　*loc. n.*, 3S

(to the) left, left side　ひだりがわ（左側）　*loc. n.*, 3

leaf　はっぱ　*n.*, 1P

leg, foot　あし（足/脚）　*n.*, 1P, 10

leisure　レジャー　*n.*, 7

letter　てがみ（手紙）　*n.*, 6

lettuce　レタス　*n.*, 7

library　としょかん（図書館）　*n.*, 4

light, electricity　でんき（電気）　*n.*, 3S

light (weight)　かるい（軽い）　い-*adj.*, 12

light blue　みずいろ（水色）*n.*, 4S

light green　きみどり（黄緑）*n.*, 4S

liked (very much)　だいすき（な）（大好きな）*な-adj.*, 7

like　すき（な）（好きな）*な-adj.*, 4P, 7

lip　くちびる（唇）*n.*, 10S

(to) listen　きく（聞く）*う-v.*, 11S

literature　ぶんがく（文学）*n.*, 2

a little; a few　すこし（少し）*adv.*, 7

a little bit　ちょっと　*adv.*, 9

a little more　もうすこし（もう少し）*adv.*, 8

(to) live, (to) reside　すむ（住む）*う-v.*, 10

(to) live in a foreign country　がいこくにすむ（外国に住む）*exp.*, 11S

(to) live in an apartment　アパートにすんでいる（アパートに住んでいる）*exp.*, 10

lively　にぎやか（な）（賑やかな）*な-adj.*, 3S

live/s, reside/s　すんでいます（住んでいます）*る-v.*, 3P, 10

living-room　リビングルーム　*n.*, 3S

lonely　さびしい（寂しい）*い-adj.*, 11

long　ながい（長い）*い-adj.*, 1P, 10

long, elongated　ほそながい（細長い）*い-adj.*, 10

(to) look older than (one's) age　としうえにみられる（年上にみられる）*exp.*, 10P

(to) lose consciousness　きをうしなう（気を失う）*exp.*, 12S

(to) lose weight　やせる、*る-v.*, 10

a lot, much, many　たくさん　*adv.*, 4P, 8

low; short (height)　ひくい（低い）*い-adj.*, 1P, 3S, 10

lower back, hip　こし（腰）*n.*, 10S, 12

lunch　ひるごはん（昼御飯）*n.*, 5

M

magazine　ざっし（雑誌）*n.*, 1P, 6

main entrance　せいもん（正門）*n.*, 4S

major　せんこう（専攻）*n.*, 2

(to) make　つくる（作る）*う-v.*, 6

(to) make (a telephone call)　（電話を）かける *る-v.*, 6

male　おとこ（男）*n.*, 2

man　おとこのひと（男の人）*n.*, 2

manager　マネージャー　*n.*, 10S

mandarin orange　みかん　*n.*, 7S

man's dress shirt　ワイシャツ　*n.*, 8S

many, much, a lot　たくさん, *adv.*, 4P, 8

map　ちず　*n.*, 1P

March　さんがつ（三月）*n.*, 5S

(to) marry　けっこんする（結婚する）*ir. v.*, 10

mathematics　すうがく（数学）*n.*, 2S

matter, thing (intangible, often refers to activities and happenings)　こと　*n.*, 11

May　ごがつ（五月）*n.*, 5S

May I do～?/Is it okay to do ～?　～てもいいですか／いいでしょうか／かまいませんか　*exp.*, 12

May I do～?/Is it okay to do ～? (Polite)　～てもよろしいですか／よろしいでしょうか　*exp.*, 12S

May I help you?　なにか　おさがしでしょうか。*exp.*, 8P

measles　はしか　*n.*, 12P

measure　はかる（計る）*う-v.*, 12

meat　にく（肉）*n.*, 1P, 7

medical science　いがく（医学）*n.*, 2S

medicine, drug　くすり（薬）*n.*, 1P, 12

(to) meet　あう（会う）*う-v.*, 9

Meiji Era, the (1868–1911)　めいじ（明治）*n.*, 11P

melon　メロン　*n.*, 7S

memories　おもいで（思い出）*n.*, 11P

menswear　しんしふく（紳士服）*n.*, 8

menswear department　しんしふくうりば（紳士服売り場）*n.*, 8

Mexican　メキシコじん（メキシコ人）*n.*, 2

Mexican cuisine　メキシコりょうり（メキシコ料理）*n.*, 9S

Mexico　メキシコ　*n.*, 2

microwave oven　でんしレンジ（電子レンジ）*n.*, 3S

milk　ミルク、ぎゅうにゅう　*n.*, 1P, 7S, 9

～ minute/s　～ふん（～分）*count.*, 5

(fashion) model　モデル　*n.*, 10P
Monday　げつようび（月曜日）*n.*, 5
money　（お）かね（お金）*n.*, 11
(specific) month　〜がつ（〜月）*count.*, 11
month/s (duration)　〜かげつ（〜か月）
　　count., 6, 11
moon　つき（月）*n.*, 1P
more　もっと, *adv.*, 8
morning　あさ（朝）*n.*, 1, 5
most, best　いちばん（一番）*adv.*, 4P
(someone else's) mother　おかあさん（お母
　　さん）*n.*, 1P, 10
(the speaker's) mother　はは（母）*n.*, 2P, 10
mountain　やま（山）*n.*, 1P, 7
mouth　くち（口）*n.*, 1P, 10
movie　えいが（映画）*n.*, 5
Mr./Mrs./Miss/Ms.　〜　〜さん　*suf.*, 1
much more, by far　ずっと　*adv.*, 7
much, many, a lot　たくさん　*adv.*, 4P, 8
museum　はくぶつかん（博物館）*n.*, 11
music　おんがく（音楽）*n.*, 2S, 6
music department　レコードうりば（レコ
　　ード売り場）*n.*, 8
musical instrument　がっき（楽器）*n.*, 1P
mustache, beard　ひげ（髭）*n.*, 1P, 10S
mustard　からし　*n.*, 1P
My name is 〜. Is 〜 home?　〜ですが、
　　〜さんは　いらっしゃいますか。
　　exp., 9

N

nail　つめ（爪）*n.*, 10S
name　なまえ（名前）*n.*, 2
name (Polite)　おなまえ（御名前）*n.*, 2P
name of the current reign　へいせい（平成）
　　n., 11P
narrow, cramped　せまい（狭い）*い-adj.*,
　　3
national flag　こっき（国旗）*n.*, 1P
nationality　〜じん（〜人）*suf.*, 2
near; vicinity　ちかく（近く）*loc. n.*, 3
neat, clean; pretty　きれい（な）*な-adj.*, 3
neck　くび（首）*n.*, 10S, 12S
necklace　ネックレス　*n.*, 8
neighborhood　きんじょ　*n.*, 1P

(someone else's) nephew　おいごさん（甥
　　子さん）*n.*, 10S
(the speaker's) nephew　おい（甥）*n.*, 10S
new　あたらしい（新しい）*い-adj.*, 3
New Year's card　ねんがじょう（年賀状）
　　n., 9P
New Year's Day　（お）しょうがつ（（お）
　　正月）*n.*, 1P, 11P
New Zealand　ニュージーランド　*n.*, 2
newspaper　しんぶん（新聞）*n.*, 6
next　つぎ（次）*n.*, 8P
next month　らいげつ（来月）*n.*, 11
next time, this time　こんど（今度）*adv.*,
　　11
next to　となり（隣り）*loc. n.*, 3
next to, at the side of　よこ（横）*loc. n.*, 3
next week　らいしゅう（来週）*n.*, 6
nice, attractive　すてき（な）（素敵な）
　　な-adj., 3
(someone else's) niece　めいごさん（姪子
　　さん）*n.*, 10S
(the speaker's) niece　めい（姪）*n.*, 10S
night　よる（夜）*n.*, 1P
night, evening　ばん（晩）*n.*, 5
nineteenth (day), the　じゅうくにち（十九
　　日）*n.*, 5S
ninth (day), the　ここのか（九日）*n.*, 5S
no　いいえ　*interj.*, 2
No, I don't mind. (Yes, please.)　はい／え
　　え、かまいません。*exp.*, 12
No, I still have a long way to go.　いいえ、
　　まだまだです。*exp.*, 10
No, not (to) that extent.　いいえ、それほ
　　どじゃありません。*exp.*, 10
No, thank you.　いいえ、けっこうです。
　　exp., 9
No, that's not so.　いいえ、そうじゃあり
　　ません。*exp.*, 2
No, that's not the case.　いいえ、そんなこ
　　とは　ありません。*exp.*, 10
(Japanese buckwheat) noodles　そば（蕎麦）
　　n., 9
(Japanese wheat) noodles　うどん　*n.*, 9
nose　はな（鼻）*n.*, 1P, 10

not at all (used with the negative form of verbs)　ぜんぜん（全然）*adv.*, 5

not worried about 〜　〜の　ことは　しんぱいしていません。*exp.*, 6P

notebook　ノート　*n.*, 4

noun modifier marker (of)　の　*part.*, 2

November　じゅういちがつ（十一月）*n.*, 5S

now　いま（今）*n.*, 2P, 5

number　ばんごう（番号）*n.*, 9

O

〜 o'clock　〜じ（〜時）*count.*, 5

ocean, sea　うみ（海）*n.*, 11

October　じゅうがつ（十月）*n.*, 5S

off-white, cream　クリームいろ（クリーム色）*n.*, 4S

often　よく，*adv.*, 5

oh　ああ　*exp.*, 3

old　ふるい（古い）い-*adj.*, 3

(someone else's) older brother　おにいさん（お兄さん）*n.*, 1P, 10

older person　としうえ（年上）*n.*, 10P

(someone else's) older sister　おねえさん　*n.*, 1P, 10

(the speaker's) older sister　あね（姉）*n.*, 1P, 10

on; at; in　で　*part.*, 5

on foot　あるいて（歩いて）*adv.*, 6

on, above, over　うえ（上）*loc. n.*, 3

one person　ひとり（一人）*count.*, 10

onion　たまねぎ　*n.*, 7S

open　あける（開ける）る-*v.*, 12P

opening phrase of a letter　はいけい（拝啓）*n.*, 11P

(abbreviated) opening phrase of a letter　ぜんりゃく（前略）exp., 9P, 11P

ophthalmology　がんか（眼科）*n.*, 12P

opposite side, across (the street)　むかい（向かい）*loc. n.*, 3S

orange　オレンジ　*n.*, 4S, 7

orange juice　オレンジジュース　*n.*, 9

order　ちゅうもんする（注文する）*ir. v.*, 9

orthopedics; reconstructive surgery　せいけいげか（整形外科）*n.*, 12P

other than 〜　ほかに，*conj.*, 12P

otorhinolaryngology　じびいんこうか（耳鼻咽喉科）*n.*, 12P

outside　そと（外）*loc. n.*, 3

over; above; on　うえ（上）*loc. n.*, 3

over there, that place　あそこ　*demo.*, 3

overstrain; overwork　むり（無理）*n.*, 12

(to) overstrain, (to) overwork　むりをする（無理をする）*exp.*, 12

(to) own; (to) have　もっている（持っている）る-*v.*, 8

P

painful, hurting　いたい（痛い）い-*adj.*, 12

pants, trousers　ズボン　*n.*, 8

paper sliding door　しょうじ（障子）*n.*, 3S

(the speaker's) parents　りょうしん（両親）*n.*, 6

(someone else's) parents　ごりょうしん（御両親）*n.*, 6

park　こうえん（公園）*n.*, 4

parking lot/garage　ちゅうしゃじょう（駐車場）*n.*, 4S

part-time job　アルバイト　*n.*, 5P, 6

particularly, especially　とくに（特に）*conj.*, 7P

partner　パートナー　*n.*, 2P

party　パーティ　*n.*, 7

pasta　パスタ　*n.*, 9S

pediatrics　しょうにか（小児科）*n.*, 12P

pencil　えんぴつ（鉛筆）*n.*, 1P, 4

people, person　ひと（人）*n.*, 1P, 2, 2P

permanent job, work　しごと（仕事）*n.*, 6

person (polite version of ひと)　かた（方）*n.*, 10

person, people　ひと（人）*n.*, 1P, 2, 2P

〜 people　〜にん（〜人）*count.*, 10

personality　せいかく（性格）*n.*, 10

photograph　しゃしん（写真）*n.*, 1P, 3

physics　ぶつりがく（物理学）*n.*, 2S

picture　え（絵）n., 1P, 3, 7

pie　パイ　*n.*, 9S

pink　ピンク　*n.*, 4S

pizza　ピザ　*n.*, 9

place　ところ（所）　*n.*, 4

(to) play a game　ゲームをする　*exp.*, 7S

(to) play pachinko　パチンコを　する, *n.*, 7S

(to) play the piano　ピアノを　ひく　*n.*, 7S

(to) play; (to) have fun　あそぶ（遊ぶ）う-*v.*, 7

player (on a sports team)　せんしゅ（選手）　*n.*, 10P

playing catch　キャッチボール　*n.*, 7S

please　どうぞ, *adv.*, 3

Please come in.　どうぞ　あがってください。　*exp.*, 3

Please don't bother.　どうぞ　おかまいなく。　*exp.*, 9

Please exhale.　いきを　はいてください。　*exp.*, 12S

Please give me 〜.　〜を　ください（〜を下さい）　*exp.*, 8

Please hold your breath.　いきを　とめてください。　*exp.*, 12S

Please lie down.　よこに　なってください。　*exp.*, 12S

Please lie face down.　うつぶせに　なってください。　*exp.*, 12S

Please lie on your back.　あおむけに　なってください。　*exp.*, 12S

Please listen.　きいて　ください。（聞いて下さい。）　*exp.*, 1

Please look (at it).　みて　ください。（見て下さい。）　*exp.*, 1

Please open your mouth wide.　くちを　おおきく　あけてください。（口を大きくあけてください。）　exp., 12S

Please read.　よんで　ください。（読んで下さい。）　*exp.*, 1

Please say it again.　もう　いちど　いってください。（もう一度言って下さい。）　*exp.*, 1

Please say it simply.　やさしい　ことばでいってください。　*exp.*, 8

Please say it slowly.　ゆっくり　いってください。　*exp.*, 1

Please say it. /Repeat after me.　いって ください。　*exp.*, 1

Please speak loudly.　おおきい　こえではなして　ください。　*exp.*, 1

Please speak slowly.　ゆっくり　はなしてください。　*exp.*, 1

Please take a deep breath.　おおきく　いきを　すってください。（大きくいきをすってください。）　*exp.*, 12S

Please take off your top (shirt, blouse, etc.).　うえだけ　ぬいでください。（上だけぬいでください。）　*exp.*, 12S

Please turn around.　うしろを　むいてください。　*exp.*, 12S

Please wait a moment. (Polite)　しょうしょう　おまちください。　*exp.*, 8P

Please write.　かいて ください。　*exp.*, 1

Pleased to meet you.　どうぞ　よろしく。　*exp.*, 1

police box　こうばん（交番）　*n.*, 4

polite prefix　お〜（御〜）*pref.*, 2P, 5, 9

political science　せいじがく（政治学）　*n.*, 2S

pond　いけ（池）　*n.*, 1P

pops (popular music)　ポップス　*n.*, 7

pork　ぶたにく（豚肉）　*n.*, 7S

pork cutlet (breaded and deep-fried)　とんかつ（豚かつ）　*n.*, 9S

post office　ゆうびんきょく（郵便局）　*n.*, 4

postcard　はがき（葉書）　*n.*, 9

potted plants　はちうえ（鉢植え）　*n.*, 3S

present　プレゼント　*n.*, 8P

pretty; clean　きれい（な）　*な-adj.*, 3

private tutor　かていきょうし　*n.*, 5R

professor, teacher　せんせい（先生）　*n.*, 2

Professor 〜　〜せんせい（〜先生）　*suf.*, 1

professor's office; research room　けんきゅうしつ（研究室）　*n.*, 4

psychiatry　せいしんか（精神科）　*n.*, 12P

psychology　しんりがく（心理学）　*n.*, 2S

purple　むらさき（紫）*n.*, 4S
(to) put in　いれる（入れる）る-*v.*, 8
(to) put on (glasses)　かける、る-*v.*, 10
(to) put on (a hat, a cap)　かぶる、う-*v.*, 10
(to) put on (a skirt, pants, socks)　はく、う-*v.*, 10
(to) put on (a sweater, shirt, jacket)　きる（着る）る-*v.*, 10

Q

question marker　か　*part.*, 2
quiet　しずか（な）（静かな）な-*adj.*, 3
quite　ずいぶん, *adv.*, 4P

R

radio cassette player　ラジカセ　*n.*, 3S
rain　あめ　*n.*, 1P
ramen (Chinese noodles in soup)　ラーメン　*n.*, 9
(to) read　よむ（読む）う-*v.*, 5
Really?/I see./Is that so.　そうですか。*exp.*, 2P
reconstructive surgery; orthopedics　せいけいげか（整形外科）*n.*, 12P
record　レコード　*n.*, 8
red　あかい（赤い）い-*adj.*, 1P, 4
refrigerator　れいぞうこ（冷蔵庫）*n.*, 3S
(someone else's) relatives　ごしんせき（ご親戚）*n.*, 10S
(the speaker's) relatives　しんせき（親戚）*n.*, 10S
rent/s a video　ビデオをかります（ビデオを借ります）*exp.*, 6
report, term paper　レポート　*n.*, 6
research room; professor's office　けんきゅうしつ（研究室）*n.*, 4
(to) reside, (to) live　すむ（住む）う-*v.*, 10
(to) rest　やすむ（休む）う-*v.*, 12
rest room　おてあらい（お手洗）*n.*, 3P
restaurant　レストラン　*n.*, 4
resultant state　〜ている　*aux.*, 10
(to) return, (to) go home　かえる（帰る）う-*v.*, 5
(to) ride, (to) get on　のる（乗る）う-*v.*, 11
right angle　ちょっかく　*n.*, 1P

right end, the　みぎはし（右端）*loc. n.*, 3S
(to the) right, right side　みぎがわ（右側）*loc. n.*, 3
ring　ゆびわ（指輪）*n.*, 8S
river　かわ（川）*n.*, 1P
rock and roll　ロック　*n.*, 7
room　へや（部屋）*n.*, 3
(Japanese-style) room　わしつ（和室）*n.*, 3S
(Western-style) room　ようしつ（洋室）*n.*, 3S
roommate　ルームメート　*n.*, 6
round　まるい（丸い）い-*adj.*, 10
routine, daily life/activities　せいかつ（生活）*n.*, 5
(to) run a fever　ねつがでる（熱が出る）*exp.*, 12
Russia　ロシア　*n.*, 2S
Russian cuisine　ロシアりょうり（ロシア料理）*n.*, 9S

S

sad　かなしい（悲しい）い-*adj.*, 11
sake　さけ　*n.*, 1P
salad　サラダ　*n.*, 9
sales clerk　てんいん（店員）*n.*, 7P, 8P
sales tax　しょうひぜい（消費税）*n.*, 8P
salt　しお　*n.*, 1P
sandal　サンダル　*n.*, 8S
sandwich　サンドイッチ　*n.*, 9
sashimi (filet of fresh raw fish, such as tuna)　（お）さしみ（御刺身）*n.*, 9
Saturday　どようび（土曜日）*n.*, 5
scallion　ねぎ　*n.*, 7S
scarf　スカーフ　*n.*, 8S
school　がっこう（学校）*n.*, 1P, 4
school cafeteria (often shortened to がくしょく)　がくせいしょくどう（学生食堂）*n.*, 4S
school of ～　～がくぶ（～学部）*suf.*, 4
school of economics　けいざいがくぶ（経済学部）*n.*, 4
school of engineering　こうがくぶ（工学部）*n.*, 4

school of liberal arts　きょうようがくぶ（教養学部）*n.*, 4

sea, ocean　うみ（海）*n.*, 11

season　きせつ（季節）*n.*, 11

second (day), the　ふつか（二日）*n.*, 5S

second-year student, sophomore　にねんせい（二年生）*n.*, 2

(to) see, (to) watch　みる（見る）る-*v.*, 5

See you later.　じゃあ、また。*exp.*, 1

self-employed　じえいぎょう（自営業）*n.*, 10S

senior high school　こうこう（高校）*n.*, 10P

senior high school student　こうこうせい（高校生）*n.*, 10P

senior, fourth-year student　よねんせい（四年生）*n.*, 1

September　くがつ（九月）*n.*, 5S

serious (injury)　ひどい　い-*adj.*, 11

serious (sickness); heavy　おもい（重い）い-*adj.*, 12

(lunch, dinner) set　ていしょく（定食）*n.*, 9S

seventeenth (day), the　じゅうしちにち（十七日）*n.*, 5S

seventh (day), the　なのか（七日）*n.*, 5S

Shinto shrine　じんじゃ（神社）*n.*, 11

shirt　シャツ　*n.*, 8

shoes　くつ（靴）*n.*, 8

(Japanese) shoe-shelf　げたばこ（下駄箱）*n.*, 3S

shopping　かいもの（買物）*n.*, 6

short (height); low　ひくい（低い）い-*adj.*, 9

short (length)　みじかい（短い）い-*adj.*, 1P, 10

shorts, briefs　パンツ　*n.*, 7

shoulder　かた（肩）*n.*, 12S

show　みせる（見せる）る-*v.*, 7

Showa Era, the (1926–1989)　しょうわ（昭和）*n.*, 11P

shower　シャワー　*n.*, 3S, 5

shrimp　えび（海老）*n.*, 7S

shrimp (fried breaded)　えびフライ　*n.*, 9S

(to) become sick　びょうきに　なる（病気になる）*exp.*, 11S

sickness　びょうき（病気）*n.*, 1P, 12

(at the) side of, next to　よこ（横）*loc. n.*, 3

silk　シルク　*n.*, 8S

similarity marker (also, too)　も　*part.*, 1

sing　うたう（歌う）う-*v.*, 7

(someone else's) sisters　ごしまい（御姉妹）*n.*, 10

(the speaker's) sisters　しまい（姉妹）*n.*, 10

sixteenth (day), the　じゅうろくにち（十六日）*n.*, 5S

sixth (day), the　むいか（六日）*n.*, 5S

skating　スケート　*n.*, 7S

skiing　スキー　*n.*, 7

skillful, good at　じょうず（な）（上手な）な-*adj.*, 10

skirt　スカート　*n.*, 8

slippers　スリッパ　*n.*, 8S

small　ちいさい（小さい）い-*adj.*, 1P, 3

smart; intelligent　あたまがいい（頭がいい）*exp.*, 10

(to) smile; (to) laugh　わらう（笑う）う-*v.*, 11

(to) smoke, (to) inhale　すう（吸う）う-*v.*, 11

(to) smoke a cigarette　たばこをすう（たばこを吸う）*exp.*, 11

sneaker　スニーカー　*n.*, 8S

snow　ゆき　*n.*, 1P

snow festival in Sapporo　ゆきまつり（雪祭り）*n.*, 11P

so　そう　*pron.*, 2

so, therefore　ですから　*conj.*, 5P

soap　せっけん（石鹸）*n.*, 1P, 3S, 8

soccer　サッカー　*n.*, 7S

sociology　しゃかいがく（社会学）*n.*, 2S

socks　くつした（靴下）*n.*, 8

sofa　ソファ　*n.*, 3

softball　ソフトボール　*n.*, 7S

sometimes　ときどき（時々）*adv.*, 5

son　むすこ（息子）*n.*, 3P

song　うた（歌）*n.*, 7

sophomore, second-year student　にねんせい（二年生）*n.*, 2

Sorry. (Colloquial)　ごめんなさい。（御免なさい。）*exp.*, 10P

sorry, unfortunate　ざんねん（な）（残念な）な-*adj.*, 6

soup　スープ　*n.*, 9

South Korea　かんこく（韓国）*n.*, 2

spacious, wide　ひろい（広い）い-*adj.*, 3

spaghetti　スパゲティ　*n.*, 9

Spain　スペイン　*n.*, 2

Spanish cuisine　スペインりょうり（スペイン料理）*n.*, 9S

Spanish language　スペインご（スペイン語）*n.*, 2

spinach　ほうれんそう　*n.*, 7S

splendid, fine　りっぱ（な）（立派な）な-*adj.*, 3

splendid, great, impressive　すごい　い-*adj.*, 12P

sports　スポーツ　*n.*, 7

(to) sprain　ねんざする（捻挫する）*exp.*, 12S

spring　はる（春）*n.*, 11

spring vacation　はるやすみ（春休み）*n.*, 11

square　しかくい（四角い）い-*adj.*, 10

St. Valentine's Day　バレンタインデー　*n.*, 11P

stamp　きって　*n.*, 1P

star　ほし　*n.*, 1P

state (in the United States, Canada, and Australia)　しゅう（州）*n.*, 7P

station　えき（駅）*n.*, 1P, 4

stationery　ぶんぼうぐ（文房具）*n.*, 8

stationery department　ぶんぼうぐうりば（文房具売り場）*n.*, 8

stereo　ステレオ　*n.*, 3

stomach　い（胃）*n.*, 12S

stomach, belly　おなか（お腹）*n.*, 10S, 12

(to) stop　とまる（止まる）う-*v.*, 8P

storage　ものおき（物置）*n.*, 3S

strange　へん（な）（変な）な-*adj.*, 11

strawberry　いちご（苺）*n.*, 7S

street　とおり　*n.*, 1P

(to) stroll, (to) go for a walk　さんぽをします（散歩をします）*exp.*, 6S

student　がくせい（学生）*n.*, 1P, 2

-student　〜せい（〜生）*suf.*, 2

student union　がくせいかいかん（学生会館）*n.*, 4

study　べんきょう（勉強）*n.*, 5

study for entrance examination　じゅけんべんきょう（受験勉強）*n.*, 11P

study of 〜　〜がく（〜学）*suf.*, 2

(to) stuff　つまる（詰まる）う-*v.*, 12

subject marker　が　*part.*, 4

(to) suffer, (to) be annoyed, be troubled　こまる（困る）う-*v.*, 12

sugar　さとう　*n.*, 1P

suit (clothing)　スーツ　*n.*, 10

summer　なつ（夏）*n.*, 11

summer vacation　なつやすみ（夏休み）*n.*, 11

Sunday　にちようび（日曜日）*n.*, 5

supermarket　スーパー　*n.*, 4

supper, dinner　ばんごはん（晩御飯）*n.*, 5

Sure./Yes, of course.　はい／ええ　もちろん。*exp.*, 12

surgery　げか（外科）*n.*, 12P

surgical operation　しゅじゅつ（手術）*n.*, 7P

sushi　（お）すし（御寿司）*n.*, 9

(to) sweat　あせをかく（汗をかく）*exp.*, 12S

sweater　セーター　*n.*, 8

(to) swim　およぐ（泳ぐ）う-*v.*, 7

swimming　すいえい（水泳）*n.*, 7S

switch　スイッチ　*n.*, 3S

symptom　しょうじょう（症状）*n.*, 12

T

T-shirt　Tシャツ　*n.*, 8

table　テーブル　*n.*, 3

tableware　しょっき（食器）*n.*, 1P, 8P

tail　しっぽ　*n.*, 1P

Taishō Era, the (1912–1925)　たいしょう（大正）*n.*, 11P

Taiwan　たいわん（台湾）*n.*, 2P
(to) take, (to) get　とる（取る）う-*v.*, 7, 8
(to) take (a bath); (to) enter　はいる（入る）
　う-*v.*, 5
(to) take (a picture)　（しゃしんを）とる
　（写真を）とる　*exp.*, 7
(to) take (a shower)　あびる（浴びる）る-
　v., 5
Take good care of yourself.　おからだをた
　いせつに（お体を大切に）*exp.*, 11P
Take good care of yourself.　おだいじに
　（お大事に）*exp.*, 12
(to) take out the trash　ゴミを　だします
　（ゴミを出します）*exp.*, 6S
(to) talk　はなす（話す）う-*v.*, 6
tall, high　たかい（高い）い-*adj.*, 1P, 3
tasty, delicious, good　おいしい　い-*adj.*, 7
tatami mat　たたみ（畳）*n.*, 3S
teacher, professor　せんせい（先生）、き
　ょういん（教員）*n.*, 1P, 2, 10S
telephone　でんわ（電話）*n.*, 1P, 3
telephone number　でんわばんごう（電話
　番号）*n.*, 9
television　テレビ　*n.*, 3
temperature (body), fever　ねつ（熱）*n.*, 12
tennis　テニス　*n.*, 7
tempura　てんぷら（天麩羅）*n.*, 1P, 9
tempura dinner　てんぷらていしょく（て
　んぷら定食）*n.*, 9S
the tenth (day)　とおか（十日）*n.*, 5S
term paper, report　レポート　*n.*, 6
test, examination　しけん（試験）*n.*, 6
test　テスト　*n.*, 6
textbook　きょうかしょ（教科書）*n.*, 4
～ th (ordinal)　～ばんめ（～番目）
　count., 10
Thank you.　ありがとうございます。
　exp., 1
Thank you (for allowing me to come in).　お
　じゃまします。*exp.*, 3
Thank you. (It is I who should be saying that.)
　こちらこそ。*exp.*, 2
Thank you for waiting.　たいへん　おまた
　せいたしました。*exp.*, 8P

Thank you very much.　どうも　ありがと
　うございます。*exp.*, 3
Thanksgiving　サンクスギビング　*n.*, 11P
that + noun　その　*demo.*, 3
that + noun over there　あの　*demo.*, 3
that, that one close by　それ　*demo.*, 4
that, that one over there　あれ　*demo.*, 4
there, that place　そこ　*demo.*, 3
therefore, so　ですから，*conj.*, 5P
thing (tangible)　もの（物）*n.*, 11
thing, matter (intangible, often refers to
　activities and happenings)　こと（事）*n.*,
　11
third (day), the　みっか（三日）*n.*, 5S
third-year student, junior　さんねんせい
　（三年生）*n.*, 2
thirteenth (day), the　じゅうさんにち（十
　三日）*n.*, 5S
thirtieth (day), the　さんじゅうにち（三十
　日）*n.*, 5S
thirty-first (day), the　さんじゅういちにち
　（三十一日）*n.*, 5S
This is my first time . . .　はじめてなんです
　が。*exp.*, 12
this + noun　この　*demo.*, 3
this person; this way　こちら　*demo.*, 2
this place, here　ここ　*demo.*, 3
this side　てまえ（手前）*loc. n.*, 3S, 4P
this time; next time　こんど（今度）*adv.*,
　11
this way; this person　こちら　*demo.*, 2
this week　こんしゅう（今週）*n.*, 6
this year　ことし（今年）*n.*, 11
this, this one　これ　*demo.*, 4
three hundred　さんびゃく（三百）*n.*, 1P
throat　のど（咽）*n.*, 1P, 10S, 12
Thursday　もくようび（木曜日）*n.*, 5
ticket　きっぷ（切符）*n.*, 1P
tidy/tidies up a room　へやをかたづけます
　（部屋を片付けます）*exp.*, 6
tie　ネクタイ　*n.*, 8
time (frequency)　～ど（～度）*count.*, 6
time frame　に　*part.*, 6
at the time of ～　～のとき（～の時）
　exp., 6

~ time/s (frequency)　～かい（～回）
count., 6

(to) become tired　つかれる（疲れる）る-
v., 12

to (goal activity + に)　に　part., 5

to (indirect object marker person + に)　に
part., 6

tobacco　タバコ／たばこ　n., 11

today　きょう（今日）　n., 1P, 5

together　いっしょに, adv., 9

toilet　トイレ　n., 3P

tomato　トマト　n., 7

tomorrow　あした（明日）　n., 6

tonight　こんばん（今晩）　n., 5

tooth　は（歯）　n., 10S, 12

topic marker　は　part., 2

tough, hectic, hard　たいへん（な）（大変
な）な-adj., 6

towel　タオル　n., 8P

town　まち（町）　n., 4

traditional Japanese clothes; kimono　きもの
（着物）n., 11

traffic accident　こうつうじこ（交通事故）
n., 11

train　でんしゃ（電車）n., 1P, 6

traveling　りょこう（旅行）n., 1P, 7

tree　き（木）n., 1P

(to) tremble　ふるえる（震える）る-v.,
12S

trousers, pants　ズボン　n., 8

Tuesday　かようび（火曜日）n., 5

turn/s in homework　しゅくだいを　だし
ます。（宿題を出します。）exp., 6S

twelfth (day), the　じゅうににち（十二日）
n., 5S

twentieth (day), the　はつか（二十日）n.,
5S

twenty-eighth (day), the　にじゅうはちにち
（二十八日）n., 5S

twenty-fifth (day), the　にじゅうごにち
（二十五日）n., 5S

twenty-first (day), the　にじゅういちにち
（二十一日）n., 5S

twenty-fourth (day), the　にじゅうよっか
（二十四日）n., 5S

twenty-ninth (day), the　にじゅうくにち
（二十九日）n., 5S

twenty-second (day), the　にじゅうににち
（二十二日）n., 5S

twenty-seventh (day), the　にじゅうしちに
ち（二十七日）n., 5S

twenty-sixth (day), the　にじゅうろくにち
（二十六日）n., 5S

twenty-third (day), the　にじゅうさんにち
（二十三日）n., 5S

two people　ふたり（二人）count., 10

U

United States; America　アメリカ　n., 2

umbrella　かさ（傘）n., 8

(someone else's) uncle　おじさん（叔父さ
ん／伯父さん）n., 1P, 10S

(the speaker's) uncle　おじ（叔父／伯父）
n., 10S

under, beneath　した（下）loc. n., 3

(to) understand　わかる　う-v., 10

underwear　したぎ（下着）n., 8S

unfortunate, sorry　ざんねん（な）（残念
な）な-adj., 6

university, college　だいがく（大学）n., 2

until　まで　part., 6

upper back, back　せなか（背中）n., 10S,
12S

urology　ひにょうきか（泌尿器科）n.,
12P

usually　たいてい, adv., 5

V

vacation, holiday　やすみ（休み）n., 11

vegetable　やさい（野菜）n., 7

verandah　ベランダ　n., 3S

very　あまり, adv., 3

very　どうも, adv., 3

very　とても, adv., 3

vicinity; near　ちかく（近く）loc. n., 3

videotape　ビデオ　n., 6

volleyball　バレーボール　n., 7S

(to) wake up; (to) get up　おきる（起きる）る-v., 5

(to) walk　あるく（歩く）う-v., 12

warm　あたたかい（暖かい／温かい）い-adj., 11

wash/es (one's) face　かおを　あらいます（顔を洗います）exp., 6S

wash/es (one's) hands　てを　あらいます（手を洗います）exp., 6S

washbowl area　せんめんじょ（洗面所）n., 3S

washing machine　せんたくき（洗濯機）n., 3S

(to) watch, (to) see　みる（見る）る-v., 5

(to) watch sumo wrestling　すもうを　みる　exp., 11S

watch, clock　とけい（時計）n., 1P, 3

water　みず（水）n., 9

waterfall　たき　n., 1P

weak　よわい（弱い）い-adj., 12

(to) wear; (to) have　する　ir. v., 10

(to) be wearing earrings　イヤリングをしている　ir. v., 10

(to) be wearing glasses　めがねをかけている　る-v., 10

(to) be wearing a skirt　スカートをはいている　exp., 10

(to) be wearing a sweater　セーターをきている（セーターを着ている）exp., 10

Wednesday　すいようび（水曜日）n., 5

week/s　〜しゅうかん（〜週間）count., 6

weekend　しゅうまつ（週末）n., 6

Welcome.　いらっしゃいませ。exp., 8P

Welcome back./Welcome home.　おかえりなさい。exp., 3

Well, that is a little bit (troublesome).　ええっと／すみません、それは　ちょっと（こまるんですが）。exp., 12

Well. Let's see . . .　えーっと　exp., 11

(Western-style) bedroom　ベッドルーム　n., 3S

(Western-style) closet　クローゼット　n., 3S

(Western-style) room　ようしつ（洋室）n., 3S

what　なに/なん（何）q. word, 2

What do you call that/that (over there)/this in Japanese?　それ／あれ／これは　にほんごで　なんと　いいますか。exp., 1

What does 〜 mean?　〜って　なんですか。（〜って何ですか。）exp., 1

What happened?　どうしましたか。／どうしたんですか。exp., 12

What is it?　なんですか（何ですか。）q. word, 2

what kind of 〜　どんな　q. word, 3

What should I do?　どうしたらいいですか。exp., 12

What would you like to order?　ごちゅうもんは。（御注文は。）exp., 9P

when　いつ　q. word, 5

when, at the time when 〜　のとき（時）n., 11

when I was a child　こどものとき（子供の時）exp., 11

when I was in high school　こうこうのとき（高校の時）exp., 6

where　どこ　q. word, 2

where (more polite than どこ); which way　どちら　q. word, 2

which (noun)　どの　q. word, 3

which, which one　どれ　q. word, 4

white　しろい（白い）い-adj., 4

white-collar worker　サラリーマン　n., 10S

who　だれ　q. word, 3

whose　だれの　q. word, 3

wide, spacious　ひろい（広い）い-adj., 3

(someone else's) wife　おくさん（奥さん）n., 3P, 10

(the speaker's) wife　かない（家内）n., 3P, 10

(the speaker's) wife　つま（妻）n., 10S

wind　かぜ（風）n., 1P

window　まど（窓）n., 3

wine　ワイン　n., 7

winter　ふゆ（冬）n., 11

winter vacation　ふゆやすみ（冬休み）n., 11

with　と　*part.*, 6
with, by means of　で　*part.*, 6
woman　おんなのひと（女の人）*n.*, 2
women's clothing　ふじんふく（婦人服）
　n., 8
women's clothing department　ふじんふく
　うりば（婦人服売り場）*n.*, 8
wool　ウール　*n.*, 8S
work, permanent job　しごと（仕事）*n.*, 6
(to) work for, (to) be employed at　つとめて
　いる（勤めている）る-*v.*, 10
world　せかい　*n.*, 1P
(to) wrap　つつむ（包む）う-*v.*, 8
wrist　てくび（手首）*n.*, 12S
wrist-watch　うでどけい（腕時計）*n.*, 8S
(to) write　かく（書く）う-*v.*, 6
writer　さっか　*n.*, 1P

Y

year (grade in school; duration; specific year)
　〜ねん（〜年）*count.*, 2, 5S, 6, 11
year before last, two years ago　おととし
　n., 11
〜 year/s old　〜さい（〜歳）*count.*, 10
yellow　きいろい（黄色い）い-*adj.*, 4
〜 yen/s　〜えん（〜円）*count.*, 8
yes　はい／ええ　*interj.*, 2

Yes, of course./Sure.　はい／ええ　もちろ
　ん。*exp.*, 12
Yes, please.　はい／ええ　どうぞ。*exp.*,
　12
Yes, that's so.　はい（ええ）、そうです。
　exp., 2
yesterday　きのう（昨日）*n.*, 6
Yokohama City　よこはま（横浜）*n.*, 11P
you　あなた　*pron.*, 2P
You are welcome.　どういたしまして。
　exp., 1
you know (emphasis marker)　よ　*part.*, 4
(someone else's) younger brother　おとうと
　さん（弟さん）*n.*, 10
(the speaker's) younger brother　おとうと
　（弟）*n.*, 1P, 10
(someone else's) younger sister　いもうとさ
　ん　*n.*, 10
(the speaker's) younger sister　いもうと（妹）
　n., 1P, 10

Z

zoo　どうぶつえん（動物園）*n.*, 11

Index

(な) Adj. = でした / じゃありませんでした (past)

(い) Adj. = です / くありません (Present)

かったです / くなかったです (past)

おおきいです / ①おおきくありません

おおきかったです / ②おおきくないです。

①おおきくありませんでした

②おおきくなかったです。

きれいです / きれいじゃありません

きれいじゃないです。

きれいでした / きれいじゃありませんでした

きれいじゃなかったです